The Brewmaster's Recipe Manual

Revised First Edition

Stephen Snyder

The Beer Garden Press

The Brewmaster's Recipe Manual, *Revised First Edition*

The Beer Garden Press, Publishers
Guttenberg, New Jersey, U.S.A.

Copyright © 1994 by Stephen Snyder
All Rights Reserved.

Technical Editors   **Dr. Alfred Haunold**
    Al Korzonas
    Paul White

Cover & Artwork Design **Melissa Snyder**

Computer Graphics   **Stacey Dunleavy**

ISBN # 1-885591-07-1

No part of this book may be reproduced or copied in any form, by any means, except where specifically noted in the text, without the express written consent of the publishers.

The publishers assume no responsibilty for typographical errors, or the use or misuse of the information contained herein.

Printed in the USA by
Morris Publishing
3212 E. Hwy 30
Kearney, NE 68847
800-650-7888

ACKNOWLEDGEMENTS

*The author would like to thank the following
for their special contributions*

Melissa for enduring non-stop "Beer Speak"
Kirsten Bespalec—*Morris Publishing*
Andy J. Janes—*Munton & Fison p.l.c.*
Axel Bachmann—*Hannen Brauerei GmbH*
Brion for German translations
The Perez Family for lagering, warehousing, & endless support
Charles & Marjorie for the Great British Pub Tour
You for enduring the word "Amber" thousands of times
Dr. Alfred Haunold—*U.S. Department of Agriculture*
Dr. Paul Bosken-Diebels—*Privatbrauerei Diebels*
G. Wohn—*Bayerische Staatsbrauerei Weihenstephan*
Hamish Sweetman—*Mountmellick Products Ltd.*
Jim & Vera for all the clippings
Craig Gilmour—*California Water Service*
Dave for books & inspiration
Daniel S. McConnell—*Yeast Lab*
David Logsdon—*Wyeast Laboratories*
Beth for peer pressure
Irish Drinking Songs
The Beer Writers et al.
The Beverage People
Wyeast Laboratories
Iain Loe—*CAMRA*
Bruce & Tracy
Jolly, Jolly Grog
The Creator of beer yeast

Questions, Comments, or Suggestions?

If you own or work in a homebrew supply shop and would like to contribute to future editions, send recipes to: **The Beer Garden Press**, P.O. Box 3120, Guttenberg, New Jersey 07093-6120.

CONTENTS

Preface 1

Introduction 2

INGREDIENT PROFILES
Malts, Adjuncts, & Specialty Grains 5
Hops 13
Yeast 19
Water 28
Additives 34
Sanitizers & Cleaners 36

BEER STYLES
Summary of Popular Styles 39
Styles at a Glance 47

RECIPES

ALE RECIPES
Brown Ale 51
Mild Ale 58
Pale Ale 61
India Pale Ale 71
Bitter 79
Porter 90
Stout 100
Oatmeal Stout 108
Scottish/Scotch Ale 112
Barleywine 119
Altbier 124
Kölsch 128
Wheat Beer 129
Belgian Ales 140
North American Ales 143

LAGER RECIPES
European Light Lager 159
Pilsner 161
Dortmunder-Export 168
Munich Helles 170
Vienna 173
Märzen/Oktoberfest 175
Münchner Dunkel 183
Bock 185
Mai Bock 190
Doppelbock 192
North American Lagers 196

CONTENTS
(Continued)

SPECIALTY RECIPES
    Christmas/Holiday Beer 207
    Fruit/Spice-Flavored Beer 211

Recipe Contributors 218

REFERENCE SECTION

GENERAL PROCEDURES
    Ale Brewing Procedures 218
    Lager Brewing Procedures 223
    Basic Infusion Mashing Procedures 225
    Basic Step-Mashing Procedures 226
    Basic Decoction Mashing Procedures 228
    Fermentation Procedures 230
    Bottling Procedures 232
    General Kegging Procedures 234
    Carbonation Chart 236
    General Conditioning & Lagering Procedures 237
    Tips for Better Homebrewing 238
    Brewing Record & Evaluation Form 242

WEIGHTS & MEASURES
    Liquid & Dry Weights 243
    Conversion Tables 244
    Specific Gravities of Wort Ingredients 245
    A Malt Extract Analysis 246

FORMULAS
    Determining Specific Gravity 247
    Determining AAUs/IBUs/HBUs 247
    Determining Alcohol Percentage 248
    Hydrometers 249

DIRECTORIES
    Homebrew Supply Shops 254
    Associations & Publications 267

BIBLIOGRAPHY 269

The Brewmaster's Recipe Manual

PREFACE

Initially, this book started out as a resource for my own personal use, but as I began collecting helpful brewing data to put in a notebook with my own recipes, I realized how much more I needed to learn, and also how much contradiction existed in the information available on brewing products. By soliciting catalogs from over 200 homebrew supply shops in an effort to gather information, I was finally able to resolve many discrepancies, and in the process, found that these shops had a lot of great recipes that they were graciously willing to share. It was then that I realized that this was information other homebrewers might find useful as well.

My hope is that this information will help you have more fun and grow as a brewer, but remember, these recipes are not sacred and do not have to be strictly adhered to. Feel free to use them as an outline for your own recipes; they are a map to guide you in discovering what works and tastes best for you. Don't forget that the foundations of homebrewing lie in trusting your own instincts, expressing your creativity, and most of all, exercising your freedom to brew the beer you want.

You will notice that the recipes given are in a variety of formats. This is the way the Homebrew Supply Shops have written them, and for the most part, I've left them that way despite my own brewing preferences or opinions. While this may prove confusing or even objectionable to some, I hope that most of you will appreciate their individuality; and see that there is always more than one way to do things. If you have not developed an unwavering method of brewing, perhaps you will appreciate one of these brewing methods and adopt it as your own.

Last, but not least, I want to preface this manual by thanking the many beer writers and brewers who shared their vast knowledge, but especially the shops who generously lent their recipes and expertise for the creation of this book. They, as my aunt Ethel would say, "Didn't know me from a sack of turnips," but they took the time to send me recipes and other information during their busiest time of year; proving the old adage, "If you want to get something done, ask a busy person to do it." I owe them a huge debt of gratitude.

The Brewmaster's Recipe Manual

INTRODUCTION

There is an old saying, "The truth is rarely pure and never simple." This is no where more appropriate than in the world of beer. Even the name of our beloved beverage is a source of contention and confusion. Many people prefer to call top-fermented beers "Ales" and bottom-fermented beers "Lagers." Others take issue with this, however, because "lager" merely comes from the German verb meaning "to store" and has nothing to do with color, content, or method of fermenting. German Altbiers are ales, after all, yet they are cold lagered; German wheats are often fermented with ale yeast then bottle conditioned with lager yeast. Furthermore, some even feel the word "Beer" should only be used to identify bottom-fermented and "Ale" should be used exclusively for top-fermented beer. In fact, "Beer" itself was once a term specifically used to differentiate malt beverages flavored with hops from Ales, which were once flavored exclusively with other herbs and spices.

The long and short of all this is that the lines between beer styles cross and criss-cross, have two or more names, or have varying fermentation and conditioning methods from country to country and region to region. Therefore, in order to simplify matters for the practical purposes of homebrewing, I refer to all beverages herein as "Beer" and have divided the recipes (five-gallon unless otherwise noted) into three main sections: Top-fermented beers will be termed "Ales" and bottom-fermented beers will be classified as "Lagers." There is also a shorter third section of "Specialty Beers" that are seasonal "Holiday Beers" or that use fruit or flavoring agents; this section includes both Ale and Lager.

You'll notice some of the recipes may fit into more than one category, particularly American versions of the classic styles. Some of these are included in the appropriate "American" sections, others in the "European" sections; in most cases, the yeast and/or hops used were the deciding factors in where the recipes would be placed. You'll also see that brand names or specific products are recommended in some recipes. This is not because we've received a handsome kickback from the manufacturer, but because it was the product used in the original recipe, it is the best one for the job in the brewer's humble opinion, or it is true to the style of the beer due to the physical properties of its ingredients (i.e., a "continental" American malt for a Steam Beer or a "maritime" German malt for a Helles). The same is true for the hop alpha acid percentages given. Since it may be difficult in future years to find hops with the exact AA% as given, use the HBU/IBU/AAU formulas on page 247 to adjust what alpha acid percent you have to the ones given in the recipe. Otherwise, use whatever you have available and what suits your personal taste. With the aid of the Homebrew Supply Shops listed on page 254, you can acquire practically any homebrewing ingredient under the sun. So, good luck and happy homebrewing!

Ingredient Profiles

The Brewmaster's Recipe Manual

MALTS, ADJUNCTS, & SPECIALTY GRAINS

Barley is an ancient and extremely hardy cereal grass that has all but vanished from our diets except in beer. Long before advanced agricultural techniques developed, barley became a staple of the human diet because of its ability to flourish under adverse conditions, particularly in Europe. Its hardiness quickly made it a favorite of ancient societies, and there is evidence that its use as a fermentable even pre-dates the baking of bread.

The rudimentary basics of barley's use in beer start with "Malting," a process where the seeds of the harvested barley grass are soaked in water until they sprout (germinate) and begin to activate enzymes that can convert starch to sugars. Beer yeast will later eat and convert those sugarsto alcohol and Carbon Dioxide (a.k.a. Carbonic Acid Gas or CO_2). The barley is then gently dried—halting the conversion process, the *acrospires* (or sprouts) are removed, and the dried malt is then cured at least one month before use. When the malted barley is mashed, the enzymes created in the malting process go to work, converting the remaining starches in the malt, and producing the sugars that the yeast will ingest.

Modern barley for homebrewing is available in 2-row and 6-row varieties. 6-row is preferred by large U.S. breweries because it has a higher starch-degrading **Enzyme Content** than 2-row, thereby making it a better choice when using inexpensive adjuncts such as rice and corn. 2-row barley is preferred by most microbrewers, continental European, and British brewers because it yields higher **Extract** and less husk material.

Besides extract yield and enzyme content, the other significant aspect of malted barley to be considered is **Modification**. Modification is defined as the level to which the starchy endosperm of the barley kernel is allowed to be altered or "modified" into the growing acrospire during the germination process. Like a chicken embryo in an egg replacing the yolk, the acrospire will continue to grow into a barley plant until all the starch is consumed; unless the maltster halts the process by heating and drying the malt. By permitting higher levels of the starch to be modified during the malting process, the mashing stage that comes later is made simpler. Starch-degrading enzymes that occur naturally in malt are activated during this process, as well as yeast nutrients that will become very valuable later in the brewing process. These "Highly-Modified Malts" are valued not only for their ease of mashing, but because they tend to create a clearer beer, and the abundant yeast nutrients lead to more a complete fermentation and a shorter "lag time" after the yeast is pitched. The down side is that during this growth process, the acrospire eats up more of the endosperm, and therefore, the level of sugar that you'll be able to extract into the wort is reduced.

Conversely, "Under-Modified Malts" whose growth process is halted early in the germination stage will give higher degrees of specific gravity per pound, but require more sophisticated mashing schedules and a protein rest. These issues, however, are mostly of concern to all-grain brewers and primarily with the malt that makes up the bulk of the grain bill or "grist" (the coarsely ground grains) not the specialty malts. Almost all American malts are highly-modified, as are most English Pale Ale Malts. Under-modification or moderate modification is becoming increasingly rare and is usually encountered in European 2-row Pilsener Malts. If in doubt about the modification of a malt you're using, consult your supplier.

MALT, ADJUNCT, & SPECIALTY GRAIN PROFILES

Below is a list of the malts commonly used in brewing, the traditional specialty grains, and the adjuncts used to adjust color, body, and head retention. There are three coloring scales used throughout this book. I have not simplified this by utilizing just one for the primary reason that all three are still widely used in homebrew supply catalogs and beer literature, and there are strong loyalties to each. They are as follows:

SRM—*The acronym for "Standard Research (or Reference) Method," a term used by the American Society of Brewing Chemists (ASBC) to denote degrees of color. In beer usage, they range on a scale of approximately 1 to 600; higher numbers being progressively darker. SRM/Lovibond are converted (approximately) to EBC by multiplying by 2.65 then subtracting 1.2 from the result.* Example: *3 SRM x 2.65 = 7.95 - 1.2 = 6.75 EBC.*

Lovibond—*An older form of color measurement, usually seen with British products, that is close enough to the SRM designation to be used interchangeably for our purposes. Expressed as Degrees Lovibond or °L. As with the SRM scale, Lovibond ranges from approximately 1 (e.g., Pilsener Malt) to 550 (e.g., Black Patent Malt) in beer usage.*

EBC—*The acronym for the European Brewing Convention (Congress), whose measurements are used primarily in continental Europe and are converted to SRM by multiplying by 0.377 then adding 0.45 to the result.* Example: *10 EBC x 0.377 = 3.77 + 0.45 = 4.22 SRM. Numbers are usually seen ranging from 3.5 (e.g., Belgian Pils Malt) to 1200 (e.g., Belgian Special B Malt).*

Amber Malt—A roasted specialty malt used primarily by British brewers for coloring and biscuity taste in Old Ale, Mild, Brown Ale, and the occasional Bitter. Created by heating cured Mild Ale malt quickly to 212°F then slowly up to 300°F. Because of its low diastatic power, it should be mashed with a diastatic malt to yield fermentable extract. It is rarely available in the U.S. Color 15-25 Lovibond/40-60 EBC.

Acid Malt—Malt containing high levels of lactic acid that is used by brewers who want to adjust malt pH without having to "sour mash" or add lactobacillus. Originally designed by brewers of pale or Pilsner beer to doctor high carbonate mash water. This malt is rarely available to (or needed by) homebrewers and is used mostly by German breweries.

Aromatic Malt—A mildly kilned Belgian barley malt that adds a strong malt aroma and deep color when used as a specialty malt. Can be used as 100% of the grist in recipes, but since it is fairly low in surplus diastatic enzymes, keep adjunct usage to below 10% of the total grist. Color 20-25 Lovibond.

Barley Syrup—A mixture of barley, corn, and wheat malt extracts used as a cheap substitute for pure malt. Rich in carbohydrates and yeast nutrients, it is highly fermentable, but should never exceed 50% usage and is generally not recommended for high quality beers.

Belgian Pils—A European 2-row malt rapidly gaining popularity because it makes a good base malt for almost any all-grain beer style, particularly Continental Lager and, because it is extremely well-modified can be easily mashed with a single temperature infusion. Color 1-2 Lovibond.

Biscuit Malt—The darker Belgian version of Victory Malt. This toasted malt provides a warm bread or biscuit flavor and aroma. Also lends a garnet to brown coloring. Use 5-15% maximum. Color 20-25 Lovibond. No enzymes. Must be mashed with malts having surplus diastatic power.

MALT, ADJUNCT, & SPECIALTY GRAIN PROFILES
(Continued)

Black Barley—Roasted unmalted barley that lends color properties similar to Black Patent Malt, but the two are not interchangeable in your recipes. A much darker form of Roasted Barley, Black Barley provides sharp, dry Stout flavor. Ideal for hearty brews. Drier than Black Patent or Chocolate Malts. 500-550+Lovibond.

Black Patent Malt (Black Malt)—Malted barley roasted at very high temperatures using the same process as Chocolate Malt except it is kilned much longer. These high temperatures destroy enzymes and much of the starch, which results in low extract yield. Black Patent Malt has no enzymes and is generally not used for its aroma, which is very aggressive. Small amounts add brown coloring, large amounts add black color and a charcoal/burnt/smokey or nutty taste that is less dry than Roasted Barley. Darkest color of all malts. Use sparingly. Good for Porters, Stouts and dark lagers. German versions and the trademarked Briess version are often called "Black Prinz" in supply catalogs. The Belgian version is called "Roasted Malt." Color 475-550 Lovibond/1250-1500 EBC.

Brewer's Sugar—See "Corn Sugar/Dextrose" and "Glucose."

Brown Malt—An old style of a roasted malted barley that was once the staple of European beer brewing, particularly in England and Germany, where it formed the basis of the famous London Porter and the Brown Beers of the Bavarian monasteries before 19th century innovations using coal as a heat source made "Pale Malt" more affordable. Technically, Brown Malt should be a smoked malt kilned over an oak, beech, ash or hornbeam fire, resulting in a rich, spicy/smokey flavor. This brand of malt is now rarely used in commercial brewing outside of the United Kingdom or Bamberg, Germany. It is still sometimes used by U.K. homebrewers primarily as a specialty malt, but is sold by only a few supply shops in the U.S., where homebrewers have taken to smoking their own malts for authenticity. Color 50-70 Lovibond/150 EBC.

Brumalt—A dark German malt (80-110 °L/30-40 EBC) developed by German breweries to darken and improve the malt flavor and aroma of Märzen/Oktoberfest and Altbiers without having to decoction mash. Rarely available to homebrewers.

Candi Sugar—A very pure, slowly crystallized dextrose/sucrose mixture used in traditional Belgian brewing that adds its own special flavor and aroma. Candi ranges in color from approximately 100 to 750 Lovibond, but is not readily available in America. Corn sugars are considered the nearest substitute for the light versions, caramel sugar for the darker styles.

Cane/Beet Sugar—A 100% fermentable refined sugar (sucrose) made from sugar cane or sugar beets that is primarily used to raise gravity and lighten body. Also known as Table Sugar. Should be dissolved before adding to the boil. Use sparingly (i.e., ≤1 lb. per 5 U.S. gallons). Beet sugar must be totally refined, but partially-refined cane sugar is available as "Raw Sugar."

Caramel—Cooked sugar (usually sucrose) used primarily in commercial brewing to darken beer and to lend a slight caramel flavor. Its use has been suggested as a possible alternative to dark candi sugar.

The Brewmaster's Recipe Manual

MALT, ADJUNCT, & SPECIALTY GRAIN PROFILES
(Continued)

Caramel Malt/Crystal Malt—Made by heating wet germinated barley (high nitrogen "green malt") to around 150°F until the enzymes in the malt convert the starches; then it is kilned at around 500°F. There are no enzymes or fermentables, but Crystal Malt's dextrines and other nonfermentables add enhanced mouthfeel, body, reddish color, head retention, caramel/nutty flavor, and sweetness to differing degrees, depending on Lovibond/EBC rating, country of origin, brand, and amount used. For example, the German "Light Crystal" version adds little sweetness. To avoid harsh flavors, use of no more than 20-30% or less than 1 pound per 5 U.S. gallons is recommended. Crystal malts can be added to the main mash or steeped alone prior to the wort boil and range in color from 10-120 Lovibond/100-300 EBC.

CaraPils®—The brand name of a Dextrine Malt made by the Briess Malting Company. See "Dextrine Malt" below. Color 1-2 Lovibond/1.5-4 EBC.

CaraMunich—A medium-amber Belgian Crystal Malt. No enzymes. Imparts a rich, caramel-sweet aroma and full flavor, as well as intense color. Not synonymous with Munich Malt. Color 53-75 Lovibond/140-160 EBC.

CaraVienne—A Belgian light Caramel Malt. Originally used by Belgian breweries in lighter Abbey or Trappiste style ales, but it is appropriate for any recipe that calls for Crystal Malt. Not synonymous with Vienna Malt. Color 12-25 Lovibond/30-60 EBC.

Chocolate Malt—A high nitrogen malt which is roasted at temperatures of up to 450°F, then rapidly cooled when the desired color is achieved. "Chocolate" refers primarily to the malt's color, not its flavor. Similar to Black Patent, but lighter and is most often used in Milds and Porters. Lends various levels of aroma, deep red color, and a nutty/roasted taste, depending on the amounts used. Color averages 350-450 Lovibond/900-1200 EBC.

Corn Sugar (a.k.a. Dextrose)—Also commonly referred to as "Brewer's Sugar." The most fermentable and commonly used adjunct, often added in lieu of the more expensive barley malts, and commonly used for priming (bottle/keg conditioning). Will lend cidery flavors and thin body if overused (i.e., >15% or more than 1 or 2 lbs. per 5 U.S. gallon batch). Increases alcohol level without increasing body.

Dark Crystal Malt—The darkest version of the Caramel Malts. Adds a deep reddish-amber color and a rich caramel sweetness. Steep or mash. Color usually 80-120 Lovibond (the German version averages 40-50 °L/105-130 EBC).

Demerara—A British term for an aromatic and softly-flavored "Raw" Brown Sugar sometimes used in English Ales. Less refined than "Table" cane sugars. Slightly subtler in flavor than the American equivalent, "Turbinado."

Dextrine Malt—Very light Caramel Malt made by drying barley malt at low temperatures. Lends body, smoother mouthfeel, and foam stability. without adding a red color or crystal malt flavor. Dextrine malts include the popular 6-row Briess Cara-Pils® and the 2-row DeWolf-Cosyns CaraPils. No enzymes. No mashing required. Use as 5 to 20% of the grist. Color 10-20 EBC/1-8 Lovibond.

The Brewmaster's Recipe Manual

MALT, ADJUNCT, & SPECIALTY GRAIN PROFILES
(Continued)

Dried Malt Extract (DME)—Malted barley, and often other coloring grains according to intended style, cooked down to a thick syrup then spray-dried to a powder form. Available with or without hop extracts added. Except for "Diastatic" malt extracts, the presence of enzymes is negligible.

English Pale Malt—Fully modified and easily converted by a single temperature mash (e.g., 150-158°F for one hour). The prefered malt for English Ales. Usually higher kilned than U.S. 2-row Pale Malts (i.e., Klages and Harrington) and lower in enzymes. Keep use of adjuncts to <15%. Color 2-4 Lovibond/4-9 EBC.

Flaked Barley—Unmalted barley often added directly to the main mashes of Bitter, Dark Mild, Porter, and Stout to lend a rich, grainy taste and to increase head retention, creaminess, and body. Does not need to be precooked, but mashing is required to avoid haze formation in the finished beer.

Flaked Maize—A virtually nitrogen-free adjunct widely used in moderate quantities to provide more depth of character to lighter beers. Contributes alcohol, but no flavor, color, or body. Overuse will impart a distinct corn taste. Must be mashed with pale malt, and as with other flaked products, doesn't need cooking beforehand.

Flaked, Rolled, and Steel Cut Oats—Used primarily in brewing Oatmeal Stouts and Belgian ales. All must be mashed and Steel-Cut Oats should be well-cooked beforehand. Adds a distinct full-bodied flavor and "chewy" texture, and can also counteract the harshness caused by hard brewing water. A long protein rest must be done to avoid a haze in pale-colored beers.

Flaked Rye—Lends dry, crisp character and strong, unique flavor that is inappropriate and overpowering in most classic beer styles. Must be mashed, preferably with highly modified malts. (See "Rye.")

Flaked Wheat—Increases head retention and body. Must be mashed, preferably with a highly modified malt. As with other flaked products, the grain is steamed then rolled flat.

German Crystal Malt—Usually found in only two varieties; "Light" (10-20 °L) and "Dark" (40-90 °L) The lower EBC/Lovibond ratings provide body without the drastic color and sweetness of British crystal malt. No enzymes. Steep or mash.

German Pale Malt (see Pilsener malt)—Produces a smooth, clean, malt flavor. Less modified varieties are best mashed by decoction. Used primarily in lagers. Color 1-2 Lovibond/1.5-4 EBC.

German Roasted Wheat—Imparts a deep brown color and a unique flavor to Dunkelweizens (dark wheat beers) and other dark beers. Color 188 Lovibond/500 EBC.

Glucose—This is term used most often in British homebrewing to refer to what Americans know as Corn or Brewer's Sugar. A monosaccharide created through hydrolisis of vegetable starch (usually corn). 100% Fermentable.

The Brewmaster's Recipe Manual

MALT, ADJUNCT, & SPECIALTY GRAIN PROFILES
(Continued)

Grits—Cereal grains (usually corn and rice) milled to small granules, giving them a larger surface area in water—making them more easily converted in one-step infusion mashes. Should be cooked beforehand.

Invert Sugar—A highly fermentable brewing/priming sugar composed of a mixture of fructose and dextrose formed when sucrose is split by acid or an enzyme. Sweeter and more soluble than sucrose. Popular in Belgian brewing because it contributes alcoholic strength without heaviness. Not generally available to homebrewers, but Corn Sugar is often recommended as a substitute.

Lager Malt—Malt that is kilned at low temperatures for lighter color and to preserve high enzyme levels. Usually 2-row German, Canadian, or American lager malt is available to homebrewers. Modern lager malts are more highly modified than the traditonal lager malts which allows single temperature infusion mashing. High levels of adjuncts can be used, but this will require more complicated stepped or decoction mashing. Appropriate as a base malt for all lagers. Color 1-2 Lovibond/3 EBC.

Malt Extract Syrup—Malted barley and/or wheat and other grains mashed and cooked down to a thick syrup to which water is added by the brewer to create wort. The recipe basis for beginning and intermediate homebrewing. When hopped and a yeast packet is included, packaged malt extract is referred to as a "kit."

Mild Ale Malt—2-row British barley of higher nitrogen content that is malted the same as Pale Ale Malt, but is then kilned at higher temperatures and for slightly longer to yield a deeper color and lower moisture content. Mild Ale Malt has lower extract yields than Pale Ale Malt, but its somewhat higher diastatic enzyme levels allow the use of greater percentages of adjuncts. Yields a malty flavor and aroma, good for English-style Mild and Brown Ales. Mashing required. Color 2-3 Lovibond/6-7 EBC.

Molasses—A thick, aromatic, and uniquely flavored syrup made from sorghum or as a residue of cane sugar refinement. Available "sulfured" or "unsulfured" and in varying degrees of intensity as Light, Medium, and Blackstrap. Use sparingly. See "Treacle."

Munich Malt—So named because this is the malt long used by Munich brewers for their dark lagers. German, Belgian, American, and Canadian varieties are now available. Higher kilning than pale malts provides a full, grainy, malty flavor and aroma, sweetness, and orange-amber color. Can make up to 100% of the grain bill, but low diastatic power makes it unsuitable for use with adjuncts. Mashing required. Color 5-8 Lovibond/14-20 EBC for imported varieties and usually 10 Lovibond/25 EBC for domestic.

Pale Malt (2-row American)—Highly modified and highly enzymatic for a 2-row variety. Suitable for ales and lagers. Mashing required. Color 2.5-4 Lovibond/7-9 EBC.

Pale Malt (6-row American)—High in enzymes, proteins, but also tannins from the greater amount of husk material (avoid over-sparging). A protein rest is recommended in all-grain brewing. Will yield less extract per pound than 2-row varieties, but is ideal for use with adjuncts (up to 50%!). Suitable for ales and lagers. Mashing required. Color 1-2 Lovibond/1.5-4 EBC.

Pale Ale Malt (2-row Belgian)—Interchangeable with British Pale Ale Malt.

MALT, ADJUNCT, & SPECIALTY GRAIN PROFILES
(Continued)

Pale Ale Malt (2-row British)—The quintessential fully-modified British malt slowly kilned at low temperatures to a 3% moisture level. Easily mashed by a single temperature infusion, 2-row Pale is suitable for both ales and lagers, but keep adjuncts to under 15% of the total grist because it has lower diastatic power than U.S. 2-row. There are less tannins and higher extract yields than with 6-row malt, but because of reduced husk material, great care must be taken when crushing to avoid a sluggish runoff in the mash. Mashing is required. Color 2-3 Lovibond/5-7 EBC.

Pilsener Malt—German/Eastern European/Belgian 2-row. Popular strains include "Moravian" and DeWolf-Cosyns' "Pils." Light color, easily mashed, and produces very malty flavor, but it is weaker in enzymes than U.S. 6-row. Large amounts of adjuncts in the mash will require addition of amylase enzyme or other highly enzymatic malts. Color 1-2 Lovibond/1.5-4 EBC.

Raw Barley—An adjunct that can compose up to 15% of the grist, but extremely skillful milling is required to preserve husk integrity while sufficiently crushing the endosperm. Raw barley performs best when decoction mashed, but can be infusion mashed by the experienced brewer. Because it is cheaper than malted barley, it is sometimes used in large commercial breweries in conjunction with industrial enzymes as a malted barley substitute.

Rice Extract/Syrup—The ingredient that gives some American and Japanese lagers (especially "Dry" Lagers) their crisp, clean taste and light body. Use instead of corn sugar and in small quantities (i.e., ≤15%).

Roasted Malt—The Belgian version of Black Patent Malt (see above).

Roasted (Unmalted) Barley—This is unmalted barley gently and gradually roasted to a rich, dark brown, but it is generally lighter than Black Barley and smoother and drier than Black Malt. It is most often used in Porters, Stouts, and Milds. No enzymes. Improves head retention and also adds reddish color when used sparingly. Imparts bitterness, roast aroma, dark color, and coffee flavor when used in greater quantities (1-4+ cups). Steep or add to main mash. Color 300-500+ Lovibond/1000-1550 EBC.

Rye—(a.k.a. "Roggen" in German). Available raw, malted, or roasted, this traditional bread grain is occasionally used to lend a unique flavor to heavier beer styles. However, because of a lack of husk material and a high water absorbtion rate, Rye is a difficult grain to use in brewing. A long protein rest is recommended.

Special B—The darkest of the Belgian Caramel Malts; on par with the darkest English or German Crystal Malts. Imparts a heavy caramel taste and is often credited with the raisin-like flavors of some Belgian Abbey beers. Larger percentages, i.e., >5%, contribute a dark brown to black color and fuller body. Color 300-500 EBC/110-225 Lovibond.

Spray Malt—The British term for Dried Malt Extract. (See above.)

Toasted Malt—Toasting of pale malted barley is easily done by the homebrewer (10-15 minutes in a 350°F oven); or it can be purchased as "Biscuit" or "Victory" malt. Adds a reddish/orange color and improved body without the sweetness of Crystal Malt. Mashing required to avoid starch haze. Color averages 25-30 Lovibond.

MALT, ADJUNCT, & SPECIALTY GRAIN PROFILES
(Continued)

Torrefied Grains—Usually wheat and rice that have been puffed like breakfast cereal or popcorn, exploding the endosperm and gelatinizing the starches. They need no further cooking, but these adjuncts used for head retention and improved mouthfeel should be mashed. Torrefied barley reportedly improves mash tun runoff and lends a drier taste than flaked barley. It is used by some British breweries in Bitters and Milds. Typically 1-1.5 °L/2-3 EBC.

Treacle—A heavy, sweet British-style mixture of molasses, invert sugar, and corn syrup often called "golden syrup." Intensely flavored, but with a very different taste profile than American-style molasses. Popular in the United Kingdom as a food product and in the brewing of some Stouts.

Turbinado—A light "Raw" Brown Sugar made from sugar cane that is minimally refined and coarsely granulated. It is usually found in vegetarian groceries and health food stores. Good for homebrewed British-style Pale Ales and possibly high gravity Belgian Ales. Use sparingly or a cloying sweetness may result. See "Demerara."

Victory Malt—A lightly toasted aroma and flavoring malt. Provides a warm biscuit aroma to dark lagers and ales such as Porter. Also lends a garnet to brown coloring, but not the sweetness of Dark Crystal. Use 5-15% maximum. Similar to Belgian Biscuit Malt, but lighter. Color 3-5 Lovibond/7-12 EBC.

Vienna Malt—A 2-row German or 6-row American roasted malt with high acidity levels. Lends a full flavor and deep amber color. Rich and aromatic, Vienna Malt is the flavorful basis for the Vienna/Märzen/Oktoberfest-style beers. Mashing required. Domestic varieties are darker. Color 3-10 Lovibond/14-16 EBC.

Wheat Malt—Made primarily from winter wheat, malted wheat is used in various amounts generally ranging from 30-70% of the grist in creating the many styles of wheat beer, and in smaller amounts (i.e., 5-10%), to aid in head retention of other beers such as Münster Alt. Mash with 2-row or 6-row barley malt to compensate for wheat's lack of husk material. Wheat malt extracts are often a combination of barley and wheat malt. Used in combination with barley, wheat malt is believed to lighten mouthfeel, improve yeast activity, and heighten thirst-quenching properties. Color 0-3 Lovibond/0-7 EBC.

Wild Rice—Adds a strong, unique, and wild flavor. Should be used in conservative amounts and, as with all rice, should be well cooked beforehand. Mashing required.

HOPS

Hops (*Humulus lupulus* L.) are a prolific, long-lived, climbing perennial vine whose flowers grow into cone-shaped structures (strobiles) on the female plant. These cones are composed of bracts and bracteoles—leaflike structures attached to a central axis. The bracteoles carry the *lupulin glands* which provide the aroma, flavor, and astringent bitterness that balances the sweetness of the malt and acts as a preservative and natural clarifier. The word "hop" comes from the Anglo-Saxon "hoppan" which means "to climb."

According to Native American and folk medicine, the hop plant is also a proven sedative, tonic, diuretic, pain-killer, hypnotic, blood purifier, intestinal cleanser, sedative, and fever reducer, as well as a treatment for jaundice, skin disease, venereal disease, tuberculosis, sleeplessness, nervous tension, anxiety, worms, dandruff, and bladder problems. Hops were used in continental Europe for beer making at least as early as the 8th century, but not in Britain until they were introduced in the 1500s by Dutch immigrants. Fierce resistance to the use of this flavoring and preservative agent in ale persisted for more than 200 years in England before the use of herbs such as Bog Myrtle, Horehound, Ground Ivy (Alehoof), and Buckbean finally diminished.

The bitterness of hops comes primarily from the *Alpha Acids* contained in the resins of the lupulin glands located at the base of the strobiles of the hop flowers. The alpha acids also provide the preservatives that retard spoilage. When boiled, the alpha acids are converted (isomerized) into iso-alpha acids, which are then water soluble. Hops also contain other acids known as *Beta Acids*, but these provide only neglible bitterness. The flavor and aroma come from the *Essential Oils* and are not measured by the *Alpha Acid Percent (AA%)* figure listed by the hop merchant. Alpha Acid Percent is only a measure of the percentage of the flower's weight that is composed of the Alpha Acid resin, a measure of bittering potential and preservative power.

Hops for homebrewing come primarily in these forms: loose *Whole Flowers*, or whole compressed flower *Plugs*, *Pelletized* powder, and *Extracts*. The form you choose will be determined by your own need to balance availability, convenience, expense, and freshness. It is important to note that there are no "fresh" hops in the same sense as you would purchase vegetables from the grocery store. All hops are dried before they are packaged to prevent spoilage. However, whole flower hops are generally freshest if purchased when they are less than a year old, but hops that are kept cold, airtight, and dark can retain their bittering, flavoring, and aromatic qualities for well over a year. Try to buy plugs or pellets that are sealed in oxygen-proof or nitrogen purged bags and, if possible, check the crop year and packaging date as hops degrade over time, especially if left unrefrigerated.

For brewing purposes, hops are classified primarily as "Bittering/Kettle" or "Aroma." Hops with high alpha acid percentages are generally used for bittering, and hops with lower alpha acid percentages are usually considered the best for aroma and flavor (collectively referred to as "Finishing"). This is a very over-simplified categorization as most hops can serve both purposes if the correct quantities are used or they are properly blended with other varieties. See "Tips for Better Homebrewing—Hops" on page 226 and the formulas for calculating hop utlization on page 247.

Whole Flowers are often considered the freshest. They are packaged in large, tight bales which the hop merchant then splits up and sells to homebrew shops or breweries in various quantities. These flowers are often repackaged in bags that are not oxygen-proof and, because of their bulkiness, are not refrigerated. As a result, they are more subject to the detrimental effects of heat and oxidation than are gas-purged pellets and plugs. They also require longer boils to fully utilize their bittering qualities—e.g., 90 minutes to achieve full utilization. However, they are ideal as flavoring and/or aroma hops and provide a good filter bed when straining wort into the primary fermenter. These whole hops are often called "fresh," "loose," or

HOPS
(Continued)

"leaf," because the petals (bracts and bracteoles) of the hop flower resemble small green leaves. "Leaf" is a misnomer because the actual leaves of the hop plant are not used in brewing. Although it may be impossible to know what condition hops will be in when mail-ordering, try to buy whole hops that are green or pale greenish-gold if you have the chance to examine them before purchase. Hops that are brown are old and no good for most brewing purposes and should be avoided. (Note: Belgian Brewers often use "stale" hops in order derive the preservative qualities without adding significant hop bitterness, aroma, or flavor.) However, almost every bag of whole hops will have a few brown petals, this is normal and should not cause concern—just remove them before use. Besides, few shops will risk their reputation by selling stale hops, but nevertheless, try to buy whole flowers that are sealed in oxygen-barrier bags. Note that there are now machines on the market for home vacuum-sealing.

Plugs (a.k.a. Type 100 Pellets) are whole hop flowers compressed into half-ounce round disks, then sealed in nitrogen-purged aluminum or mylar bags. When added to the boil, these expand to resemble whole flowers. Although some of the delicate aroma may be lost in the compression process, this form of hops is a good middle ground between the freshness of whole flowers and the convenience of pellets. If you are able to examine before buying, look for "CO_2-purged, oxygen-barrier packaging," etc. As with all hops, keep them refrigerated.

Pellets (Type 45 & Type 90) are hops which are ground very fine into powder then formed into pellets under intense pressure. This process greatly increases the shelf life of the hops and helps to increase the utilization of bittering acids by crushing the tiny lupulin glands. However, some argue that this destroys the more delicate oils and resins responsible for aroma and flavor, but this has not been proven. Despite this controversy, pellets are in wide use in the microbrewing industry for all purposes. Pellets also have the added bonus that practically all varieties are available in this form. Type 90 pellets are the form most commonly used in homebrewing. Type 45 pellets are enriched with additional lupulin for increased bittering capabilities.

Hop Oils are created by a variety of distillation processes and are used for adding aroma to fermented beer just before packaging. **Hop Extracts** are hop products derived from whole hops by cooking or with chemical or liquid CO_2 solvents. These products have the advantage of long-life, accurate measurement, and consistent quality. They usually contain only the vital alpha acids necessary for bittering and less flavor or aroma compounds. In *isomerized extracts*, the isomerization that normally occurs during boiling is already completed, thereby allowing more complete and accurate utilization in achieving desired bitterness after fermentation is complete. *Non-isomerized* extracts must be added to the brew kettle for boiling.

The two most popular ways of achieving proper hopping rates in homebrewing are by calculating **Homebrew Bittering Units (HBUs)** (a measure of hop quantity in ounces multiplied by alpha acid percentage) and **International Bittering Units (IBUs)** (a measure of actual bitterness utilized during brewing). These two methods work well together in allowing the brewer to achieve not only the appropriate level of bitterness, but also to estimate the quantity of hops needed in designing and planning a recipe. For more information on HBUs, IBUs, and their applications, see page 247. It is important to reiterate that hops are primarily meant to balance the sweetness of the malt. Therefore, try to keep in mind how attenuative your yeast is and where your original gravity (O.G.) is on the scale of a particular style. In other words, if you shoot for the upper end of a particular style's O.G., but the lower end of the style's IBUs, and vice-versa, you probably won't achieve proper bitterness and balance.

The Brewmaster's Recipe Manual

HOP PROFILES

Commonly used homebrewing hops are listed below; with countries that are the major producers, the hop's typical* alpha acid percentage, usage (bittering or finishing), characteristics, and the styles of beer most often used in. More than 20 varieties, such as Columbia, Crystal, Spalter Select, Magnum, and Talisman, have been omitted because they are generally not yet available for homebrewing or have decreased in popularity to the point of being unobtainable.

Brewers Gold (America, Britain, & Germany) (6-10%)—Second only to Northern Brewer production numbers in Germany, Brewers Gold is a good bittering hop traditionally used for *German Lagers and English Ales,* but is versatile enough for bittering usage in most recipes.

British Columbia Goldings (B.C.) (Canada & America) (4-6%)—North American version of the classic British aromatic finishing hop. (Note: A 10 acre plot is now grown in Oregon for homebrew uses.) Identical to "East Kent Goldings" below—*Pale Ales, Bitter, Porters, and Stouts, especially Dry-Hopped Ales.*

Bullion (America & Britain) (5-10%)—Primarily bittering, strong flavors, spicy, and pungent. A sister selection of Brewer's Gold and virtually identical to it in agronomic characteristics (except maturity), brewing performance, and quality. The America-grown Bullion usually has higher AA%s. A homebrewer's favorite as a good general purpose hop—*Stouts and Dark Ales.*

Bramling Cross (Canada & Britain) (5-7%)—Finishing and bittering but primarily an aroma hop. A decreasingly popular hop developed in the 1960s as a wilt resistant replacement for East Kent Goldings. Not widely available in the U.S. *Ales and Lagers.*

Cascade (America) (4-7%)—A Fuggles cross. Versatile, citrusy, and primarily a flavor and aroma finishing hop, but also an acceptable bittering hop that is a favorite of microbrewers as well as homebrewers—*Ales and Lagers.*

Centennial (America) (9-11%)—a.k.a. CFJ-90. Aromatic, but also acceptable for bittering purposes. A stronger version of Cascade—*Medium to Dark American Ales.*

Challenger (Britain) (7-10%)—A popular bittering seeded or seedless hop used primarily in the United Kingdom. A favorite of British homebrewers as a multi-purpose hop, but not generally available in the U.S. *British Ales and Lagers.*

Chinook (America) (11-13%)—Bittering, similar to Bullion, but stronger. Intense aroma. A U.S. hybrid suited for practically all *American Ales and Lagers.*

Cluster (America) (5-8%)—Primarily a mild bittering hop but with a nice floral aroma and fair to good flavor—*Light and Dark American Lagers.*

Comet (America) (9-10%)—Very bitter. Availability very spotty. *American Ales and Lagers.*

East Kent Goldings (Britain, Canada, & America) (4-6%)—The classic aromatic ale finishing hop. Unfortunately, availability is spotty and these hops store poorly. Nitrogen-purged plugs are recommended. Like Fuggles, this hop is produced mainly in the English counties of Kent, Sussex, Hereford, and Worcester but is rapidly expanding in Oregon to an estimated 80 bales (16,000 lbs.) in 1995—*Pale Ales, Bitter, Porters, and Stouts, especially Dry-Hopped Ales.*

15

HOP PROFILES
(Continued)

Eroica (America) (10-13%)—<u>Bittering</u> and good <u>aroma</u> for a high alpha variety (use sparingly). Now decreasing in popularity among growers because it matures very late, is difficult to harvest, has lower alpha acid content than Galena or Nugget, and doesn't keep as well—*Pale Ales, Dark Ales, and Stouts*.

Fuggles (Britain & America) (4-5%)—A classic <u>finishing</u> hop. Very versatile and popular, with a rounded, mild, and woody <u>aroma</u>. The British varieties have higher AA%—well suited for all *English Ales, especially Pale Ales, Porters, and Stouts*.

Galena (America) (11-14%)—<u>Very bitter</u>. Very popular because, as a bittering hop, it is said to blend well with finishing hops. *American Ales and Lagers*.

Green Bullet (New Zealand) (9-11%)—<u>Bittering</u>. When available it is usually in pellet form. *Australian-style Ales and Lagers*.

Hallertau Hersbrucker (Germany) (2-5%)—The Hallertau is an area in Bavaria extending north of Munich bounded by the rivers Isar, Vils, Rott, and Inn that is the largest single hop production region in Europe. The Hersbrucker hops grown near Nürnberg are among the finest—they are certainly the most popular aroma variety. Often used interchangeably with the scarce Mittelfrüh. Mildly aromatic, with a crisp, spicy fragrance; a versatile <u>bittering</u> and herbal <u>finishing</u> hop. *Wheats, Altbiers, Pilsners, Belgian Ales, American and German Lagers*.

Hallertau (America) (4-6%)—Without accompanying adjectives, such as "Mittelfrüh" or "Hersbrucker," this is often a U.S.-grown version of the above. Mellow, spicy fragrance, a good all-around <u>bittering</u> and <u>finishing</u> hop—*Stock Ales, Altbiers, Belgian Ales, and Continental-style Lagers*.

Hallertau Mittelfrüh (Mittelfrueh) (Germany) (4-7%)—<u>Bitttering</u>, <u>flavor</u>, and <u>aroma</u>. The legendary Mittelfrüh's share of Germany's hop production has dropped from around 90% 25 years ago to less than 5% today, largely due to low yields and susceptibility to Verticillium wilt. More pungent, assertive, and herbal than Hersbrucker, but the two have been used interchangeably by brewers. Not widely available to homebrewers. *Continental Lagers and German Ales*.

Liberty (America) (4-5%)—A very good, low alpha acid improvement of the Mt. Hood variety developed to closely approximate Hallertauer Mittelfrüh aroma. Primarily a <u>finishing</u> hop. *American and German Ales and Lagers*.

Mt. Hood (America) (4-6%)—An excellent American derivative of Hallertauer Mittelfrüh with a light, delicate aroma. "Half-sister" to the Liberty. Primarily for <u>aroma</u> and <u>flavor</u> in *American and German Ales and Lagers*.

Northdown (Britain) (8-11%)—Developed by the famous Wye College, Northdown is a versatile <u>flavor</u> and <u>aroma</u> hop that also performs well as a bittering hop. Available seeded or seedless, this derivative of the Northern Brewer variety is one of Great Britain's most popular hops.

The Brewmaster's Recipe Manual

HOP PROFILES
(Continued)

Northern Brewer (America, Britain & Germany) (7-11%)—Each country produces a distinctly different version of this versatile hop—the British variety, for example, can have as much as a 4% higher alpha acid content than the German (approximately 7%AA), and the American version has a rougher flavor and aroma than the German. Primarily for <u>bittering</u>, but with strong <u>flavors</u> and <u>very fragrant</u>. Available seeded or seedless, this is a favorite bittering hop for *California Common Beers, Dark English Ales, and German Lagers,* but is also acceptable for aroma when used very sparingly.

Nugget (America) (11-15%)—<u>Extremely bitter</u>—Rapidly gaining popularity among microbrewers for its economy. *Medium to Dark American Ales and Lagers.*

Olympic (America) (11-13%)—An aggressively flavored bittering hop. Not widely available. *American Ales and Lagers.*

Omega (Britain) (9-11%)—A newer variety of high alpha acid <u>bittering</u> hop quickly gaining favor with British commercial brewers and homebrewers alike. Available in seeded or seedless varieties.

Perle (Germany & America) (6-11%)—A Hallertau/Northern Brewer hybrid. American varieties generally have higher AA ratings. Primarily for <u>bittering</u>, but it also has good "green hop" <u>aromas</u> when used sparingly. *Lagers, Wheats, and Pilsners.*

Pride of Ringwood (Australia) (8-10%)—An acclaimed <u>bittering</u> hop grown primarily in Tasmania. Availablity spotty in the U.S. *British Ales, Australian-style Ales, and Lagers.*

Progress (Britain) (6-7%)—A disease-resistant derivative of Whitbread Goldings. Primarily an aroma variety, Progress has declined drastically since its introduction in the mid-1960s.

Saazer (Saaz) (Czech Republic & America) (3-6%)—Production of this 150-year old strain has declined in recent years, but it is still considered one of the finest varieties ever used in beer. <u>Aromatic</u>, spicy, fragrant, and <u>flavorful</u>. Higher yielding/disease-resistant American varieties are currently being tested. Saaz is the quintessential Czech *Pilsner* hop, but is also exceptionally good in other *Continental Lagers and Wheats.*

Spalter (Germany) (4-5%)—Another <u>aromatic</u> and flavorful hop that has been suggested as an alternative to Saaz because it is a member of the Saazer "Formenkreis" (or group of varieties). Although Spalter production quantity is second only to Hersbrucker in terms of aroma hops, this pungent and spicy hop is not widely available to homebrewers, and it is often found only in pellet form—so stock up when you can. Ideal for all *German Lagers.*

Sticklebract (New Zealand) (9-10%)—A reliable and popular <u>bittering</u> hop. Not widely available, and often only in pellet form. *Australian-style Ales and Lagers.*

Styrian (Slovenia) (3.5-7%)—Basically, Fuggles that were brought to the Austro-Hungarian Empire from England at the turn of the century. The term "Goldings" was arbitrarily attached by merchants years ago, but these are not a predecessor of East Kent Goldings. Strong, warm <u>aroma</u>, but like many aroma varieties, it is often used by traditional brewers to provide a "rounded" <u>bitterness</u> as opposed to the so-called "harsh" bitterness of some high alpha varieties. For finishing *English-style Ales* and often suggested for bittering *Vienna/Märzen Lagers, Belgian Ales, and Pilsners.*

HOP PROFILES
(Continued)

Target (Britain) (9-13%)—A robust and disease-resistant <u>bittering</u> hop grown primarily around the town of Wye in East Kent. This is the U.K.'s most popular hop because of its low seed count and high alpha percentage, and it accounts for nearly half of British hop production. Used primarily by British brewers; not generally available to U.S. Homebrewers. *British Ale and Lagers.*

Tettnanger (Germany & America) (4-5%)—A member of the Saazer "Formenkreis" primarily grown in the Swabian region of southern Germany around the Bodensee (Lake Constance). Can be used interchangeably with Spalter. Tettnanger is often used by traditional German brewers in aroma blends with Saazer and Spalter. Mild, floral, and <u>very aromatic</u>. Also grown on a small scale in the U.S.—*Wheats and German Lagers.*

Whitbread Golding Variety (Britain) (5-7%)—Not actually a Golding, but an <u>aroma</u> hybrid developed with Golding as a parent strain. Generally considered a Fuggles replacement. WGV is not generally available to U.S. Homebrewers and is diminishing in popularity in the U.K. *British Ales.*

Willamette (America) (4-6%)—A spicy, aromatic <u>finishing</u> hop. A popular, high-quality American derivative of Fuggles with a slightly higher AA content. *American and British Ales.*

Yeoman (Britain) (9-14%)—A popular, disease resistant <u>bittering</u> hop developed in the United Kingdom that is similar to the Target variety. Not generally available to U.S. Homebrewers. *British Ales and Continental Lagers.*

Zenith (Britain) (9-10%)—A newer <u>bittering</u> hop with fairly good aroma developed in the United Kingdom in the 1980s. Not generally available to U.S. Homebrewers. *British Ales and Continental Lagers.*

*Note: Hops, like wine grapes, are greatly influenced by climatic conditions (i.e., rainfall, temperature, days of sunshine, whether the hops are grown seeded or seedless, etc.), and therefore, AA% varies from year to year.

The Brewmaster's Recipe Manual

YEAST

Beer yeasts (primarily *Saccharomyces Cerevisiae* and *Saccharomyces Uvarum*) are simple, single-celled microscopic fungi which transform malt sugar into alcohol, carbon dioxide (CO_2), and other by-products which give beers their varied flavors. For centuries, the importance of yeast in brewing was not fully understood. In fact, the original "Reinheitsgebot" Bavarian Beer Purity Law did not even recognize yeast as one of the primary ingredients and Bavarian monks, who knew only that a pot full of this stuff pitched into fresh wort made a great beer, euphemistically referred to it as "God is good." Now we know that yeast is the most important factor in determining a beer's flavor. Although it is probably the least glamorous ingredient in beer, yeast is quickly becoming the homebrewer's greatest concern, especially for those interested in accurately brewing a classic style; where proper yeast selection is imperative.

The primary differences between the two main beer yeasts are **1)** Saccharomyces Cerevisiae or "Ale Yeast" prefers warmer temperatures and tends to settle in clumps (floccculate) on top of the beer during fermentation, and **2)** Saccharomyces Uvarum or "Lager Yeast" prefers cooler temperatures and flocculates to the bottom of the vessel during fermentation. Neither really ferments only at the top or bottom, but throughout the beer. Each yeast species has a variety of unique strains that give each beer style its characteristic flavor, body, and aroma.

In the past, controlling flavor was hindered by the scarcity of pure liquid yeast cultures; a situation that has rapidly changed. Dry yeasts have a somewhat bad reputation, due to the fact that many dry yeasts included with English malt extract kits were mixed with cheap baker's yeast and/or were contaminated with wild or mutant yeasts, not to mention the fact that they were often very old. Most of these problems have been eliminated because homebrewers are becoming more sophisticated and are demanding higher quality. 7-14 Grams are recommended for 5 U.S. gallon recipes and rehydration with warm (90-110°F) water is now universally advised. Although liquid yeasts are currently very popular with serious homebrewers; to their credit, dry yeasts are drastically cheaper and tend to be longer-lived. For these reasons, several microbreweries now use dry yeasts with excellent results. However, this applies only to quality name-brand yeasts; generic ones included in malt extract kits (e.g., marked "Beer Yeast") still should be avoided. Some popular dry yeast brands available to homebrewers include: Nottingham, Windsor, Munton & Fison, Red Star, Amsterdam (a.k.a. European), Whitbread, and Coopers.

Some Yeast Basics—Courtesy David Logsdon & Wyeast Laboratories

- A **closed fermentation under airlock** is recommended.
- **Lag time** can be reduced by starting fermentation at 75°F, bringing the fermenter to the desired temperature once fermentation activity is evident.
- Ale strains usually ferment between 60-75°F, with a few able to perform down to 55°F. **68°F** is recommended as a good average.
- Lager strains usually ferment between 32-75°F, with **50-55°F** being the norm for primary fermentation. During secondary fermentation, a slow, steady reduction to **32°F** is customary.
- Vigorousness of fermentation activity is directly related to **temperature**. Low temperatures will result in a slower fermentation.
- **Fluctuations in temperature** negatively impact yeast performance.
- **Attenuation** is normally 67-77% and is affected by wort composition and yeast strain. The degree of attenuation will influence the body and residual sweetness of the finished beer.
- The level and type of **flocculation** varies according to yeast strain, with some forming large masses while others flocculate into small, granular clumps.
- Most brewing yeast is tolerant of alcohol levels of at least **8%**, and most ale yeasts can withstand up to **12%**.

The Brewmaster's Recipe Manual

YEAST PROFILES

Following is a glossary of popular liquid yeasts tailored to the major beer styles. A special mention is made of these because of their wide variety, their proven reliability (but not infallibility), and their dominance of the market. Some of the advanced Wyeast brands require a starter, as do all of the Yeast Lab products. The BrewTek yeasts are "slants" and require the use of a yeast culturing kit to produce quantities suitable for fermentation.

ALE YEASTS
(Saccharomyces Cerevisiae)

Except where noted, these generally perform best when fermenting at 60-72 °F and aging at 40-55 °F.

Common Name(s), Wyeast (Brewer's Choice)™, BrewTek™, or Yeast Lab™ number, and a brief supplier's/manufacturer's description:

Altbier (The Yeast Culture Kit Co. #A37)—Appropriate style(s): Altbier. Origin: Bavaria. Description: The strain used by many Alt breweries. Distinct profile.

American (Chico) Ale (Wyeast #1056)—Dry, neutral-flavored. Soft, smooth, clean and well-balanced. Apparent attenuation 73-77%, low to medium flocculation. A long secondary fermentation yields a dry lager-like beer. Ferments well from 72°F down to 60°F.

American Ale (Yeast Lab #A02)—This clean strain produces a very fruity aroma, with a soft and smooth flavor when fermented cool. Medium attenuation and low flocculation. This is an all purpose ale yeast. Optimum fermentation temperature 65-66°F.

American Ale (The Yeast Culture Kit Co. #A01)—Appropriate style(s): Barleywine, Brown Ale, IPA, Pale Ale, Porter, Stout. Origin: California. Description: Clean, crisp, and neutral. Easy to use.

American Microbrewery Ale #1 (BrewTek #CL-10)—A smooth, clean, strong fermenting ale yeast that works well down to 56°F. The neutral character of this yeast makes it ideal for Cream Ales and other beers in which you want to maintain a clean malt flavor.

American Microbrewery Ale #2 (BrewTek #CL-20)— Gives an accentuated, rich and creamy malt profile with generous amounts of diacetyl. Use it in lower gravity beers where the malt character should not be missed or in Strong Ales for a robust character.

American White Ale (BrewTek #CL-980)—A smooth Wheat Beer yeast with an exceptionally round, clean malt flavor. The poor flocculation of this yeast leaves a cloudy "Hefe-Weizen" yet its smooth flavor makes it an integral part of a true unfiltered Wheat Beer.

Australian Ale (Yeast Lab #A01)—An all-purpose strain that produces a very complex, woody, and flavorful beer. Australian origin. Medium attenuation, medium flocculation. Great for Brown Ales and Porters. Optimum fermentation temperature 65-68°F.

Bavarian Weizen (Yeast Lab #W51)—This strain produces a classic German-style wheat beer, with moderately high, spicy, phenolic overtones reminiscent of cloves. Medium attenuation, moderate flocculation. Optimum fermentation temperature 66-70°F.

YEAST PROFILES
(Continued)

Bavarian Weizen (The Yeast Culture Kit Co. #A50)—Appropriate style(s): Weizen, Weizenbock (was M01). Origin: Bavaria. Description: Clove and banana esters blend well with the sweet fruitiness of wheat malt to produce a classic weizen. Recommended fermentation temperature 64-66°F.

Bavarian Wheat (Wyeast #3056)—Blend of S. Cerevisiae and S. Delbrückii for the classic phenolic and estery Bavarian Weizen with a cloying sweetness when fresh. Apparent attenuation 73-77%, medium flocculation.

Belgian Ale #1 (BrewTek #CL-300)—Produces a truly classic Belgian Ale flavor. Robust and estery with notes of clove and fruit. Recommended for general purpose Belgian Ale brewing, it also ferments high gravity worts as well. (Note: this is not Chimay!)

Belgian Ale #2 (BrewTek #CL-320)— A Flanders style yeast. Makes a terrific Strong Brown and a good base brew for fruit-flavored beers. This strong fermenting yeast attenuates well and produces a fruity, estery malt profile, but is a little slow to flocculate.

Belgian Ale #3 (BrewTek #CL-340)— Slightly more refined than the CL-300, this yeast also produces a classic Trappist character, with esters of spice and fruit. Mildly phenolic, this is a strong fermenting yeast, well suited to Trappist and other Belgian ales.

Belgian Abbey (Wyeast #1214)—Abbey Style. Use for Belgian Trappiste, Dubbels, Tripels, and Barleywines—i.e., alcohol tolerant. Apparent attenuation 71-75%, medium to high flocculation.

Belgian Ale (The Yeast Culture Kit Co. #A36)— Appropriate style(s): Belgian Ale.s Origin: Houffalize, Belgium. Description: Distinct yeast signature. Estery and fruity.

Belgian Wheat (BrewTek #CL-900)— A top-fermenting yeast which produces a soft, bread-like flavor and leaves a sweet, mildly estery finish. Lends its delicious Belgian character to any beer, especially when brewing with Belgian Pils malt, and finishing with coriander and orange peel.

Belgian Wheat (Yeast Lab #W52)—Yeast used in the production of Belgian White Beer (Wit). This strain provides a soft, elegant finish with moderate esters and mild, spicy phenols. Optimum fermentation temperature 66-70°F.

Belgian White Beer (Wyeast #3944)—Rich, slightly phenolic character for classic Belgian wheat styles and Grand Cru. Medium flocculation. Apparent attenuation 72-76%.

Belgian Wit (The Yeast Culture Kit Co. #A35)—Appropriate style(s): Belgian Wit. Origin: Central Belgium. Description: Spicy, slight phenolic character compliments orange and coriander.

British (Whitbread) Ale (Wyeast #1098)—For the classic English Pale or Bitter Ale. Apparent attenuation 73-75%, medium flocculation. Slightly tart, slight diacetyl. Dry, crisp, fruity, and well-balanced. Complex, but more neutral than Wyeast #1028-London. Ferments well from 72°F down to 65°F.

YEAST PROFILES
(Continued)

British Ale (Yeast Lab #A04)—This strain produces a great light-bodied ale, excellent for Pale Ales and Brown Ales, with a complex estery flavor. Ferments dry with a sharp finish. Medium attenuation and medium flocculation. Optimum fermentation temperature 65-68°F.

British Draft Ale (BrewTek #CL-160)—Gives a full-bodied, well-rounded flavor with a touch of diacetyl. Emphasizes malt character. Highly recommended for Porter and Bitter.

British Pale Ale #1 (BrewTek #CL-120)— Produces a bold, citrusy character which accentuates mineral and hop flavors. The distinctive character of this yeast makes it well-suited for use in your classic British Pale Ale or Bitter.

British Pale Ale #2 (BrewTek #CL-130)— A smooth, full-flavored, well-rounded yeast that accentuates caramel and other malt nuances. Mildly estery, this yeast is a strong fermenter and is highly recommended for strong or spiced ales.

Canadian Ale (BrewTek #CL-260)—A clean, strong fermenting, and well attenuating ale yeast that leaves a pleasant, lightly fruity, complex finish. Well-suited for light Canadian Ales, as well as fuller flavored Porters and other British styles such as Bitter and Pale Ale.

Canadian Ale (Yeast Lab #A07)—This strain produces a light-bodied, clean, and flavorful beer—very fruity when fermented cool. High attenuation, medium flocculation. Good for Light and Cream Ales. Optimum fermentation temperature 65-66°F.

Classic British Ale (BrewTek #CL-170)—Creates a very complex British-style ale with fruity esters for draft Bitter or Porter; it also produces a classic Scottish Heavy and plays well in high gravity worts.

Dusseldorf Ale (Yeast Lab #A06)—German Altbier yeast strain that finishes with full body, complex flavor, and spicy sweetness. Medium attenuation, high flocculation. Optimum fermentation temperature 65-68°F.

English Ale (Yeast Lab #A09)—An old English Brewery strain, this clean yeast is fairly neutral in character; producing a fruity, soft, and estery finish. A vigorous fermenter. Optimum fermentation temperature 64-66°F.

English Ale (The Yeast Culture Kit Co. #A15)—Appropriate style(s): IPA, Pale Ale, Brown Ale, English Bitter. Origin: England. Description: Complex with strong, yeasty flavors.

English Barleywine Ale (The Yeast Culture Kit Co. #A08)—Appropriate style(s): Barleywine. Origin: Dorchester, England. Description: Tends to leave a high residual sweetness.

European Ale (Alt) (Wyeast #1338)—This Wissenschaftliche strain from Munich typifies the old pre-lager style of Ale. Complex, full-bodied, sweet, and very malty, apparent attenuation 67-71%. High flocculation.

YEAST PROFILES
(Continued)

German Ale (Wyeast #1007)—Ferments dry and crisp, leaving a mild and complex flavor. Produces an extremely rocky head, ferments well down to 55°. Apparent attenuation 73-77%, high flocculation. Often confused with #1338 above.

German Ale (The Yeast Culture Kit Co. #A04)—Appropriate style(s): Kolsch, Cream Ale. Origin: Germany. Description: Clean and fruity, produces exquisitely flavorful light-bodied ales.

German Weiss (BrewTek #CL-930)—Milder than the German Wheat #920, the 930 strain from a famous German yeast-bank still produces the sought-after clove and phenol characters, but to a lesser degree, with a fuller, earthier character underneath.

German Wheat (BrewTek #CL-920)—A true, top-fermenting Weizenbier yeast. Intensely "spicy," clovey, and phenolic. This yeast is highly-attenuative and flocculates in large, loose clumps. Use for all Weizen recipes—it is particularly good in Weizenbocks.

Irish Ale (Wyeast #1084)—Dry, complex, slight residual diacetyl—fruity, good for Stouts and Strong Ales. Soft, smooth, clean, and full-bodied. Apparent attenuation 71-75%, medium flocculation. Optimum fermentation temperature 62-72°F.

Irish Ale (Yeast Lab #A05)—This top-fermenting strain is ideal for Stouts and Porters. Slightly acidic, with a hint of butterscotch in the finish, soft and full-bodied. High attenuation, high flocculation. Optimum fermentation temperature 65-68°F.

Irish Ale (The Yeast Culture Kit Co. #A13)—Appropriate style(s): Porter, Stout, Imperial Stout. Origin: Dublin, Ireland. Description: The real thing from Ireland. Nutty, woody, and complex.

Irish Dry Stout (BrewTek #CL-240)—A top-fermenting yeast which leaves a very recognizable, slightly woody character to Dry Stouts. Has a vinous, almost lactic character which blends exceptionally well with roasted malts. Highly attenuative and a true top-fermenter.

Kölsch (Wyeast #2565)—A hybrid of ale and lager characteristics. This strain develops excellent maltiness and subdued fruitiness with a crisp finish. Ferments well at moderate temperatures. Low flocculation. Apparent attenuation 73-77%.

Kölsch (BrewTek #CL-450)—Produces mild sulphur during fermentation which smooths with time into a clean, well-attenuated flavor. Mineral and malt characters come through well with a clean, lightly yeasty flavor and aroma in the finish.

London (Whiteshield) Ale (Wyeast #1028)—Rich, minerally profile, bold, woody, and spicy—slight diacetyl. Mild but complex. Apparent attenuation 73-77%, medium flocculation. Great for Porters; often confused w/Wyeast #1098.

London ESB (formerly Special London Ale) (Wyeast #1968)—Highly flocculant ale yeast with rich, malty character and balanced fruitiness. Its high degree of flocculation makes it an excellent strain for cask conditioned ales. Apparent attenuation 67-71%.

London Ale (Yeast Lab #A03)—Classic Pale Ale strain, very dry. A powdery yeast with a hint of diacetyl and a rich, minerally profile. Optimum fermentation temperature 65-68°F.

YEAST PROFILES
(Continued)

Old German Ale (BrewTek #CL-400)—For traditional Alt Biers, a strong fermenter which leaves a smooth, attenuated, yet mild flavor. Use in your favorite German Ale recipes. This yeast also makes a slightly dry but clean, quenching wheat beer.

Pale Ale (The Yeast Culture Kit Co. #A17)—Appropriate style(s): Brown Ale, English Bitter, Mild, IPA, Pale Ale. Origin: London, England. Description: Very smooth and mellow with a distinct yeast signature.

Saison (BrewTek #CL-380)—A pleasant yeast best used to recreate country French and Belgian Ales, as well as Grand Cru styles. This yeast leaves a smooth, full character to the malt with mild yet pleasant esters and flavors reminiscent of apple pie spices.

Scotch Ale (The Yeast Culture Kit Co. #A34)—Appropriate style(s): Barleywine, Scotch Ale, Scottish Bitter, Strong Ale. Origin: Edinburgh, Scotland. Description: Clean, ferments well at cool temperatures.

Scottish Ale (Wyeast #1728)—Rich, smokey, peaty character ideally suited for Scottish-style ales, smoked beers, and high gravity ales. High flocculation. Apparent attenuation 69-73%.

Stout Ale (The Yeast Culture Kit Co. #A06)—Appropriate style(s): Porter, Stout, Imperial Stout. Origin: Ireland. Description: Low attenuation, slight diacetyl.

Trappe Ale (The Yeast Culture Kit Co. #A16)—Appropriate style(s): Trappist-style Ale.s Origin: Belgian Monastery. Description: Typical Trappist esters and aromas.

Trappist Ale (Yeast Lab #A08)—This is a typical Trappist strain, producing malty flavor with a balance of fruity, phenolic overtones when fermented warm. Alcohol tolerant, high attenuation, and high flocculation. Optimum fermentation temperature 64-70°F.

Weihenstephan Wheat (Wyeast #3068)—Saccharomyces Delbrückii single-strain culture for true-to-style Bavarian wheat beers. Low flocculation. Apparent attenuation 73-77%.

Wyeast Ale Blend (Wyeast #1087)—An 80 ml highly concentrated yeast blend for large volumes of beer. Yeast blends are created to ensure quick starts, good flavor, and good flocculation. Apparent attenuation 71-75%.

The Brewmaster's Recipe Manual

YEAST PROFILES
(Continued)

LAGER YEASTS
(Saccharomyces Uvarum [Carlsbergensis])

Except where noted, these generally perform best when fermenting at 46-55°F and aging at 32-45°F.

American (New Ulm) Lager (Wyeast #2035)—Steam beers and other American Lagers—light and clean, bold, complex, and woody. Ferments dry, crisp, clean, and light, but with more aggressive flavors than in Pilsners; producing flavors characteristic of the Midwest breweries/pre-Prohibition beers. Slight diacetyl. Apparent attenuation 73-77%, medium flocculation.

American Megabrewery Lager (BrewTek #CL-620)—A smooth yeast with a slightly fruity character when fresh which lagers into a smooth, clean-tasting beer. Use for your lightest, cleanest lagers or those in which you want an unobtrusive yeast character.

American Microbrewery Lager (BrewTek #CL-630)—A strong fermenter leaving a clean, full-flavored, malty finish. Slightly attenuative, this yeast is very versatile for most lager styles requiring a clean, full flavor.

Bavarian Lager (Wyeast #2206)—Rich flavor, smooth, clean, full-bodied—malty, unsurpassed for Bocks and Vienna/Oktoberfest/Märzen. Apparent attenuation 73-77%, medium flocculation. Used by many Bavarian breweries.

Bavarian Lager (Yeast Lab #L32)—Use this classic strain for medium-bodied lagers and Bocks, as well as Vienna and Märzen styles. Rich in flavor with a clean, malty sweetness. Medium attenuation and medium flocculation. Optimum fermentation temperature 48-52°F.

Bohemian Lager (Wyeast #2124)—A popular strain for a drier Pilsen-style beer than with the #2278 "Czech Pils." Ferments clean with a rich, residual maltiness. Apparent attenuation 69-73%, medium flocculation.

California Esteem Lager (BrewTek #CL-690)—Use to recreate California Common Beers, leaves a slightly estery, well-attenuated finish. The character of this yeast is quite distinct, try it in American or robust Porters for a new and unique flavor profile.

California Lager (Wyeast #2112)—For warm fermenting (58-62°F) "Steam" and California styles; malty profile, clears brilliantly. Apparent attenuation 72-76%, high flocculation.

California Lager (Yeast Lab #L35)—A "California Common Beer" strain, malty with a sweet, woody flavor and subtle fruitiness. Medium attenuation and high flocculation. Optimum fermentation temperature 64-66°F.

Czech Pils (Wyeast #2278)—Classic Czech Saaz style. Good choice for Pilsners and Bock beers. Sulphur produced during fermentation dissipates with conditioning. Medium to high flocculation. Apparent attenuation 70-74%.

Danish Lager (Wyeast #2042)—Continental European/North German-style accenting hop character. Rich, crisp, and dry. Produces strong fermentation odors which soon fade. Apparent attenuation 73-77%, low flocculation.

YEAST PROFILES
(Continued)

East European Lager (BrewTek #CL-680)—Imparts a smooth, rich, almost creamy character, emphasizing a big malt flavor and clean finish. For brewing lagers in which the malt character should be full and smooth as in Märzen/Oktoberfest.

German Lager (The Yeast Culture Kit Co. #L09)—Appropriate style(s): German lagers & Bocks, most other lager styles. Origin: Bavaria. Description: Common strain used in many German lager breweries.

Munich Lager (Wyeast #2308)—Well-rounded, malty, smooth and soft, but sometimes unstable, Wissenschaftliche #308. Recommended for Dunkels, Bocks, and heavier German beers, but also makes a nice Vienna/Oktoberfest. Apparent attenuation 73-77%, medium flocculation.

Munich Lager (Yeast Lab #L33)—Wissenschaftliche strain for medium-bodied lagers and Bocks, subtle and complex flavors, smooth and soft, with a hint of sulfur when fresh. Medium attenuation and medium flocculation. Optimum fermentation temperature 50-52°F.

North German Lager (BrewTek #CL-660)—Exhibits a clean, crisp, traditional lager character. A strong fermenting and forgiving lager yeast. Excellent for general-purpose lager brewing of German Pils, as well as Mexican and Canadian lagers.

Original Pilsner (BrewTek #CL-600)—Leaves a full-bodied lager with a sweet, underattenuated finish and subdued diacetyl character. Use in classic Czech Pilsners or any lager in which you want to emphasize a big, malty palate.

Pilsen Lager (Wyeast #2007)—a.k.a. St. Louis. Ferments dry, crisp, clean, and light. Ferments well down to 40°F. Apparent attenuation 71-75%. Medium flocculation. For American Pilsners and "Steam" beers.

Pilsen Lager (The Yeast Culture Kit Co. #L17)—Appropriate style(s): American Lager, Pilsner. Origin: Plzen. Description: Extremely clean, malty, and full-bodied. Ferments well to 48°F.

Pilsner Lager (Yeast Lab #L31)—This classic strain produces a lager that is light in both flavor and body, fermenting dry and clean. High attenuation and medium flocculation. Optimum fermentation temperature 50-52°F.

St. Louis Lager (Yeast Lab #L34)—This strain produces a rounded, very crisp and clean, fruity flavor, with medium body that is good for American-style lagers. High attenuation and medium flocculation. Optimum fermentation temperature 50-52°F.

Wyeast Lager Blend (Wyeast #2178)—An 80 ml highly concentrated yeast blend for large volumes of beer. Yeast blends are created to ensure quick starts, good flavor, and good flocculation. Apparent attenuation 71-75%.

SPECIAL PURPOSE YEASTS & BACTERIA

Brettanomyces Bruxellensis (Wyeast #3273)—Belgian Lambic-style "wild" yeast with rich, earthy, odoriferous character and acidic finish. Advanced Brewing Culture that must be cultured-up before use.

Brettanomyces Lambicus (BrewTek #CL-5200 & Yeast Lab #3220)—"Wild yeast" added during various stages of fermentation (depending on your opinion of what works best) in the creation of Belgian Lambics. Starter often requires one week to culture up.

YEAST PROFILES
(Continued)

Champagne (The Yeast Culture Kit Co. #W06)—Appropriate style(s): Mead, wine. Origin: Montreal. Description: A vigorous and thorough fermenter, very alcohol tolerant.

Dry Mead (Yeast Lab #M61 & Wyeast #3632)— Very alcohol tolerant, ferments dry, fruity and clean, yet leaves noticeable honey flavor and aroma. Optimum fermentation temperature 65-70°F.

Pasteur Champagne Yeast (Wyeast #3021)—"Prise de Mousse." Sold on the *Vintner's Choice* label. Crisp and dry. Recommended for high-gravity beers, Meads, and Barleywines. A good flocculating, low foaming, excellent barrel fermenter. Ferments well down to 55°F.

Pediococcus Cerevisiae (Wyeast & Yeast Lab #3200)—A bacteria often added during the secondary fermentation to produce lactic sourness in the creation of Belgian Lambics—usually after a primary fermentation with an ale yeast. Starter often requires one week to culture up.

Pediococcus Damnosus (BrewTek #CL-5600)— A lactic acid and diacetyl producing bacteria added prior to the Brettanomyces in the secondary fermentation of Belgian Lambics and Oud Bruins.

Sweet Mead (Yeast Lab #M62 & Wyeast #3184)— This strain has reduced alcohol tolerance and therefore, produces a very fruity, sweet Mead with tremendous honey aromas. Optimum fermentation temperature 65-70°F.

Nine Steps to Yeast Success—Courtesy David Logsdon & Wyeast Laboratories

• **Use the freshest yeast possible**—Yeast is very sensitive to temperature extremes and light. Keep refrigerated and use within 30 days of manufacture date, if possible.
• **Culture up yeast that isn't at peak freshness**—Yeast more than 1 month old should be rejuvenated with a 1.020-1.025 S.G. 1/2 liter starter; sterilized, then cooled to exactly 75°F before pitching in yeast.
• **Use sufficient quantities**—Yeast quantities provided by manufacturers are generally for standard gravity beers. Wyeast recommends doubling the pitching rate for every 0.008 increase above 1.048.
• **Pitch at the right time**—The high krausen stage of yeast reproduction 36-72 hours after making your starter or activating your "slap pack" is the optimum time to pitch into wort or a larger starter.
• **Use the proper strain for the beer you are brewing**—Select the appropriate yeast not only for the style you want, but also for the actual temperature at which you'll be fermenting. More flocculant ale yeast produces maltier, clearer beers. Less flocculant ale yeast produces drier beers, but they are often more estery and fruity. More flocculant lager strains produce clearer, fuller-bodied beers, and ferment best at 48°F or above. Less flocculant lager yeasts usually produce drier, colder fermenting beers, but take longer to clear.
• **Use the optimum fermentation temperature**—Culture yeast at 75°F, not at fermentation temperature. Introduce this starter into your wort when both are at 75°, then adjust to proper fermentation temperature.
• **Perform proper aeration**—Lack of aeration increases lag time, prolongs fermentation, results in high final gravities, and causes off-flavors. As long as wort is cooled to 75°F, there is no threat of oxidation from vigorous aeration. The CO_2 produced during fermentation will purge any oxygen. Highly flocculant yeasts need greater aeration, medium and low flocculators need less.
• **Keep fermentation temperature steady**—Changes in fermentation temperature (at night, for example) can result in premature flocculation and stuck fermentation, particularly with high flocculators.
• **Don't rack prematurely**—Transferring beer too early can result in a high final gravity. Wait until 90% of the sugars are attenuated before racking to a secondary fermenter. Also, top-fermenting yeast should not be harvested before at least 50% of the sugars are attenuated.

WATER

Although an in-depth scientific discussion of water chemistry is beyond the scope of this book, there are a few facts about this most basic beer ingredient that every brewer should know. Below is a brief discussion and glossary of water terms, and how they apply to homebrewing.

The main reason that the properties of brewing water (called "liquor") are considered at all by brewers is because of the effect its various ions have on the vital starch-degrading **enzymes** in malt. The levels of the six main ions directly affect the water's pH, which in turn determines the effectiveness of the enzymes to do their job of making maltose. Therefore, achieving the correct balance among these ions will greatly influence the extract yield of the malt. In malt extract-based brewing, the concerns of water used in mashing and brewing down the wort into syrup or powder are taken care of by the manufacturer. However, if you are adding your own malts, specialty grains, or hops, the water you use is of importance.

The second major consideration of water is perhaps the most obvious—**flavor**. As long as your water is free of organic or man-made contaminants, its flavor will in large part be influenced by the same six ions that influence enzyme activity. If you've been plagued by unsatisfactory "house flavors," these may relate to an imbalance in the ions of the water you are using.

The third consideration of a particular water's makeup is its ability to provide necessary **nutrients** to the yeast that will ferment the wort. This is definitely the least of a homebrewer's concern, as yeast requires only trace amounts of these ions, which are generally present in more than sufficient quantities in well-modified malts and in all water sources except, of course, distilled water.

Below is a list of the six main ions and their effects on brewing liquor:

Carbonate/Bicarbonate (CO_3 or HCO_3)—The ions that determine Temporary or "Carbonate" Hardness. Expressed as "Total Alkalinity" on most water analysis sheets, the presence (or lack of) bicarbonate is considered the most crucial factor in brewing liquor. Too little and the mash acidity will be too high, especially when using darker malts. (High levels in Munich's water are largely responsible for the famous softness of Münchner Dunkel). Too much counteracts the calcium ion acidification process, resulting in poor extract yields from malted grain. Levels should generally be no higher than 25-50 mg/l for pale beers, 100-300 mg/l for dark beers.

Sodium (Na)—Contributes body, full mouthfeel, and character. Overuse of sodium in liquor treatment will lead to a noticeable "sea water" taste. Levels generally range from 10-70 mg/l in good brewing liquor.

Chloride (Cl)—Found in common table salt, this ion brings out malt sweetness, and like sodium, contributes to the overall mouthfeel and complexity of the beer. Levels generally can range from 1-100 mg/l in good brewing liquor, but should always stay below 150 mg/l to avoid salty flavors.

Sulfate (SO_4)—Although secondary to calcium in lowering pH, this is the main water element influencing hopping rates as it brings out a sharp, dry bitterness if IBUs are too high. Levels below 10 mg/l are recommended for Pilsners, around 25-50 mg/l for most light or amber lagers, and 30-70 mg/l for most ales. Notable exceptions include Burton-on-Trent style Pale Ales (500-700 mg/l), and Dortmunder and Vienna Lagers (100-130 mg/l).

The Brewmaster's Recipe Manual

WATER
(Continued)

Calcium (Ca)—This most important "Permanent Hardness" element in brewing liquor helps lower pH to the optimum 5.0-5.5 range and encourages the precipitation of proteins ("the break") during the boiling process. A good level for most ales and lagers is generally considered to be around 100 mg/l. Too much will create a harsh, bitter taste, especially in amber lagers.

Magnesium (Mg)—Valued primarily as a yeast nutrient, this ion is usually increased by the addition of Epsom Salts, but addition of magnesium is usually advised against by many experts, especially when brewing light lagers. Levels above 30 mg/l will lend a dry, astringent bitterness to your brew. Levels in the great brewing waters of the world usually hover around 20-30 mg/l.

All of the above ions, along with other trace elements, determine the water's Total Hardness and Total Dissolved Solids (TDS). TDS and Total Hardness are arrived at by complex laboratory methods of titration and filtration and generally cannot be calculated at home if you only know the free ion levels. In the United States, water is generally grouped according to its TDS into one of the four categories below:

Soft—0 to 75 mg/l (ppm) TDS
Moderate—75 to 150 mg/l (ppm) TDS
Hard—150 to 300 mg/l (ppm) TDS
Very Hard—Above 300 mg/l (ppm) TDS

Temporary Hardness: Also referred to as "Carbonate Hardness," this refers to the level of carbonates/bicarbonates in a water sample. Temporary Hardness can be removed by boiling your brewing liquor for 10 minutes, but the liquor should then be transferred off the powdery, white salts precipitated behind. Water high in Temporary Hardness is good for Porters, Stouts, Munich Dunkel, and Schwarzbier.

Permanent Hardness: This pertains to the levels of calcium and magnesium ions that contribute to a water sample's "Total Hardness." These cannot be removed by boiling and, therefore, are called "permanent." Water with a high degree of Permanent Hardness is good for brewing Burton-style ales and Dortmund-style lagers.

Note: *You can obtain a water analysis from your local Water Board or Health Department, or you can test your own water to a certain degree with kits purchased from local Hot Tub and Swimming Pool Suppliers, and some Hardware Stores.*

Water Treatments

These additives, commonly sold by Hombrew Supply Shops, can help you adjust your ion concentrations and pH levels.

Burton Water Salts—A combination of Gypsum, Magnesium Sulfate, and Sodium Chloride added in the mash tun or brew kettle.

Gypsum ($CASO_4$)—Increases Calcium and Sulfate ions, primarily used to lower the pH in the mash. Not generally recommended in large amounts for lager brewing.

WATER
(Continued)

Table Salt (NaCl)—Increases Sodium and Chloride ions. Addition is usually advised against unless you are certain of the results. In any event, addition should be below 1 teaspoon per 5 U.S. gallons.

Epsom Salts (MgSO$_4$)—Increases Magnesium and Sulfate ions. For Permanent Hardness in the brew kettle or mash tun to imitate Burton-on-Trent water.

Calcium Carbonate (CaCO$_3$)—Increases Temporary Hardness in the mash and raises pH (increases alkalinity/lowers acidity). One teaspoon raises the Carbonate level 60ppm and the Calcium level 36ppm (per 5 U.S. gallons). This may also be referred to in water analysis sheets as Bicarbonate (a.k.a. HCO$_3$).

Calcium Chloride (CaCl$_2$)—Increases Calcium and Chloride ions. Preferable to Calcium Sulfate for pH adjustment because of the side effect of harshness contributed by Sulfate.

"Water Salts" are often sold as additives containing the above ingredients alone, in combination, or sometimes with other products such as supplementary yeast nutrients and haze reducers added. There are several books containing information on the use of water salts to achieve proper ion concentrations, particularly Clive LaPensee's *The Historical Companion to House-Brewing*, Gregory Noonan's *Brewing Lager Beer*, and Charlie Papazian's *The New Complete Joy of Homebrewing*. It is recommended that you first learn what your water contains, then learn what additions will yield the proper results. Consulting works on a particular style, such as the Brewer's Publications' *Beer Style Series,* is highly recommended for this.

It is usually safe to add the standard pre-packaged dosage of water hardening salts in brewing a Burton-style Pale Ale or a Dortmunder, since most of us start with treated municipal water that is fairly soft, but when brewing other styles where water hardness should be in the medium or soft range, adjustment will be trickier. Above all else, remember that homebrewing is more of an art than a science when compared to commercial brewing, so use the tried-and-true "artistic methods" of (1) trial and error; and (2) practice, practice, practice!

Important Points to Remember About Brewing Liquor

•Dark malts counteract the effects of alkaline water, and vice-versa. This includes lower Lovibond rated malts such as Vienna and Munich. Therefore, beers with more than 5-15% dark malt in the grist should have some level of Temporary Hardness.

•Chlorine in public drinking water supplies lends significant off-flavors to beer, especially light lagers. Boiling is the most effective means of removing chlorine from water, but it also reduces Temporary Hardness, which may not be desirable. Aerating cold water, then waiting 24 hours before using, reduces chlorine without reducing Temporary Hardness.

•pH is measured on a scale of 1-14. 7 is neutral, the accepted ideal for brewers <u>prior</u> to adding malt, which lowers pH to the 5.0-5.5 range. Temporary Hard water has a pH of approximately 7.8—after boiling 10 minutes, this falls to 7. The brewing process only deals with pH levels in the 4-8 range.

•Reduce hops if using water with Temporary Hardness greater than 100-150 mg/l.

WATER
(Continued)

•Add water treatments to the mash or to the wort, not raw water. Some salts, like NaCl will dissolve in plain water, but $CaCO_3$, for example, will not.

•These basic water principles apply not only to the mash and brew liquor, but to sparge liquor as well.

•Top-fermenting yeasts are not as sensitive to improper wort pH as bottom-fermenting yeasts and, therefore, can tolerate a wider range of water salt levels.

The *International Bottled Water Association* gives these definitions for the major bottled water products and processes, all of which must meet FDA standards.

•**Spring Water** is defined as coming from an underground formation which flows naturally to the earth's surface. Like most bottled waters, spring water is disinfected with ozone (O_3), a form of oxygen which leaves no chemical residue, aftertaste, or aroma.

•**Natural Water** is spring, mineral, artesian well, or well water which is derived from an underground formation and is not taken from a municipal or public water supply, has not been modified by the addition or deletion of dissolved solids, except for ozonation (non-chlorine disinfection).

•**Mineral Water** is defined as coming from a geologically or physically protected undergound source. It should be clearly distinguishable from other water types by the level of minerals and trace elements. Total Dissolved Solids must appear on the label stated in mg/l.

•**Distilled Water** is vaporized, then condensed, leaving the water free of dissolved minerals. Also know as "Purified Water."

•**Deionization** is a process where water is filtered through resins which remove most of the dissolved minerals. This also creates "Purified Water."

•**Reverse Osmosis** is a process where water is forced under pressure through membranes which remove 90% of the dissolved minerals. This also creates "Purified Water."

Beer Trivia—*The pH scale, now indispensable to the scientific world, was invented by Danish biochemist S.P.L. Sørenson (1868-1939) originally for the purpose of—you guessed it—brewing beer.*

The Brewmaster's Recipe Manual

WATER ANALYSES OF SELECTED U.S. CITIES

These are <u>average</u> figures (often from combined groundwater and surface water sources) that indicate the approximate levels at the consumer's faucet. These will often be quite different from the raw, untreated levels. (All numbers expressed in milligrams per liter, which is equivalent to parts per million.)

	TH	Sodium	Chloride	Sulfate	Calcium	Magnesium	pH	TDS	Hardness
Atlanta, GA	19	3	NA	7	6	1	7.2	37	24
Boston, MA	10	10	14	8	4	1	7.9	NA	15
Charlotte, NC	17	9	6	8	8	1	8.8	NA	28
Chicago, IL	106	6	11	25	34	11	8.1	NA	131
Cleveland, OH	70	11	16	25	33	8	7.3	176	7
Dallas, TX	45	17	34	44	24	3	9.0	150	74
Hackensack, NJ	87	69	120	0	40	7	8.4	310	133
Las Vegas, NV	105	103	92	279	80	30	7.7	NA	329
Los Angeles (East)	NA	84	99	151	63	22	7.9	531	256
L.A. (West & S. F. Valley)	105	68	85	75	32	14	7.8	347	139
Memphis, TN	53	8	4	7	8	5	7.2	74	46
Milwaukee, WI	107	7	16	26	96*	47*	7.5	NA	143
New York City	29	11	21	12	13	4	7.2	102	47
Pittsburgh, PA	252	5	7	12	145	17	7.9	200	238
Portland, OR	9	2	2	0	2	1	6.7	24	9
Richmond, VA	29	NA	13	NA	15	3	8.0	94	49
Salt Lake City, UT	252	5	7	12	30	17	7.9	238	145
Seattle, WA	18	4	4	2	17*	1	7.8	41	21
S. San Francisco	NA	28	39	39	24	15	8.2	212	143

TH—Temporary Hardness—A term used primarily in brewing texts as a measure of the carbonate/bicarbonate level. Temporary Hardness is usually expressed on a water analysis as Bicarbonate Hardness or Total Alkalinity (as $CaCO_3$).

TDS—Total Dissolved Solids.

NA—Levels not tested, levels too low for current testing methods, or current data not available.

Hardness—Total Hardness—a measure of Calcium (as $CaCO_3$) and Magnesium (as $CaCO_3$). This will be significantly different from the free ion totals of Calcium and Magnesium alone.

*Expressed as $CaCO_3$, which can be three times higher than the "free ion" level.

ANALYSES OF SELECTED BOTTLED SPRING WATERS
(Expressed in milligrams per liter, which is equivalent to parts per million)

	TH	Sodium	Chloride	Sulfate	Calcium	Magnesium	pH	TDS
Deer Park®	32.9	2.8	0.5	6.0	3.8	1.17	7.6	50.0
Great Bear®	110.0	3.9	5.6	14.0	42.0	7.3	7.0	153.0
Naya®	243.0	6.0	1.0	14.0	38.0	22.0	7.0	NA
White Rock®	2.0	0.6	0.7	5.4	1.2	0.9	5.7	19.0
Poland Spring®	22.0	3.0	5.1	5.0	19.0	1.2	6.5	38.0
Vermont Pure®	NA	1.6	1.5	12.5	58.3	5.3	7.0	97.0

Note: The FDA classifies "sodium-free" as less than 5 milligrams per 8 oz. serving.

ANALYSES OF FAMOUS BREWING WATERS

Unlike the U.S. city numbers, these figures generally represent the approximate raw, untreated, and unfiltered groundwater sources.

	TH	Sodium	Chloride	Sulfate	Calcium	Magnesium
Burton-on-Trent	200	40	35	660	295	55
Dortmund	180	69	106	260	261	23
Dublin	319	12	19	54	117	4
London	156	99	NA	77	52	16
Munich	152	10	2	8	75	18
Pilsen	14	2	5	5	7	2

TH—Temporary Hardness—A term used primarily in brewing texts as a measure of the carbonate/bicarbonate level. Temporary Hardness is usually expressed on a water analysis as Bicarbonate Hardness or Total Alkalinity (as $CaCO_3$).

NA—Levels not tested, levels too low for current testing methods, or current data not available.

Beer (Water) Trivia—*Americans drink approximately 2 billion gallons of non-sparkling bottled water a year. Approximately 1 out of 6 American households use non-sparkling bottled water. In California, which consumes 36% of all bottled water in the U.S., the ratio is 1 out of 3.*

ADDITIVES

Below are products intended to improve the overall quality of your beer or to solve common problems such as poor head retention, thin body, or haze.

Amylase Enzyme—One of the diastatic enzymes (naturally occurring in malted barley) that converts starch to maltose (sugar) and allows better conversion when using low enzyme malts or high percentages of adjuncts. Produces light and dry characteristics in beer. Use in the mash.

Ascorbic Acid (Vitamin C)—Reduces oxidation in the bottle. Overuse will lend citrusy flavors.

Burton Water Salts—Used to harden brewing liquor for creating Burton-on-Trent style Pale Ales or "Hard Water" beers. (See "Water" section.)

Calcium Carbonate (Powdered Chalk)—Used in mash to add "temporary hardness" and to raise pH. (See "Water" section.)

Citric Acid—Anti-haze and pH balance.

Epsom Salts—Magnesium Sulfate (Sulphate), used in mash or kettle to provide "permanent hardness." (See "Water" section.)

Fermax—A yeast nutrient/dietary supplement for Meads and low gravity/low malt beers.

Gelatin—Promotes clearing by settling yeast and reduces haze by removing suspended proteins. Added before bottling—colorless and tasteless.

Gypsum (Calcium Sulfate)—Used to harden soft brewing liquor and settle out suspended particulate matter, specifically in Pale Ales. Lowers pH. (See "Water" section.)

Heading Agents—Helps beers develop and retain a creamy head; especially in low gravity and high-adjunct beers.

Irish Moss—A negatively-charged, dried seaweed that attracts positively-charged suspended beer proteins in the final (15-20) minutes of a wort boil to aid clearing. Active ingredient *Carrageenan* deters chill-haze. "Red" Irish moss is a similar, but more finely powdered version. One teaspoon per 5 gallons is recommended.

Isinglass—A yeast-settling, gelatinous fining agent made from the linings of fish swim bladders. Aids in clarification. Use of Isinglass during the secondary fermentation or conditioning stage is permitted under the Reinheitsgebot.

Juniper Berries—Good for flavoring Holiday Beers, Stouts, and Porters. Use sparingly.

Lactic Acid—For lowering pH when brewing with hard water. (See "Water" section.)

Lactose (Milk Sugar)—A mildly sweet, nonfermentable carbohydrate found only in milk. It is used primarily in Stouts and Porters to lend residual sweetness. Lactose has approximately 17% of the sweetness of Table Sugar.

Licorice Sticks—Adds a special, smooth flavor to Stouts, Porters, and flavored beers. Chop up 2-5 inches, then boil in brew kettle for 20 minutes.

ADDITIVES
(Continued)

Malto-Dextrin—Nonfermentable, tasteless carbohydrate that adds smoothness to beer. Can cause haze in light beers. Primarily for extract-based recipes to improve mouthfeel.

Oak Chips—A flavoring additive used to add hints of spiciness—as in India Pale Ale or Belgian Ale—to simulate oak cask conditioning. One ounce per 5 gallons is typical.

Papain—Derived from the juice of unripe papaya. Usually seen as a meat tenderizer. Prevents chill-haze in beer.

Pectic Enzyme—Removes the haze caused by the pectin carbohydrates contained in fruits and berries. Used primarily in winemaking, but can be used in fruit-flavored beers.

Polyclar®—A polymer (plastic powder) that prevents chill haze and oxidation.

Spruce Essence—Adds a unique flavor to Porters, Holiday Beers, and Honey Lagers. Use sparingly!

Water Crystals/Salts (Magnesium Sulfate & Gypsum)—Water hardener used for imitating Burton-on-Trent brewing liquor. Aids enzymes during the mash. Often contains other haze preventing ingredients. (See "Water" section.)

Yeast Nutrient—Aids fermentation in low gravity worts and Meads by providing essential foods for rapid yeast growth.

Beer Trivia—*In Bavaria, the annual per capita beer consumption is approximately 58 gallons.*

The Brewmaster's Recipe Manual

SANITIZERS & CLEANSERS

Sanitation is probably the single most crucial factor in the final outcome of your beer. Some of the more popular and widely available products for cleaning and sanitizing your equipment are as follows:

B-Brite—Product name of a cleaner/sanitizer that removes beer stone (hardened yeast) and other fermentation residues, but needs thorough rinsing. Its active oxygen cleans without chlorine or bisulfite and is especially useful in cleaning hard-to-reach places like carboy necks, but this may require an overnight soak. One tablespoon per gallon of water is recommended. Environmentally friendly.

BTF-Iodophor—Sanitizer. Product name of an iodine solution used in many breweries as a line cleaner because it won't corrode stainless steel or kegs. Requires no rinsing if properly diluted. Often recommended after using B-Brite. One-half ounce per 5 gallons is recommended. Not environmentally friendly and can permanently stain clothing.

Campden Tablets (Potassium or Sodium Metabisulfite)—Inhibits harmful bacteria and yeast. Use only in wine. One tablet per gallon is recommended. Allow to air dry for 24 hours. Contains sulfites which many people are extremely allergic to. It is often recommended that asthmatics avoid sulfite (sulphite) based products.

Chlorine/Household Bleach—Although very effective in sanitizing, it is very environmentally unfriendly. One teaspoon per gallon recommended. When using chlorine, adequate ventilation is highly recommended.

CL-9 Sanitizer—Concentrated chlorine-based sanitizer in a granular form.

One Step—Product name of a non-toxic, environmentally friendly sanitizer. No rinsing required after washing bottles or equipment. A good iodophor substitute, but extended soaking can leave a residue. One tablespoon per gallon of warm water is recommended.

Potassium Metabisulfite—Antibacterial agent that produces bacteria/yeast-inhibiting sulphur dioxide gas. Same uses as sodium metabisulfite, but adds no sodium. Use in wine "must" only, should not be put into beer wort.

Sodium Metabisulfite—Sanitizer. Inhibits bacterial & yeast growth. No longer widely used because many consider them dangerous and ineffective. See "Campden Tablets."

Straight-A—Product name of a cleaner similar to B-Brite. Environmentally friendly. Rinsing required.

Soda Ash (Sodium Carbonate)/Washing Soda—Cleaner used primarily in winemaking to "sweeten" new oak barrels, but also for cleaning primary and secondary fermenters, and for "beer clean" glassware.

Beer Styles

The Brewmaster's Recipe Manual

SUMMARY OF POPULAR STYLES

Abbey Beer—Although there are no rigid guidelines for what constitutes an Abbey Beer, it is generally accepted as a rich, full-flavored Belgian ale meant to approximate the Trappiste style (see "Trappiste"); often with a vinous quality due to high alcohol content. These beers are called "Abbey" simply because they often have the name of an old monastery attached—usually by a commercial brewery who pays a royalty for the privilege. Abbey beers run the gamut from deep gold to dark reddish brown and are generously carbonated. Esters, malt aroma, and some phenols usually dominate. Abbeys classified as "Dubbel" or "Tripel" sometimes have hop aroma. Alcohol averages 6-8% v/v.

Altbier—Also known as Düsseldorfer Alt. "Altbier" means "Old" or "Traditional" beer in German, referring to the old way that beers (i.e., ales) were top-fermented prior to the lagering revolution of the 19th century. These ales were originally lagered for long periods in ice filled caves after a warm primary ferment, which served to subdue the fruitiness. These beers have intense bitterness, with subdued hop flavor and aroma compared to a Pils (but to what degree is hotly debated by brewers). Full-bodied, bitter, and a deep, reddish-amber to brown color, but drier and more carbonated than an English-style ale. It should be noted that Altbier is not an appellation and, therefore, the term "alt" can be incorporated in the brand names of various beers not in the Dusseldorfer style e.g., Münster Alt, Altmünchener, Kloster Altbier, Alt Bayerische, etc., and often merely indicates an old style ale or a dark lager.

American Microbrewed Ale—With the renaissance of craft beers in the U.S., these beers are now typified by, but are by no means exclusively, full-bodied, medium-dry, moderately alcoholic, and well-hopped variations of classic British styles. In a sense, micro/regional brewers often strike a balance between the American taste for a drier, more carbonated beer and the freshness and character of Old World brews not previously available in the U.S.

American Microbrewery Lager—Originally, most microbrews were patterned after English-style ales using simple, single-step infusion mashing, as opposed to the more complex and expensive methods of programmed temperature and decoction, but now many American lagers that borrow from pre-Prohibition and modern European temperature-controlled mashing methods are being microbrewed. As in American ale brewing, American lager brewers often rely heavily on homegrown hop varieties such as Cascade, Willamette, Mt. Hood, Eroica, Chinook, etc., as well as American yeast strains which tend to be more neutral than their European counterparts.

American Pilsner—Also referred to as "American Premium Lager." Lightly colored and hopped, these often include adjuncts such as corn and rice for their character, and bear little resemblance to authentic Czech Pilsner. They are usually highly carbonated and served ice-cold. These generally are the products of the "giants" (Coors, Budweiser, Miller, etc.) that have grown progressively lighter and blander over the past 30 years, but still dominate the marketplace.

Australian/New Zealand Ales and Lagers—Tend to be light straw to amber colored, are often dry, full-bodied, and well-hopped with the locally grown Pride of Ringwood or Sticklebract. Although they have a reputation for being very strong, Australian beers are usually moderately alcoholic, and draw from both British and German brewing traditions.

Barleywine—British Strong Ale with high, wine-like alcohol content (6-12%). Usually reddish amber or copper w/O.G.s of 1.065 to 1.120 and often fermented with an alcohol-tolerant champagne yeast. High final gravities give this beer a sweetness that is balanced by high hopping rates. Best when aged 6 months to several years. Often a special occasion/holiday brew.

The Brewmaster's Recipe Manual

SUMMARY OF POPULAR STYLES
(Continued)

Belgian Red Ale—A West Flanders ale deriving its reddish color from large portions of Vienna malt, and its trademark acidity from bulk aging for 1-1/2 years in oak tuns. Belgian Red (a.k.a. "Old Red") is sometimes blended with new beer to reduce the acidity level.

Belgian Strong Ale—An alcoholically strong Belgian ale (6-12% v/v) similar to English Strong Ale that varies in color from pale amber to deep brown. The use of various refined sugars gives these vinous beers strength without the heaviness found in some Stouts and Bocks.

Bière de Mars—Light seasonal French ales homebrewed from the best of the summer barley and autumn hops. These beers are subjected to a long, slow fermentation over the winter and have been drunk in celebration of the arrival of spring since the late 14th century.

Bière de Garde/Bière de Paris—French Country/Parisian Ale that usually occupies the middle ground in body and maltiness. The hop bitterness, flavor, and aroma are also mild to moderate. Often characterized by a smooth, sweet, fruity, and earthy taste, these beers borrow heavily from Belgian brewing traditions. Color most often is deep amber to reddish brown. Traditionally, the majority of these unique "farmhouse" beers are brewed in the area near the Belgian border, bottled with corks in 750ml wine bottles and then aged for months, or even years, to mellow out the estery/phenolic overtones.

Bitter—A well-hopped, cask-conditioned, English draught ale. Lightly carbonated, and not as bitter as the name would suggest, but more often spicy from English hops and only slightly drier than standard Pale Ale. Varying in color from bronze to deep reddish copper. This very popular "Pub" style encompasses three sub-styles classified according to original gravity: **Ordinary Bitter**, **Special Bitter**, and **Extra Special Bitter/Best Bitter**. Alcohol generally ranges from 3.5% for the Ordinary to 5+% v/v for the ESB.

Bock—Rich, malty, brown German lager of 6.5+% alcohol by volume that is traditionally brewed in fall and winter for consumption in spring. Originally consumed during the season of Lent by monks—these beers provided a good source of nutrition during fasts. Contemporary American Bocks (O.G. 1.065) are usually lighter in body and color than the original, dark German Bocks. Doppelbocks or "Double Bocks" start w/O.G.s of around 1.075 (alcohol @7.5% v/v) and feature intense maltiness. Bock can also be homebrewed with top-fermenting yeast at cooler temperatures while still remaining true to style. Weizenbock is a German wheat beer that ranges from a deep, reddish-amber to black, but these are usually much lighter in body and intensity than the standard all barley malt Bock.

Brown Ale—Southern English Brown Ales are generally dark, sweet, and low alcohol. The northern English version is often drier and stronger in alcohol. Both are made with softer water than Pale Ales, and from O.G.s of 1.035 - 1.050. Their commercial popularity has waned considerably over the past few centuries, but Brown Ales are probably the easiest and most forgiving style to homebrew. They are enjoying currently enjoying somewhat of a revival among homebrewers and craft brewers. American Brown typically has more pronounced hop bitterness, flavor, and aroma—masking any diacetyl/estery qualities.

Burton Pale Ale—First brewed at Burton-on-Trent, England, this beer became the hallmark for the wildly popular new style "Pale Ale" that supplanted the Porters, Browns, and Milds. A full-bodied light amber ale with definite hop character. Addition of Burton Water Salts ("Burtonisation") is often recommended to approximate the high sulfate water used in the original.

The Brewmaster's Recipe Manual

SUMMARY OF POPULAR STYLES
(Continued)

California Common Beer—A uniquely American lager style fermented at the lower range of ale fermenting temperatures or the upper range for lagers (i.e., 55 to 60°) with a clean lager yeast strain, then cold lagered—resulting in low esters/diacetyl. Pale to dark straw or copper in color, medium-full flavor and body, and usually well-hopped in bitterness, flavor, and aroma. These well-carbonated lagers were nicknamed "Steam Beer" in the 19th century.

Canadian Ales and Lagers—Similar to U.S. versions in the use of adjuncts, etc. but usually with much more hop character. The ales have clean, crisp, lager characteristics, but exported megabrewery versions of both ales and lagers are often considered inferior to those found close to home in Canada.

Continental Dark Lager—A broad generalization encompassing lagers from continental Europe (i.e., not Britain) featuring a deep amber to brown color (sometimes from caramel coloring), subtle maltiness, well balanced with mellow European hops such as Hallertau or Saaz. Munich Dunkel is largely considered the pinnacle of the style.

Continental Light Lager—A very broad style category encompassing the many variations of light lager brewed primarily on the European continent, such as Dutch Light Lager, Munich Helles, Czech Pilsner, etc.

Cream Ale—An American mild, golden, full-bodied pale ale generally brewed with North American-grown barley and hops, and with an alcohol content of around 4.5-4.75% v/v. Typically top-fermented, then cold aged like a lager or even blended with lager.

Czech/Bohemian Pilsner (Pilsener)—Possibly the world's most famous and popular beer style, originally brewed in the Bohemian city of Plzen (Pilsen) in 1842. This is the classic European lager that others raced to imitate in the 19th century lagering revolution—straw to deep gold in color with a flowery Saaz hop aroma, a dry finish, and extremely well-balanced maltiness. More complex and full-bodied than the European or American imitators.

Dortmunder-Export—A popular style of beer originally brewed in the area around the city of Dortmund in western Germany. Typically, a full-bodied, "premium" lager occupying the middle ground between the dryness of German Pils and the sweeter maltiness of Munich Helles. Alcohol 5-6% by volume. Referrred to simply as "Export" in Germany, this is not to be confused with Export-Dunkel, a Bavarian/Munich dark lager.

Dubbel (Double)—A more clearly defined sub-style of the Belgian Trappiste/Abbey style that originally had approximately double the original gravity of the "Simple" beers of medieval Belgium. With original gravities of 1.063-1.070, these fairly sweet, dark, reddish-brown beers fall in the mid-range of "standard" Abbey strength.

Erlanger—A dark German lager from the Bavarian city of Erlangen that is both heavier and darker than Munich Dunkel, but has lower gravity and lighter color than Kulmbacher.

Eis Bock—German for "Ice Bock." A lager beer created by freezing Doppelbock after fermentation is complete. The resulting ice is removed and, therefore, much of the water, resulting in a much sweeter, heavier, and alcoholically strong beer.

The Brewmaster's Recipe Manual

SUMMARY OF POPULAR STYLES
(Continued)

Faro—A pale to brown Belgian Lambic (originally served exclusively on draft in and around Brussels) fermented with wild yeast and bacteria, of course, and refermented/sweetened with Candi sugar. The result is a lively, faintly sweet, but lactic and acidic ale with a soft, wine-like character. Faro is hard, but not impossible, to find outside of Belgium and France. One unique example imported to the U.S. is aged for 2 years in oak casks, then blended with wheat ale before bottling. It is also spiced with curaçao orange peel and the pre-hops bitterer, gentian root. Alcohol 4.5-5.5% v/v.

Fest Bier (festbiere)—A term commonly used to describe "special occasion" German beer such as Märzen, but it also refers to German Christmas (Weinachten) or Easter (Ostern) beer and a variety of beers commemorating lesser feast days. Typically, Fest Biers are ruddy, malty, rich lagers sold only during holidays. These slightly stronger than normal beers are usually on draft, but are sometimes bottled.

Flanders Brown—A smooth, malty Brown Ale (a.k.a. "Oud Bruin") with a slight lactic sourness that originally was brewed in the Flemish-speaking region of Belgium. Only slightly darker than the "typical" Abbey style, and characteristically low in hop bitterness, flavor, and aroma.

Framboise—Belgian fruit Lambic flavored with raspberries. Like other styles of Lambic, this is also effervescent, tart, turbid, and very lightly hopped. Not to be confused with Liefman's *Frambozen,* an Oud Bruin flavored with raspberries.

German/North European Pils—A lighter, drier, hoppier, more effervescent and less-smooth version of the malty Czech Pilsner. There are four classes of German Pils: *Klassische Pilsener, Suddeutschen Pilsener, Sauerlander Pilstypus,* and *Hanseatische Pilsenertyp.* These range in O.G. from 1.044-56, have alcohol levels of 4.8-5.7% v/v, vary in maltiness and hoppiness, and have water hardnesses ranging from 200-400 ppm.

Gueuze—Non-flavored old Lambic (2-4 years old) and young Lambic (3 months to 1 year old) that are blended, then aged at least 1 more year before drinking. Pronounced "Gurrs."

Grand Cru—A term for Belgian "special occasion" beer in no particular style that is often arbitrarily bestowed on a brewery's strongest beer. Originally brewed for weddings, village celebrations, and other important events, Grand Cru can sometimes be a "Zuur" (lactic acid) Ale blended with Lambic that produces a beer gold in color, with bready/grain flavor, spicy yeast presence, malt dominating, and no hop bouquet. High in alcohol ($\geq 6\%$ v/v).

Ice Beer—The result of a fermentation process developed by Labatt's Brewery of Canada. The lager is force-fermented with specially-designed yeasts engineered to work at low temperatures in order to produce a very clean, dry, and smooth product. The subsequent removal of ice crystals from the chilled beer similar to the method of creating Eis Bock is meant to produce less of the watery flavor found in "Dry" or "Light" beers (in some brands, water is put back in). Alcohol is typically 5-5.6% v/v.

India Pale Ale (IPA)—A sub-style of English Pale Ale whose textbook definition has traditionally been of a premium, high gravity, extremely well-hopped ale, although there are many commercial brands that do not fit this description. IPA gained its name because of its popularity with the British troops in colonial India. Its alcoholic strength and high hopping rates helped it withstand the long ocean voyage from England. This is a beer now found mostly in bottled form, although it was originally cask-conditioned for several months (and with estimated hopping rates of up to 200 IBUs.)

Irish Red Ale—A slightly sweet, red-hued (from the use of roasted barley) Irish cousin of English Pale Ale/Bitter. Greatly influenced by the Scottish Ales, Irish Reds are malty, lightly hopped, light to medium bodied, and have a slight buttery quality. Top or bottom-fermented commercial versions can be found.

SUMMARY OF POPULAR STYLES
(Continued)

Kellerbier—A fruity, dry lager brewed primarily in Franconia around Buttenheim and Bamberg. Kellerbier averages 4.5-5% alcohol by volume, and is highly hopped and lightly carbonated. Bottled versions do exist, but this unfiltered or minimally filtered beer is usually served on draft in local village "bräustüberls."

Klosterbier—Literally, "Cloister Beer," denoting a beer that is now or sometime in the past was brewed in a monastery or convent.

Kölsch—A pale, often cloudy, and blonde "old style" German ale originally brewed in the Köln (Cologne) area before the lagering revolution. Moderately or lightly hopped in the boil, dry with a slight lactic taste, and moderately high in alcohol (4-5.5% v/v).

Kriek—Belgian cherry-flavored Lambic made by putting macerated cherries in the secondary fermenter—usually after an extended primary ferment.

Kulmbacher—Dark German lager from the town of Kulmbach in northern Bavaria that is both heavier and darker than Erlanger, as well as the more popular Münchner Dunkel.

Lambic—Belgian wheat beer spontaneously fermented with wild airborne yeast and bacteria. The style originated in the town of Lembeek in the Pajottenland and by law must contain a minimum of 30% wheat, usually unmalted. It is cloudy yellow, very lightly hopped, frothy, and slightly sour or citric in taste. Lambic is often flavored with fruits such as peaches ("Pêche"), cherries ("Kriek"), or raspberries ("Framboise") and is cooled in large, open vats, then fermented from start to finish in large, oak wine casks.

Light Beer—A wildly successful American invention that has spread worldwide. Typically thin, tasteless, and watery (O.G.s @1.030), and intended to be low in alcohol (1-2.5% v/v) and/or low calorie (90-110 calories per serving). The low flavor profile requires that these beers be served ice-cold.

Malt Liquor—An American term whose legal definition varies from state to state, but typically refers to lagers with a minimum of 4% and a maximum of 6% alcohol by volume. In some states, imports with these alcohol levels, such as Bavarian Oktoberfest, must contain the words "malt liquor" on the label. As a style definition, "Malt Liquor" is equated with the low-quality, alcoholic, rough-flavored, and highly carbonated lagers of the American megabreweries.

Mars—A rare "March" beer from the region around the famous Belgian brewing town of Louvain (Leuven) that is no longer brewed commercially. Traditionally, a "small beer" brewed from the low-gravity runoff of the mash, which is then aged several months before summer consumption.

Märzen—A German lager "festbiere." Similar to the Vienna style, but now generally regarded to be a slightly darker, stronger beer. True Märzen, by the German definition, is brewed in March and aged until late September/early October. Amber, smooth, and malty, but well-balanced by German or Czech hops.

Mexican Beer—Originally, these were basically German or Vienna-style lagers brewed by German immigrants. Most modern varieties, however, have moved closer to American mega-brewery lagers in body, flavor, carbonation, and alcohol content due in large part to the recent popularity of *Corona*, a high-adjunct beer originally brewed in the 1920s to be an inexpensive, blue collar beer.

The Brewmaster's Recipe Manual

SUMMARY OF POPULAR STYLES
(Continued)

Mild Ale—Mild Ales are low alcohol English beers (roughly 3-3.5% v/v) that have medium-light body and a slightly sweet finish. Some are copper colored, but most are actually lower-gravity, dark Brown Ales. They were originally just green ("mild" once meant immature) beers of normal or even high gravity, but are now "mild" in terms of strength and hop bitterness, not age.

Münchner Dunkel—The Bavarian version of Continental Dark Lager also referred to simply as "Dunkel" (German for "dark"). Mastery of this beer style is credited to Spaten Brewery's Gabriel Sedlmayr in the mid-19th century. His initials can still be found on the Spaten label. Malty in aroma and taste, but well-balanced by German hops—not at all bitter or heavy.

Munich Helles—Munich-style light lager developed in the 1920s as an answer to the overwhelming demand for Pilsen-style beers. Basically, a lighter version of the renowned Munich Dunkel already in existence. These gold to straw-colored lagers are noted for their smooth, well-balanced maltiness and unaggressive hop bitterness.

Oktoberfest—An American term denoting the style of beer traditionally served at Oktoberfest celebrations in Bavaria. Bavarians refer to this beer as "Märzen."

Old Ale—A medium-strong British dark ale also called "Stock Ale," usually with O.G.s between 1.040-1.064 and around 6% alcohol v/v. This beer was named "Old" because centuries ago it was Mild Ale aged a year or more before drinking. A mixture of expensive Old Ale and inexpensive Mild became the basis for the Porter style.

Oud Bruin (Old Brown)—Dark reddish-brown to black East Flanders ale (a.k.a. "Flanders Brown") that is subjected to a long primary ferment, and an even longer secondary ferment, often in wooden casks where it is exposed to beer souring bacteria. The result is a well-aged, slightly sour, and acidic beer with a vinous nature, but like Belgian ales in every style category, no two are ever alike. Some Oud Bruins are also flavored with raspberry or cherry.

Pale Ale—The classic British ale developed in 18th century that is well-hopped, full-bodied, and bronze, golden, or copper in color. Originally, Pale Ales were cask conditioned and many in the U.K. still are; in the U.S. they are primarily kegged or bottled, although there is a growing interest in cask conditioning, particularly in the Pacific Northwest. By modern standards, these ales are far from pale, but the name was first used in comparison to the really dark Stouts and Porters. Pale Ales are brewed from harder waters than most ales and typically with O.G.s of 1.040-1.055. (See "India Pale Ale" and "Bitter.")

Porter—London's claim to brewing fame. A dark, moderately strong ale (O.G.s 1.048-1.060) that was born as an inexpensive mixture of green beer (Mild and/or Brown Ale) with aged beer (Old Ale). Porter has a spicy, chocolatey character and is hopped with English varieties such as Fuggles. Gypsum, chocolate malt, black malt, dark unrefined sugar, licorice root, wormwood, and roasted barley have all contributed to the recipes of this Stout predecessor. Dark malt flavors dominate, yet Porter is lighter in body and malt character than Stout. American Porter is sometimes fermented with lager yeast. This slightly bitter, dark ale is quickly regaining widespread popularity among microbreweries and homebrewers alike.

Radler—The strange and unlikely mixture of draft Pils and Sprite® that is popular in southern Germany—primarily among teenagers. This could probably be best described as Germany's answer to "Lawnmower Beer." Usually served in a 1 liter maß.

The Brewmaster's Recipe Manual

SUMMARY OF POPULAR STYLES
(Continued)

Rauchbier—German "smoke beer." These flavored lagers were made famous in the city of Bamberg in northern Bavaria and go well with the intensely flavored sausages made there. Seasonal Märzen and Bock-strength versions can also be found in the region. The smoke character originally was a by-product of the ancient practice of drying malts over oak or beechwood fires, but authentic flavor can be achieved by homebrewers through the use of "liquid smoke" flavoring or simply by home-smoking lager malt.

Roggenbier/Rye Beer—A rare specialty beer made from 60% malted and roasted rye in one Bavarian version to produce a dry, grainy, and unique brew. This exported version from Regensburg also uses wheat beer yeast for fermentation. Several American craft brewers also produce beers with rye as a principal ingredient. The traditional Finnish "farmhouse" brew, **Sahti**, is often brewed with rye and juniper, then fermented with wild yeasts.

Saison—A smooth, mellow, lightly hopped, slightly estery, and acidic "summer" ale from the French speaking region of Belgium, particularly the town of Liège. Traditionally, these complex, thirst quenching ales are brewed by "farmhouse" breweries in winter and aged several months before serving. Top-fermented, dry-hopped, and bottle-conditioned with alcohol around 6% v/v.

Scottish/Scotch Ale—The standard gravity Scottish Ales include the sub-categories Light, Heavy, and Export (a.k.a. 60 Shilling, 70 Shilling, and 80 Shilling, respectively). Scottish Ale is typically black or deep, walnut brown from the use of roasted barley or dark malts in addition to pale ale malt, and is low in hop bitterness, flavor, and aroma—reflecting Scotland's history of being unsuitable for hop cultivation. A fourth category, Strong (90 Shilling) is a dark, rich, creamy ale of varying strengths that is often called "Scotch Ale" or "Wee Heavy" and approaches Barleywine strength. The taste is complex, with hints of raisin, plum, currant, or jam.

Schwarzbier—Literally, "Black Beer." A dark German lager that often has bittersweet, dark chocolate flavors. These are generally darker, more robust, and less delicate than Munich Dunkel. The modern benchmarks of the style are now brewed in Japan as well as eastern Germany.

Steam Beer—Technically, the name "Steam®" now belongs to Anchor Brewing Company of San Francisco, but is used colloquially in the homebrewing community to refer to California Common Beer (see above). Theories abound concerning the origin and reason for the moniker "steam" being attached to this style of lager beer; ranging from the 19th century use of steam for industrial brewery power, to the high temperature of the primary fermentation, and even the sound created when casks of the lively beer was broached. Several Bavarian brewers have also revived a style called **Dampfbier** (German for "steam beer") in the past two decades. Produced mainly around the Bavarian towns of Bayreuth and Zweisel, these are fruity, top-fermented, but cold-lagered beers.

Steinbier—A specialty beer from Altenmünster whose character is drawn from an ancient method of bringing large quantities of wort to a boil in a wooden vessel. "Steinbier" literally means "stone beer" in German, and refers to the fact that porous greywacke stones are heated to 1200°C, then are dunked into the wort (or more recently, have the wort poured over them), causing the sugars to scorch and crystallize. The stones are allowed to cool, then returned to the young beer so the caramelized sugars can be fermented out—giving the beer a sweet, smokey flavor.

Strong Ale—Full-bodied, malty English ale, generously hopped for balance, with alcohol levels running from 6-8% v/v. As an older style with only a few commercial examples, Strong Ale has more recently been grouped together with the Barleywine style. (See also "Belgian Strong Ale" above.)

SUMMARY OF POPULAR STYLES
(Continued)

Stout—Another beer style with its roots in English Mild. This derivative of Porter is a dark, heavy, opaque ale with a high percentage of roasted grains (5-10% roasted/unmalted barley). Stouts may be "Sweet" (also called "European"—the old description "Milk Stout" was banned by British food trade law), "Dry" (Irish), or "Imperial" and range in strength from a low 3.5% alcohol to 10% v/v. Dry Stout is often dispensed with a high pressure nitrogen/CO_2 mixture to give it the traditional intense, creamy, tan head without overcarbonating the beer. In Ireland, Dry Stout is served at room temperature and is usually low in alcohol to make it a better "session beer." The Sweet Stout category also includes Oatmeal Stout.

Trappiste Ale—An "appellation" or protected class of top-fermented, bottle conditioned, and (usually) lightly hopped Belgian Ale. By law, only beers produced by Trappist monasteries (five in Belgium, one in the Netherlands) have the right to be called "Trappiste," which is more indicative of a brewing location than an actual style. Although widely varying in character, even among the various brands of a single monastery, these world renowned ales are generally regarded as strong (alcohol 6-10% v/v), estery, phenolic, and complexly malty, with higher alcohol flavors often in evidence. The higher gravity Trappiste beers typically use adjuncts such as invert or candi sugar to provide increased alcohol without the heavy maltiness associated with Bock. See the sub-categories "Dubbel," "Tripel," and "Belgian Strong Ale."

Tripel—A sub-style of Belgian beers with Trappiste origins and original gravities that are approximately triple the original specific gravities of the "Simple" beers of medieval Belgium. Referred to as "Triple" by the French-speaking Belgians, these beers are typically in the 1.070-1.095 O.G. range and are made from very pale malt and a generous quantity of refined sugar. Tripel is alcoholically stronger than Dubbel, but drier and much lighter in color than British ales of similar strength, such as Barleywine. Alcohol is usually 7-10% v/v.

Vienna—Vienna is a style of lager beer developed by brewing pioneer Anton Dreher in Vienna, Austria during the mid-19th century lagering revolution. This commercially produced lager evolved from the old tradition of brewing a special, higher gravity beer in March and cold aging it until the autumn harvest celebrations. A friend of Dreher's, Gabriel Sedlmayr of Spaten Brewery, is credited with being the first to successfully utilize the technology necessary for these and other lagers to be brewed and drunk year-round. Pale red to deep amber in color, moderately strong (4.5-6% alcohol v/v), light to moderately hopped, and malty. The darker, stronger Märzen lagers are based on the Vienna style, as are the traditional, dark Mexican lagers.

Wheat/Weizen Beer—Made from widely varying percentages of malted wheat and barley; depending on sub-style and country of origin, "Wheat Beer" is an enormous style category encompassing vastly differing beers ranging from the tart, refreshing Berliner Weisse to the dark, malty Bavarian Weizenbock. Colors range from pale, whitish gold to ruddy orange to dark brown. Bavarian-style wheats, particularly Hefe (pronounced "HAY-Fuh") Weizen, are now enjoying a dramatic comeback worldwide after more than a century of near extinction. American wheat is much milder in flavor and usually lacks the distinctive clove and banana notes of the Bavarian-style varieties, but has the same refreshing taste and generous carbonation. Other major sub-styles include: Kristall, a clear, filtered wheat beer krausened with bottom-fermenting yeast for more lager-like character; and Dunkelweizen, a maltier, darker variation of Hefe-Weizen.

SUMMARY OF POPULAR STYLES
(Continued)

Wit (White) Bier—A Belgian-style wheat beer also known as "Biere Blanche," that originated around Louvain and Hoegaarden. Cloudy, frothy, and pale, with a low flavor and aroma profile. O.G.s are usually around 1.045-1.049. Lactobacillus bacteria, special ale yeast strains, unmalted ("raw") wheat, and spices such as coriander, cumin, and curaçao bitter orange peel are often used in addition to malted barley for Witbier's unique flavor.

Zoigl—A beer rarely produced by commercial breweries, but mainly "homebrewed" in small towns in the Oberfalz region of Northern Bavaria. Zoigl may be top or bottom-fermented, but it is usually amber to dark brown, full-bodied, unfiltered, dry, and served vom faß (on draft). Its availablity is heralded when the farmhouse brewer displays an ancient, six-pointed alchemist's sign resembling the Star of David. The commercial, bottled version from the village of Friedenfels has an alcohol level of 5.2% v/v.

STYLES AT A GLANCE

Use these general guidelines demonstrated by modern commercial beers in creating your own recipes, but bear in mind that these numbers are merely averages and cannot tell of the quality ingredients, proper balance of flavor, and attention to detail needed for success. Sample some good microbrews or fresh imported versions to guide you in crafting your own recipes. (See explanation of column headings below.)

STYLE	OG	IBU	SRM	Alc.v/v
Altbier	1.043-48	28-60	10-16	4.5-5%
Barleywine	1.065-1.120+	50-100	8-22	7-12%
Bavarian Hefe-Weizen	1.048-55	10-18	3-10	4.5-5.5
Belgian Ale	1.044-54	20-30	3.5-12	4-6.2%
Belgian Dubbel	1.050-70	18-25	10-14	6-7.5%
Belgian Trappiste/Abbey	1.050-95	20-45	3.5-23	5-11%
Belgian Tripel	1.070-95	20-25	3.5-5.5	7-10%
Berliner Weisse	1.028-32	3-6	2-4	2.8-3.4%
Bière de Garde	1.060-80	25-30	8-12	4.5-8%
Bitter (Ordinary)	1.035-38	20-25	8-12	3-3.5%
Bitter (Special)	1.038-42	25-30	12-14	3.5-4.5%
Bitter (Extra Special)	1.042-55	30-35	12-15	4.5-6%
Bock	1.065-74	20-35	9.5-22	6.6-7.5%
Bohemian (Czech) Pilsner	1.043-49	30-43	4-4.5	4-4.5%
Brown Ale (American)	1.038-55	25-55	15-25	3.5-5.5%
Brown Ale (English)	1.038-50	14-38	18-34	3.5-4.5%
California Common	1.040-55	35-45	8-17	3.6-5%
Continental Light	1.044-52	18-25	5.5-13	4.5-5.5%
Cream Ale	1.044-55	10-22	2-4	4.5-7%
Doppelbock	1.074-80	17-27	12-30	6.5-8%
Dortmunder-Export	1.050-60	24-37	3-5	5-6%
Dunkelweizen	1.048-56	10-15	17-22	4.8-5.4%
Eis Bock	1.092-1.116	28-40	18-50	8.6-14.4%
Faro	1.044-56	11-23	6-13	5-6%
Gueuze	1.044-56	11-23	6-13	5-6%
Imperial Stout	1.072-80	50-80	20-50	7-9%
India Pale Ale	1.050-65	40-60	8-14	5-6.5%
Japanese-style Dry	1.040-50	15-23	2-4	4-5%
Kölsch	1.042-47	16-34	3.5-5.5	4.5-5%

STYLES AT A GLANCE
(Continued)

STYLE	OG	IBU	SRM	Alc.v/v
Kristall-Weizen	1.045-55	10-19	3.5-5	5-5.5%
Lambic (Fruit-Flavored)	1.040-72	15-21	5-10	5-7%
Light Beer	1.024-40	8-15	2-4	2.9-4.2%
Mai Bock	1.066-68	20-35	4.5-6	6-7.5%
Malt Liquor	1.045-70	7-22	2.5-3.5	5.3-6%
Märzen/Oktoberfest	1.050-60	20-25	8-12	5-6%
Mild Ale	1.030-37	10-30	10-26	3-3.5%
Münchner Dunkel	1.049-60	25-30	14-20	5-6%
Munich Helles	1.045-52	25-30	3-4.5	4.5-5.5%
Oatmeal Stout	1.044-48	27-31	30-40	3.7-4.5%
Old Ale	1.055-75	30-40	10-16	6-8%
Oud Bruin	1.044-56	15-25	12-18	4.8-5.2%
Pale Ale (American)	1.044-56	20-40	4-11	4.5-5.5%
Pale Ale (English)	1.045-55	25-45	6-12	4.5-5.5%
Pils	1.044-50	30-40	2.5-4	4-5%
Porter	1.048-60	35-40	20-40	5-6%
Rauchbier	1.048-52	20-30	10-20	4.3-4.8%
Saison	1.044-54	20-30	3.5-12	4-6%
Schwarzbier	1.044-52	22-30	25-30	3.8-5%
Scottish Light	1.030-35	8-18	7-18	3-4%
Scottish Heavy	1.035-40	10-15	10-20	3.5-4%
Scottish Export	1.040-50	15-20	10-20	4-4.5%
Scotch Ale	1.072-85	25-40	15-50	6-8%
Stout (Dry)	1.040-50	30-50	35-70	4-5.5%
Stout (Sweet)	1.045-56	15-25	40+	3-6%
Strong Ale (Belgian)	1.063-95	20-30	3.5-20	7-12%
Strong Ale (English)	1.060-75	30-40	10-16	6.5-8.5%
U.S. Pilsner (Bud, Coors, etc.)	1.044-48	11-16	2-2.5	4-5%
Vienna	1.048-55	22-28	8-12	4.4-6%
Weizenbock	1.066-80	10-20	7-30	6.5-7.5%
Wit Bier	1.044-50	15-25	2-4	4.5-5.2%

OG—<u>Original Gravity</u>. A measure of the fermentables in the wort prior to fermentation.
IBUs—<u>International Bitterness Units</u>. See page 14.
SRM—<u>Standard Reference (Research) Method</u>. See page 5.
Alc. v/v—<u>Alcohol by Volume</u>. (ABV in the U.K.) Expressed as a percentage, this is figure is often confused with the <u>Alcohol by Weight (w/v)</u> figure used by U.S. breweries.

Beer Trivia—*The Weihenstephan Bayerische Staatsbrauerei is the world's oldest operating brewery—established in the year 1040! Here is a brief profile of some of their beers:*

	°Plato	Alc. % (v/v)	IBUs
Leicht (Light Weißbier)	7.9	2.9	15
Hefe-Weißbier Dunkel	12.4	5.4	14
WeizenBier-Kristall	12.7	5.4	16
Korbinian Starkbier (Doppelbock)	18.3	7.4	32
Edel-Pils	12.2	5.2	38
Original (Lager)	11.8	4.9	26
Hefe-Weißbier	12.2	5.4	14
Export Dunkel	12.8	5.2	24

Ale Recipes

BROWN ALE

These sweet, full-bodied, and moderately alcoholic British ales are a venerable old style that represents what most beer was like for centuries; simple, wholesome, and easy to make at home. Original Gravities for modern versions of this beer hover around 1.040 for the southern English version, 1.050 for the northern; English hops such as East Kent Goldings, Fuggles, etc. are recommended, and the use of small amounts of refined sugar is also acceptable. Water high in temporary hardness and sodium chloride is traditional, but overall, the water should be softer than for Burton-style ales. Good versions to enjoy while waiting for yours to ferment include Watney's *Brown Ale, Old Peculier, Newcastle Brown,* and Samuel Smith's *Nut Brown Ale.* American microbrewed varieties of English Brown include *Steelhead Nut Brown Ale* and *Bond Street Brown Ale.*

BROWN ALE
Compliments of Sloan S. Venables
BREWMASTER—San Leandro, CA

Ingredients
6 lbs. British Light Malt Syrup
1 lb. Dark Brown Sugar
1 lb. Crystal Malt—40L (Steeped 30 min.)
1/2 lb. Chocolate Malt (Steeped 30 min.)
1 oz. Fuggle Hops—Bittering Hops (Boiled 60 min.)
1 oz. Fuggle Hops—Bittering/Flavoring Hops (Boiled 25 min.)
1 oz. Fuggle Hops—Aromatic Hops (End of Boil or Dry-Hopped)
Ale Yeast—Wyeast #1028 London Ale or Nottingham Ale Yeast
3/4 cup Corn Sugar at bottling

Starting Gravity: 1.048
Bittering Units: 28
Finishing Gravity: 1.012-1.014
Fermentation Temperature: 65-70°

Instructions
(Refer to *General Ale Brewing Procedures* section beginning on page 218.)

NUT BROWN ALE
S. SNYDER

Ingredients:

1, 3.3 lb. Telford's Nut Brown Ale Kit
3.25 lbs. Munton & Fison light DME
2 cups English 40L crystal malt
1/4 oz. Fuggles plug 4.2%AA (boil) 60 min.
1/2 oz. Fuggles plug 4.2%AA (boil) 30 min.
1 oz. Fuggles plugs 4.2% (flavor) 10 min.
1/2 oz. Fuggles plug 4.2%AA (aroma) steep 30 min.
Wyeast #1028 "London" yeast
3/4 cup corn sugar for priming

O.G. ~1.050
F.G. ~1.015 Potential alcohol 4.5% v/v

Instructions
(Refer to *General Ale Brewing Procedures* beginning on page 218.)

BROWN ALE
Compliments of Dick Foehringer
THE BREWMEISTER—*Folsom, CA*

"Our Brown Ale features a strong, rummy flavor from the brown sugar. Mild and sweet with a medium hoppiness in between *Newcastle* and *Watney's Brown Ale."*

6 lbs. Amber Malt Extract Syrup
14 oz. Crystal Malt
2 oz. Black Patent Malt
1/2 teaspoon Citric Acid
1 teaspoon Calcium Carbonate
4 oz. Lactose
8 oz. Dark Brown Sugar
1-1/2 oz. Northern Brewer Hops (Boiling)
1/2 oz. Northern Brewer Hops (Aromatic)
Ale Yeast
1 teaspoon Gelatin
1 tsp. Irish Moss
3/4 cup Bottling Sugar

Original Gravity: ~1.050
Final Gravity: ~1.012

Put the crushed crystal and black patent malts in a grain bag. Place bag and 1-1/2 to 2-1/2 gallons of cold water in your brewpot. Bring to a near boil (~160°F). Shut off heat and steep the grain for 30 minutes. Remove grains. Stir in extract and thoroughly dissolve. Return to heat and add lactose, brown sugar, citric acid, and calcium carbonate. Bring to a boil for 15 minutes. Add boiling hops and boil 30 minutes. Add Irish moss and boil 15 minutes. Turn off heat and add the aromatic hops. Steep 15 minutes. Cold break by placing the pan into a sink full of cold water. When wort is below 100°F, strain the wort into your primary fermenter. Add enough cold water to make 5-1/2 gallons. Rehydrate yeast by dissolving in 1 cup warm water. Let stand for 15 minutes. When wort is cool (below 85°F), pitch yeast. Ferment in a cool place (~70°F). When fermentation is complete, rack into secondary, leaving all sediment behind. Prepare gelatin by dissolving in 1 cup hot water and stir into secondary. When clear (3-5 days) rack again, leaving sediment behind. Prepare bottling sugar by dissolving in 1 cup hot water. Stir dissolved bottling sugar into clear beer, bottle, and cap.

Age a minimum of 2-3 weeks.

Beer Trivia—*The word "ale" is derived from the Scandinavian word for the Viking drink, "Øl."*

BROWN ALE
Compliments of David Ruggiero
BARLEYMALT & VINE—Newton, MA

Ingredients:
2 cans (3.3 lbs.) Light Malt Extract
OR 6.6 lbs. bulk light extract
1/2 lb. Crystal Malt 90L
1 oz. Mt. Hood Hops
1 tsp. Sodium Chloride (NaCl), for sweetness
1 tsp. Irish Moss (for clarifying the wort)
1 pkg. Edme Ale Yeast
3/4 cup Corn Sugar (for priming)
1 Muslin Bag

Original Gravity (O.G.) 1.040-1.042   Final Gravity (F.G.) 1.010-1.012
H.B.U.s~6 to 12 or I.B.U.s~15 to 30
Alcohol 4.5% by Volume

Directions for Brewing:
1. Secure grains in muslin bag and place into a pot with 2 gallons of water.
2. Steep the grain while water is heating, remove before a boil commences.
3. Dissolve all malt extracts and the NaCl into the brewpot and re-establish the boil.
4. A total elapsed brewing time of 30 minutes is required in order to:
    - Reconstitute the malt extracts.
    - Sterilize the ingredients.
    - Clarify the wort (this is known as a Hot Break).
    - Extract hop bitterness and aromatic properties.
5. The following additions to the brewpot must be made at the specified times:
ELAPSED TIME   0 minutes, add the NaCl and the Mt. Hood hops.
                      15 minutes, add the Irish Moss.
                      30 minutes, remove the brewpot from the stove.
6. Transfer the wort to a sanitized fermenter, straining out hop pellets if possible.
7. Add enough cold water to the fermenter to equal 5 gallons, when the temperature falls below 75°F, add the yeast.
8. Secure the airlock and ferment as usual (refer to the *General Fermentation Procedures* section beginning on page 230);
    - Single stage fermentation techniques last 7 to 10 days.
    - Two stage fermentation techniques last 3 to 5 days in the primary and 5 days to 3 weeks in the secondary.
    - Influencing factors that can shorten or prolong your beer's fermentation cycle are; temperature, yeast selection and viability, wort gravities, oxygen uptake and general sanitation procedures.
9. When all fermentation activity has ceased, check your final gravity. It should be within .002 degrees of the recipe's suggested reading. Prepare to bottle if it is. (Refer to the *General Bottling Procedures* section beginning on page 232.)

NUTTY BROWN BEAR ALE
Recipe of the Month
BEER & WINE HOBBY—Woburn, MA

2 cans John Bull Light Plain Malt
1/2 lb. English Crystal Malt
1/4 lb. Chocolate Malt
2 ozs. Roasted Barley
3/4 lb. Belgian Grain Mix
1 cup Brown Sugar
1 package Burton Water Salts
1 teaspoon Irish Moss
2 ozs. Styrian Goldings Hop Pellets
1 oz. Fuggles Hop Pellets
1 Muslin Bag
3/4 cup Priming Sugar
Yeast: AO1 Australian or 1028 London- **Starter Required**

S.G. 1.045-1.048
F.G. 1.010-1.014

Crush grains and place crushed grains in Muslin Bag. Place bag into 1-1/2 gallons of cold water and heat water to 155°F. Remove from heat and let steep for 20 minutes. Remove grains and discard. Add 2 cans malt, Brown Sugar, Burton Water Salts and bring to a boil. Add 2 ozs. Styrian Goldings Hop Pellets and Irish Moss, boil for 25 minutes. Add 1/2 oz. Fuggles Hop Pellets and continue to boil for 20 minutes more. Add remaining 1/2 oz. Fuggles Hop Pellets and boil for 5 minutes more. Put 3-1/2 gallons cold water in primary fermenter and add the boiled liquid and bring total to 5-1/4 gallons. Cool to 70-75°F. Pitch prepared yeast starter and ferment as usual (either single or two-stage). Prime with 3/4 cup priming sugar and bottle.

EAST COAST NEWCASTLE BROWN ALE
EAST COAST BREWING SUPPLY—Staten Island, NY

Makes 12 gallons O.G. 1.044

MALT:
Sour Mash
1 lb. Klages 2 Row soured 2 days at 120°F

Main Mash
12.0 lbs.	Klages 2 Row
1. lb.	Crystal 40L
0.5 lbs.	Chocolate
0.25 lbs.	Black Patent
0.25 lbs.	Roast Barley

HOPS:
Centennial	2.0 ozs. for 60 mins.
Willamette	1.5 ozs. for 20 mins.

OTHER INGREDIENTS
4 tsps. Gypsum in the boil
2 tsps. Irish Moss for 30 mins.

YEAST:
Wyeast 1028 - London Ale
Wyeast 1098 - British Ale

PROCEDURE:
Main Mash

Dough in and protein rest	122°F	30 mins.
Saccharification rest	150 - 152	60 mins.
Mash out	168	10 mins.

Boil 90 mins.

FERMENTATION

Primary	4 days	64-75°F
Secondary	2 weeks	54-59°F

Keg or bottle with 0.5 cup corn sugar per 5 gallons.

COMMENTS
Good brown color.

PIRATES BREW NUT BROWN ALE
Compliments of Jay Garrison
BREW BUDDYS—Redondo Beach, CA

Ingredients

6 lbs. Amber Liquid Extract
1 can Alexander Dark
1 lb. Crystal Malt (120L)
1 lb. Munich Malt
2 oz. Chocolate Malt
1-1/2 ozs. Perle Hops
1/2 oz. Willamettte Hops
1/2 oz. Mt. Hood Hops
Irish Moss
Gypsum
Wyeast #1084 Irish Ale, #1028 London Ale or Dry Ale Yeast

Instructions

1) If you selected the Wyeast liquid yeast, you must break the inner packet before you begin to brew. Allow 1 day for each month after the manufacture date printed on the front. If you're using the dry yeast that came with the Pirates Brew Kit, go ahead and get to it.
2) Prepare the grains. The grains should be crushed; if you did not get the grains crushed at the shop, crush it with some sort of rolling pin. You can either mix the grains with 2 quarts of water and heat it until it starts to boil, or heat it to about 165°F and steep for about 15 minutes.
3) Strain the grains, collecting the liquid into your brew pot. Rinse the grains (sparge) with 2 quarts of hot (170-180°F) water.

4) Add the bag and can of extract and 1 gallon of water to the brew pot. (You might want to rest the bag of extract in hot water for awhile to soften it up.) Bring the wort to a soft rolling boil.
5) Add the Perle hops to the wort, and boil for 40 minutes. Stir occasionally.
6) Add the Willamette hops and Irish moss to the wort, and boil for 20 minutes. Stir occasionally.
7) Add the Mt. Hood hops to the wort, turn off the heat; stir and let sit (covered, if possible) for 10 minutes.
8) Add the boiled wort to your sanitized, rinsed fermenter. Add ice-cold water to make 5 gallons. When the temperature drops to 75°F or less, add the yeast.
9) If you use liquid yeast, open the swollen packet and add to the wort. If you use dry yeast, add the yeast to 1 cup of 90°F water for a few minutes before adding to the wort. (You can add the yeast directly to the wort and let it sit for a few minutes also, but rehydrating the yeast in warm water will improve the fermentation.) Stir the wort thoroughly with a sanitized spoon.
10) Put the lid on the fermenter tightly, and insert the fermentation lock with the stopper into the hole in the lid and fill it up about 3/4 of the way with water or vodka. Let the wort ferment for a week or two until the fermentation ceases.
11) When fermentation is complete, syphon the beer into a sanitized bottling bucket. Boil the corn sugar in about a cup of water; cool; stir gently into the beer. This provides the nutrients necessary for the yeast to carbonate the beer in the bottle.
12) Insert one end of the sanitized and rinsed hose into the bottling spigot and the other end to the bottle filler. Push the bottle filler down onto the bottom of the bottle and open the bottling spigot. 5 gallons of beer will make about 2 cases, so make sure you sanitize this amount beforehand. Leave about 1/2-3/4 inch of space at the top of the bottle. Cap the bottles.
13) Let the beer age for 2 weeks to 6 months. Chill and enjoy.

Note: The normal phase of fermentation will be a lag phase, usually 2 hours to 1.5 days. Followed by a steady increase in intensity, usually lasting anywhere from 1 to 4 days. Fermentation abruptly slows down after this and tapers off to an occasional bubble being pushed out of the fermentation lock every 30 seconds or so. The main contributing factors to these fluctuations are the strain and initial amount of yeast being used, sanitation, and temperature intensity and consistency. For ale yeast, try and maintain temperatures between 65° and 75°. For lagers, temperatures of 65° down to 32° work best to maintain lager characteristics.

DUBLIN DARK*
Compliments of Peter Hood
BREWING SUPPLIES—Stockport/Altrincham, England

*For 5 Imperial Gallons

No. 1—5 lb. SFX Malt Extract
No. 2—1 lb. Dark Dried Malt Extract Powder
No. 3—8 oz. Patent Black
No. 4—8 oz. Crystal Malt
No. 5—8 oz. Brown Sugar
No. 6—4 oz. Hops
No. 7—Yeast
No. 8—2 Level Teaspoons "Brewery Heading Powder"

1. Boil No. 1, 2, 3, 4, and 6 in as much water as possible (about 3 gallons is best, but you can use much less).
2. After 40 mins., strain off into clean, sterilised bucket and add No. 5. Stir well to dissolve.
3. Make up to 5 gallons with cold water and leave to cool below 75°F.
4. Add yeast and leave to ferment for about 7 days or until all signs of fermentation have finished (bubbles stop rising).
5. Syphon off into barrel or bottles adding 1/2 tsp. sugar per pint of beer to prime bottles—or 2 to 4 oz. sugar to a 5 gallon pressure barrel.
6. Leave in a warm place for 4-5 days, then a cool place to clear—CHEERS!

Notes: It's best to add **Brewing Supplies'** Finings to the barrel. For better head retention, use **Brewing Supplies'** Brewery Heading Powder.

Beer Trivia—*The decline of wine's popularity as the common man's drink, and the subsequent rise of malt beverages, is largely attributed to the rapid changes in climate that occurred in 14th century Europe. The increased rainfall and slight lowering of temperatures made many places, such as England, unsuitable for growing high quality wine grapes.*

MILD ALE

One of the oldest styles of British ale, Mild (an archaic term meaning "new" or "fresh") in its original form was merely a green, immature ale as opposed to an ale that would be cellared for a year or more before it was sold. For reasons no one is completely sure of, probably an expanding population and the growing demand for beer, Mild beers began to be sold before they were ready, and at a considerably lower cost than mature beer. Eventually, this led to the harsh, sour Mild being mixed with a small portion of the Old (or "stale") Ale in order to make it more palatable. This 9:1 mixture was the origin of an ale called "Porter's Ale," because it was a good-tasting beer still affordable by the working class, particularly London's porters.

As Porter developed into a distinct style of its own, brewers began to formulate recipes of Mild that didn't require the addition of matured ale to improve the taste. These recipes included the addition of chocolate malt, torrefied barley, black malt, oatmeal, and roasted barley. Mellower hop varieties were used, hopping rates were reduced, more flocculant yeast was developed, and finings were employed to evolve Mild into its present form.

"Mild" now means lightly hopped and can be considered a mellower, lighter bodied, but darker version of English Brown Ale—many experts consider Mild to be nothing more than the draft version of Brown Ale. In any event, traditional Milds had original gravities of 1.060 or greater, but have fallen in the last century to 1.037-1.030; mainly to avoid high excise taxes. Although this lightly carbonated beer style is far less popular than the pub-dominating Bitter, it can be widely found in Wales and northwestern England and seems to be making a comeback throughout Britain in the wake of the "Real Ale" movement. Its low alcohol strength (around 3.5% v/v) makes this an excellent "session" beer.

Modern Milds are often crafted from Maris Otter malt, amber malt, black malt, torrefied wheat, and caramel malts, as well as Fuggles, Challenger, and Goldings hops. Historically, waters rich in calcium sulfate and calcium chloride were used, but the water should be softer than for brewing an English Pale Ale. Popular commercial examples (which Americans will probably have to travel to the U.K. for) include: *Bass Highgate Dark, Theakston Traditional, Tetley Mild, XXX Dark Mild, Ansells, Brain's Dark, McMullen's AK,* and *Thwaites*.

PREMIUM AMBER ALE
Recipe of the Month
BEER & WINE HOBBY—Woburn, MA

1 - 3.3 lb can Amber Plain Malt Extract
3 lbs. Dutch Amber Dry Malt
    reserve 1-1/4 cup for bottling
1/2 lb. English Crystal Malt
1/2 lb. Dextrine Malt (Carapils)
1-1/2 oz. Fuggles loose or pellet hops (Boil)
1/2 oz. Cascade plugs (finish)
1 package Burton Water Salts
1 teaspoon Irish Moss
3 Muslin Bags
Yeast: AO4 British - **Starter Required**
1-1/4 cup dry malt for priming

S.G. 1.035-1.040
F.G. 1.008-1.010

Add 2 gallons of cold water to your pot; put 1/2 lb. crushed English Crystal Malt, 1/2 lb. crushed Dextrine Malt into muslin bag and tie. Place bag in cold water and bring to a boil. When water comes to a boil, remove from heat and let grains steep for 5 minutes. Remove grains and discard, return pot to heat and bring to a boil. Add 1 can of Amber Malt, Dutch Dry Malt (minus the 1-1/4 cup), and 1-1/2 oz. of Fuggles hops tied in a muslin bag and boil for 45 minutes. During the last 15 minutes, add Irish Moss and the package of Burton Water Salts. During the last 5 minutes of the boil, add 1/2 oz. Cascade hops tied in a muslin bag. Remove from heat. Discard hops and cool. In primary fermenter add cold water and boiled liquid, bring total volume of liquid to 5-1/4 gallons. When wort has cooled to between 65-75°F, pitch prepared yeast starter and proceed as usual. Finish fermenting. Prime with 1-1/4 cup dry malt dissolved in some beer and proceed with bottling.

NORTHERN MILD
Compliments of Peter Hood
BREWING SUPPLIES—Stockport/Altrincham, England

For 5 Imperial Gallons

No. 1—2 lb. Dark Powder Malt
No. 2—2 lb. SFX Malt Extract
No. 3—2 lb. Glucose Sugar
No. 4—2 oz. Northern Brewer Hops
No. 5—4 oz. Crystal Malt
No. 6—Yeast

1. Boil No. 1, 3, 4, and 5 in a large pan or boiler with as much water as possible. Use 2 pans if you want.
2. After 30 mins., strain off into clean, sterilised bucket and add No. 3. Stir well to dissolve.
3. Make up to 5 gallons with cold water and leave to cool below 75°F.
4. Add yeast and leave to ferment for about 7 days or until all signs of fermentation have finished (bubbles stop rising).
5. Syphon off into barrel or bottles adding 1/2 tsp. sugar per pint of beer to prime bottles—or 2 to 4 oz. sugar to a 5 gallon pressure barrel.
6. Leave in a warm place for 4-5 days, then a cool place to clear—CHEERS!

Notes: It's best to add **Brewing Supplies'** Finings to the barrel. For better head retention, use **Brewing Supplies'** Brewery Heading Powder.

CARDIFF DARK*
Compliments of Duncan Hook
THE CELLARS—Cardiff, Wales

*For 5 Imperial Gallons

"This Recipe is for a 'Mild Ale' (only in the Cardiff area are Milds referred to as 'Darks'). Hop Variations—Liberty is obvious, Willamette should be good. U.K. Northern Brewer has also been used."—*Duncan Hook*

If possible you should use fresh brewer's yeast from your local brewery, as your beer will tend to develop the character of the beer from that brewery. A proportion of your yeast may be retained from the first brew by storing in a polythene bag in the freezing compartment of a household fridge. If liquid yeast is unobtainable you can use a good commercial dried variety. This will produce a good beer but will lack some of the traditional "Cardiff" character. The first recipe shown is the ideal way to produce this distinctive dark beer, but if you do not feel confident enough to try mashing, follow our second recipe for a very acceptable brew using malt extract. For both recipes you should must use fairly soft water to which has been added a good rounded teaspoon of common salt (5ml).

Traditional Brewing Method and Recipe

5 lbs. Crushed Pale Malt
5 ozs. Cracked Black Malt
5 ozs. Cracked Crystal Malt
1 lb. Demerara Sugar
2 ozs. Whole (or plug) Fuggle Hops
Fresh Brewer's Yeast

Mashing

Mash the grains in about 2 gallons of salted water. Keep the temperature at a constant level of 145 to 148°F for 3 hours. This is important, especially for the first half hour. Sparge the grain with water at 170°F to collect 5-1/2 gallons of wort. Bring the wort to the boil. Add sugar and hops, fast boil for 2 hours and add the Irish Moss half an hour before the end of the boil. Allow the wort to settle for 1/2 hour after the boil is completed. Open the boiler tap to draw off the clear wort, using the settled bed of hops as a filter. If the wort does not run clear, return the liquid to the boiler and draw offf again until clear wort is obtained. Make quantity back up to five gallons with cold water (use sanitary ice if possible) and cool as rapidly as you can. Pitch yeast when temperature has dropped below 80°F. When the fermentation is underway reduce temperature to, and maintain at, an ideal of 60 to 65°F. A heavy yeast deposit will form on top of the beer. Do not disturb this yeast cap, but remove any brown scum that forms on the sides of the vessel. Stir the brew daily, taking care not to disturb the yeast cap too much. After 5 days skim off the yeast. Retain some of the yeast (about the size of a walnut will do) for pitching your next brew. Transfer the beer to a sterile, closed 5-gallon container and fit with an airlock. Leave beer to fall bright. Use beer finings if necessary. This should take a week to 10 days. When beer is clear, rack off. Prime the beer with 4 ozs. white sugar (made into a syrup) and put in cask or bottle to mature (2 weeks in cask or 4 weeks in bottle). This beer continues to mature and improve, being superb after 3 months.

Malt Extract Equivalent Recipe and Method

4 lbs. Pale Dried Malt Extract
8 ozs. Cracked Crystal Malt
5 ozs. Cracked Black Malt
1-1/2 lbs. Demerara Sugar
Hops, Irish Moss, Yeast, and Water as in first recipe

Put all the ingredients except the yeast and Irish Moss into the boiler. Pour on 5-1/2 gallons of boiling water (salted). Boil for two hours. Add the Irish Moss 1/2 hour from the end of boil as above to produce bright wort. If you do not have a proper boiler, a large saucepan can be used. Boil using as much water as possible, strain the wort through the hops in a straining bag, and make up the quantity to 5 gallons with cold water. Once the bright wort is obtained, proceed as in first recipe above.

PALE ALE

This English-born beer is the world's most popular style of ale, and deservedly so. A good Pale Ale represents everything a beer should be; malty, but not too sweet, refreshing, but not too bitter, lively but not over-carbonated, full-bodied, but not heavy.

Unlike the Germans, the British are more liberal in their categorization of beers and you'll be hard pressed to scientifically pin down exactly what separates a Pale Ale from an India Pale Ale and what separates these two from Bitter, except that the latter is usually served on draft and the former are usually bottled. In reality, these ales are simply what the brewer arbitrarily decides to name them. For this same reason, there may be some Pale Ale recipes here that are closer to the American version of Pale Ales included in the "North American Ale" section, and vice versa, but we have tried to put them in the category they fit the closest. These beers are generally made from hard water that is rich in calcium, sulfate, and bicarbonate. A study of Burton-on-Trent's water will give you a good idea of proper levels.

Some of the many fine examples of English-style Pale Ale include: Eldridge Pope's *Royal Oak Pale Ale*, *Worthington White Shield* (bottle conditioned), Samuel Smith's *Old Brewery Pale Ale*, Bass *Pale Ale*, Fuller's *London Pride*, Young's *Special London Ale*, *Pike Place Pale Ale*, and *Burning River Ale*.

PALE ALE
Compliments of Sloan S. Venables
BREWMASTER—San Leandro, CA

Ingredients

6lbs. John Bull Light Malt Syrup
1-1/2 lbs. Light Dried Malt Extract
1 lb. Crystal Malt—10L (Steeped 30 Min.)
1/2 lb. Crystal Malt—20L (Steeped 30 Min.)
1-1/4 oz. Cascade Hops—Bittering Hops (Boiled 60 Min.)
1 oz. Cascade Hops—Bittering /Flavoring Hops (Boiled 30 Min.)
1 oz. Cascade Hops—Aromatic Hops (End Of Boil Or Dry-Hopped)
Ale Yeast—Wyeast #1056 or Dried Ale Yeast
3/4 cup Corn Sugar at bottling

Starting Gravity: 1.054
Bittering Units: 35

Finishing Gravity: 1.012-1.014
Fermentation Temperature: 65-70°F

Instructions
(Refer to *General Ale Brewing Procedures* beginning on page 218.)

YELLOW DOG PALE ALE
THE HOME BREWERY—Ozark, MO

Ingredients:

6.6 lbs. (2 packs) Yellow Dog Malt Extract
3/4 oz. Kent Goldings Hop Pellets (bittering)
3/4 oz. Kent Goldings Hop Pellets added 1/2 hour before the end of the boil
1/2 tsp. Irish Moss added 15 minutes before the end of the boil
3/4 oz. Willamette Hop Pellets (finishing)
2 packs Doric Ale Yeast
3/4 cup corn sugar for priming

Starting Gravity ~1.047
Final Gravity ~1.012
Alcohol ~4.6% v/v

Instructions:

Heat 5 gallons of water in a large kettle. Many people don't have a kettle that large, but heat as much as you can (at least 2 gallons). When the water is boiling, turn off the heat and add the Malt Extract to the water. Use a spoon and stir until you are sure no Malt Extract is sticking to the bottom of the kettle. Then turn the heat back on.

Bring the kettle back to a boil, and stir occasionally so the ingredients won't burn on the bottom of the kettle. If your recipe calls for Bittering Hops, now is the time to add them and stir them in. Watch out for a boil-over. In the early part of the boil, the kettle usually tries to boil over once or twice, so control this by adjusting the heat. Later in the boil, the surface tension changes and boiling over is not a problem. Keep stirring occasionally, and let the beer (wort) boil hard for one hour. Stir in the 1/2 tsp. of Irish Moss in your recipe about 15 minutes before the end of the boil.

If Finishing Hops are called for in your recipe, stir them in 2 minutes before the end of the boil. Using Finishing Hops at the end of the boil adds a fresh aroma and flavor to the beer, and the use of finishing hops is appropriate in most beer styles.

Pour the hot beer (wort) into the primary fermenter. It is not necessary to strain the wort if you used hop pellets. Add cold water to bring the total volume up to 5 gallons. If you are using our #B3a Fermenter (the one in the kits) the 5-gallon mark is the bottom ring. Cover the fermenter and wait until the temperature is down to 75°F. If you have a Wort Chiller (#C44), use it to bring the temperature down quickly. At 75° or less, add the Yeast in your recipe. Just tear open the pack(s) and sprinkle it on the wort. Close the fermenter with the lid, stopper, and airlock. Remember to put water (or Vodka) in the airlock. Vodka evaporates more quickly, but bacteria won't live in it.

Fermentation should start within 24 hours, and may continue for between one day and two weeks, depending on the type of yeast, the recipe, and the temperature. Leave the beer alone and don't open the lid. When the airlock has not bubbled for several days and the beer is flat, still, and clearing, it is ready to bottle.

To bottle, siphon about one pint of beer into a pan and warm it on the stove. Add exactly 3/4 cup of Corn Sugar to the pan and stir until it is dissolved. Pour this back into the beer and stir gently but well to distribute the sugar. Siphon or tap into clean sanitized bottles and cap. Keep the bottles at room temperature. After a week, put a bottle in the refrigerator and try it. It will be best in about three weeks.

SPRING PALE ALE
THE VINEYARD—Upton, MA

Ingredients:

5.4 lbs. Alexanders pale malt extract
1 lb. light dry malt extract
1/3 cup light brown sugar
1 lb. pale malt grain
1/2 lb. crystal malt grain
1-1/2 oz. Northern Brewer hop pellets (boiling)
1/2 oz. Golding hop plug (10 minutes)
1/2 oz. Golding hop plug (5 minutes)
1 tsp. Burton Water Salts
1 tsp. Irish moss
1 pkt. Whitbread Ale Yeast
3/4 cup corn sugar for priming

Original Specific Gravity: 1.050-1.052
Terminal Specific Gravity: 1.010-1.012
Primary fermentation: 4 days at 70°F
Secondary Fermentation: 8 days at 70°F
Boil Time: 30 minutes

Procedure: Crush and put all grains into 1-1/2 gallons cold water with 1 tsp. Burton Water Salts for 10 minutes, then raise temperature to a boil slowly. Once boiling commences, remove from heat. Strain liquid into boiling pot. Add 1/2 gallon water, bring to boil and add 5.4 lbs. Alexanders malt extract, 1lb. dry malt and 1/3 cup light brown sugar. Bring back to a boil and add 1-1/2 oz. Northern Brewer hops, start timing 30 minutes. Add Irish moss last 15 minutes of boil. Add Goldings hops last 10 minutes of boil. Add 1/2 oz. Goldings hops last 5 minutes of boil. Strain into sanitized primary fermenter and add cold water to make 5 gallons and let cool. Pitch yeast when temp. drops below 80°F. At bottling time boil 3/4 cup priming sugar with 1 cup water for bulk priming.

CLASSIC PALE ALE
Compliments of Dick Foehringer
THE BREWMEISTER—Folsom, CA

7 lbs. Pale Malt Extract
3/4 lb. Crystal Malt
3/4 lb. Carapils Malt
1 oz. Northern Brewer Hops (60 min.) Boiling
1 oz. Cascade Hops (15 min.) Aromatic
1 oz. Cascade Hops (end of boil)
2 teaspoon Gypsum
1 teaspoon Irish Moss (15 min.)
1 Wyeast American Ale Liquid Yeast
1 teaspoon Gelatin
3/4 cup Bottling Sugar

Original Gravity ~1.055
Final Gravity ~1.014

Put the crystal and carapils malted grains into a grain bag. Place 1-1/2 to 2 gallons of cold water in your brew pot. Place grain bag in water and bring to a near boil (160-170°F). Turn off heat and allow grains to steep for 30 minutes. Drain and remove grain. Dissolve extract and gypsum thoroughly and then return mixture to heat. Bring to a boil. Add 1 oz. of boiling hops and boil for 45 minutes. Add the aromatic hops, and Irish moss and boil, for 15 minutes. Add the "end of boil" hops, turn off heat, and steep for 15 minutes. Cold break the wort to below 100°F by setting your pan of wort into a sink full of cold water. Put the cooled wort into your primary fermenter and add cold water to make 5-1/2 gallons. When cooled below 85°F, pitch your yeast. (**Note:** You must start the liquid yeast 1-2 days prior to brewing to allow it to culture up. Follow the instructions on the package for preparation.) Ferment in a cool (65-75°F), dark place. When fermentation has ceased, transfer to the secondary, leaving all the sediment behind. Dissolve gelatin in 1 cup hot water and stir into secondary. Allow beer to clear, typically 3-5 days. Rack again, leaving sediment behind. Dissolve bottling sugar in 1 cup of hot water and stir into beer. Bottle and cap. Allow to age/carbonate in the bottles for 2-4 weeks. Enjoy!

LIGHT ALE
Compliments of Sloan S. Venables
BREWMASTER—San Leandro, CA

Ingredients

6 lbs. Light Malt Extract Syrup
1 lb. Crystal Malt—10L (Steeped 30 min.)
1 oz. Fuggle Hops—Bittering Hops (Boiled 60 min.)
1/2 oz. Fuggle Hops—Bittering/Flavoring Hops (Boiled 30 min.)
1/2 oz. Fuggle Hops—Aromatic Hops (End of Boil)
Ale Yeast—Wyeast #1098 British Ale or Nottingham Ale Yeast
3/4 cup Corn Sugar at bottling

Starting Gravity: 1.044　　　**Finishing Gravity: 1.010-1.012**
Bittering Units: 20　　　**Fermentation Temperature: 65-70°F**

Instructions
(Refer to *General Ale Brewing Procedures* beginning on page 218.)

PIRATES BREW PALE ALE
Compliments of Jay Garrison
BREW BUDDYS—Redondo Beach, CA
Ingredients

6 lbs. Light Liquid Extract
1/2 lb. Crystal Malt 40L
3/4 oz. Centennial Hops
1 oz. Hallertau Hops
Irish Moss
Wyeast #1098 British Ale or Dry Ale Yeast

Instructions

1) If you selected the Wyeast liquid yeast, you must break the inner packet before you begin to brew. Allow 1 day for each month after the manufacture date printed on the front. If you're using the dry yeast that came with the Pirates Brew Kit, go ahead and get to it.

The Brewmaster's Recipe Manual

2) Prepare the grain. The grain should be crushed; if you did not get the grain crushed at the shop, crush it with some sort of rolling pin. You can either mix the grain with 2 quarts of water and heat it until it starts to boil, or heat it to about 165°F and steep for about 15 minutes.
3) Strain the grain, collecting the liquid into your brew pot. Rinse the grain (sparge) with 2 quarts of hot (170-180°F) water.
4) Add the bag of extract and 1 gallon of water to the brew pot. (You might want to rest the bag of extract in hot water for awhile to soften it up.) Bring the wort to a soft rolling boil.
5) Add the Centennial hops to the wort and boil for 40 minutes. Stir occasionally.
6) Add 3/4 of the Hallertau hops to the wort and boil for 20 minutes. Stir occasionally.
7) Add the last 1/4 of the Hallertau hops to the wort, turn off the heat; stir and let sit (covered, if possible) for 10 minutes.
8) Add the boiled wort to your sanitized, rinsed fermenter. Add ice-cold water to make 5 gallons. When the temperature drops to 75°F or less, add the yeast.
9) If you use liquid yeast, open the swollen packet and add to the wort. If you use dry yeast, add the yeast to 1 cup of 90°F water for a few minutes before adding to the wort. (You can add the yeast directly to the wort and let it sit for a few minutes also, but rehydrating the yeast in warm water will improve the fermentation.) Stir the wort thoroughly with a sanitized spoon.
10) Put the lid on the fermenter tightly, and insert the fermentation lock with the stopper into the hole in the lid and fill it up about 3/4 of the way with water or vodka. Let the wort ferment for a week or two until the fermentation ceases.
11) When fermentation is complete, syphon the beer into a sanitized bottling bucket. Boil the corn sugar in about a cup of water; cool; stir gently into the beer. This provides the nutrients necessary for the yeast to carbonate the beer in the bottle.
12) Insert one end of the sanitized and rinsed hose into the bottling spigot and the other end to the bottle filler. Push the bottle filler down onto the bottom of the bottle and open the bottling spigot. 5 gallons of beer will make about 2 cases, so make sure you sanitize this amount beforehand. Leave about 1/2-3/4 inch of space at the top of the bottle. Cap the bottles.
13) Let the beer age for 2 weeks to 6 months. Chill and enjoy.

Note: The normal phase of fermentation will be a lag phase, usually 2 hours to 1.5 days. Followed by a steady increase in intensity, usually lasting anywhere from 1 to 4 days. Fermentation abruptly slows down after this and tapers off to an occasional bubble being pushed out of the fermentation lock every 30 seconds or so. The main contributing factors to these fluctuations are the strain and initial amount of yeast being used, sanitation, and temperature intensity and consistency. For ale yeast, try and maintain temperatures between 65° and 75°. For lagers, temperatures of 65° down to 32° work best to maintain lager characteristics.

ENGLISH REAL ALE
Recipe of the Month
BEER & WINE HOBBY—Woburn, MA

1 can English Light Malt, 3.3 lbs.
1 can English Amber Malt, 3.3 lbs.
1/2 lb. English Crystal Malt
1/2 lb. Victory Malt
1 cup Brown Sugar
4 oz. Malto-Dextrine
1-1/2 oz. Fuggles Hop Pellets (Boil)
1 oz. Kent Goldings Hop Plug, *last 2 minutes*
1 pkg. Burton Water Salts
1 teaspoon Irish Moss
2 Muslin Bags
3/4 cup Corn Sugar
Yeast: Wyeast Special London Ale or Yeast Lab AO9 English Ale *(starter required)*

S.G. 1.040-1.044
F.G. 1.009-1.013

IMPORTANT NOTE: Please read all instructions before starting!

Crush grains, place in Muslin Bag and tie. Add grains to 2 gallons of cold water and bring to a boil. When water comes to a boil, remove from heat and discard grains. Add 2 cans of liquid malt, 1 cup Brown Sugar, 4 oz. Malto-Dextrine, 1-1/2 Fuggles Hop Pellets. Put back on heat and return to a boil; boil for 20 minutes. Add 1 teaspoon Irish Moss and package of Burton Water Salts; put back on heat and return to boil. Continue to boil for 15 minutes more. During the last 2 minutes add 1 oz. Kent Goldings Hop Plug tied in Muslin Bag. Remove from heat and add to primary fermenter containing enough cold water to bring total volume to 5-1/4 gallons. Remove hop bag and discard. When wort has cooled to between 65° - 75°F, pitch prepared yeast (instructions included). Proceed as usual. Finish fermenting. Prime with 3/4 cup priming sugar and bottle.

PALE ALE
Compliments of David Ruggiero
BARLEYMALT & VINE—Newton, MA

Ingredients:

1 Can (3.3 lbs.) Light Malt Extract
2 lbs. Dry Malt Extract
OR 6 lbs. Bulk Light Malt Extract
1/2 lb. Crystal Malt
1 oz. Bullion Hops (for bittering, yielding ~ 9 H.B.U.s)
1 oz. Kent Hops (for aroma)
1 pkg. Water Crystals (for hardening water)
1 tsp. Irish Moss (for clarifying the wort)
3/4 cup Corn Sugar (for priming)
1 Muslin Bag

Original Gravity (O.G.) 1.040-1.042   Final Gravity (F.G.) 1.010-1.012
Alcohol 4.0% by Volume

The Brewmaster's Recipe Manual

Directions for Brewing:
1. Secure grains in muslin bag and place into a pot with 2 gallons of water.
2. Steep the grain while water is heating, remove before the boil commences.
3. Dissolve all malt extracts into the brewpot and re-establish the boil.
4. A total elapsed brewing time of 30 minutes is required in order to:
    - Reconstitute the malt extracts.
    - Sterilize the ingredients.
    - Clarify the wort (this is known as a Hot Break).
    - Extract hop bitterness and aromatic properties.
5. The following additions to the brewpot must be made at each of the specified times:
ELAPSED TIME: 0 minutes, add Water Crystals and Bullion hops.
                     15 minutes, add Irish Moss & 1/2 oz. Kent hops.
                     25 minutes, add 1/2 oz. Kent hops.
                     30 minutes, remove brewpot from the stove.
6. Transfer the wort to a sanitized fermenter, straining out hop pellets if possible.
7. Add enough cold water to the fermenter to equal 5 gallons, when the temperature falls below 75°F, add the yeast.
8. Secure the airlock and ferment as usual (refer to the *General Fermentation Procedures* section beginning on page 230);
    - Single stage fermentation techniques last 7 to 10 days.
    - Two stage fermentation techniques last 3 to 5 days in the primary and 5 days to 3 weeks in the secondary.
    - Influencing factors that can shorten or prolong your beer's fermentation cycle are; temperature, yeast selection and viability, wort gravities, oxygen uptake and general sanitation procedures.
9. When all fermentation activity has ceased, check your final gravity. It should be within .002 degrees of the recipe's suggested reading. Prepare to bottle if it is. (Refer to the *General Bottling Procedures* section beginning on page 232.)

JUPITER ALE
Compliments of Dick Foehringer
THE BREWMEISTER—Folsom, CA

"Jupiter Ale is a Pale Ale with moderate/strong hop bitterness and a hint of chocolate malt. The combination of the British Ale yeast and the generous dry hops gives the beer a citrus-like aroma."

6 lbs. Light Extract Syrup
1/4 lb. Chocolate Malt
1/2 lb. Crystal Malt
1-1/2 oz. Northern Brewer Hops (Boiling)
2 oz. Willamette Hops (Dry Hopping/Aromatic)
1 teaspoon Irish Moss
1 teaspoon Gelatin
3/4 cup bottling sugar
1 liquid yeast (British Ale)

Original Gravity ~1.046
Final Gravity ~1.010

Put crystal and chocolate malt in boiling bag into your brew kettle with 1-1/2 to 2-1/2 gallons of cold water. Bring to a near boil and turn off heat. Let grain steep for 30 minutes. Remove and discard grains. Stir in extract and thoroughly dissolve. Return heat and add boiling hops. Boil 45 minutes. Add Irish moss and boil an additional 15 minutes. Remove from heat and cold break the wort. When wort is cool strain into primary fermenter. Add enough water to make 5 gallons. Pitch yeast when cool (below 85°F). **Note:**

You must start the yeast 1-2 days before you brew. See the instructions on the yeast pouch. After fermentation slows, rack to secondary and dry hop. (mix the Willamette hops with 1/2 cup of hot water and stir into secondary.) Allow dry hopping for 1-2 weeks. Rack again, stir in dissolved gelatin, when clear (3-5 days) rack once more, stir in dissolved bottling sugar, bottle and cap.

Age a minimum of 3-4 weeks.

PALE ALE (PARTIAL MASH)
NORTHEAST BREWERS SUPPLY—West Kingston/Narragansett, RI

"Pale Ale is stronger with more hop flavor than its cousin, English Bitter. This partial mash recipe will provide more malt character than our all-extract kit of the same style. The original gravity should be about 1.046. Finishing gravity should be 1.012. If you want to use liquid yeast for this brew, we recommend Wyeast #1056 or #1028."

Ingredients

  3.3 lb. Can Light Malt Extract
  4-1/2 lb. Pale Ale Grain Mix (3 lbs. Harrington 2-row
    & 1-1/2 lbs. Crystal Malt)
  (2) oz. Boiling Hops
  (1-1/2) oz. Finishing Hops
  (1/2) tsp. Irish Moss
  (2) Boiling Bags
  (1) Pack Ale Yeast
  (58) Crown Caps
  (3/4) cup Corn Sugar (priming)

1. Add 5 quarts of water to your mash tun. Heat the water to about 120°F. Crush the grains. Mix well and hold the temperature at 120° for about 20 minutes. Bring the temperature up to 152°. Maintain the temperature at 152° for one hour. Stir the mash every 5 minutes.

2. Carefully transfer the mash to the lauter tun (another 5 gallon bucket with a false bottom). Start draining the water off the mash. Initially, this water should be recirculated through the mash to "set" the filter bed. The idea is to let the small particles in the mash collect at the bottom and create a filter. Once the filter is set (you can tell when the run-off starts to look clean—without particles and sediment) it is very important not to disturb it by letting it dry out or by forcing the sparge water through it too quickly. It should take about 45 minutes to sparge 5-1/2 gallons of water through the grain. Collect the runnings into your brewpot.

3. When you're finished sparging, it's time to start the boil. (If you're using the NBS Mashing Kit, you can start raising the temperature in the brewpot while you're waiting for the sparge to finish.) When the water starts to boil, add the malt extract and the boiling hops. To prevent scorching, turn off the heat before adding the extract and turn it back on after the extract is well mixed. Put the boiling hops into a boiling bag and drop into the pot. When the water starts boiling again, set your timer for <u>25 minutes</u>.

4. After 25 minutes have elapsed, add the Irish Moss and set your timer for an additional <u>20 minutes</u>.

5. After you've boiled the wort for a total of 45 minutes, put the finishing hops into a bag, drop them in, and boil for an additional 2 minutes. Remove from heat.

6. Cool the wort. There are a couple of ways to do this. If you have a wort chiller this process takes about 10 minutes. If you're boiling a small quantity of wort (1-1/2 to 3 gallons) you can add it to cold water in

your primary fermenter to make up 5 gallons. Whatever method you use, remember the time between the end of the boil and pitching the yeast is when your brew is most susceptible to contamination. Therefore, extra care is warranted during this time to protect the wort from exposure to undesirable microorganisms. Be sure to sanitize everything that comes into contact with your beer with boiling water, chlorine, or iodophor.

7. When the wort has been added to the primary fermenter and cooled to 70-80°F, add the yeast.

8. Ferment at 65-70° F (in a single or two-stage fermenting system—your choice) until the specific gravity falls to below 1.015. This should take approximately 1-2 weeks.

9. When you're ready to bottle, dissolve the corn sugar in 2 cups of boiling water. Add to the brew and mix well without disturbing the sediment. This is easy if you first siphon your beer into a bottling bucket and then mix in the sugar solution.

10. Bottle, cap, and put in a warm (65-75°F) environment for at least 6 days. Your Pale Ale will be ready to drink in about 2 weeks and will improve with age. *Cheers!*

CLASSIC ENGLISH PALE ALE
February's Brew of the Month
E.C. KRAUS—Independence, MO

Description: Classic English Pale Ale is a more hoppy, drier version of English Bitter. It tends to be higher in alcohol. While it is called "pale" its color is closer to light amber. Its most prevalent character is the clean, dry, hoppy finish.

General Profile: Starting Gravity: 44-56
Finished Alcohol: 4.5 - 5.5%
Bittering: 20-40 IBUs
Color: 4-11 SRM/5.5-13°L

Ingredients: 3.3 lbs. Light Unhopped Malt Extract
2.5 lbs. Light Dried Malt Extract (6 cups)
8 ozs. Dark Caramel Malted barley
4 ozs. Malto-Dextrin (5 min. Boil Time)
1-1/4 ozs. Brewers Blend Pelletized Hops (60 min. boil time)
1/2 oz. Fuggles Pelletized Hops (Finish-steep 15 min.)
14 grams Whitbread Ale Yeast
3/4 cup Priming Sugar (Bottling Time)

Directions:

1. Lightly crack malted barley and put with 1-1/2 gallons of cold water in a cooking pan. Slowly bring to a boil over a 30-45 minute period.

2. Strain the grain out by use of a colander and discard.

3. Bring the liquid back to a boil and add both the liquid and dried malt extracts. Bring back to a boil again.

4. Once boiling, add Brewers Blend hops and boil for 60 minutes. During the last 5 minutes of boil, fold in Malto-Dextrin.

5. Once the boiling is complete, add the Fuggles hops, turn off the burner and allow to steep for 15 minutes with a lid on.

6. Now add the wort to your fermenter with cold water up to 5 gallons. Make sure it has cooled below 80°F and sprinkle on yeast.

7. Attach air-lock to fermenter and allow to ferment for 7-10 days or until finished, then bottle with priming sugar as normal.

PALE ALE (ALL-GRAIN)
Compliments of Sloan S. Venables
BREWMASTER—San Leandro, CA

Ingredients

10 lbs. 2-Row Pale Malted Barley
1 lb. Crystal Malt—10L
1/2 lb. Crystal Malt—40L
1-1/4 oz. Cascade Hops—Bittering Hops (Boiled 60 min.)
1 oz. Cascade Hops—Bittering/Flavoring Hops (Boiled 25 min.)
1 oz. Cascade Hops—Aromatic Hops (End of Boil or Dry-Hopped)
Ale Yeast—Wyeast #1056 American Ale or Dried Ale Yeast
3/4 cup Corn Sugar at bottling

Starting Gravity: 1.054-1.057   **Finishing Gravity: 1.012-1.014**
Bittering Units: 35   **Fermentation Temperature: 65-70°F**

Mashing Procedure

1. Put Pale Malted Barley in large pot (7 gallons or larger)
2. Initial Strike Water: 6.5 Qts. @ 170°F
3. Initial Rest: 30 minutes @ 125-130°F
4. Starch Conversion Infusion: 6.5 Qts. @ 200°F
5. Starch Conversion Rest: Hold @ 155°F for 1 hour (**Note**—To maintain Mash Temperature at 155°F, either put pot in pre-heated oven or add heat via stove top)
6. Mash Out: Add Crystal Malts and 2 Qts. water @ 200°F. Mix well, then heat on stove to 170°F and hold for 10 minutes
7. Sparge Water: 14 Qts. @ approximately 200°F and pH 5-5.5
8. Recirculate first 3 to 4 Qts. of Sparge run-off
9. Sparge slowly so that it takes at least 30 minutes
10. Water at start of boil: 6 gallons (add to sparge if necessary)
11. Bring wort to a boil and proceed as in extract brewing

Instructions

(Refer to *General Ale Brewing Procedures* beginning on page 218.)

INDIA PALE ALE (IPA)

India Pale Ale, so named because it was a Pale Ale brewed strong and heavily hopped in order to withstand the rigorous ocean voyage to the British troops stationed in colonial India. Modern Special or Best Bitters are sometimes considered the "true" descendants of the original India Pale Ales. Oak chips are often added by homebrewers to create a spicy flavor obtained when beer is aged in oak casks. However, this should be done very sparingly (i.e., 1 oz. or less) because the American and French oak chips available to homebrewers are very pungent. Some English beer authorities insist that oak flavor is inappropriate to IPA because pitch-lined English oak barrels impart little flavor to the beer. Others, however, assert that the barrels used to ship beer to India were probably not coated with pitch and, therefore, would have had some oak flavor notes. No matter which stance you take, IPAs should be in the O.G. range of 1.050-65, with IBUs at 40-60, alcohol 5-6.5 v/v, and equal to or lighter than standard Pale Ales in color.

Because of the American love affair with hops, India Pale Ale is enjoying a wide resurgence of popularity in the U.S. among homebrewers, microbrewers, and brewpubs alike. A few of the great examples, American and British, by which to judge your homebrewed IPA include: Brooklyn Brewery's *East India Pale Ale*, *Ushers India Pale Ale*, *Flowers IPA*, *Bass IPA*, *Charrington IPA*, *Greene King IPA*, *Long Trail IPA*, *Punjabi Pale Ale*, and *Liberty Ale*.

INDIA PALE ALE
Yankee Brewer Recipe of the Month
BEER & WINEMAKING SUPPLIES, INC.—*Northampton, MA*

Ingredients:

7 lbs. British Pale Malt Extract
1 lb. British Pale Malt Grain
8 oz. medium amber U.K. Crystal Malt
8 oz. British Dextrin Malt
3 oz. U.K. Kent Goldings whole hops (for bittering)
1 oz. U.K. Kent Goldings hop pellets (for aroma)
2 tsp. Gypsum/water treatment
3/4 cup corn sugar for bottling
10-14 grams dry ale yeast OR Brewer's Choice #1098 (English/Whitbread Ale), #1028 (London/Bass/Whiteshield Ale), or #1084 (Irish Ale) liquid yeast culture

O.G.: 1.050-52   F.G.: 1.012-14

(Refer to *General Ale Brewing Procedures* beginning on page 218.)

INDIA PALE ALE
Compliments of David Ruggiero
BARLEYMALT & VINE—Newton, MA

Ingredients:
2, 4lb. cans, Alexander's pale malt extract
OR 8 lbs. bulk light malt extract
1/2 lb. Munich malt
1 oz. Chinook hops (for bittering)
1 oz. B.C. Kent hops (for aroma)
1/2 oz. Kent Golding hop plug (for dry hopping)
1 Tbsp. Water Crystals
1 tsp. Irish Moss (for clarifying the wort)
1 pkg. Edme Ale Yeast
3/4 cup Corn Sugar (for priming)
1 Muslin Bag

Original Gravity (O.G.) 1.060-1.062   Final Gravity (F.G.) 1.012-1.014
H.B.U.s~12 to 25 or I.B.U.s~30 to 60
Alcohol 6.0% by Volume

Directions for Brewing:
1. Secure grains in muslin bag and place into a pot with 2 gallons of water.
2. Steep the grain while water is heating, remove before a boil commences.
3. Dissolve all malt extracts into the brewpot and re-establish the boil.
4. A total elapsed brewing time of 60 minutes is required in order to:
   - Reconstitute the malt extracts.
   - Sterilize the ingredients.
   - Clarify the wort (this is known as a Hot Break).
   - Extract hop bitterness and aromatic properties.
5. The following additions to the brewpot must be made at each of the specified times:
ELAPSED TIME   0 minutes, add the Chinook hops and the Water Crystals.
                        30 minutes, add 1/2 of the BC Kent Goldings and
                          the Irish Moss.
                        55 minutes, add the remaining BC Kent hops.
                        60 minutes, remove the brewpot from the stove.
6. Transfer the wort to a sanitized fermenter, straining out hop pellets if possible.
7. Add enough cold water to the fermenter to equal 5 gallons, when the temperature falls below 75°F, add the yeast.
8. Secure the airlock and ferment as usual (refer to the *General Fermentation Procedures* section beginning on page 230;
   - Single stage fermentation techniques last 7 to 10 days.
   - Two stage fermentation techniques last 3 to 5 days in the primary—5 days to 3 weeks in the secondary.
   - Influencing factors that can shorten or prolong your beer's fermentation cycle are; temperature, yeast selection and viability, wort gravities, oxygen uptake and general sanitation procedures.
9. Add the Golding Hop Plug to the fermenter 3 to 5 days before bottling.
10. When all fermentation activity has ceased, check your final gravity. It should be within .002 degrees of the recipe's suggested reading. Prepare to bottle if it is. (Refer to the *General Bottling Procedures* section beginning on page 232.)

The Brewmaster's Recipe Manual

PIRATES BREW I.P.A.
Compliments of Jay Garrison
BREW BUDDYS—Redondo Beach, CA

6 lbs. Amber Liquid Extract
1 can Alexander Amber
1 lb. Crystal Malt
1 oz. Cascade Hops
1 oz. Chinook Hops
1/2 oz. Oak Chips
Wyeast #1098 British Ale or Dry Ale Yeast

Instructions

1) If you selected the Wyeast liquid yeast, you must break the inner packet before you begin to brew. Allow 1 day for each month after the manufacture date printed on the front. If you're using the dry yeast that came with the Pirates Brew Kit, go ahead and get to it.
2) Prepare the grain. The grain should be crushed; if you did not get the grain crushed at the shop, crush it with some sort of rolling pin. You can either mix the grain with 2 quarts of water and heat it until it starts to boil, or heat it to about 165°F and steep for about 15 minutes.
3) Strain the grain, collecting the liquid into your brew pot. Rinse the grain (sparge) with 2 quarts of hot (170-180°F) water.
4) Add the bag and can of extract and 1 gallon of water to the brew pot. (You might want to rest the bag of extract in hot water for awhile to soften it up.) Bring the wort to a soft rolling boil.
5) While waiting for the wort to boil, steam the oak chips for 10 minutes, then bake in a 350°F oven for 20 minutes.
6) Add the Chinook hops to the wort and boil for 40 minutes. Stir occasionally.
7) Add 3/4 of the Cascade hops and oak chips to the wort and boil for 20 minutes. Stir occasionally.
8) Add the remaining Cascade hops to the wort, turn off the heat; stir and let sit (covered, if possible) for 10 minutes.
9) Add the boiled wort to your sanitized, rinsed fermenter. Add ice-cold water to make 5 gallons. When the temperature drops to 75°F or less, add the yeast.
10) If you use liquid yeast, open the swollen packet and add to the wort. If you use dry yeast, add the yeast to 1 cup of 90°F water for a few minutes before adding to the wort. (You can add the yeast directly to the wort and let it sit for a few minutes also, but rehydrating the yeast in warm water will improve the fermentation.) Stir the wort thoroughly with a sanitized spoon.
11) Put the lid on the fermenter tightly, and insert the fermentation lock with the stopper into the hole in the lid and fill it up about 3/4 of the way with water or vodka. Let the wort ferment for a week or two until the fermentation ceases.
12) When fermentation is complete, syphon the beer into a sanitized bottling bucket. Boil the corn sugar in about a cup of water; cool; stir gently into the beer. This provides the nutrients necessary for the yeast to carbonate the beer in the bottle.
13) Insert one end of the sanitized and rinsed hose into the bottling spigot and the other end to the bottle filler. Push the bottle filler down onto the bottom of the bottle and open the bottling spigot. 5 gallons of beer will make about 2 cases, so make sure you sanitize this amount beforehand. Leave about 1/2-3/4 inch of space at the top of the bottle. Cap the bottles.
13) Let the beer age for 2 weeks to 6 months. Chill and enjoy.

Note: The normal phase of fermentation will be a lag phase, usually 2 hours to 1.5 days. Followed by a steady increase in intensity, usually lasting anywhere from 1 to 4 days. Fermentation abruptly slows down after this and tapers off to an occasional bubble being pushed out of the fermentation lock every 30 seconds or so. The main contributing factors to these fluctuations are the strain and initial amount of yeast being used, sanitation, and temperature intensity and consistency. For ale yeast, try and maintain temperatures between 65° and 75°. For lagers, temperatures of 65° down to 32° work best to maintain lager characteristics.

EAST COAST AMERICAN PALE ALE
EAST COAST BREWING SUPPLY—Staten Island, NY

Makes 12 gallons O.G. 1.050-52

MALT:

17.0 lbs.	Klages 2 Row
1. lb.	Crystal 90L

HOPS:

Cluster	2.0 ozs. for 60 mins.
Cascade	2.5 ozs. for 60 mins.
Cascade	1.5 ozs. for 20 mins.
Cascade	1.0 oz. steeped for 30 mins. after boil
Cascade	1.0 oz. dry hopped in secondary

OTHER INGREDIENTS
4 tsps. Gypsum in the boil
2 tsps. Irish Moss for 30 mins.

YEAST:
Wyeast 1056 - American Ale

PROCEDURE:
Dough in grain at 127°F in 4.5 gallons. Hold protein rest for 30 min. Raise temp. to 148° with 2.25 gallons of 200° water. Heat to 150° - 152°. Mash for 1 hour. In 10 mins. mash out at 168°. Sparge with 9 gallons of 170° water. Collect 13 to 13.3 gallons. Boil for 1.5 hours. Add hops as listed. Adjust volume in boiler to 12.25 to 12.5 gallons (1.048 gravity). Settle trub for 30 minutes. Cool with counterflow chiller. Collect 11 gallons in 2 fermenters. Pitch yeast.

FERMENTATION

Primary	3 - 4 days	64-73°F
Secondary	2 weeks	64-73°F

Keg or bottle with 0.75 cup corn sugar per 5 gallons.

COMMENTS
Use 90L Crystal for more amber color. Light body due to low mash. Hops very bright. Great head. More hop flavor, but less bitter than classic. Could cut back on hops a little if desired.

Excellent extraction rate; 36 - 37 O.G. points per lb. per gallon. Zappap method or Phil's lauter tun will give 27 to 30 max.

The Brewmaster's Recipe Manual

INDIA PALE ALE
Compliments of Ric Genthner
WINE BARREL PLUS—Livonia, MI

"This India Pale Ale is a special variety of British Ale and is a relative of the English Bitter. The characteristic of the IPA makes this beer more hoppy and alcoholic (5.5% - 7%) than the English Bitter. Use authentic varieties of British malt extracts, hops and pure liquid brewing yeast."

This brew contains:
  6 lbs. amber plain malt extract
  1 lb. crystal malt
  1/2 lb. toasted malt
  2 oz. Northern Brewer hops (boiling)
  1 oz. Kent Goldings hops (finishing)
  1 package of liquid ale yeast
  1 tsp. Irish moss
  3/4 cup corn sugar (for bottling)

O.G.: 1.055 - 1.065
F.G.: 1.015

Directions

Add the crystal and toasted malt to 1-1/2 gallons of water and bring to a boil. Remove the grain when the boiling starts.
Add the malt extracts and the Northern Brewer hops and boil for 60 minutes.
Add the Cascade hops and the add the Irish moss to the boil for the last 15-20 minutes.
Pour immediately into primary fermenter with cold water and top up to make 5 gallons.
Add yeast when cool.
Bottle with 3/4 cup of corn sugar when fermentation is complete.

Beer Trivia—*The cultivation of hops was forbidden in England under King Henry VI and its use in ale was forbidden by Henry VIII.*

INDIA PALE ALE
Compliments of Mike Knaub
STARVIEW BREW—Mt. Wolf, PA

This recipe won the 1994 "Hail to Ale Competition" for Mike's homebrew club, the York Area Homebrewers Association of York, Pennsylvania.

Beer Type	India Pale Ale	Amount—5 gal.	Boil Time 90 mins
Malt Extract	Geordie dry light plain	2 lbs.	
Malt Grains	Hugh Baird Pale Ale 1/2 lb. Crystal 1/2 lb. Toasted	9 lbs.	
Steep			
Mash In		2-1/2 gal. @ 175°	
Protein Rest			
Sach. Rest	60 mins. @ 150°		
Mash Out	10 mins. @ 165°		
Sparge		4 gal @ 170°	
Hops			
Boil	Bullion leaf	13 HBU	60 mins.
Flavor	Cascade leaf	13 HBU	15 mins.
Aroma	Cascade leaf	2 ozs.	Dry hop secondary
Yeast	Yeast Lab London Ale	1-1/2 pints starter	
Water		1 gal. for boil	
Misc.	Irish Moss Burton Water Salts Liquid Isinglass	1 teaspoon 1 teaspoon 2 oz.	last 15 mins. 60 mins. 10 days secondary
O.G. = 1.059	Primary = 12 days @ 70°		
T.G. = 1.017	Secondary = 20 days @ 40° (15 days for dry hops)		
Brew Date =	Bottled =		

The Brewmaster's Recipe Manual

INDIA PALE ALE
Compliments of Dick Foehringer
THE BREWMEISTER—Folsom, CA

7 lbs. Light Malt Extract Syrup
1 lb. Crystal Malt
1/2 lb. Toasted Malted Barley
2 teaspoons Gypsum
1-1/2 oz. Northern Brewer Hops (Boiling)
3/4 oz. Cascade Hops (Aromatic)
1 teaspoon Irish Moss
1 teaspoon Gelatin
3/4 cup Bottling Sugar
1/3 cup Oak Chips
1 Ale Yeast

Original Gravity ~1.056
Final Gravity ~1.014

Toast malted barley in oven of 350 degrees on cookie sheet for 10 minutes. Put the crystal and toasted barley into the boiling bag. Add 1-1/2 to 2-1/2 gallons of cold water and slowly bring to a near boil (~160°F). Shut off heat and let grain steep for 30 minutes. Remove grain bag and drain it completely. Dissolve malt extract and then return pot to the heat. Add gypsum bring to boil. Add boiling hops, boil 45 minutes. Add the Irish moss and boil an additional 15 minutes. Add aromatic hops and remove from heat. Prepare wood chips by boiling in 2 cups of water. Strain "tea" into hot wort. Let aromatic hops steep for 15 minutes. Cool the wort by placing the pan into a sink of cold water. When temp is below 100°F, strain into primary fermenter. Add cold water to make 5-1/2 gallons. Rehydrate yeast by dissolving it in 1 cup warm water and letting it stand for 15 min. When wort is cooled below 85°F, pitch yeast. Ferment in cool place (~70°F). When fermentation ceases, rack into secondary, leaving all sediment behind. Prepare gelatin by dissolving in 1 cup hot water. Stir in dissolved gelatin into secondary. When clear (3-5 days) rack again leaving sediment behind. Prepare bottling sugar by dissolving in 1 cup hot water. Stir into clear beer, bottle and cap.

Age a minimum of 3-4 weeks. (1-2 months is perfect.)

EAST COAST IPA
EAST COAST BREWING SUPPLY—Staten Island, NY

Ingredients (12 Gallon Yield)

Grain:
    20.0 lbs. Klages 2-Row Malt (crushed)
    1.0 lbs. Crystal Malt (40L)

Hops:
    2.0 oz. Cluster (60 mins.)
    3.5 oz. Cascade (60 mins.)
    1.5 oz. Cascade (20 mins.)
    1.0 oz. Cascade (steeped 30 mins. after boil)
    1.0 oz. Cascade (dry hopped in secondary)

Additives:
    2 tsp. Gypsum in boiler
    2 tsp. Irish Moss with 30 mins. left in boil

Yeast:
    Wyeast American Ale

Procedure: Mash, 2 step infusion. Protein rest at 122°F with 4 gallons of water for 25 mins. Raise to 154°F with 2.5 gallons of 200°F water for 1 hour. Sparge with 10 gallons of 170°F water. Yield: 13 gallons of wort.

Boil 1 hour to reduce to 12 gallons. Allow hot break to settle for 30 mins. Use counterflow chiller to cool to 76°F. Collect in 2, 6-gallon carboys. Pitch yeast. **Original Gravity is 1.060.**

Ferment 3 days in primary and rack to secondary for 3 weeks. Keg and artificially carbonate.

BITTER

Technically a sub-style of Pale Ale, this style of beer is the favorite of the British pubs. Like the textbook descriptions of Pale Ale, the term "Bitter" is a little tough to pin down and is often used interchangeably with "Pale Ale." Northern English Bitter is generally different from its southern counterpart in hopping rates, water profiles, and have creamier heads provided by a different dispensing system. Yorkshire Bitters traditionally also have a unique, yeasty, dry character derived from the use of "Yorkshire Stone Square" fermenters. Some Englishmen will insist that for a beer to qualify as a true Bitter, it must be served on draft. Bitter's sub-categories include: Ordinary Bitter, Special Bitter, Extra Special Bitter (a.k.a. Best Bitter or Strong Bitter)—and practically every brewery interprets them somewhat differently. However, to make things easier, the *American Homebrewers Association* uses these guidelines for classifying English Bitter:

Ordinary: O.G. 1.035-1.038, 20-25 IBUs, & Alcohol 3-3.5%v/v
Special: O.G. 1.038-1.042, 25-30 IBUs, & Alcohol 3.5-4.5%v/v
Extra Special: O.G. 1.042-1.055, 30-35 IBUs, & Alcohol 4.5-6%v/v

CAMRA, on the other hand, categorizes Bitter in this way:

Bitter: O.G. less than 1.040
Best Bitter: O.G. 1.040-1.045
Strong Bitter: O.G. 1.046-1.054

English malts, hops, and yeast strains are recommended, as is water rich in dissolved salts similar to that used for Burton-style ales. Brakspear's *Bitter*, Webster's *Yorkshire Bitter*, Samuel Smith's *OBB*, Timothy Taylor *Landlord Best Bitter, Barnsley Bitter*, St. Austell *Bosun's Bitter, Riding Bitter, Mansfield Bitter*, Adnam's *Bitter*, Young's *Ram Rod*, Greene King *Abbot Ale*, Fuller's *ESB*, and the American microbrews *Emerald Special Bitter* and *Boston's Best Burton Bitter* are but a few of the many, many excellent commercial examples.

ENGLISH BITTER*
Compliments of David Gourley
THE MAD CAPPER—Glastonbury, CT

Ingredients:

1-1/2 lbs. Munton & Fison light spray malt (3.6 cups)
4 lbs. Pale barley malt (16 cups)
1/2 lb. Cara-pils (2 cups)
1/4 lb. Wheat (1 cup)
1/4 lb. Munich (1 cup)
1/2 lb. Crystal malt (2 cups)
1/2 oz. Fuggles hops & 1/2 oz. Kent Goldings (Boil)—60 min.
3/4 oz. Fuggle hops & 1/2 oz. Kent Goldings (Flavor)—30 min.
1 oz. Kent Goldings hops (Aroma)—1 min.
1 teaspoon Irish Moss—30 min.
1 pkg. liquid or dry English Ale Yeast
1 tsp. Gypsum
5 gallons water

O.G. 1.041
Potential alcohol 3.5-4%

INSTRUCTIONS
1 TSP Gypsum to mash
Infusion mash: 135°F—15 min.
                 150°F—1 hour
                 168°F—5 min.
Sparge with 175-180°F water
1 TSP gypsum (boil)
Force carbonate with CO_2.

This recipe won David a Third Place award in the 1991 AHA Nationals.

JOLLY BREWERS BEST BITTER*
Compliments of Penelope S.J. Coles
JOLLY BREWER—Wrexham Clwyd, Wales

* <u>For 5 Imperial Gallons</u>

5 lbs. Dark Malt Extract SFX
2.5 lbs. Sugar
3 oz. Goldings Hops
1 lb. Crushed Crystal Malt
5 Gallons Water
Beer Yeast

1. Pour about 1 gallon of water into a 2 gallon capacity pan. Bring to the boil.
2. Weigh the malt extract, add to the pan of water, stir very well.
3. Weigh 1.5 oz. of Hops and 1 lb. Crystal Malt, put them in a muslin bag, and tie the neck.
4. Drop the bag into the pan, bring the contents of the pan to the boil, simmer for one hour.
5. Weigh the sugar and put it into a clean, sterile fermenting bucket. Pour two pints of water onto the sugar and stir to dissolve.
6. Pour six pints of cold water into the bucket (to prevent the plastic softening), then add the boiling wort, retaining the muslin bag in the pan. Stir very well.
7. Pour 1 gallon of water into the pan, bring to the boil, give the muslin bag a good pummel, and stir.
8. Simmer for half an hour, then pour the wort into the fermenting bucket, leaving the muslin bag in the pan.
9. Weigh the remaining 1.5 oz. of Hops, put them in a muslin bag and drop them into the pan. Add one teaspoon of Irish Moss. Top up the pan again with 1 gallon of water, bring to the boil and simmer for half an hour.
10. Pour the wort into the fermenting bucket with cold water to the five gallon mark, stir and leave to cool to 20 degrees centigrade.
11. Add the Yeast and ferment, barrel, and prime as usual.

The Brewmaster's Recipe Manual

SEATTLE STYLE BITTER
THE CELLAR HOMEBREW—Seattle, WA

1 can Alexander's Pale malt syrup
3 lbs. Light dry malt extract
1/2 lb. German Light Crystal malt (crushed)
1 tsp. Gypsum
1-1/2 oz. Eroica or Chinook hops (boiling)
1-1/2 oz. Cascade hops (finishing)
1 pkg. dry ale or European Ale liquid yeast
1-1/4 tsp. Yeast Nutrient

<u>Brewing Directions</u>

1) Place any crushed Specialty Grains in a strainer bag. Add this bag of grain to your brewing kettle, which contains 2 to 2-1/2 gallons brewing water.
2) Bring the brewing water to a boil, then remove the bag of grains.
3) Remove the brewing kettle from the burner and add any Malt Syrup and Dry Malt Extract. Stir thoroughly and return the kettle to the burner. Continue heating and stirring this wort until it boils.
4) At boiling point, add any Yeast Nutrient, Water Salts, and Boiling Hops. Hops can be placed in a hop bag or added loose, to be later strained out after the boil using a strainer bag. Time the boil for about one hour, stirring occasionally. After the first 10 minutes of this boil, remove two cups of wort in measuring cup, and cover with foil or plastic. Cool to 90°F for use in step #5 below.
5) Making the Yeast Starter: For dry yeast, use 1/2 cup warm tap water (90 to 100°F). Sprinkle the contents of yeast packet into that water, cover for at least fifteen minutes, and then add to the two cups of wort you prepared in step #4. Cover and set aside for use in step #9 below. For liquid yeast, prepare one to three days ahead of brewing time per package instructions.
6) After the wort has boiled for that one hour, add Finishing Hops. Place them in the hop bag, which has been emptied of the spent boiling hops, and place them in the boiling kettle or just add the Finishing Hops directly to the brewing kettle.
7) Let the boil continue for 5 minutes. Remove the pot from the burner and let it cool, covered, for about 20 minutes.
8) Pour three gallons of cold water into the sanitized open fermenter fitted with strainer bag, if loose Finishing Hops were used in step #6, strain the warm wort from step #7 into the cold water. Top up the fermenter to 5-1/2 gallons using cold tap water. Cover the fermenter and cool the wort as rapidly as possible.
9) When the wort has cooled to about 80° add the Yeast Starter and ferment as you usually do.

PIRATES BREW BITTER
Compliments of Jay Garrison
BREW BUDDYS—Redondo Beach, CA

Ingredients

6 lbs. Amber Liquid Extract
8 oz. Scottish Crystal Malt
1 oz. Nugget Hops
1 oz. Willamette Hops
Wyeast #1098 British Ale or Dry Ale Yeast

The Brewmaster's Recipe Manual

Instructions

1) If you selected the Wyeast liquid yeast, you must break the inner packet before you begin to brew. Allow 1 day for each month after the manufacture date printed on the front. If you're using the dry yeast that came with the Pirates Brew Kit, go ahead and get to it.
2) Prepare the grain. The grain should be crushed; if you did not get the grain crushed at the shop, crush it with some sort of rolling pin. You can either mix the grain with 2 quarts of water and heat it until it starts to boil, or heat it to about 165°F and steep for about 15 minutes.
3) Strain the grain, collecting the liquid into your brew pot. Rinse the grain (sparge) with 2 quarts of hot (170-180°F) water.
4) Add the bag of extract and 1 gallon of water to the brew pot. (You might want to rest the bag of extract in hot water for awhile to soften it up.) Bring the wort to a soft rolling boil.
5) Add the Nugget hops to the wort, and boil for 40 minutes. Stir occasionally.
6) Add 1/2 of the Willamette hops to the wort and boil for 20 minutes. Stir occasionally.
7) Add 1/2 of the Willamette hops to the wort, turn off the heat; stir and let sit (covered, if possible) for 10 minutes.
8) Add the boiled wort to your sanitized, rinsed fermenter. Add ice-cold water to make 5 gallons. When the temperature drops to 75°F or less, add the yeast.
9) If you use liquid yeast, open the swollen packet and add to the wort. If you use dry yeast, add the yeast to 1 cup of 90°F water for a few minutes before adding to the wort. (You can add the yeast directly to the wort and let it sit for a few minutes also, but rehydrating the yeast in warm water will improve the fermentation.) Stir the wort thoroughly with a sanitized spoon.
10) Put the lid on the fermenter tightly, and insert the fermentation lock with the stopper into the hole in the lid and fill it up about 3/4 of the way with water or vodka. Let the wort ferment for a week or two until the fermentation ceases.
11) When fermentation is complete, syphon the beer into a sanitized bottling bucket. Boil the corn sugar in about a cup of water; cool; stir gently into the beer. This provides the nutrients necessary for the yeast to carbonate the beer in the bottle.
12) Insert one end of the sanitized and rinsed hose into the bottling spigot and the other end to the bottle filler. Push the bottle filler down onto the bottom of the bottle and open the bottling spigot. 5 gallons of beer will make about 2 cases, so make sure you sanitize this amount beforehand. Leave about 1/2-3/4 inch of space at the top of the bottle. Cap the bottles.
13) Let the beer age for 2 weeks to 6 months. Chill and enjoy.

Note: The normal phase of fermentation will be a lag phase, usually 2 hours to 1.5 days. Followed by a steady increase in intensity, usually lasting anywhere from 1 to 4 days. Fermentation abruptly slows down after this and tapers off to an occasional bubble being pushed out of the fermentation lock every 30 seconds or so. The main contributing factors to these fluctuations are the strain and initial amount of yeast being used, sanitation, and temperature intensity and consistency. For ale yeast, try and maintain temperatures between 65° and 75°. For lagers, temperatures of 65° down to 32° work best to maintain lager characteristics.

BAKES' BITTER
Compliments of Chris Baker
BREWMASTER—San Leandro, CA

Ingredients

22 lbs. Great Western Domestic 2-Row
1/4 lb. 40L Crystal Malt
2/3 lb. 80L Crystal Malt
1.6 oz. Galena
2.4 oz. Cascade
1 pack Wyeast #1098

Mash all grain with 7 gallons water to strike temperature of 151°. Hold for 1 hour

Instructions
(Refer to *General Ale Brewing Procedures* beginning on page 218.)

BEST BITTER
Compliments of Peter Hood
BREWING SUPPLIES—Stockport/Altrincham, England

<u>For 5 Imperial Gallons</u>

No. 1—4 lb. Diamalt Extract
No. 2—2 lb. Glucose Sugar
No. 3—4 oz. Hops
No. 4—8 oz. Crystal Malt
No. 5—Yeast

1. Boil No. 1, 4, and 3 in as much water as possible (about 3 gallons is best but you can use much less).
2. After 30 mins., strain off into clean, sterilised bucket and add No. 2. Stir well to dissolve.
3. Make up to 5 gallons with cold water and leave to cool below 75°F.
4. Add yeast and leave to ferment for about 7 days or until all signs of fermentation have finished (bubbles stop rising).
5. Syphon off into barrel or bottles adding 1/2 tsp. sugar per pint of beer to prime bottles—or 2 to 4 oz. sugar to a 5 gallon pressure barrel.
6. Leave in a warm place for 4-5 days, then a cool place to clear—CHEERS!

Notes: It's best to add **Brewing Supplies'** Finings to the barrel. For better head retention, use **Brewing Supplies'** Brewery Heading Powder.

EAST COAST ORDINARY BITTER
EAST COAST BREWING SUPPLY—Staten Island, NY

Makes 5 gallons (5.5 in fermenter) O.G. 1.032-36

MALT:

3.3 lbs.	Northwestern amber
1.5 lbs.	DME gold
0.25 lb.	Crystal 40L
0.25 lb.	Toasted
0.25 lb.	Dark Molasses, unsulphured

HOPS:
Bullion	1.25 ozs. for 60 mins.
Fuggles	0.5 oz. for 20 mins.

OTHER INGREDIENTS
1 tsp. Gypsum in the boil
1 tsp. Irish Moss for 30 mins.

YEAST:
Wyeast 1098 - British Ale

PROCEDURE:
Toast malt for 10 mins. at 350°F. Add grains to brew water. Raise to 170°F and remove grain.
Add malt and molasses at boil. Boil for 1.0 hour. Add hops as listed. Cool with counterflow chiller. Collect 5.5 gallons in fermenter. Pitch yeast.

FERMENTATION
Primary	2 days	65-73°F
Secondary	5 days	65-73°F

Keg or bottle with 0.5 cup corn sugar per 5 gallons.

COMMENTS
Use 90L Crystal Malt for deeper amber color. Should be light bodied with lots of flavor. Bitter but have malty/molasses nose and taste.

EAST COAST EXTRA SPECIAL BITTER
EAST COAST BREWING SUPPLY—Staten Island, NY

Makes 5 gallons (5.5 in fermenter) O.G. 1.048-52

MALT:

3.3 lbs.	Northwestern amber
3.3 lbs.	Northwestern gold
0.5 lb.	Crystal 40L
0.25 lb.	Toasted
0.25 lb.	Dark Molasses, unsulphured
0.5 lb.	Dextrin powder

HOPS:
    Bullion   2.0 ozs. for 60 mins.
    Fuggles   0.75 oz. for 20 mins.

OTHER INGREDIENTS
    2 tsps. Gypsum in the boil
    1 tsp. Irish Moss for 30 mins.

YEAST:
    Wyeast 1098 - British Ale or 1028 - London Ale

PROCEDURE:
    Toast malt for 10 mins. at 350°F. Add grains to brew water. Raise to 170°F and remove grain. Add malt and molasses at boil. Boil for 1.0 hour. Add hops as listed. Cool with counterflow chiller. Collect 5.5 gallons in fermenter. Pitch yeast.

FERMENTATION

Primary	3 - 4 days	65-73°F
Secondary	2 weeks	65-73°F

Keg or bottle with 0.75 cup corn sugar per 5 gallons.

COMMENTS
    Should be full bodied with good hop bitterness. Malty/molasses nose and taste.

EXTRA SPECIAL BITTER
THE CELLAR HOMEBREW—Seattle, WA

1 can Geordie Scottish malt syrup
3 lbs. Amber dry malt extract
1/2 lb. English Crystal malt
2 tsp. Burton water salts
1 oz. Fuggle or Willamette hops (boiling)
1 oz. Tettnang hops (finishing)
1 pkg. dry ale or London Ale yeast
1-1/4 tsp. Yeast Nutrient

<u>Brewing Directions</u>

1) Place any crushed Specialty Grains in a strainer bag. Add this bag of grain to your brewing kettle, which contains 2 to 2-1/2 gallons brewing water.
2) Bring the brewing water to a boil, then remove the bag of grains.
3) Remove the brewing kettle from the burner and add Malt Syrup and Dry Malt Extract. Stir thoroughly and return kettle to the burner. Continue heating and stirring this wort until it boils.
4) At boiling point, add any Yeast Nutrient, Water Salts, and Boiling Hops. Hops can be placed in a hop bag or added loose, to be later strained out after the boil using a strainer bag. Time the boil for about one hour, stirring occasionally. After the first 10 minutes of this boil, remove two cups of wort in measuring cup, and cover with foil or plastic. Cool to 90°F for use in step #5.
5) Making the Yeast Starter: For dry yeast, use 1/2 cup warm tap water (90 to 100°F). Sprinkle the contents of yeast packet into that water, cover for at least fifteen minutes, and then add to the two cups of wort you prepared in step #4. Cover and set aside for use in step #9 below. For liquid yeast, prepare one to three days ahead of brewing time per package instructions.

6) After the wort has boiled for that one hour, add Finishing Hops. Place them in the hop bag, which has been emptied of the spent boiling hops, and place them in the boiling kettle or just add the Finishing Hops directly to the brewing kettle.

7) Let the boil continue for 5 minutes. Remove the pot from the burner and let it cool, covered, for about 20 minutes.

8) Pour three gallons of cold water into the sanitized open fermenter fitted with strainer bag, if loose Finishing Hops were used in step #6, strain the warm wort

from step #7 into the cold water. Top up the fermenter to 5-1/2 gallons using cold tap water. Cover the fermenter and cool the wort as rapidly as possible.

9) When the wort has cooled to about 80° add the Yeast Starter and ferment as you usually do.

STOCKPORT STYLE BITTER*
Compliments of Peter Hood
BREWING SUPPLIES—Stockport/Altrincham, England

*For 5 Imperial Gallons

8 lbs. Pale Malt, crushed (Maris Otter is best)
10 ozs. Crystal Malt, crushed
5 ozs. Goldings (go for the ones in the best condition)
Dried Ale Yeast (or the residue from a Coopers bottle works well)

1. Raise 3 gallons of water to 75°C.
2. Throw in the crushed pale malt and crystal. Cover and leave for 2 hours.
3. Jug wet grain through a sparge bag and sparge with boiling water until you get 5 gallons of liquor.
4. Boil with 4 ozs. Hops for 1 hour, add 1 oz. Hops and boil for 5 mins.
5. Strain into bucket and ferment out as normal.

NEW YORKSHIRE SPECIAL BITTER
S. SNYDER

INGREDIENTS:

2 lbs. Munton & Fison Amber DME
2.5 lbs. Munton & Fison Light DME
1 lb. English 40L Crystal Malt
1 oz. Fuggles Hop plugs @ 4.2% AA (boil) 60 min.
1 oz. Fuggles Hop plugs @ 4.2% AA (boil) 30 min.
1 oz. East Kent Goldings Hop plugs @ 5.0% AA (flavor) 7 min.
1 oz. East Kent Goldings Hop plug (aroma) 1 min.
Wyeast #1098 (Whitbread/British Ale) liquid yeast with starter
2 tsp. Irish Moss (20 minutes)
3/4 cup Corn Sugar for priming
Muslin or Nylon Hop Bag

O.G. 1.040 **F.G.** 1.011
Potential alcohol 4% v/v
IBUs 30   **HBUs** 16

Instructions
(Refer to *General Ale Brewing Procedures* beginning on page 218.)

EARTHQUAKE (ESB) ALE
Courtesy of Bruce Brode
WOODLAND HILLS HOME BREWING—Woodland Hills, CA

GENERAL INFORMATION:
Gravity   1.055
Color   5 SRM
IBUs   32

INGREDIENTS:

Grain Bill	Weight (lb.-oz.)	Mash Time (min.)	Color (SRM)	Specific Gravity
Scottish Carastan	8 oz.	30	0.8	1.003
Cara-Pils	8 oz.	30	0.1	1.003
Corn	4 oz.	30	0.0	1.001

Extracts				
Bierkeller 2 cans Light Syrup	6 lbs. 10 oz.		2.7	1.048

Hopping Schedule	Weight (lb.-oz.)	Boil Time (min.)	Alpha Acid	IBUs	Type
Kent Goldings	0.75 oz.	75	5.7%	18.6	Pellet
Pride of Ringwood	1.0	20	8.0%	11.5	Pellet
Fuggles	0.5	0	4.9%	1.7	Pellet

Finings	Amount
Irish moss	1 teaspoon

Yeast	
	Wyeast London Ale

COMMENTS: Steep grains at 150 degrees for 30 minutes. Sparge with same temp. water. Pitch (add) yeast when wort is 70 degrees. Ferment at 60-65 degrees.

GOOD KETTLE WORK:
1—Vigorous, rolling boil.
2—Skim all foam before starting hop seqeunce.
3—Add Irish moss last 20 minutes.

LONDON CALLING ORDINARY BITTER
Courtesy of Al Korzonas
SHEAF & VINE BREWING SUPPLY—Countryside, IL

NOTE: 15 gallon batch size

15.5 gallons Chicago water (see page 32)
3# DeWolf-Cosyns Cara-Vienne Crystal Malt
1# DeWolf-Cosyns Cara-Munich Crystal Malt
12# Northwestern Gold Extract Syrup
2# Laaglander Light Dried Malt Extract
15 grams Gypsum (added to boil)
4.25 grams Non-iodized Sodium Chloride (added to boil)
4.5 oz. Mt. Hood Pellets (4.1% AA) (60 min.)
2.25 oz. East Kent Goldings Plugs (4.1% AA) (15 min.)
1.5-liter starter from Wyeast Irish Ale #1084
1 oz. Styrian Goldings Plugs (dry hopped 2 weeks)

Boil 7.5 gallons of water the day before and add to the 20 gallon, sanitized fermenter to cool overnight. On brewing day, steep the crushed grains in 3 gallons of water at 170°F, remove the grains, add the final 4.5 gallons of water, brewing salts, and extracts. Bring to a boil. Boil 15 minutes. Add the boiling hops. Boil 45 minutes. Add the flavor hops, boil 15 minutes. Remove hops (I used hops bags for easier cleanup), chill with a wort chiller down to 70°F. Pour the wort and starter into the fermenter. Ferment 2 weeks at 62-65°F.

OG = 1.042   FG = 1.015

"The brewing salt additions in the recipe are based upon Chicago water. You should adjust them for your own water. The target water I was trying to get was:
- 100ppm of Ca
- 10ppm of Mg
- 30ppm of Na
- 225ppm of SO_4
- 35ppm of Cl

CO_3 should be kept as low as reasonable —if your water is high in Carbonates, you should add some Calcium Chloride and boil the water to get the Calcium Carbonate to precipitate out. After boiling, decant the water off the precipitate. You see, if you just use the water, the carbonate will dissolve back into the wort.

I call this an Ordinary even though its OG is in the Special Bitter range because the Laaglander and Crystal malts keep the unfermentables high (thereby putting the alcohol level down around 3.3% v/v). A great session beer, but be aware that it's meant to consumed young. The best way to enjoy this beer would be hand-pulled (from a cask) using a beer engine. Barring that, you could keg it (priming very lightly) and then release all the pressure from the keg when you're not serving. Despite the fact that this beer is low in alcohol, it is not low in flavor."—*Al Korzonas*

BOLTON BEST BITTER
S. SNYDER

5.5 lbs. Munton & Fison Light DME
1/8 lb. Turbinado
1/2 lb. English 60L Crystal Malt
1/4 lb. Wheat Malt
1/2 oz. Styrian Goldings 5.3% AA 45 min.
1/2 oz. Fuggles Whole Hops 4.4% AA (boil) 45 min.
1 oz. Fuggles Whole Hops 4.4% AA (boil) 30 min.
1 oz. East Kent Goldings Whole Hops 5.0% AA (flavor) 15 min.
1 oz. East Kent Goldings Whole Hops (aroma) 1 min.
Yeast Lab #AO 3 & 4 (London/British Ale mixed) liquid yeast starter
2 teaspoons calcium carbonate added to mash water
2 teaspoons Burton Water Salts added to mash water
1 tsp. Irish Moss (15 minutes)
1/3 cup Corn Sugar for priming kegs
Nylon Hop Bag
4, 1.25 Gallon Mini-Kegs (or bottle with 3/4 cup corn sugar)

O.G. 1.044 **F.G.** 1.010 **Potential alcohol** 4.5% **IBUs** 33.5
Instructions
(Refer to *General Ale Brewing Procedures* beginning on page 218.)

BABY'S BEST BITTER*
Compliments of Brian & Donna Lynn Johnson
FERMENTATION FRENZY—Los Altos, CA

Ingredients
13 lb. Munton & Fison Pale Ale Malt
1 lb. Carapils Malt
1 lb. 20°L Crystal Malt
1 lb. Victory Malt
1/3 lb. UK Pale Malt
1/2 lb. Flaked Barley
1/4 lb. Wheat Flakes
2 oz. Perle Hops
1 oz. Cascade Hops
1 tsp. Irish Moss
1 pkg. Wyeast American Ale yeast #1056

Starting Gravity = 1.047
Final Gravity = 1.012

Instructions Note: This recipe is for ten (10) gallons!
Mash the above grains at 157°F for 90 minutes. Sparge with 170° water. Bring wort to a boil and make the following additions:
   2 oz. Perle Hops (alpha acid = 7.6%) (Boil for 45 minutes);
   Irish Moss (Add last fifteen minutes);
   1 oz. Cascade Hops (At end of Boil).
Cool rapidly with wort chiller and pitch the ale yeast of your choice. Donna Lynn recommends a starter using Wyeast's 1056 American liquid ale yeast, with about 700ml pitched into each 5-gallon glass carboy.
This recipe won brewer Donna Lynn Johnson a First Place award in the English Bitter category of the 1993 AHA Nationals.

PORTER

Born as a mixture of inexpensive Mild and expensive Old Ale, Porter is a full-bodied, dark ale accentuating crystal, black, and roasted malts and medium to high hop bitterness. Originally named "Porter's Ale" because of its popularity among London's market porters, this beer dominated the working class market in the 18th and 19th centuries because it was cheap, and because it was one of the first beers to be available in sufficient quantities year-round—due in large part to the industrial revolution. Porter gave rise to an even stronger and heavier ale called "Stout Porter," which eventually was shortened to "Stout." Porter became almost extinct when faster maturing Pale Ales, Stouts, and then lagers became more popular. The final blow came with Great Britain's *Beer Orders of 1915 & 1916*, which placed restrictions on specific gravities and the use of raw materials during World War I. Stout rebounded after the war, Porter did not. However, recently renewed interest in the style has introduced Porter to a whole new generation of craft-beer lovers in the U.S.

Porters are generally brewed with large percentages of roasted malts and water rich in bicarbonates, sodium, and chloride. Just a few of the commercial versions include *Harvey's 1859 Porter, Ushers Dark Horse Porter, Samuel Smith's The Famous Taddy Porter,* and the American brewed *Edmund Fitzgerald Porter, Point Reyes Porter, Yuengling Porter,* and *Tower Dark Ale.*

LONDON PORTER
THE HOME BREWERY—Ozark, MO

Ingredients:

3.3 lbs. (1 pack) Home Brewery Hopped Dark Malt Extract
3.3 lbs. (1 pack) Home Brewery Unhopped Dark Malt Extract
1.7 lbs. (1/2 pack) Yellow Dog Malt Extract
1 oz. Cascade Hop Pellets (bittering)
1/2 tsp. Irish Moss added 15 minutes before the end of the boil.
3/4 oz. Tettnanger Hop Pellets (finishing)
2 packs Doric Ale Yeast
3/4 cup corn sugar for priming

Starting Gravity ~1.060
Final Gravity ~1.016
Alcohol ~5.6% v/v

Instructions:

Heat 5 gallons of water in a large kettle. Many people don't have a kettle that large, but heat as much as you can (at least 2 gallons). When the water is boiling, turn off the heat and add the Malt Extract to the water. Use a spoon and stir until you are sure no Malt Extract is sticking to the bottom of the kettle. Then turn the heat back on.

Bring the kettle back to a boil, and stir occasionally so the ingredients won't burn on the bottom of the kettle. If your recipe calls for Bittering Hops, now is the time to add them and stir them in. Watch out for a boil-over. In the early part of the boil, the kettle usually tries to boil over once or twice, so control this by adjusting the heat. Later in the boil, the surface tension changes and boiling over is not a problem. Keep stirring occasionally, and let the beer (wort) boil hard for one hour. Stir in the 1/2 tsp. of Irish Moss in your recipe about 15 minutes before the end of the boil.

If Finishing Hops are called for in your recipe, stir them in 2 minutes before the end of the boil. Using Finishing Hops at the end of the boil adds a fresh aroma and flavor to the beer, and the use of finishing hops is appropriate in most beer styles.

Pour the hot beer (wort) into the primary fermenter. It is not necessary to strain the wort if you used hop pellets. Add cold water to bring the total volume up to 5 gallons. If you are using our #B3a Fermenter (the one in the kits) the 5-gallon mark is the bottom ring. Cover the fermenter and wait until the temperature is down to 75°F. If you have a Wort Chiller, use it to bring the temperature down quickly. At 75° or less, add the Yeast in your recipe. Just tear open the pack(s) and sprinkle it on the wort. Close the fermenter with the lid, stopper, and airlock. Remember to put water (or Vodka) in the airlock. Vodka evaporates more quickly, but bacteria won't live in it.

Fermentation should start within 24 hours, and may continue for between one day and two weeks, depending on the type of yeast, the recipe, and the temperature. Leave the beer alone and don't open the lid. When the airlock has not bubbled for several days and the beer is flat, still, and clearing, it is ready to bottle.

To bottle, siphon about one pint of beer into a pan and warm it on the stove. Add exactly 3/4 cup of Corn Sugar to the pan and stir until it is dissolved. Pour this back into the beer and stir gently but well to distribute the sugar. Siphon or tap into clean sanitized bottles and cap. Keep the bottles at room temperature. After a week, put a bottle in the refrigerator and try it. It will be best in about three weeks.

HONEY PORTER
Compliments of Sloan S. Venables
BREWMASTER—San Leandro, CA

Ingredients

6 lbs. Light Malt Syrup
1 lb. Clover Honey
1 lb. Crystal Malt—20L (Steeped 30 min.)
1 lb. Chocolate Malt (Steeped 30 min.)
8 oz. Black Patent Malt (Steeped 30 min.)
3/4 oz. Kent Goldings Hops—Bittering Hops (Boiled 60 min.)
3/4 oz. Kent Goldings Hops—Bittering/Flavoring Hops (Boiled 30 min.)
1/2 oz. Cascade Hops—Bittering Flavoring Hops (Boiled 30 min.)
1 oz. Cascade Hops—Aromatic Hops (End of Boil)
Ale Yeast—Wyeast #1098 British Ale or Nottingham Ale Yeast
3/4 Corn Sugar at bottling

Starting Gravity: 1.048   **Finishing Gravity: 1.012-1.014**
Bittering Units: 30   **Fermentation Temperature: 65-70°F**

Instructions
(Refer to *General Ale Brewing Procedures* beginning on page 218.)

PORTER
THE VINEYARD—Upton, MA

Ingredients:

3.3 lbs. Superbrau Amber Malt Extract unhopped
3 lbs. Amber dry malt extract
1 lb. black malt grain
4 oz. crystal malt grain
2 oz. Northern Brewer hop pellets
1/2 oz. Fuggles hop plug (last 5 minutes)
1 pkt. Nottingham Ale Yeast
1/2 cup corn sugar for priming

Original Specific Gravity: 1.052-54
Terminal Specific Gravity: 1.010-1.014
Primary Fermentation: 4 days at 70°F
Secondary Fermentation: 8 days at 70°F
Boil Time: 40 minutes

Procedure: Crush and put all grains into 2 quarts cold water for 10 minutes, then raise temperature to a boil slowly. Once boiling commences, remove from heat. Strain liquid into boiling pot. Add up to 2 gallons water. Add Superbrau malt, amber dry malt and bring to boil. Once boiling starts add Northern Brewer hop pellets. Last 5 minutes add Fuggles hops. At end of boil, strain into primary fermenter and add cold water to make 5 gallons. Pitch yeast when temperature drops below 90°F. At bottling time boil 1/2 cup priming sugar with 1 cup water for bulk priming.

PIRATES BREW PORTER
Compliments of Jay Garrison
BREW BUDDYS—Redondo Beach, CA

Ingredients

6 lbs. Dark Liquid Extract
1 can Alexander Dark
7 oz. Chocolate Malt
1 oz. Perle Hops
1/2 oz. Willamette Hops
Wyeast #1028 London Ale or Dry Ale Yeast

Instructions

1) If you selected the Wyeast liquid yeast, you must break the inner packet before you begin to brew. Allow 1 day for each month after the manufacture date printed on the front. If you're using the dry yeast that came with the Pirates Brew Kit, go ahead and get to it.
2) Prepare the grain. The grain should be crushed; if you did not get the grain crushed at the shop, crush it with some sort of rolling pin. You can either mix the grain with 2 quarts of water and heat it until it starts to boil, or heat it to about 165°F and steep for about 15 minutes.
3) Strain the grain, collecting the liquid into your brew pot. Rinse the grain (sparge) with 2 quarts of hot (170-180°F) water.
4) Add the bag and can of extract and 1 gallon of water to the brew pot. (You might want to rest the extract in hot water for awhile to soften it up.) Bring the wort to a soft rolling boil.
5) Add the Perle hops to the wort and boil for 40 minutes. Stir occasionally.

6) Add 1/2 of the Willamette hops (1/4 oz.) to the wort and boil for 20 minutes. Stir occasionally.
7) Add 1/2 of the Willamette hops (1/4 oz.) to the wort, turn off the heat; stir and let sit (covered, if possible) for 10 minutes.
8) Add the boiled wort to your sanitized, rinsed fermenter. Add ice-cold water to make 5 gallons. When the temperature drops to 75°F or less, add the yeast.
9) If you use liquid yeast, open the swollen packet and add to the wort. If you use dry yeast, add the yeast to 1 cup of 90°F water for a few minutes before adding to the wort. (You can add the yeast directly to the wort and let it sit for a few minutes also, but rehydrating the yeast in warm water will improve the fermentation.) Stir the wort thoroughly with a sanitized spoon.
10) Put the lid on the fermenter tightly, and insert the fermentation lock with the stopper into the hole in the lid and fill it up about 3/4 of the way with water or vodka. Let the wort ferment for a week or two until the fermentation ceases.
11) When fermentation is complete, syphon the beer into a sanitized bottling bucket. Boil the corn sugar in about a cup of water; cool; stir gently into the beer. This provides the nutrients necessary for the yeast to carbonate the beer in the bottle.
12) Insert one end of the sanitized and rinsed hose into the bottling spigot and the other end to the bottle filler. Push the bottle filler down onto the bottom of the bottle and open the bottling spigot. 5 gallons of beer will make about 2 cases, so make sure you sanitize this amount beforehand. Leave about 1/2-3/4 inch of space at the top of the bottle. Cap the bottles.
13) Let the beer age for 2 weeks to 6 months. Chill and enjoy.

Note: The normal phase of fermentation will be a lag phase, usually 2 hours to 1.5 days. Followed by a steady increase in intensity, usually lasting anywhere from 1 to 4 days. Fermentation abruptly slows down after this and tapers off to an occasional bubble being pushed out of the fermentation lock every 30 seconds or so. The main contributing factors to these fluctuations are the strain and initial amount of yeast being used, sanitation, and temperature intensity and consistency. For ale yeast, try and maintain temperatures between 65° and 75°. For lagers, temperatures of 65° down to 32° work best to maintain lager characteristics.

PORTER
Compliments of David Ruggiero
BARLEYMALT & VINE—Newton, MA

Ingredients:
2 containers (6.6) lbs. light malt extract
OR 6.6 lbs. Bulk Light Malt Extract
1 lb. Crystal Malt
1/2 lb. Chocolate Malt
1 oz. Cluster Hops (for bittering)
1 oz. Chinook Hops (for bittering & aroma)
1/2 tsp. Calcium Carbonate, CaCO3 (reduces malt acidity)
1 tsp. Irish Moss (for clarifying the wort)
1 pkg. M&F Ale Yeast
3/4 cup Corn Sugar (for priming)
1 Muslin Bag

Original Gravity (O.G.) 1.048-1.050 Final Gravity (F.G.) 1.016-1.018
H.B.U.s~7 to 9 or I.B.U.s~21 to 27
Alcohol 5.0% by Volume

Directions for Brewing:
1. Secure grains in muslin bag and place into a pot with 2 gallons of water.
2. Steep the grain while water is heating, remove before a boil commences.
3. Dissolve all malt extracts and the CaCO3 into the brewpot and re-establish the boil.
4. A total elapsed brewing time of 30 minutes is required in order to:
   • Reconstitute the malt extracts.
   • Sterilize the ingredients.
   • Clarify the wort (this is known as a Hot Break).
   • Extract hop bitterness and aromatic properties.
5. The following additions to the brewpot must be made at each of the specified times:
ELAPSED TIME   0 minutes, add the Cluster hops.
                      15 minutes, add the Irish Moss.
                      25 minutes, add the Chinook hops.
                      30 minutes, remove the brewpot from the stove.
6. Transfer the wort to a sanitized fermenter, straining out hop pellets if possible.
7. Add enough cold water to the fermenter to equal 5 gallons, when the temperature falls below 75°F, add the yeast.
8. Secure the airlock and ferment as usual (refer to the *General Fermentation Procedures* section beginning on page 230);
   • Single stage fermentation techniques last 7 to 10 days.
   • Two stage fermentation techniques last 3 to 5 days in the primary and 5 days to 3 weeks in the secondary.
   • Influencing factors that can shorten or prolong your beer's fermentation cycle are; temperature, yeast selection and viability, wort gravities, oxygen uptake and general sanitation procedures.
9. When all fermentation activity has ceased, check your final gravity. It should be within .002 degrees of the recipe's suggested reading. Prepare to bottle if it is. (Refer to the *General Bottling Procedures* section beginning on page 232.)

PORTER
Compliments of Dick Foehringer
THE BREWMEISTER—Folsom, CA

7 lbs. Amber Bulk Extract Syrup
1/2 lb. Chocolate Malt
1/2 lb. Black Patent Malt
1/2 teaspoon Citric Acid
1 teaspoon Calcium Carbonate
1 teaspoon Irish Moss
2 oz. Hallertauer Hops — Boiling
1 oz. Fuggles Hops — Aromatic
Ale Yeast
1 teaspoon Gelatin
3/4 cup Bottling Sugar

Original Gravity ~1.053
Final Gravity ~1.014

Put the chocolate and black patent grains into your brew pot (best to put the grain in a hop boiling bag) with 1-1/2 to 2-1/2 gallons cold water and bring to a near boil. Remove from heat and allow grains to steep for 30 minutes, remove chocolate malt and black patent grains. Dissolve bulk malt extract, citric acid and calcium carbonate. Return to heat and boil for 30 minutes. Add the Irish Moss and boil 15 minutes. Total Boiling time 1 hour. Turn off heat, add the aromatic hops, cover and let steep for 15 minutes. Cold break and strain the wort into your primary fermenter. Add cold water to make 5-1/2 gallons. When cool, pitch the yeast and ferment in a cool place. When fermentation is complete, rack to secondary and stir in dissolved gelatin. When clear (3-5 days) rack again and add dissolved bottling sugar. Bottle and cap. Age a minimum of 2 weeks.

BLACK DOG PORTER
THE HOME BREWERY—Ozark, MO

Ingredients:

1/2 lb. Dark Crystal Malt, crushed
1/4 lb. Black Patent Malt, crushed
1/3 lb. Chocolate Malt, crushed
   Remove grains from kettle at 170°
6.6 lbs. (2 packs) Yellow Dog Malt Extract
3/4 oz. Northern Brewer Pellets (8.1% AA) in boil
1/2 oz. Tettnanger Hop Pellets (5.0% AA) finishing
1/2 oz. Hallertauer Hop Pellets (5.1% AA) after heat is off
2 packs Doric Ale Yeast <u>or</u> 1 Wyeast Liquid Ale
3/4 cup Corn Sugar for priming

Starting Gravity ~1.060
Final Gravity ~1.020
Alcohol ~5.5% v/v

Instructions:

Heat 5 gallons of water in a large kettle. Add crushed grains. Many people don't have a kettle that large, but heat as much as you can (at least 2 gallons). When the water is boiling, turn off the heat and add the Malt Extract to the water. Use a spoon and stir until you are sure no Malt Extract is sticking to the bottom of the kettle. Then turn the heat back on.

Bring the kettle back to a boil, and stir occasionally so the ingredients won't burn on the bottom of the kettle. If your recipe calls for Bittering Hops, now is the time to add them and stir them in. Watch out for a boil-over. In the early part of the boil, the kettle usually tries to boil over once or twice, so control this by adjusting the heat. Later in the boil, the surface tension changes and boiling over is not a problem. Keep stirring occasionally, and let the beer (wort) boil hard for one hour. Stir in the 1/2 tsp. of Irish Moss in your recipe about 15 minutes before the end of the boil.

If Finishing Hops are called for in your recipe, stir them in 2 minutes before the end of the boil. Using Finishing Hops at the end of the boil adds a fresh aroma and flavor to the beer, and the use of finishing hops is appropriate in most beer styles.

Pour the hot beer (wort) into the primary fermenter. It is not necessary to strain the wort if you used hop pellets. Add cold water to bring the total volume up to 5 gallons. If you are using our #B3a Fermenter (the one in the kits) the 5-gallon mark is the bottom ring. Cover the fermenter and wait until the temperature is down to 75°F. If you have a Wort Chiller (#C44), use it to bring the temperature down quickly. At 75° or less, add the Yeast in your recipe. Just tear open the pack(s) and sprinkle it on the wort. Close the fermenter with the lid, stopper, and airlock. Remember to put water (or Vodka) in the airlock. Vodka evaporates more quickly, but bacteria won't live in it.

Fermentation should start within 24 hours, and may continue for between one day and two weeks, depending on the type of yeast, the recipe, and the temperature. Leave the beer alone and don't open the lid. When the airlock has not bubbled for several days and the beer is flat, still, and clearing, it is ready to bottle.

To bottle, siphon about one pint of beer into a pan and warm it on the stove. Add exactly 3/4 cup of Corn Sugar to the pan and stir until it is dissolved. Pour this back into the beer and stir gently but well to distribute the sugar. Siphon or tap into clean sanitized bottles and cap. Keep the bottles at room temperature. After a week, put a bottle in the refrigerator and try it. It will be best in about three weeks.

CRICKET'S PORTER
JASPER'S HOME BREW SUPPLY—Hudson, NH

Ingredients:

John Bull dark hopped malt
2 lbs. Munton & Fison dark dried malt extract
1 lb. crushed Crystal malt
1/2 lb. crushed Black Patent malt
1 oz. Cascade hops (boil)
1/2 oz. Cascade hops (finishing)
Munton & Fison Ale yeast
4 oz. priming sugar
1 muslin bag (for grains)

O.S.G. 1.050-1.054
F.S.G. 1.011-1.022

Put crushed grains in muslin bag, put into 1 gallon cold water and bring to a boil, remove grains. Take pot off the flame and add syrup and dried malt to boiled water, stir until dissolved. Put back on the flame. Add 1 oz. Cascade hops and boil for 45-60 minutes. The last 2-3 minutes add 1/2 oz. cascade hops. Add to 4 gallons of cold water, when cooled to below 80°F pitch yeast.

PORTER
THE CELLAR HOMEBREW—Seattle, WA

6.6 lbs. British bulk malt syrup (unhopped)
1/2 lb. English Crystal malt (crushed)
1/4 lb. Chocolate malt (crushed)
1/4 lb. Black Patent (crushed)
2 tsp. Burton water salts
1-1/2 oz. Fuggle hops (boiling)— 1/2 oz. Tettnang hops (boiling)
1/2 oz. Willamette hops (finishing)—1 oz. Tettnang hops (finishing)
1 pkg. dry ale yeast or Irish Ale liquid yeast
1-1/4 tsp. Yeast Nutrient

<u>Brewing Directions</u>

1) Place any crushed Specialty Grains in a strainer bag. Add this bag of grain to your brewing kettle, which contains 2 to 2-1/2 gallons brewing water.
2) Bring the brewing water to a boil, then remove the bag of grains.
3) Remove the brewing kettle from the burner and add any Malt Syrup and Dry Malt Extract. Stir thoroughly and return the kettle to the burner. Continue heating and stirring this wort until it boils.

4) At boiling point, add any Yeast Nutrient, Water Salts, and Boiling Hops. Hops can be placed in a hop bag or added loose, to be later strained out after the boil using a strainer bag. Time the boil for about one hour, stirring occasionally. After the first 10 minutes of this boil, remove two cups of wort in measuring cup, and cover with foil or plastic. Cool to 90°F for use in step #5 below.

5) Making the Yeast Starter: For dry yeast, use 1/2 cup warm tap water (90 to 100°F). Sprinkle the contents of yeast packet into that water, cover for at least fifteen minutes, and then add to the two cups of wort you prepared in step #4. Cover and set aside for use in step #9 below. For liquid yeast, prepare one to three days ahead of brewing time per package instructions.

6) After the wort has boiled for that one hour, add Finishing Hops. Place them in the hop bag, which has been emptied of the spent boiling hops, and place them in the boiling kettle or just add the Finishing Hops directly to the brewing kettle.

7) Let the boil continue for 5 minutes. Remove the pot from the burner and let it cool, covered, for about 20 minutes.

8) Pour three gallons of cold water into the sanitized open fermenter fitted with strainer bag, if loose Finishing Hops were used in step #6, strain the warm wort from step #7 into the cold water. Top up the fermenter to 5-1/2 gallons using cold tap water. Cover the fermenter and cool the wort as rapidly as possible.

9) When the wort has cooled to about 80° add the Yeast Starter and ferment as you usually do.

ORFORDVILLE PORTER (revisited)
Compliments of Paul White
THE SEVEN BARREL BREWERY SHOP—*Lebanon, NH*

The Tea

8 oz. Crystal Malt
4 oz. Chocolate Malt
2 oz. Black Patent

Put crushed grains into 2 quarts cold water and raise temperature to 160°F. Cover and steep for 20 minutes. Strain the grains and sparge with 1 quart of 170°F water.

The Boil

1 can John Bull Dark Hopped syrup
1 can John Bull Light Hopped syrup

Add more hot water and stir in extracts. Bring to a boil and boil for 15 minutes. Cool and ferment with Edme ale yeast. Bottle when ready and age for as long as you can stand it. (Usually 1 week.)

Brewer's Notes: "You can change anything in this recipe except the can of John Bull Dark. It's a tried and true ingredient that has always given the best flavor in this recipe."

PORTER
Recipe of the Month
BEER & WINE HOBBY—Woburn, MA

2 cans Light Malt Extract
1/2 lb. English Crystal Malt
1/2 lb. Chocolate Malt
1/4 lb. Biscuit Malt
1 oz. Perle Hops (Boil)
1/2 oz. Tettnang Hops (Flavor)
1/2 oz. Tettnang Hops (Finishing)
1 Burton Water Salts
1 Muslin Bag
1 teaspoon Irish Moss
Yeast: Australian or American Liquid Ale
3/4 cup Corn Sugar

S.G. 1.040-1.044
F.G. 1.009-1.013

Add 2 gallons of cold water to your pot; put 1/2 lb. crushed English Crystal Malt, 1/2 lb. crushed Chocolate Malt and 1/4 lb. crushed Biscuit Malt into your Muslin Bag and tie. Place bag in cold water and bring almost to a boil. Remove from heat and let grains steep for 15 minutes. Remove grains and discard. Add 2 cans of Light Malt Extract, 1 oz. of Perle Hops, 1 Burton Water Salts and dissolve. Return to boil for 40 minutes. At this point add 1 teaspoon of Irish Moss, 1/2 oz. of Tettnang Hops and boil for 20 more minutes. Add the remaining 1/2 oz. of Tettnang Hops during the final 2 minutes of the boil. Remove from heat. Put 3 gallons of cold water in your primary fermenter, add boiled wort and top off to 5-1/4 gallons total volume. When wort has cooled to between 65-75°F, pitch prepared yeast starter and proceed as usual. Ferment to completion. Prime with 3/4 cup of Corn Sugar and bottle.

BODIAM CASTLE BROWN PORTER
Courtesy of Al Korzonas
SHEAF & VINE BREWING SUPPLY—Countryside, IL

NOTE: 8.5 gallon batch size

7.5 gallons Chicago water (extract boil)
1.5 gallons Chicago water (mash)
2.5 gallons Chicago water (sparge)
4# DeWolf-Cosyns Aromatic Malt
6# Northwestern Dark Extract
3.3# Northwestern Amber Extract
3 grams Non-iodized table salt in boil
10 grams Calcium Carbonate in boil
2.4 oz. Mt. Hood Pellets (3.5% AA) (60 min.)
2.6 oz. Fuggle Pellets (3% AA) (15 min.)
1 oz. Brewer's Gold Pellets (8% AA) (2 minutes in extract boil)
2 packages rehydrated Red Star Ale Yeast

The mash was:
    40 min. at 100°F
    1 hr. at 158°F
    15 min. at 170°F
    Sparge at 165°F.

OG = 1.052   FG = 1018

"This beer is not as dark as most commercial Porters, so don't be surprised if it seems light coloured. It approximates the colour much more of an original Porter. This beer is relatively full-bodied and sweet for its original gravity, but has a bitterness level of approximately 30 IBUs, so the sweetness is not cloying. The Aromatic Malt lends a nice toasty flavor which fits this style well. If you prefer to make this beer all-extract, you could substitute 1.75 pounds of Laaglander Light Dried Malt Extract and 3/4 pound of CaraMunich Malt in place of the Aromatic Malt (also, reduce the water by one gallon)."—*Al Korzonas*

Beer Trivia—*In the year 1814, eight people were drowned and several houses were destroyed when a 20,000 barrel Porter aging vat burst in London. Widespread inebriation was also reported as people drank freely from the gutters.*

STOUT

"Stout," an archaic term meaning "strong," was once used to describe high alcohol beers in a variety of styles. Stout, as we know it today, originated from a Porter of high gravity called "Stout Porter." The most famous is Guinness, which has dominated the market since its introduction in 1759. This "Dry" (because of its hop bitterness) or "Irish Stout" is served at room temperature (68°F) in Ireland and generally at cellar temperatures (50-57°F) or colder in the U.K. and elsewhere. *Russian Imperial Stout* is actually the trade name of a bottle-conditioned product of the Courage Ltd. company that was originally exported to the Royal Court of Czarist Russia. However, the term "Imperial Stout" is often used colloquially and by other breweries to describe a similarly sweet, high alcohol ale that is technically a Barleywine. So called "Foreign Export Stout," such as those popular in Belgium and Africa, are merely more alcoholic versions of Dry Stout, and are usually contract-brewed around the world by British and Irish firms. Practically all Stouts have been made less assertive in recent years to accommodate what marketing directors feel are the tastes of younger drinkers and women.

Noteworthy commercial examples in the Dry Stout category include: *Murphy's Irish Stout, Guinness Extra Stout* , of course, and the American microbrewed *Old No. 38 Stout,* and *Ryan's Irish Stout.* In the Sweet Stout category: *Mackeson's Sweet Stout* and *Zoser Stout.* In the Imperial Stout category, *Russian Imperial Stout* and *Samuel Smith's Imperial Stout.* The rare microbrewed example is well represented by Pacific Coast Brewing's *Imperial Stout.*

Homebrewers should aim for a full-bodied, black beer made from English or Scottish malts that is low in hop flavor and aroma, but high <u>or</u> low in hop bitterness, depending on the sub-style. Emphasize the malty, caramel, and roasted barley qualities, but use water with enough temporary hardness to counteract the acidity of the dark malts. A long primary fermentation in the cooler range of ale temperatures is advised to keep diacetyl levels low. Carbonation should be high, with a thick, lacey head that lasts until the end.

STOUT
Compliments of David Ruggiero
BARLEYMALT & VINE—Newton, MA

Ingredients:
2, 3.3 lb. cans dark malt extract
OR 6.6 lbs. Bulk Dark Malt Extract
1/2 lb. Crystal malt
1/2 lb. Roasted malt
1/2 lb. Chocolate malt
1/3 lb. Flaked barley
1 tsp. of Calcium Carbonate, CaCO3, (reduces malt acidity)
1 oz. Nugget hops (yielding~11 H.B.U.s of bitterness)
1 pkg. Edme ale yeast
1 Grain Bag
3/4 cup corn sugar (for priming)

Original Gravity (O.G.) 1.050-1.052   Final Gravity (F.G.) 1.016-1.018
H.B.U.s~10 to 13 or I.B.U.s~25 to 30
Alcohol 4.5% by Volume

The Brewmaster's Recipe Manual

Directions for Brewing:
1. Secure grains in muslin bag and place in brewpot with 2 gallons of cold water.
2. Steep the grain while water is heating, remove before a boil commences.
3. Dissolve all malt extracts into the brewpot and allow the boil to re-establish.
4. A total elapsed brewing time of 30 minutes is required in order to:
   - Reconstitute the malt extracts.
   - Sterilize the ingredients.
   - Clarify the wort (this is known as Hot Break).
   - Extract hop bitterness and aromatic properties.
5. The following additions to the brewpot must be made at the specified times:
ELAPSED TIME: 0 minutes, add CaCO3 and the Nugget hops.
                       30 minutes, remove the brewpot from the stove.
6. Transfer the wort to a sanitized fermenter, straining out hop pellets if possible.
7. Add enough cold water to the fermenter to equal 5 gallons, when the temperature falls below 75°F, add the yeast.
8. Secure the airlock and ferment as usual;
   - Single stage fermentation techniques last 7 to 10 days.
   - Two stage fermentation techniques last 3 to 5 days in the primary and 5 days to 3 weeks in the secondary.
   - Influencing factors that can shorten or prolong your beer's fermentation cycle are; temperature, yeast selection and viability, wort gravities, oxygen uptake and general sanitation procedures.
9. When all fermentation activity has ceased check your final gravity. It should be within .002 degrees of the recipe's suggested reading. Prepare to bottle if it is. (Refer to the *General Bottling Procedures* section beginning on page 232.)

DEEP WINTER STOUT
THE VINEYARD—Upton, MA

Ingredients:

3.3 lbs. Northwestern Gold unhopped
3.1 lbs. Superbrau Dark unhopped
1/2 lb. roasted barley
1/2 lb. black malt
1/2 lb. chocolate malt
1 lb. crystal malt
2 oz. Northern Brewer Hop pellets (boiling)
1/2 oz. Fuggles hops plug (last 10 minutes)
1 pkt. Whitbread ale yeast
1/2 cup priming sugar

Original Specific Gravity: 1.056
Terminal Specific Gravity: 1.014
Primary fermentation: 4 days at 60-65°F
Secondary Fermentation: 10 days at 60-65°F
Boil Time: 40 minutes

Procedure: Crush and put all grains into 2 gallons cold water for 10 minutes, then raise the temperature to a boil slowly. Once boiling commences, remove from heat. Strain liquid into boiling pot. Add 1/2 gallon water, Northwestern and Superbrau malt extracts, 2 oz. Northern Brewer hop pellets, and bring to a boil for 40 minutes. Add 1/2 oz. Fuggles last 10 minutes of the boil. Strain into primary fermenter and add cold water to make 5 gallons and let cool. Pitch yeast when temp. drops below 80°F. At bottling time boil 1/2 cup priming sugar with 1 cup water for bulk priming.

PIRATES BREW IRISH STOUT
Compliments of Jay Garrison
BREW BUDDYS—Redondo Beach, CA

Ingredients

6 lbs. Dark Liquid Extract
1 lb. Crystal Malt 120L
5 oz. Roasted Barley
2 oz. Black Patent Malt
2-1/2 oz. Cluster Hops
Wyeast #1084 Irish Ale or Dry Ale Yeast

Instructions

1) If you selected Wyeast liquid yeast, you must break the inner packet before you begin to brew. Allow 1 day for each month after the manufacture date printed on the front. If you're using the dry yeast that came with the Pirates Brew Kit, go ahead and get to it.
2) Prepare the grains. The grain should be crushed; if you did not get the grains crushed at the shop, crush it with some sort of rolling pin. You can either mix the grain with 2 quarts of water and heat it until it starts to boil, or heat it to about 165°F and steep for about 15 minutes.
3) Strain the grains, collecting the liquid into your brew pot. Rinse the grain (sparge) with 2 quarts of hot (170-180°F) water.
4) Add the bag of extract and 1 gallon of water to the brew pot. (You might want to rest the bag of extract in hot water for awhile to soften it up.) Bring the wort to a hard rolling boil.
5) Add 2 oz. of the Cluster hops to the wort and boil for 40 minutes. Stir occasionally.
6) Add the remaining 1/2 oz. of the Cluster hops to the wort and boil for 20 minutes. Stir occasionally.
7) Add the boiled wort to your sanitized, rinsed fermenter. Add ice-cold water to make 5 gallons. When the temperature drops to 75°F or less, add the yeast.
8) If you use liquid yeast, open the swollen packet and add to the wort. If you use dry yeast, add the yeast to 1 cup of 90°F water for a few minutes before adding to the wort. (You can add the yeast directly to the wort and let it sit for a few minutes also, but rehydrating the yeast in warm water will improve the fermentation.) Stir the wort thoroughly with a sanitized spoon.
9) Put the lid on the fermenter tightly, and insert the fermentation lock with the stopper into the hole in the lid and fill it up about 3/4 of the way with water or vodka. Let the wort ferment for a week or two until the fermentation ceases.
10) When fermentation is complete, syphon the beer into a sanitized bottling bucket. Boil the corn sugar in about a cup of water; cool; stir gently into the beer. This provides the nutrients necessary for the yeast to carbonate the beer in the bottle.
11) Insert one end of the sanitized and rinsed hose into the bottling spigot and the other end to the bottle filler. Push the bottle filler down onto the bottom of the bottle and open the bottling spigot. 5 gallons of beer will make about 2 cases, so make sure you sanitize this amount beforehand. Leave about 1/2-3/4 inch of space at the top of the bottle. Cap the bottles.
12) Let the beer age for 2 weeks to 6 months. Chill and enjoy.

Note: The normal phase of fermentation will be a lag phase, usually 2 hours to 1.5 days. Followed by a steady increase in intensity, usually lasting anywhere from 1 to 4 days. Fermentation abruptly slows down after this and tapers off to an occasional bubble being pushed out of the fermentation lock every 30 seconds or so. The main contributing factors to these fluctuations are the strain and initial amount of yeast being used, sanitation, and temperature intensity and consistency. For ale yeast, try and maintain temperatures between 65° and 75°. For lagers, temperatures of 65° down to 32° work best to maintain lager characteristics.

INSPIRATION STOUT
Compliments of Jeff Pzena
THE MODERN BREWER CO. INC.—*Cambridge, MA*

Ingredients:

1 lb. Roasted Barley
8.5 lbs. Pale Barley Malt
0.125 lb. Black Patent Malt
0.5 lb. Wheat Malt
0.5 lb. Steel Cut Oats
0.5 lb. Crystal Malt
0.5 lb. Dark Brown Sugar
1.25 oz. Chinook Hops (Boil) 11.9% AA (50 minutes)
1 oz. Cascade Hops (Flavor) 5.9%AA (20 minutes)
0.5 oz. Mt. Hood Hops (Aroma) (5 minutes)
1 Pkg. Wyeast #1007 Liquid Ale Yeast (German Ale/Mild Alt)
0.5 oz. Water Crystals
1.25 cups Dried Malt for Priming
1 tablespoon Irish Moss for Fining

Original Specific Gravity: 1.060
Terminal Specific Gravity: 1.013-1.017
Potential Alcohol by Volume: 6%

Instructions: Add cracked grains to 3.5 gallons of 173° water and stir thoroughly. Put in oven on hold (warm) and let mash for 90 minutes (mash temp. settles to 151-153°F). Put mash on stove and slowly heat to 165°F. Sparge with 4.25 gallons of 168° water. Bring to boil, add brown sugar. When boil resumes, begin the hop additions and add water crystals and Irish moss. At end of boil, chill as quickly as possible (wort chiller or ice water bath). Funnel into fermenter and add pre-started yeast culture. Ferment 7 days at approximately 67°F then rack into clean carboy and let sit as cold as possible (refrigerate) for 7 days. Rack, prime, bottle and let condition for 4 weeks at 67°F.

IRISH CREAM STOUT
Recipe of the Month
BEER & WINE HOBBY—Woburn, MA

Ingredients

2 cans of Mountmellick Dark Plain Malt
1/2 lb. English Crystal Malt
1/4 lb. Chocolate Malt
1/4 lb. Roasted Barley
2-1/2 oz. Bullion Loose Hops (boil) (15 HBU) or 1-1/2 oz. pellets
1/2 oz. Kent Golding (last 10 minutes)
1-1/2 oz. Kent Golding Plug (dry hop)
1/2 lb. Lactose
1 pkg. Burton Water Salts
4 Muslin bags
3/4 cup Priming Sugar
Yeast: Yeast Lab AO3 London—Starter Required

SG 1.045-1.050
FG 1.010-1.014

Instructions

Add 2 gallons of cold water to your pot, put 1/2 lb. of crushed English Crystal, 1/4 lb. Chocolate Malt, and 1/4 lb. crushed Roasted Barley into muslin bag and tie. Place bag in cold water and bring to a boil. When water comes to a boil, remove from heat and let steep for 5 minutes. Remove grains and discard, return pot to heat and bring to a boil. Add 2 cans of Mountmellick Dark Plain Malt and 2-1/2 oz Bullion loose hops (in muslin bag) and boil for 45 minutes. During the last ten minutes of the boil, add 1/2 oz. plug of Kent Golding tied into a muslin bag, 1/2 lb. Lactose and 1 package of Burton Water Salts. Remove from heat, discard hops and cool. In primary fermenter, add some cold water and boiled liquid, bring total volume of liquid to 5-1/4 gallons. When wort has cooled to between 65-75°F, add prepared yeast (instructions included). Prepare dry hops - place 1-1/2 oz. of Kent Golding Plugs in muslin bag, tie and place in primary fermenter, stir and allow hops to float. After 3 days of fermentation, remove hops and gently syphon beer into secondary fermenter. Finish fermenting. Prime with 3/4 cup corn sugar, bottle, and cap. For best results age a minimum of 4 weeks.

Beer Trivia—*In 1873 the U.S. had over 4,000 breweries. By the 1960s, there were less than 100.*

MARK'S RYE STOUT
Compliments of Mark Larrow
BEER & WINEMAKING SUPPLIES, INC.—Northampton, MA

Ingredients

8 lbs. British Pale Malt Extract
12 oz. Roasted Barley
4 oz. Flaked Barley
2 oz. Roasted Rye
2 oz. Malted Rye
2 oz. Bullion/Northern Brewer hops
1/2 oz. Fuggles aroma hops
3/4 cup corn sugar for bottling
10-14 grams dry ale yeast OR 1 Brewer's Choice (Wyeast) liquid yeast

O.G.: 1.050   **F.G.: 1.014**

(Refer to *General Ale Brewing Procedures* beginning on page 218.)

SWEET STOUT
Compliments of Dick Foehringer
THE BREWMEISTER—Folsom, CA

7 lbs. Amber Malt Extract Syrup
3.3 lbs. Telford or Edme Dark Extract Syrup
1/4 lb. Black Patent Malt
1/4 lb. Roasted Barley
1/4 lb. Flaked Barley
1/2 lb. Cara-Pils Malt
1 oz. Bullion Hops (Boiling)
1 oz. Fuggles (Boiling)
1/2 oz. Cascade Hops (Aromatic)
2 oz. Lactose
1 Irish Moss
1 teaspoon Gelatin
1 Ale Yeast
1 Bottling Sugar

Original Specific Gravity: 1.078
Terminal Specific Gravity: 1.026

Put grains in 1-1/2 to 2-1/2 gallons of cold water. (Use a grain bag if you have one.) Bring to a near boil and turn off heat. Steep grain for 30 minutes, remove grain. Dissolve malt extract syrups, lactose and return to heat. Bring to a boil. Add boiling hops and boil 45 minutes. Add Irish Moss, boil 5 minutes. Add Aromatic hops, boil 10 minutes. Total boiling time of 60 minutes. Cold break and strain wort into primary fermenter. Add cold water to make 5-1/2 gallons. When cool (below 85°F) pitch yeast. Ferment in a cool, dark place. When fermentation stops, transfer to secondary. Stir in dissolved gelatin and allow to clear (3-5 days). When cleared, rack again, stir in bottling sugar, bottle and cap.

Age a minimum of 2-4 weeks.

STOUT
Compliments of Sloan S. Venables
BREWMASTER—San Leandro, CA

Ingredients

6 lbs. Pale Malt Syrup
3 lbs. Dark Dried Malt Extract
1 lb. Crystal Malt—40L (Steeped 30 min.)
1/2 lb. Roasted Barley (Steeped 30 min.)
1/2 lb. Black Patent (Steeped 30 min.)
1 oz. Perle Hops—Bittering Hops (Boiled 60 min.)
1 oz. Perle Hops—Bittering/Flavoring Hops (Boiled 25 min.)
1 oz. Kent Goldings Hops—Aromatic Hops (End of Boil)
Ale Yeast—Wyeast #1084 Irish Ale or Dried Ale Yeast
3/4 cup Corn Sugar at bottling

Starting Gravity: 1.066 **Finishing Gravity: 1.014-1.016**
Bittering Units: 50 **Fermentation Temperature: 65-70°F**

Instructions
(Refer to *General Ale Brewing Procedures* beginning on page 218.)

The Brewmaster's Recipe Manual

RUSSIAN IMPERIAL STOUT
Compliments of Mike Knaub
STARVIEW BREW—Mt. Wolf, PA

Beer Type	Russian Imperial Stout	Amount	Boil Time 60 mins.
Malt Extracts	M&F extra light plain malt extract	2-3.3 lb. cans	
	Dutch dry malt light plain	4 lbs.	
Malt Grains	Crystal	1 lb.	
	Black Patent	1/3 lb.	
	Roasted Barley	1/3 lb.	
Steep		2 gal.	30 mins. @ 160°
Hops			
Boil	Chinook pellet	25 HBU	60 mins.
Flavor			
Aroma	Cascade leaf	1/2 oz.	5 min.
Yeast	Yeast Lab Irish Ale	1-1/2 pints starter	
Water		4 gal.	
Misc.	Lactose	1 lb.	
	Briar Rabbit Molasses	1-1/2 cup	
O.G. = 1.087	Primary = 10 days @ 70°		
T.G. = 1.018	Secondary = 14 days @ 70°		
Brew Date =	Bottled =		

Add grains to 2 gallons of cold water. Raise to 160° and steep for 30 mins. Sparge grains, add the other 4 gallons of water and bring to a boil. Add extracts, lactose, and molasses. Bring back to a boil, add boil hops and boil for 60 minutes. Cool down to 70° and add active starter culture.

OATMEAL STOUT

Oatmeal Stout is a member of the "Sweet Stout" sub-category that traces its roots back to Mild Ales that were brewed with a portion of oatmeal to cut the green beer harshness. Oatmeal Stout's new popularity among homebrewers demands that it be given a section of its own. Oatmeal Stout has more body than Irish Stout, is smoother, slightly sweeter, and often stronger; with a clean, roasted, malty flavor, and a "chewy" texture from the rolled or steel-cut oats. Hops should be used only to bitter, otherwise, the full roasted malt and oatmeal flavors, which should prevail, will be masked. Low to medium carbonate water and fermentation temperatures between 60-66°F are recommended. *Samuel Smith's Oatmeal Stout* and the American microbrewed *Seabright Oatmeal Stout* are good commercial examples of this style to enjoy while brewing your own.

OATMEAL STOUT
WILLIAM'S BREWING—San Leandro, CA

Ingredients:

6 lbs. William's Oatmeal Dark
1 lb. William's American Dark
4 oz. Lactose
1/4 oz. English Fuggle Hops AA 6.7% (boil) 60 minutes.
1 oz. English Fuggle Hops AA 6.7% (flavor) 30 minutes
1 pkg. liquid Burton Ale Yeast
4-1/2 oz. Corn Sugar for priming

O.G. 1.047
F.G. 1.016
Potential alcohol **4%** by volume

Procedure: Boil for 1 hour with at least 3 gallons of water, adding hops as indicated. Add the Lactose during the last 10 minutes of the boil. Cool and add to a fermenter, adding water if needed to make 5 gallons.

Add the swollen pack of Burton Ale Yeast (started two or three days in advance). Allow to ferment at 60 to 75° F (ideally 65°F) for 12 days before checking with a hydrometer to see if the finishing gravity has been reached.

After the finishing gravity has been reached, prime and bottle. Age 2 weeks in a dark place before drinking, ideally at 60 to 65°F.

Notes: "A rich and smooth Stout in the English tradition. This recipe is not overly sweet, yet it lacks the roasted character of a Dry Stout. Hops are used minimally to balance the sweetness, and aromatic hops are not used, as they detract from the oatmeal and malt character."—*William's Brewing*

The Brewmaster's Recipe Manual

PIRATES BREW OATMEAL STOUT*
Compliments of Jay Garrison
BREW BUDDYS—Redondo Beach, CA

Ingredients

6 lbs. Dark Liquid Extract
1 can Alexander Dark
6 oz. Crystal Malt 80 L
5 oz. Chocolate Malt
4 oz. Roasted Barley
8 oz. Flaked Oatmeal
1 oz. Chinook Hops
1 oz. Perle Hops
1/2 oz. Hallertau Hops
Gypsum
Wyeast #1084 Irish Ale or Dry Ale Yeast

Instructions

1) If you selected the Wyeast liquid yeast, you must break the inner packet before you begin to brew. Allow 1 day for each month after the manufacture date printed on the front. If you're using the dry yeast that came with the Pirates Brew Kit, go ahead and get to it.
2) Prepare the grains. The grains should be crushed; if you did not get the grains crushed at the shop, crush it with some sort of rolling pin. You can either mix the grains and oatmeal flakes with 2 quarts of water and heat it until it starts to boil, or heat it to about 165°F and steep for about 15 minutes.
3) Strain the grains and flakes, collecting the liquid into your brew pot. Rinse the grain (sparge) with 2 quarts of hot (170-180°F) water.
4) Add the bag and can of extract, the gypsum, and 1 gallon of water to the brew pot. (You might want to rest the bag of extract in hot water for awhile to soften it up.) Bring the wort to a soft rolling boil.
5) Add the Chinook hops to the wort and boil for 30 minutes. Stir occasionally.
6) Add the Perle hops to the wort and boil for 30 minutes. Stir occasionally.
7) Add the Hallertau hops to the wort, turn off the heat; stir and let sit (covered, if possible) for 10 minutes.
8) Add the boiled wort to your sanitized, rinsed fermenter. Add ice-cold water to make 5 gallons. When the temperature drops to 75°F or less, add the yeast.
9) If you use liquid yeast, open the swollen packet and add to the wort. If you use dry yeast, add the yeast to 1 cup of 90°F water for a few minutes before adding to the wort. (You can add the yeast directly to the wort and let it sit for a few minutes also, but rehydrating the yeast in warm water will improve the fermentation.) Stir the wort thoroughly with a sanitized spoon.
10) Put the lid on the fermenter tightly, and insert the fermentation lock with the stopper into the hole in the lid and fill it up about 3/4 of the way with water or vodka. Let the wort ferment for a week or two until the fermentation ceases.
11) When fermentation is complete, syphon the beer into a sanitized bottling bucket. Boil the corn sugar in about a cup of water; cool; stir gently into the beer. This provides the nutrients necessary for the yeast to carbonate the beer in the bottle.
12) Insert one end of the sanitized and rinsed hose into the bottling spigot and the other end to the bottle filler. Push the bottle filler down onto the bottom of the bottle and open the bottling spigot. 5 gallons of beer will make about 2 cases, so make sure you sanitize this amount beforehand. Leave about 1/2-3/4 inch of space at the top of the bottle. Cap the bottles.
13) Let the beer age for 2 weeks to 6 months. Chill and enjoy.

Note: The normal phase of fermentation will be a lag phase, usually 2 hours to 1.5 days. Followed by a steady increase in intensity, usually lasting anywhere from 1 to 4 days. Fermentation abruptly slows down after this and tapers off to an occasional bubble being pushed out of the fermentation lock every 30 seconds or so. The main contributing factors to these fluctuations are the strain and initial amount of yeast being used, sanitation, and temperature intensity and consistency. For ale yeast, try and maintain temperatures between 65° and 75°. For lagers, temperatures of 65° down to 32° work best to maintain lager characteristics.

Brew Buddys customer Steve Crawford took first place at the LA County Fair with this recipe.

XXX OATMEAL COOKIE CHOCOLATE MILK STOUT
Recipe of the Month
BARLEYMALT & VINE—Newton, MA

"Milk Stouts, Oatmeal Stouts, chocolate malt and oatmeal cookies; four singular ingredients now combined in one great beer. This twisted take-off of a traditional Milk Stout is full bodied and sweet due to the use of lactose, also its sharp character and unique mouthfeel are contributed by the rolled oats. BM&V believes that our Stout honors the long-held belief that Milk Stouts have nutritional value. Also, with the addition of an oatmeal cookie, it is not only nutritious, but delicious as well."

BM&V Style Specs: O.G. 1.050-55, T.G. 1.018-25, AAU 7-10, IBU 27-30, %Alc 3-4

Ingredients: 1# Oatmeal, 1/2 # Crystal malt (90L), 1/2 # Chocolate malt, muslin bag, 6# dark malt extract, 1# Lactose, 1 oz. Cluster hops, 1 tsp. $CaCO_3$, London Ale yeast, priming sugar.

Brewing Specifics: Mash the grain in 3 quarts of 150°F water for 30 minutes, add the $CaCO_3$ to this water. Rinse/sparge the grains with 170°F water and collect 2 gallons of runoff. Dissolve the malt extract and bring to a boil. Add the hops and boil for an additional 5 minutes. Cool and top up to 5 gallons. Rehydrate the yeast and add it to the cooled wort. Ferment as usual, bottle when ready. Condition for 2-4 weeks.

The Brewmaster's Recipe Manual

OATMEAL STOUT—Best of Show Winner, 1988
BREWERS RESOURCE—Camarillo, CA

Brewers Resource says, "In an Oatmeal Stout recipe you will want to emphasize the roasted malt and thick oatmeal flavor. Keep it full and slightly sweet by using original gravity between 1.050 and 1.060. Balance the Roast Barley with Chocolate Malt for complexity. So as not to mask the malt flavor, use hops only to bitter. You should use a clean ale yeast, preferably one that will produce a full bodied beer. Fermentation temperatures should be kept between 60° and 66°F to minimize excessive ester production, and use a low to medium carbonate water for brewing this style of beer."

Malt Extract Recipe:
6-1/2 lbs. Light dry malt extract or 8lbs. pale syrup malt extract.
8 oz. Roast barley.
6 oz. Chocolate malt—crushed.
8 oz. Regular rolled oats.
38 I.B.U.s Northern Brewer (i.e., 1-1/4 oz. @ 7.5%AA).
BrewTek American Microbrewery Ale yeast (CL-10) or
Wyeast American Ale (Y-1056).
3/4 cup (4 oz.) Corn sugar to prime at bottling.
(Refer to *General Ale Brewing Procedures* beginning on page 218.)

Mash-Extract Recipe:
4-1/2 lbs. light dry malt extract or 5-1/2 lbs. pale syrup malt extract
8 oz. Roast barley.
6 oz. Chocolate malt—crushed.
8 oz. Regular rolled oats, steeped with pale malt below.
3 lbs. crushed British pale ale malt, mashed in 4 liters of water at 152°F for 45 minutes.
38 I.B.U.s Northern Brewer (i.e., 1-1/4 oz. @ 7.5%AA).
BrewTek American Microbrewery Ale yeast (CL-10) or Wyeast American Ale (Y-1056).
3/4 cup (4 oz.) Corn sugar to prime at bottling.

Steep crushed grains in mini-mash bucket (Q-80) and sparge to collect 3 gallons of wort. Add the malt extract and brew recipe as you normally would or see *General Ale Brewing Procedures* beginning on page 218.

All Grain Recipe:
9 lbs. Pale crushed Klages or, preferably, British pale ale malt.
8 oz. Roast barley.
6 oz. Chocolate malt—crushed.
8 oz. Regular rolled oats, steeped with pale malt below.
38 I.B.U.s Northern Brewer (i.e., 1-1/4 oz. @ 7.5%AA).
BrewTek American Microbrewery Ale yeast (CL-10) or
Wyeast American Ale (Y-1056).
3/4 cup (4 oz.) Corn sugar to prime at bottling.

In mash/lauter bucket stir crushed malts into 10 liters of 168°F water to rest out at about 154°. Cover and rest for 45 minutes. Sparge to 6 gallons into kettle. Bring to a boil and add hops. Brew to completion as you normally would or see *General Ale Brewing Procedures* beginning on page 218. **Recipe Variations:** You may experiment with the recipes below by increasing or decreasing the ratios of Roasted Malts and Oatmeal, or try a touch of Black Patent Malt. Experiment with different original gravities and hop varieties. We prefer a malty Oatmeal Stout, but you may experiment with different yeast strains or mash temperatures for more complexity and variety.

SCOTTISH/SCOTCH ALE

Scottish Ale is traditionally brewed rich, malty, dark, and smooth. Products of Barleywine strength are often labeled "Scotch Ale." Strong Scotch Ale ("Wee Heavy") is compared to English Strong or Old Ale, but has no real equivalent in taste. The sub-categories of Scots Ale are: Scottish Light (60 Shilling), which is light in gravity, not color; Scottish Heavy (70 Shilling); Scottish Export (80 Shilling); and Wee Heavy (90 Shilling).

Originally, beers of the Scottish style were brewed mostly with brown malt, with bog myrtle for bitterness, a high temperature mash, and a lengthy, cool ferment. Later, brewers began to use more pale malts with roasted malts or roasted barley for color. Scottish Ales are low in hop bitterness, with noticeable fruitiness and diacetyl, and a subtle smokey taste. *MacAndrew's Scotch Ale, McEwan's Scotch Ale,* and *Traquar House Ale* represent some of the legendary Scottish versions—*Auld Tartan Wee Heavy* and *Grant's Scottish Ale* are noteworthy American microbrewed versions.

The Scottish microbrewed *Golden Promise* is a prime example of the Scottish style of ale patterned after English Pale Ale. *Legacy Red Ale, Sonoma Irish Ale, Golden Gate Red Ale,* and *Wrigley Red* are all highly praised American microbrewed versions of the malty, reddish Irish Pale Ales which are heavily influenced by the lightly hopped Scottish Ales. I have included recipes for these beers in this section as well.

FIRESIDE SCOTCH ALE
Recipe of the Month
BEER & WINE HOBBY—Woburn, MA

2 cans Light Liquid Malt
2 lbs. Dry Light Malt
1 lb. 2 oz. Special Grain Mix
2 oz. Peat Smoke Malt
1 oz. Northern Brewer Hops
3/4 cup Priming Sugar
1 Muslin Bag
Yeast: 1728 - **Starter Required**

S.G. 1.058-1.062
F.G. 1.014-1.016

Combine Special Grain Mix and Peat Smoke Malt in large plastic bag and crush with rolling pin. Place crushed grains in the muslin bag and tie. Add grains to 2 gallons of cold water and bring to a boil. When water comes to a boil, remove from heat and discard grains. Add 2 cans of light malt, 2 pound s of light dry malt and 1 ounce of Northern Brewer hops. Put back on heat and bring back to a boil; boil for 45 minutes. Remove from heat and add to primary fermenter containing enough cold water to bring total volume to 5-1/4 gallons. When wort has cooled to between 65 and 75°F, pitch prepared yeast. Proceed as usual. Finish fermenting. prime with 3/4 cup priming sugar and bottle.

STRONG SCOTCH ALE
Compliments of Sloan S. Venables
BREWMASTER—San Leandro, CA

Ingredients

6 lbs. British Light Malt Syrup
3 lbs. Light Dried Malt Extract
1 lb. Dark Brown Sugar
1 lb. British Crystal Malt—90L (Steeped 30 min.)
1 lb. Chocolate Malt (Steeped 30 min.)
1/4 lb. Black Patent Malt (Steeped 30 min.)
1 oz. Kent Goldings Hops—Bittering Hops (Boiled 60 min.)
1 oz. Kent Goldings Hops—Flavoring Hops (Boiled 25 min.)
1 oz. Fuggle Hops—Aromatic Hops (End of Boil)
Ale Yeast—Wyeast #1098 British Ale or Dried Ale Yeast
3/4 Corn Sugar at bottling

Starting Gravity: 1.075
Bittering Units: 30

Finishing Gravity: 1.018-1.020
Fermentation Temperature: 65-70°F

Instructions
(Refer to *General Ale Brewing Procedures* beginning on page 218.)

SCOTS BROWN ALE
THE HOME BREWERY—Ozark, MO

Ingredients:

3.3 lbs. (1 pack) Home Brewery Hopped Light Malt Extract
3.3 lbs. (1 pack) Home Brewery Hopped Dark Malt Extract
1.7 lbs. (1/2 pack) Yellow Dog Malt Extract
No bittering hops.
1/2 tsp. Irish Moss added 15 minutes before the end of the boil.
1/2 oz. Willamette Hop Pellets (finishing)
2 packs Doric Ale Yeast
3/4 cup corn sugar for priming

Starting Gravity ~1.060
Final Gravity ~1.016
Alcohol ~5.6% v/v

Instructions:

Heat 5 gallons of water in a large kettle. Many people don't have a kettle that large, but heat as much as you can (at least 2 gallons). When the water is boiling, turn off the heat and add the Malt Extract to the water. Use a spoon and stir until you are sure no Malt Extract is sticking to the bottom of the kettle. Then turn the heat back on.

Bring the kettle back to a boil, and stir occasionally so the ingredients won't burn on the bottom of the kettle. If your recipe calls for Bittering Hops, now is the time to add them and stir them in. Watch out for a boil-over. In the early part of the boil, the kettle usually tries to boil over once or twice, so control this by adjusting the heat. Later in the boil, the surface tension changes and boiling over is not a problem. Keep stirring occasionally, and let the beer (wort) boil hard for one hour. Stir in the 1/2 tsp. of Irish Moss in your recipe about 15 minutes before the end of the boil.

If Finishing Hops are called for in your recipe, stir them in 2 minutes before the end of the boil. Using Finishing Hops at the end of the boil adds a fresh aroma and flavor to the beer, and the use of finishing hops is appropriate in most beer styles.

Pour the hot beer (wort) into the primary fermenter. It is not necessary to strain the wort if you used hop pellets. Add cold water to bring the total volume up to 5 gallons. If you are using our #B3a Fermenter (the one in the kits) the 5-gallon mark is the bottom ring. Cover the fermenter and wait until the temperature is down to 75°F. If you have a Wort Chiller (#C44), use it to bring the temperature down quickly. At 75° or less, add the Yeast in your recipe. Just tear open the pack(s) and sprinkle it on the wort. Close the fermenter with the lid, stopper, and airlock. Remember to put water (or Vodka) in the airlock. Vodka evaporates more quickly, but bacteria won't live in it.

Fermentation should start within 24 hours, and may continue for between one day and two weeks, depending on the type of yeast, the recipe, and the temperature. Leave the beer alone and don't open the lid. When the airlock has not bubbled for several days and the beer is flat, still, and clearing, it is ready to bottle.

To bottle, siphon about one pint of beer into a pan and warm it on the stove. Add exactly 3/4 cup of Corn Sugar to the pan and stir until it is dissolved. Pour this back into the beer and stir gently but well to distribute the sugar. Siphon or tap into clean sanitized bottles and cap. Keep the bottles at room temperature. After a week, put a bottle in the refrigerator and try it. It will be best in about three weeks.

SCOTTISH LIGHT 60°/-
March's Brew of the Month
E.C. KRAUS—Independence, MO

Description: Scottish Light is a lightly hopped but very full bodied beer. Its color is a light translucent amber and has a lasting lacy head of foam. Its most prevalent character is its malty attack, but it still leaves a clean tasting finish.

General Profile: Starting Gravity: 30-35
Finished Alcohol: 3-4%
Bittering: 9-15 IBUs
Color: 8-17 SRM/12-30°L

Ingredients: 3.3 lbs. Light Unhopped Malt Extract
.5 lb. Light Dried Malt Extract (1-1/4 cups)
4 ozs. Brown Sugar
8 ozs. Crystal Malted Barley
1 oz. Chocolate Malted Barley
4 ozs. Malto-Dextrin (5 min. Boil Time)
3/4 oz. Fuggles Pelletized Hops (45 min. boil time)
2 ozs. Dried Oak Chips
14 grams Ale Yeast or Wyeast #1728 Scottish Ale
3/4 cup Priming Sugar (Bottling Time)

The Brewmaster's Recipe Manual

Directions:

1. Lightly crack malted barley s and put with 1-1/2 gallons of cold water in a cooking pan. Slowly bring to a boil over a 30-45 minute period.

2. Strain the grains out by use of a colander and discard.

3. Add the liquid and dried malt extracts and the Brown Sugar to the mixture. Now bring back to a boil once again.

4. Once boiling, add Fuggles hops and boil for 45 minutes. During the last 5 minutes of boil, fold in Malto-Dextrin.

5. When the boiling is complete, add the wort to your fermenter with cold water up to 5 gallons.

6. Boil Oak Chips in a small amount of water for about 10 minutes. Strain the chips off the water, then add them to the wort.

7. Make sure the wort has cooled below 80°F and sprinkle yeast on top.

8. Attach air-lock to fermenter and allow to ferment for 7-10 days or until finished.

9. Bottle with priming sugar as normal and condition 2-4 weeks.

SCOTTISH ALE—Best of Show Winner, 1992
BREWERS RESOURCE—Camarillo, CA

Brewers Resource says, "In designing a Scottish Ale you will want to emphasize the rich malt flavor. An original gravity between 1.055 and 1.065 is fine. It's important to use a strong, slightly estery ale yeast. Fermentation temperatures should be kept between 62° and 68°F to ensure a strong fermentation and allow some ester production. Use low to medium carbonate water for brewing this style of beer."

Malt Extract Recipe:
7 lbs. light dry malt extract or 9 lbs. pale, syrup malt extract.
10 oz. dark crystal malt (120 L)—crushed.
31 I.B.U.s Fuggles (i.e., 1-1/2 oz. @ 5%AA).
BrewTek British Draft Ale yeast (CL-26) or Wyeast American Ale (Y-1056).
3/4 cup (4 oz.) Corn sugar to prime at bottling.

(Refer to *General Ale Brewing Procedures* beginning on page 218.)

Mash-Extract Recipe:
4-1/2 lbs. light dry malt extract or 6 lbs. pale syrup malt extract.
10 oz. dark crystal malt (120 L)—Crushed and steeped with pale malt below.
3 lbs. crushed British pale ale malt, mashed in 4 liters of water at 152°F for 45 min.
31 I.B.U.s Fuggles (i.e., 1-1/2 oz. @ 5%AA).
BrewTek British Draft Ale yeast (CL-26) or Wyeast American Ale (Y-1056).
3/4 cup (4 oz.) Corn sugar to prime at bottling.

Steep crushed grains in mini-mash bucket (Q-80) and sparge to collect 3 gallons of wort. Add malt extract and brew as you normally would or see *General Ale Brewing Procedures* beginning on page 218.

All Grain Recipe:

In mash/lauter bucket stir crushed malts into 11 liters of 168°F water to rest out at about 156°. Cover and rest for 45 minutes. Sparge to 6 gallons into kettle. Bring to boil and add hops as per directions. Cool wort and transfer to fermenter. Pitch yeast, ferment, and bottle. **Recipe Variations:** You may experiment with the recipes below by trying a touch of Chocolate or Black Patent Malt, or try lighter or darker crystal malts. Experiment with different O.G.s and different hop varieties (but always stick with British hops). Also, experiment with different mash temperatures and yeast strains. Try to find a yeast that really produces a full malt flavor, and has a nice ester and diacetyl character.

SCOTCH ALE
Compliments of Mike Knaub
STARVIEW BREW—Mt. Wolf, PA

Beer Type	Scotch Ale	Amount—5.5 gal.	Boil Time 90 mins
Malt Grains	Hugh Baird Pale " " Crystal Durst Munich Durst Pilsner	13 lbs. 4 lbs. 2 lbs. 3 lbs.	Toasted at 350° for 20 mins.
Steep			
Mash In		5-1/2 gal @ 180°	
Protein Rest			
Sach. Rest	85 mins. @ 156°		
Mash Out	10 mins. @ 165°		
Sparge		6 gal. @ 170°	
Hops			
Boil	Kent Goldings leaf	15 HBU	60 mins.
Flavor	" "	5 HBU	20 mins.
Aroma			
Yeast	Yeast Lab Irish Ale		
Water			
Misc.	Irish Moss	1 teaspoon	15 mins.
O.G. = 1.088	Primary		
T.G. = 1.028	Secondary		

The Brewmaster's Recipe Manual

IRISH RED ALE
THE VINEYARD—Upton, MA

Ingredients:

6.6 lb Northwestern hopped gold malt extract
1/2 lb. light crystal malt grain
2 oz. roasted barley
1 tsp. Irish moss (last 15 minutes)
1/2 oz. Hersbrucker hop plug (last 5 minutes)
1 pkt. Whitbread Ale yeast
1/2 cup corn sugar for priming

Original Specific Gravity: 1.042
Terminal Specific Gravity: 1.010-1.012
Primary fermentation: 4 days at 70°F
Secondary Fermentation: 8 days at 70°F
Boil Time: 40 minutes

Procedure: Crush and put grains into 1 gallon cold water for 10 minutes, then raise temperature to a boil slowly. Once boiling commences, remove from heat. Strain liquid and sparge grains with one gallon hot water into boiling pot. Add 1/2 gallon water, 6.6 lbs. malt extract, and bring to a boil. Once boil begins start timer for 40 minutes. Last 15 minutes add Irish moss. Last 5 minutes add Hersbrucker hops. Strain into sanitized primary fermenter and add cold water to make 5 gallons and let cool. Pitch yeast when temperature drops below 80°F. At bottling time boil 1/2 cup priming sugar with 1 cup water for bulk priming.

BARLEY-WHEAT "RED" ALE
Compliments of Dick Foehringer
THE BREWMEISTER—Folsom, CA

"For all of you "Red" Ale drinkers, this recipe is for you. Barley-Wheat Red Ale is, as its name implies, reddish in color due to the roasted barley. The half wheat/barley combination gives excellent body with high alcohol strength. The Fuggles hops provide a good balanced bitterness in the brew. This brew is patterned after *Australian Redback Ale.*"

4 lbs. Alexander's Pale Malt Extract
4 lbs. Alexander's Wheat Malt Extract
1/4 lb. Roasted Barley
1-1/2 oz. Fuggles Hops (60 min.) Boiling
1/2 oz. Fuggles Hops (5 min.) Aromatic
1 teaspoon Irish Moss (15 min.)
1 Doric Dry Ale Yeast
1 teaspoon Gelatin
3/4 cup Bottling Sugar

Original Gravity: ~1.057
Final Gravity: ~1.014

Put the roasted barley into a grain bag. Place 1-1/2 to 2 gallons of cold water in your brew pot. Place grain bag in water and bring to a near boil (160°F). Turn off heat and allow grains to steep for 30 minutes. Drain and remove grain. Dissolve extract thoroughly and then return mixture to heat. Bring to a boil. Add the 1-1/2 oz. of hops and boil for 45 minutes. Add Irish moss and boil for 10 minutes. Add the remaining 1/2 oz. of aromatic hops and boil for 5 minutes. Cold break the wort to below 100°F by setting your pan of wort into a sink full of cold water. Put the cooled wort into your primary fermenter and add cold water to make 5-1/2 gallons. When cooled below 85°F, pitch your yeast. (**Note:** Rehydrate your yeast by dissolving it in 1 cup warm water and allowing it to sit for 10 minutes before pitching). Ferment in a cool (65-75°F), dark place. When fermentation has ceased, transfer to the secondary, leaving all the sediment behind. Dissolve gelatin in 1 cup hot water and stir into secondary. Allow beer to clear, typically 3-5 days. Rack again, leaving sediment behind. Dissolve bottling sugar in 1 cup of hot water and stir into beer. Bottle and cap.

Allow to age/carbonate in the bottles for 2-4 weeks. Enjoy!

"RED" ZEPPELIN ALE
Compliments of Dick Foehringer
THE BREWMEISTER—Folsom, CA

"Red Zeppelin Ale is reddish in color due to the roasted barley. The generous amount of crystal and Munich malts lends a residual sweetness that is well balanced with the hop bitterness. The Fuggles aromatics, along with moderate-high alcohol strength, will make you rock-on!"

7 lb. Pale Malt Extract
1/4 lb. Roasted Barley
1 lb. 20L Crystal Malt
1/2 lb. Munich Malt
1 oz. Northern Brewer Hops (60 min.) Boiling
1 oz. Northern Brewer Hops (30 min.) Boiling
1 oz. Fuggles Hops (2 min.) Aromatic
1 teaspoon Irish Moss (15 min.)
1 Doric Dry Ale Yeast
1 teaspoon Gelatin
3/4 cup Bottling Sugar

Original Gravity ~1.056
Final Gravity ~1.014

Put the roasted barley, crystal, and Munich malted grains into a grain bag. Place 1-1/2 to 2 gallons of cold water in your brew pot. Place grain bag in water and bring to a near boil (160-170°F). Turn off heat and allow grains to steep for 30 minutes. Drain and remove grain. Dissolve extract thoroughly and then return mixture to heat. Bring to a boil. Add the 1 oz. of hops and boil for 30 minutes. Add the second 1 oz. of hops and boil for 15 minutes. Add Irish moss and boil for 15 minutes. Add the remaining aromatic hops and boil for 2 minutes. Cold break the wort to below 100°F by setting your pan of wort into a sink full of cold water. Put the cooled wort into your primary fermenter and add cold water to make 5-1/2 gallons. When cooled below 85°F, pitch your yeast. (**Note:** Rehydrate your yeast by dissolving it in 1 cup warm water and allowing it to sit for 10 minutes before pitching) Ferment in a cool (65-75°F), dark place. When fermentation has ceased, transfer to the secondary, leaving all the sediment behind. Dissolve gelatin in 1 cup hot water and stir into secondary. Allow beer to clear, typically 3-5 days. Rack again, leaving sediment behind. Dissolve bottling sugar in 1 cup of hot water and stir into beer. Bottle and cap.Allow to age/carbonate in the bottles for 2-4 weeks. Enjoy!

BARLEYWINE

Technically, these malty-sweet ales belong in the British Strong Ale category that includes Winter Warmers and Strong Christmas Ales, but their extremely high original and final gravities, not to mention their popularity among homebrewers in recent years, have earned them a style category of their own. The traditional ingredients have included, but are in no way limited to, British 2-row pale ale malt, crystal malt, chocolate malt, roasted barley, and black malt. Adjuncts and sugars such as treacle are often used, but the color should be deep amber to deep copper and not dark brown/black as in the case of Bock or Stout. These beers should also be balanced with enough hop bitterness to avoid an overwhelming sweetness inappropriate for the style. An alcohol-tolerant yeast such as Wyeast #3021 Pasteur Champagne is often recommended, especially in the conditioning phase. *Thomas Hardy's Ale*, Young's *Old Nick*, Woodeford's *Headcracker*, Marston's *Owd Rodger*, and Gibbs Mew Brewery's *The Bishop's Tipple* are British standouts. There are also several excellent American microbrewed versions available including: *Belle Dock, Old Crustacean Barley Wine, Old Bawdy Barley Wine, Old Wooly,* and *Big Foot Barleywine*.

BARLEYWINE
Compliments of Sloan S. Venables
BREWMASTER—San Leandro, CA

Ingredients

12 lbs. Light Malt Syrup
1-1/2 lbs. Light Clover Honey
1 lb. Crystal Malt—40L (Steeped 30 min.)
1-1/2 oz. Chinook or Nugget Hops—Bittering Hops (Boiled 60 min.)
3 oz. Fuggle Hops—Flavoring Hops (Boiled 30 min.)
1 oz. Fuggle Hops—Aromatic Hops (End of Boil)
2 pkgs. Dried Champagne Yeast or Liquid Champagne Yeast
3/4 cup Corn Sugar at bottling

Starting Gravity: 1.090
Bittering Units: 75
Finishing Gravity: 1.020-1.025
Fermentation Temperature: 65-70°F

Instructions
(Refer to *General Ale Brewing Procedures* beginning on page 218.)

Beer Trivia—*It is now largely accepted as fact that the main reason the Pilgrims ended their journey to Virginia prematurely at Plymouth Rock was that they had run out of ale. At the time, ale was a staple of every man, woman, and child's diet and was a valued food source consumed with every meal.*

BARLEY WINE
NORTHEAST BREWERS SUPPLY—West Kingston/Narragansett, RI

"A classic English style, this very strong ale offers a huge body that is dominated by a malty sweetness. Barley Wines are often aged for months or years, allowing the hop character to fade away. To combat this tendency, this recipe calls for dry-hopping in the secondary fermenter. To avoid problems with stuck fermentation with this high gravity recipe, a yeast starter must be used for the liquid yeast that comes with this kit. Prepare the yeast starter according to the instructions given on the following page. We consider this kit to be more advanced than our standard Ale kits.

This recipe for 'Barley Wine' uses 9.6 lbs. of malt extract to make 5 U.S. gallons of homebrew. Starting specific gravity should be approximately 1.086 with a resulting alcohol content of about 8% by volume."

Ingredients

(2) 3.3 lb cans Light Malt Extract
(1) 3 lbs. Amber Dry Malt Extract
(1) lb. Barley Wine Grain Mix (crushed Crystal Malt)
(3) oz. Boiling Hops (Northern Brewer)
(1) oz. Flavoring Hops (Northern Brewer)
(1-1/2) oz. Finishing Hops for Dry-Hopping (Cascade)
(1/2) lb. Malto Dextrin
(4) Boiling Bags
(1) Pack Liquid Ale Yeast
(1) Pack NBS Magnificent Media
(58) crown caps
(3/4) cup Corn Sugar (priming)

1. About 2 days before you're ready to brew, take the liquid yeast out of the refrigerator and pop the inner bag (according to instructions on the package) to get it started. To improve performance of liquid yeast with this recipe, you must use a yeast starter. Instructions for preparing a yeast starter are given below.

2. When you're ready to brew, put the crushed Grain Mix into one of the boiling bags. Tie off the top of the bag and put it into the biggest stainless steel or enameled pot you can find. Add water to the pot, leaving space for the malt (approx. 3/4 gallon) and a couple of inches at the top for the boil. Apply heat.

3. When the water starts to boil, remove the grains and discard. Add the 3 cans of malt extract (to prevent scorching, turn off heat before adding malt—turn it back on after the malt is well mixed). Put the boiling hops into a bag and drop them into the pot. When the water starts boiling again, set your timer for <u>30 minutes</u>.

4. After 30 minutes have elapsed, put the Flavoring Hops into a boiling bag and drop them into the pot. Set your timer for an additional <u>30 minutes</u>.

5. After you've boiled the wort for a total of 60 minutes, turn off the heat.

6. Cool the wort. There are a couple of ways to do this. If you have a wort chiller this process takes about 10 minutes. If you're boiling a small quantity of wort (1-1/2 to 3 gallons) you can add it to cold water in your primary fermenter to make up 5 gallons. Whatever method you use, remember the time between the end of the boil and pitching the yeast is when your brew is most susceptible to contamination. Therefore, extra care is warranted during this time to protect the wort from exposure to undesirable microorganisms. Be sure to sanitize everything that comes into contact with your beer with boiling water, chlorine, or iodophor.

7. When the wort has been added to the primary fermenter and cooled to 70-80° F, shake it up for about 5 minutes. After the wort is sufficently cooled and aerated, add the yeast.

8. Ferment in the primary fermenter for at least a week at room temperature. Rack to the secondary fermenter. Before installing the airlock and stopper (or cover, if you're using a bucket), put the Finishing Hops into a hop bag and drop them into the fermenter. The finishing gravity is difficult to predict. Optimally, it should finish around 1.020. If it doesn't drop below 1.030, don't worry—it will still turn out great.

9. When you're ready to bottle, dissolve the corn sugar in 2 cups of boiling water. Add to the brew and mix well without disturbing the sediment. This is easy if you first siphon your beer into a bottling bucket and then mix in the sugar solution.

10. Bottle, cap, and put in a warm (65-75°F) environment for at least a week. Start enjoying your Barley Wine after it's been in the bottle for at least 3 months. You will find that it will improve with age. *Cheers!*

Preparing a Yeast Starter

Our **NBS-1Y** Yeast Culturing Kit was designed to simplify the process of preparing yeast starters. It's a small investment that will pay dividends if you use a lot of liquid yeast.

One of the problems with using liquid yeast is that if you use it straight from the pouch after it expands, you don't start out with very much yeast. This may cause excessive lag time and problems with stuck fermentation. The idea of using a yeast starter is to grow more yeast to increase your pitching rate. This is accomplished by adding yeast to a small amount of **aerated** sterile wort and giving it time to grow. Aeration is important because yeast needs oxygen to reproduce.

Take a 1 quart mason jar and fill it to about 2/3 with tap water. Add a package of NBS Magnificent Media (or 3 tablespoons of dry malt extract). Cover the top of the jar with tin foil and put it into a pot. Put a couple of inches of water into the pot, but not too much or it will cause the jar to tip over once the water starts to boil. Cover the pot and turn on the heat. When the water starts to boil, turn down the heat and let it simmer for 20 minutes. The wort in the mason jar is now sterile. When it cools down to room temperature, swirl it around to aerate it. Carefully lift the tin foil cover and quickly add the liquid yeast from the **expanded** pouch. Put the tin foil back on to keep the nasties out. After a day or two in a warm place, you'll have plenty of yeast for pitching into 5 gallons of wort.

BARLEYWINE
Compliments of David Ruggiero
BARLEYMALT & VINE—Newton, MA

Ingredients For <u>Three</u> (3) Gallons:

6.6 lbs. Light Malt Extract
1 lb. Corn Sugar
1/2 lb. Munich Malt
1/2 lb. Crystal Malt
1/2 lb. Wheat Malt
1 oz. Eroica hops (for bittering)
1 oz. Cluster hops (for aroma)
Water Crystals
Irish Moss (for clarifying the wort)
Pasteur Champagne Yeast
Muslin Bag

Original Gravity (O.G.) 1.095-1.100   Final Gravity (F.G.) 1.015-1.020
H.B.U.s~15 to 35 or I.B.U.s~50 to 100
Alcohol 10.5% by Volume

Directions for Brewing:
1. Secure grains in muslin bag and place into a pot with 2 gallons of water.
2. Steep the grain while water is heating, remove before a boil commences.
3. Dissolve all malt extracts into the brewpot and re-establish the boil.
4. A total elapsed brewing time of 60 minutes is required in order to:
    • Reconstitute the malt extracts.
    • Sterilize the ingredients.
    • Clarify the wort (this is known as a Hot Break).
    • Extract hop bitterness and aromatic properties.
5. The following additions to the brewpot must be made at each of the specified times:
ELAPSED TIME   0 minutes, add the Water Crystals and the Eroica hops.
                        40 minutes, add the Irish Moss.
                        45 minutes, add the Cluster hops.
                        60 minutes, remove the brewpot from the stove.
6. Transfer the wort to a sanitized fermenter, straining out hop pellets if possible.
7. Add enough cold water to the fermenter to equal 3 gallons, when the temperature falls below 75°F, add the yeast.
8. Secure the airlock and ferment as usual (refer to the *General Fermentation Procedures* section beginning on page 230);
    • Single stage fermentation techniques last 7 to 10 days.
    • Two stage fermentation techniques last 3 to 5 days in the primary and 5 days to 3 weeks in the secondary.
    • Influencing factors that can shorten or prolong your beer's fermentation cycle are; temperature, yeast selection and viability, wort gravities, oxygen uptake and general sanitation procedures.
9. When all fermentation activity has ceased, check your final gravity. It should be within .002 degrees of the recipe's suggested reading. Prepare to bottle if it is. (Refer to the *General Bottling Procedures* section beginning on page 232.)

CALIFORNIA BARLEY WINE
Compliments of Dick Foehringer
THE BREWMEISTER—*Folsom, CA*

"This is a Barley Wine style beer noted for its malty richness and high alcohol strength. Its full, rich body is balanced with a higher hopping rate; making this a winter warmer that will light up your tree! Patterned after the celebrated *Sierra Nevada Big Foot*."

7 lb. Pale Malt Extract
2 lb. Light Dry Malt Extract
1 lb. 20L Crystal Malt
1/2 lb. Carapils Malt
1/4 Chocolate Malt
2 oz. Northern Brewer Hops (60 min.) Boiling
1 oz. Hallertauer Hops (5 min.) Aromatic
2 teaspoons Gypsum
1 teaspoon Irish Moss (15 min.)
1 teaspoon Gelatin
3/4 Bottling Sugar
1 Dry Ale Yeast

Original Gravity: ~1.074
Final Gravity: ~1.019

Put the crystal malt, carapils, and chocolate malt grains into a grain bag. Place 1-1/2 to 2 gallons of cold water in your brew pot. Place grain bag in water and bring to a near boil (160-170°F). Turn off heat and allow grains to steep for 30 minutes. Drain and remove grain. Dissolve extract thoroughly and then return mixture to heat. Bring to a boil. Add the Northern Brewer hops and boil for 45 minutes. Add Irish moss and boil for 10 minutes. Add the aromatic hops and boil for 5 minutes. Cold break the wort to below 100°F by setting your pan of wort into a sink full of cold water. Put the cooled wort into your primary fermenter and add cold water to make 5-1/2 gallons. When cooled below 85°F, pitch your yeast. (**Note:** Rehydrate your yeast by dissolving it in 1/2 cup warm water and allowing it to sit for 10 minutes before pitching). Ferment in a cool (65-75°F), dark place. When fermentation has ceased, transfer to the secondary, leaving all the sediment behind. Dissolve gelatin in 1 cup hot water and stir into secondary. Allow beer to clear, typically 3-5 days. Rack again, leaving sediment behind. Dissolve bottling sugar in 1 cup of hot water and stir into beer. Bottle and cap.

Allow to age/carbonate in the bottles for 2-4 weeks. Enjoy!

Beer Trivia—*Medieval monasteries often had their famous beers "contract-brewed" by local village women (who were the recognized brewing experts of the time).*

ALTBIER

I will leave the description of this beer style to Dr. Paul Bösken-Diebels of *Privatbrauerei Diebels* in Issum, Germany, who writes: "With the explanation given below, it will be possible for a well-trained homebrewer to produce a good Alt.

"Alt," the German word for "old," is a synonym for the traditional, old way of brewing beer. This type of dark, top-fermented beer has been brewed in the areas of mild climate in Germany since the very first days of brewing. Its brewing method has been kept unchanged in the lower Rhein region until today. In the past, in regions with cold winters brewers could control fermentation and storage temperatures of their lager-beer with ice cut with saws from frozen lakes. In the Rhein area, however, winters are too mild to produce enough natural ice.

Alt is produced in a quantity of approximately 4 million hectoliters per annum–mainly in Nordrhein-Westfalen. Various little breweries share the market with the main brand, our Diebels Alt, brewed in Issum. Privatbrauerei Diebels Alt sales exceeeded 1.7 million hectoliters in 1992.

Alt is brewed according to the "Reinheitsgebot" of 1516 from water, malt, hops, and yeast with an original gravity of 11.0-12.0 °P (1.043- 1.047). Alt is always dark (~30-35 EBC) (12-14 SRM), quite contrary to Kölsch, another top-fermented beer being brewed in Cologne with light color. Alt is a dry and bitter beer with approximately 28-38 IBU. The color derives from roasted malt while the main quantity of the malt used is normal malt. The necessary quantity of roasted malt to be added depends on the color intensity of this malt.

By an intensive mash program a complete saccharification is intended. Lautering and wort boiling will be made according to the existing facilities of the brewery. The starting fermentation temperature is higher than for lager type beers and varies between 14 °C and 18 °C (57-64 °F). A special strain of top-fermenting saccharomyces cerevisiae must be used (e.g., Wyeast's #1338 or 1007, BrewTek CL-400, or Yeast Lab A06—ed.).

According to the high fermentation temperatures, the fermentation period is rather short. After diacetyl reduction, the beer will be cooled, separated from the yeast–the yeast will not settle–and lagered at temperatures of about 0 °C (32 °F) for approximately three weeks. When filtered and bottled, a tasty, wholesome beer is ready for the first trial."

Harpoon Alt, Butterfield Brewing's *Alt, Schmaltz's Alt, Alt Noveau, Widmer Alt, St. Stan's Alt,* and Boston Beer Works' *Centennial Alt* represent good American versions, although some experts argue that these generally have more hop aroma and flavor than the German originals, such as *Diebels Alt* and *Hannen Alt*.

GERMAN ALTBIER
Compliments of Dick Foehringer
THE BREWMEISTER—Folsom, CA

Ingredients
7 lbs. Amber Malt Extract
1/2 lb. Munich Malt
1/2 lb. 20L Crystal Malt
2 oz. Tettnanger (60 min.) Boiling
1 teaspoon Irish Moss (15 min.)
1 Wyeast #1007 German Ale Liquid Yeast
1 teaspoon Gelatin
3/4 cup Bottling Sugar

Original Gravity: ~1.050
Final Gravity: ~1.012

Put the crystal malt and Munich malt grains into a bag. Place 1-1/2 to 2 gallons of cold water in your brew pot. Place grain bag in water and bring to a near boil (160°F). Turn off heat and allow grain to steep for 30 minutes. Drain and remove grain. Dissolve liquid extract thoroughly and then return mixture to heat. Bring to a boil. Add the 2 oz. of hops and boil for 45 minutes. Add Irish moss and boil for 15 minutes. Cold break the wort to below 100°F by setting your pan of wort into a sink full of cold water. Put the cooled wort into your primary fermenter and add cold water to make 5-1/2 gallons. When cooled below 85°F, pitch your yeast. (**Note:** You must start the liquid yeast 1-2 days prior to brewing to allow it to culture up. Follow the instructions on the package for preparation.) Ferment in a cool (65-75°F), dark place. When fermentation has ceased, transfer to the secondary, leaving all the sediment behind. Dissolve gelatin in 1 cup hot water and stir into secondary. Replace airlock and allow beer to clear, typically 3-5 days. Rack again, leaving sediment behind. Dissolve bottling sugar in 1 cup of hot water and stir into beer. Bottle and cap.

Allow to age/carbonate in the bottles for 2-4 weeks. Enjoy!

GERMAN ALT
THE VINEYARD—Upton, MA

Ingredients:

6.6 lb. Ireks Munich light malt extract
2 lbs. dry light malt extract
6 oz. crystal malt grain
3 oz. toasted malt grain
2 oz. German Hallertau hop pellets (boiling)
1.5 oz. Fuggles hop plugs (1 oz. last 10 minutes; 1/2 oz. last 5 minutes)
1 tsp. Irish moss
1 pkt. Whitbread ale yeast
1/2 cup priming sugar

Original Specific Gravity: 1.054
Terminal Specific Gravity: 1.012-1.014
Primary Fermentation: 4 days at 70°F
Secondary Fermentation: 8 days at 70°F
Boil Time: 30 minutes

Procedure: Crush and put all grains into 2 quarts cold water for 10 minutes, then raise temperature to a boil slowly. Once boiling commences remove from heat. Strain liquid into boiling pot. Add up to 2 gallons water. Add Ireks malt extract and dry malt and bring to boil. Once boiling starts add German Hallertau hops. Last 15 minutes of the boil add Irish moss. Last 10 minutes of the boil add 1/2 oz. Fuggles hops. At end of boil, strain into primary fermenter and add cold water to make 5 gallons. Pitch yeast when temperature drops below 90°F. At bottling time boil 1/2 cup priming sugar with 1 cup water for bulk priming.

GERMAN ALT
Recipe of the Month
BEER & WINE HOBBY—Woburn, MA

2 cans Bierkeller Light Liquid Malt
1 lb. Light Dry Malt
1/2 lb. German Crystal Dark Malt
2 ozs. Chocolate Malt
1 oz. Perle Hop Pellets (boil)
1 oz. Tettnang Hop Pellets (boil)
1 oz. Tettnang Hop Pellets (last 2 minutes)
1 package Burton Water Salts
1 teaspoon Irish Moss
1 Muslin Bag
3/4 Priming Sugar
Yeast: AO6 Dusseldorfer Alt - **Starter Required**

S.G. 1.040-1.045
F.G. 1.010-1.014

IMPORTANT NOTE: PLEASE READ ALL INSTRUCTIONS BEFORE STARTING

Crush grains, place in Muslin Bag and tie. Add grains to 2 gallons of cold water and bring to a boil. When water comes to a boil, remove from heat and discard grains. Add 2 cans of German Light Malt, 1 lb. Light Dry Malt, 1 oz. Perle Hop Pellets and 1 oz. Tettnang Hop Pellets. Put back on heat and return to a boil; boil for 20 minutes. Add 1 tsp. Irish Moss and package of Burton Water Salts; continue to boil for 15 minutes more. During the last 2 minutes add 1 oz. Tettnang Hop Pellets. Remove from heat and add to primary fermenter containing enough cold water to bring total volume to 5-1/4 gallons. When wort has cooled to between 65-75°F, pitch prepared yeast. Proceed as usual. Finish fermenting. Prime with 3/4 cup priming sugar and bottle.

GERMAN ALT
S. SNYDER

INGREDIENTS:

1 lb. Munton & Fison Amber DME
4 lbs. Laaglander Light DME
1/2 lb. (2 cups) 10L Light Crystal Malt
1/4 lb. (1 cup) Vienna Malt
1/4 lb. (1 cup) Munich Malt
6 oz. English Pale Ale Malt
1/2 oz. Spalter Hop pellets 4.5%AA (boil) 60 min.
1 oz. Hallertau Hersbrucker Hop plugs 2.9%AA (boil) 60 min.
1 oz. Hallertau Hersbrucker Hop plugs 2.9%AA (boil) 30 min.
Wyeast #1007 (German Ale/Mild Alt) liquid yeast with starter
1.25 cups Dutch Light DME for priming
Muslin or Nylon Hop Bag

O.G. ~1.046
F.G. ~1.013
Potential alcohol 4.5% v/v
IBUs 28 **HBUs** 8

Special Instructions: Warm-condition 7 days at room temperature (68°F). Store cold (33-45°F) a minimum of 3 weeks.

EIN ALT BITTE*
Compliments of Paul White
THE SEVEN BARREL BREWERY SHOP—Lebanon, NH

The Mash

7-1/2 lbs. 2-Row Pale
1 lb. Malted Wheat
12 oz. Crystal Malt
4 oz. Dextrine
8 oz. Flaked Barley

Mash in 3 gallons at 148°F for 1-1/2 hours. Mash out and sparge to collect 6 gallons.

The Boil

Bring to a boil and after 15 minutes add 12 AAUs of Northern Brewer Flowers. Boil for 55 minutes, adding 1 tsp. of Irish moss at 45 minute mark. Add 5-6 AAUs of Casacade Flowers for 5 minutes. End boil, cool to 70°F, pitch a German Ale culture or Edme Ale Yeast. Ferment, bottle and age at least 2 months.

Brewer's Notes: (*Translation: An Alt Bier Please!) "The name comes from all I needed to know how to say during a week in Germany."—Paul

Beer Trivia—*Vermont has more breweries per capita than any other state in the U.S.*

KÖLSCH

A pale golden or blonde German Ale with a subdued malt flavor, moderate hop bitterness, and low hop flavor and aroma. Like Alt Bier, this is a beer from the "old" brewing tradition before lagers took over. Traditional German recipes include very hard water, Vienna malt, wheat malt, Pilsener malt, crystal malt, and German hop varieties. Warm primary and secondary fermentations should be followed by three to six weeks of cold lagering as with Alt. Bottling with lager yeast will greatly improve clarity, but a slight cloudiness is normal. If you are interested in crafting your own Kölsch, but are unsure that you'll like this unique taste, sample the excellent microbrewed version, Goose Island's *Kölsch Beer*.

KÖLSCH—GERMAN PALE ALE
Compliments of Dick Foehringer
THE BREWMEISTER—Folsom, CA

"Kölsch is a pale version of German Alt beer from the region around Cologne. It is a light, fruity, medium-hopped dry ale, excellent for summer quaffing!"

Ingredients

7 lbs. Pale Malt Extract
1/2 lb. Munich Malt
1/2 lb. 20L Crystal Malt
2 oz. Tettnanger (60 min.) Boiling
1 teaspoon Irish Moss (15 min.)
1 Wyeast #1007 German Ale Liquid Yeast
1 teaspoon Gelatin
3/4 cup Bottling Sugar

Original Gravity: ~1.052
Final Gravity: ~1.014

Instructions

Put the crystal malt and Munich malt grains into a bag. Place 1-1/2 to 2 gallons of cold water in your brew pot. Place grain bag in water and bring to a near boil (160°F). Turn off heat and allow grain to steep for 30 minutes. Drain and remove grain. Dissolve liquid extract thoroughly and then return mixture to heat. Bring to a boil. Add the 2 oz. of hops and boil for 45 minutes. Add Irish moss and boil for 15 minutes. Cold break the wort to below 100°F by setting your pan of wort into a sink full of cold water. Put the cooled wort into your primary fermenter and add cold water to make 5-1/2 gallons. When cooled below 85°F, pitch your yeast. (**Note:** You must start the liquid yeast 1-2 days prior to brewing to allow it to culture up. Follow the instructions on the package for preparation.) Ferment in a cool (65-75°F), dark place. When fermentation has ceased, transfer to the secondary, leaving all the sediment behind. Dissolve gelatin in 1 cup hot water and stir into secondary. Replace airlock and allow beer to clear, typically 3-5 days. Rack again, leaving sediment behind. Dissolve bottling sugar in 1 cup of hot water and stir into beer. Bottle and cap.

Allow to age/carbonate in the bottles for 2-4 weeks. Enjoy!

The Brewmaster's Recipe Manual

WHEAT BEER

Wheat beer in its modern form, also known as Weizen (German for wheat), Weisse, or Weissbier (white beer), gained a fanatical following in Bavaria during the later part of the 17th century. Wheat beers are now enjoying a renewed popularity worldwide, especially in Germany (Weissbiers now account for 50% of Spaten Brewery's production). Beers typical of the style are made with roughly a 50/50 mixture of wheat and barley malt. They are also characterized by phenolic flavors and estery aromas provided primarily by special top-fermenting yeast strains. Weissbiers are made from a wide range of brewing waters commercially and require no special parameters.

Freshness is more important to this style than any other, primarily due to the low hop content. In Germany, Wheat Beers are usually full-flavored ales with hints of clove and spice esters. American Wheats tend to be cleaner and softer in flavor without the wild yeast influences and are included with the "North American Ales." All wheat beers should be well-carbonated and low in hop bitterness, aroma, and flavor. *Franziskaner Hefe-Weissbier, Maisel's Hefe-Weisse, Heartland Weisse, Tabernash Weiss, Heavenly Hefe Weizen, Schneider Weisse,* and *Paulener Hefe-Weißbier* are among the multitude of good commercial brands.

NORTHWESTERN WHEAT
Compliments of Paul White
THE SEVEN BARREL BREWERY SHOP—Lebanon, NH

O.G.: ~1.046
F.G.: ~1.014

Ingredients
6.6 lbs. Northwestern Weizen Malt Extract
1-1/2 oz. Hallertau (Bittering) 5-6 AAU
1/2 oz. Hallertau (Flavoring)
Yeast Labs W51 Yeast (for German style)
Ale Yeast (for American style)

Instructions
Mix extract well with hot water, then bring to a boil. When the boil is under control, add bittering hops and start timing. Total length of boil will be 60 minutes.

If using Irish moss, add 2 tsp. 20 minutes before the end of the boil.

Add flavoring hops 15 minutes before the end of boil.

Cool to achieve 70 to 80 degrees, after topping up in the fermenter, and pitch yeast.

GERMAN WEIZENBIER
THE HOME BREWERY—Ozark, MO

Ingredients:

3.3 lbs. (1 pack) Home Brewery Unhopped Wheat Extract
3.3 lbs. (1 pack) Home Brewery Hopped Wheat Extract
3/4 oz. Hallertauer Hop Pellets (bittering)
1/2 tsp. Irish Moss added 15 minutes before the end of the boil
3/4 oz. Saaz Hop Pellets (finishing)
2 packs Doric Ale Yeast
3/4 cup corn sugar for priming

Starting Gravity ~1.048
Final Gravity ~1.013
Alcohol ~4.6% v/v

Instructions:

Heat 5 gallons of water in a large kettle. Many people don't have a kettle that large, but heat as much as you can (at least 2 gallons). When the water is boiling, turn off the heat and add the Malt Extract to the water. Use a spoon and stir until you are sure no Malt Extract is sticking to the bottom of the kettle. Then turn the heat back on.

Bring the kettle back to a boil, and stir occasionally so the ingredients won't burn on the bottom of the kettle. If your recipe calls for Bittering Hops, now is the time to add them and stir them in. Watch out for a boil-over. In the early part of the boil, the kettle usually tries to boil over once or twice, so control this by adjusting the heat. Later in the boil, the surface tension changes and boiling over is not a problem. Keep stirring occasionally, and let the beer (wort) boil hard for one hour. Stir in the 1/2 tsp. of Irish Moss in your recipe about 15 minutes before the end of the boil.

If Finishing Hops are called for in your recipe, stir them in 2 minutes before the end of the boil. Using Finishing Hops at the end of the boil adds a fresh aroma and flavor to the beer, and the use of finishing hops is appropriate in most beer styles.

Pour the hot beer (wort) into the primary fermenter. It is not necessary to strain the wort if you used hop pellets. Add cold water to bring the total volume up to 5 gallons. If you are using our #B3a Fermenter (the one in the kits) the 5-gallon mark is the bottom ring. Cover the fermenter and wait until the temperature is down to 75°F. If you have a Wort Chiller (#C44), use it to bring the temperature down quickly. At 75° or less, add the Yeast in your recipe. Just tear open the pack(s) and sprinkle it on the wort. Close the fermenter with the lid, stopper, and airlock. Remember to put water (or Vodka) in the airlock. Vodka evaporates more quickly, but bacteria won't live in it.

Fermentation should start within 24 hours, and may continue for between one day and two weeks, depending on the type of yeast, the recipe, and the temperature. Leave the beer alone and don't open the lid. When the airlock has not bubbled for several days and the beer is flat, still, and clearing, it is ready to bottle.

To bottle, siphon about one pint of beer into a pan and warm it on the stove. Add exactly 3/4 cup of Corn Sugar to the pan and stir until it is dissolved. Pour this back into the beer and stir gently but well to distribute the sugar. Siphon or tap into clean sanitized bottles and cap. Keep the bottles at room temperature. After a week, put a bottle in the refrigerator and try it. It will be best in about three weeks.

BAVARIAN WHEAT BEER
Compliments of Sloan S. Venables
BREWMASTER—San Leandro, CA

Ingredients

6 lbs. Dried Wheat Extract (60% Wheat - 40% Barley)
1/2 lb. Crystal Malt—10L (Steeped 30 min.)
1 lb. Carapils/Dextrin Malt (Steeped 30 min.)
4 oz. Wheat Flakes—Added for last 10 minutes of boil
3/4 oz. Tettnanger Hops—Bittering Hops (Boiled 60 min.)
3/4 oz. Tettnanger Hops—Bittering/Flavoring Hops (Boiled 25 min.)
1/2 oz. Tettnanger Hops—Aromatic Hops (End of Boil)
Yeast—Wyeast #3056 Bavarian Wheat Beer Yeast
3/4 cup Corn Sugar at bottling

Starting Gravity: 1.050
Bittering Units: 24
Finishing Gravity: 1.014
Fermentation Temperature: 65-70°F

Instructions
(Refer to *General Ale Brewing Procedures* beginning on page 218.)

WHEAT BEER—Winner of numerous 1st Place Awards
BREWERS RESOURCE—Camarillo, CA

Brewers Resource says, "In designing a Wheat beer recipe you may want a clean malt flavor or a full, clovey beer like the Germans or Belgians brew. Concentrate on the yeast strain rather than the recipe for these differences. The yeast strain you choose is of the greatest importance in Wheat beers. The original gravity should be kept between 1.040 and 1.050 while fermentation temperatures should be between 64° and 72°F, to promote a strong fermentation and to allow traditionally slow working wheat strains to ferment."

Malt Extract Recipe:

3.5 lbs. dry wheat extract plus 2 lbs. DME or 3.3 lbs. syrup wheat extract and 3.3 lbs. pale syrup malt extract.
19 I.B.U.s Hallertau (i.e., 1 oz. @ 4.5% AA)—Bittering Hops
1/4 Saaz Finishing Hops
Brew-Tek® German Wheat (CL-62) or Belgian Wheat yeast (CL-60), or Wyeast Bavarian Wheat yeast (#3056)
1 Cup (5 oz.) Corn Sugar to prime at bottling

(Refer to *General Ale Brewing Procedures* beginning on page 218.)

The Brewmaster's Recipe Manual

Mash-Extract Recipe:

3 lbs. Light Dried Wheat Extract or 3.3 lbs. Syrup Wheat Extract
2 lbs. Crushed German Pale Malt
1 lb. crushed Wheat malt, Mashed in 3 liters of Water at 152°F for 45 min.
19 I.B.U.s Hallertau (i.e., 1 oz. @ 4.5% AA)—Bittering Hops
1/4 oz. Saaz—Finishing Hops
Brew-Tek® German Wheat (CL-62) or Belgian Wheat yeast (CL-60), or Wyeast Bavarian Wheat yeast (#3056)
1 Cup (5 oz.) Corn Sugar to prime at bottling

Steep crushed grains in mini-mash bucket and sparge to collect 3 gallons of wort. Continue with recipe as you normally would or see *General Ale Brewing Procedures* beginning on page 218.

All Grain Recipe:

3 lbs. Crushed Wheat Malt
3 lbs. Crushed Klages or, preferably, German Pale Malt
14 I.B.U.s Hallertau (i.e., 3/4 oz. @ 4.5% AA)—Bittering Hops
1/4 oz. Saaz—Finishing Hops
Brew-Tek® German Wheat (CL-62) or Belgian Wheat yeast (CL-60), or Wyeast Bavarian Wheat yeast (#3056)
1 Cup (5 oz.) Corn Sugar to prime at bottling

In mash/lauter bucket stir crushed pale malt into 8 liters of 166°F water to rest out at about 152°F. Cover and rest for 45 minutes. Sparge to 6-1/2 gallons into kettle. Bring to boil and add hops. Continue with recipe as you normally would or see *General Ale Brewing Procedures* beginning on page 218. Cool wort and transfer to fermenter. Pitch yeast, ferment, and bottle.

Recipe Variations: You may experiment with the recipes below by varying the wheat to malt ratio (try 40 to 70% wheat), add 4 oz. each of Crystal and Chocolate Malt for a dark wheat beer. Add a teaspoon of crushed coriander seed for a Belgian wheat style and try different finishing hops (traditionally, not used).

"KILLER" WHEAT BEER
Compliments of Joe Marleau
THE CELLAR HOMEBREW—Seattle, WA

1 can Alexander's Wheat malt extract
1 can Alexander's Wheat "Kicker"
1/4 lb. German Light Crystal malt (crushed)
1/4 lb. Dextrine malt (crushed)
1 oz. Chinook hops (boiling)
1 oz. Hallertau Hersbrucker hops (finishing)
1 pkg. dry ale or Bavarian Weizen liquid yeast
1-1/4 tsp. Yeast Nutrient

<u>Brewing Directions</u>

1) Place any crushed Specialty Grains in a strainer bag. Add this bag of grain to your brewing kettle, which contains 2 to 2-1/2 gallons brewing water.
2) Bring the brewing water to a boil, then remove the bag of grains.
3) Remove the brewing kettle from the burner and add any Malt Syrup and Dry Malt Extract. Stir thoroughly and return the kettle to the burner. Continue heating and stirring this wort until it boils.

4) At boiling point, add any Yeast Nutrient, Water Salts, and Boiling Hops. Hops can be placed in a hop bag or added loose, to be later strained out after the boil using a strainer bag. Time the boil for about one hour, stirring occasionally. After the first 10 minutes of this boil, remove two cups of wort in measuring cup, and cover with foil or plastic. Cool to 90°F for use in step #5 below.

5) Making the Yeast Starter: For dry yeast, use 1/2 cup warm tap water (90 to 100°F). Sprinkle the contents of yeast packet into that water, cover for at least fifteen minutes, and then add to the two cups of wort you prepared in step #4. Cover and set aside for use in step #9 below. For liquid yeast, prepare one to three days ahead of brewing time per package instructions.

6) After the wort has boiled for that one hour, add Finishing Hops. Place them in the hop bag, which has been emptied of the spent boiling hops, and place them in the boiling kettle or just add the Finishing Hops directly to the brewing kettle.

7) Let the boil continue for 5 minutes. Remove the pot from the burner and let it cool, covered, for about 20 minutes .

8) Pour three gallons of cold water into the sanitized open fermenter fitted with strainer bag, if loose Finishing Hops were used in step #6, strain the warm wort from step #7 into the cold water. Top up the fermenter to 5-1/2 gallons using cold tap water. Cover the fermenter and cool the wort as rapidly as possible.

9) When the wort has cooled to about 80° add the Yeast Starter and ferment as you usually do.

BAVARIAN WHEAT BEER
NORTHEAST BREWERS SUPPLY—West Kingston/Narragansett, RI

"Sometimes called the 'Champagne of Beer,' Wheat Beer is known for its crisp, refreshing character. Lightly hopped, this brew should be served cold and perhaps with a slice of lemon. We supply liquid Bavarian Wheat Beer yeast from Wyeast with this kit because it is the yeast, rather than the wheat, that provides this style with its unique character. As an Ale, this recipe is a quick, easy and satisfying beverage for the homebrewer.

This recipe for 'Bavarian Wheat Beer' uses 7.0 lbs. of malt extract to make 5 U.S. gallons of homebrew. Starting specific gravity should be approximately 1.052 with a resulting alcohol content of about 5.0% by volume."

Ingredients

(1) 4.0 lb. Alexanders Pale Malt Extract
(2) 1.5 lb. Alexanders Wheat Kickers
1/2 lb. Light Crystal Malt
(2) oz. Boiling Hops (Hallertau Whole Hops)
(1/2) tsp. Irish Moss
(2) Boiling Bags
(1) Package Bavarian Wheat Liquid Yeast #3056
(58) crown caps
(3/4) cup Corn Sugar (priming)

1. About 2 days before you're ready to brew, take the liquid yeast out of the refrigerator and pop the inner bag (according to instructions on the package) to get it started. To improve performance of liquid yeast, it is recommended that you use a yeast starter. Instructions for preparing a yeast starter are given below.

2. When you're ready to brew, put the crushed Grain Mix into one of the boiling bags. Tie off the top of the bag and put it into the biggest stainless steel or enameled pot you can find. Add water to the pot, leaving space for the malt (approx. 3/4 gallon) and a couple of inches at the top for the boil. Apply heat.

3. When the water starts to boil, remove the grains and discard. Add the 3 cans of malt extract and kickers (to prevent scorching, turn off heat before adding malt—turn it back on after malt is well mixed). Put the

boiling hops into a bag and drop them into the pot. When the water starts boiling again, set your timer for 25 minutes.

4. After 25 minutes have elapsed, add the Irish Moss and set your timer for an additional 20 minutes.

5. After you've boiled the wort for a total of 45 minutes, turn off the heat.

6. Cool the wort. There are a couple of ways to do this. If you have a wort chiller this process takes about 10 minutes. If you're boiling a small quantity of wort (1-1/2 to 3 gallons) you can add it to cold water in your primary fermenter to make up 5 gallons. Whatever method you use, remember the time between the end of the boil and pitching the yeast is when your brew is most susceptible to contamination. Therefore, extra care is warranted during this time to protect the wort from exposure to undesirable microorganisms. Be sure to sanitize everything that comes into contact with your beer with boiling water, chlorine, or iodophor.

7. When the wort has been added to the primary fermenter and cooled to 70-80°F, add the yeast.

8. Ferment at 65-70° F (in a single or two-stage fermenting system—your choice) until the specific gravity falls to below 1.015. This should take approximately 1-2 weeks.

9. When you're ready to bottle, dissolve the corn sugar in 2 cups of boiling water. Add to the brew and mix well without disturbing the sediment. This is easy if you first siphon your beer into a bottling bucket and then mix in the sugar solution.

10. Bottle, cap, and put in a warm (65-75°F) environment for at least 2 days. Your Wheat Beer will be ready to drink in about 2 weeks and will improve with age. *Cheers!*

Preparing a Yeast Starter

Our **NBS-1Y** Yeast Culturing Kit was designed to simplify the process of preparing yeast starters. It's a small investment that will pay dividends if you use a lot of liquid yeast.

One of the problems with using liquid yeast is that if you use it straight from the pouch after it expands, you don't start out with very much yeast. This may cause excessive lag time and problems with stuck fermentation. The idea of using a yeast starter is to grow more yeast to increase your pitching rate. This is accomplished by adding yeast to a small amount of aerated sterile wort and giving it time to grow. Aeration is important because yeast needs oxygen to reproduce.

Take a 1 quart mason jar and fill it to about 2/3 with tap water. Add a package of NBS Magnificent Media (or 3 tablespoons of dry malt extract). Cover the top of the jar with tin foil and put it into a pot. Put a couple of inches of water into the pot, but not too much or it will cause the jar to tip over once the water starts to boil. Cover the pot and turn on the heat. When the water starts to boil, turn down the heat and let it simmer for 20 minutes. The wort in the mason jar is now sterile. When it cools down to room temperature, swirl it around to aerate it. Carefully lift the tin foil cover and quickly add the liquid yeast from the expanded pouch. Put the tin foil back on to keep the nasties out. After a day or two in a warm place, you'll have plenty of yeast for pitching into 5 gallons of wort.

The Brewmaster's Recipe Manual

HONEY WEISS BEER
April's Brew of the Month
E.C. KRAUS—Independence, MO

Description: While not a defined AHA beer style, this is certainly a beer that brings its own reward. It is very similar to the summertime weiss of Germany. Light florescent yellow with a distinct clovey aroma which is further enhanced by the addition of honey. The hops are detectable but remain subdued by other characteristics.

General Profile: Starting Gravity: 50-55
Finished Alcohol: 4.5 - 5.5%
Bittering: 13-17 IBUs
Color: 3-8 SRM/4-12°L

Ingredients: 3.3 lbs. Barley/Wheat Mix Extract
1.0 lb. Light Dried Malt Extract (2-1/2 cups)
1.0 Honey (Clove Spun Preferred)
1.0 lb. Six-Row Barley (Mini Mashed)
1.0 lb. Malted Wheat (Mini Mashed)
1-1/4 ozs. Hallertau Pelletized Hops (45 min. Boil Time)
1/4 oz. Hallertau Pelletized Hops (Finish)
1 Tbsp. Irish Moss (15 min. Boil Time)
1/3 oz. Burton Water Salts
3/4 cup Priming Sugar (Bottling Time)
1 pkg. Wyeast #3068 Weihenstephan Wheat

Directions:

1. Lightly crack malted grains and put with 1-1/2 gallons of warm water in a cooking pan. Bring temperature to 122-125°F and hold for 30 min. Then bring the same mixture to 155-160°F and hold for 45 min.

2. Strain the grains out by use of a colander and discard.

3. Bring the liquid back to a boil and add both the liquid and dried malt extracts. Bring back to a boil again.

4. Once boiling, add Hallertau hops and boil for 45 minutes. During the last 15 minutes of boil, add Irish Moss and Honey. During the last 1 minute of the boil, add the Finishing hops and Burton Salts.

5. Once the boiling is complete, add the wort to your fermenter with cold water up to 5 gallons. Make sure it has cooled below 80°F and add yeast.

6. Attach air-lock to fermenter and allow to ferment for 7-10 days or until finished.

7. Bottle with priming sugar as normal and allow to condition for 4-6 weeks.

PIRATES BREW WHEAT
Compliments of Jay Garrison
BREW BUDDYS—Redondo Beach, CA

Ingredients

1 can Telfords Wheat Extract
2 lbs. Wheat Malt
2 lbs. Pale Malt (6-row)
1-1/4 oz. Hallertau Hops
Irish Moss
Wyeast #3056 Bavarian Wheat or Dry Ale Yeast

Instructions

1) If you selected the Wyeast liquid yeast, you must break the inner packet before you begin to brew. Allow 1 day for each month after the manufacture date printed on the front. If you're using the dry yeast that came with the Pirates Brew Kit, go ahead and get to it.
2) Prepare the grains. The grains should be crushed; if you did not get the grains crushed at the shop, crush it with some sort of rolling pin. You can either mix the grains with 2 quarts of water and heat it until it starts to boil, or heat it to about 165°F and steep for about 15 minutes.
3) Strain the grains, collecting the liquid into your brew pot. Rinse the grains (sparge) with 2 quarts of hot (170-180°F) water.
4) Add the can of extract and 1 gallon of water to the brew pot. (You might want to rest the can of extract in hot water for awhile to soften it up.) Bring the wort to a soft rolling boil.
5) Add the 1 oz. Hallertau hops to the wort and boil for 40 minutes. Stir occasionally.
6) Add 1/4 of the Hallertau hops and the Irish moss to the wort and boil for 20 minutes. Stir occasionally.
7) Turn off the heat; stir and let sit (covered, if possible) for 10 minutes.
8) Add the boiled wort to your sanitized, rinsed fermenter. Add ice-cold water to make 5 gallons. When the temperature drops to 75°F or less, add the yeast.
9) If you use liquid yeast, open the swollen packet and add to the wort. If you use dry yeast, add the yeast to 1 cup of 90°F water for a few minutes before adding to the wort. (You can add the yeast directly to the wort and let it sit for a few minutes also, but rehydrating the yeast in warm water will improve the fermentation.) Stir the wort thoroughly with a sanitized spoon.
10) Put the lid on the fermenter tightly, and insert the fermentation lock with the stopper into the hole in the lid and fill it up about 3/4 of the way with water or vodka. Let the wort ferment for a week or two until the fermentation ceases.
11) When fermentation is complete, syphon the beer into a sanitized bottling bucket. Boil the corn sugar in about a cup of water; cool; stir gently into the beer. This provides the nutrients necessary for the yeast to carbonate the beer in the bottle.
12) Insert one end of the sanitized and rinsed hose into the bottling spigot and the other end to the bottle filler. Push the bottle filler down onto the bottom of the bottle and open the bottling spigot. 5 Gallons of beer will make about 2 cases, so make sure you sanitize this amount beforehand. Leave about 1/2-3/4 inch of space at the top of the bottle. Cap the bottles.
13) Let the beer age for 2 weeks to 6 months. Chill and enjoy.

Note: The normal phase of fermentation will be a lag phase, usually 2 hours to 1.5 days. Followed by a steady increase in intensity, usually lasting anywhere from 1 to 4 days. Fermentation abruptly slows down after this and tapers off to an occasional bubble being pushed out of the fermentation lock every 30 seconds or so. The main contributing factors to these fluctuations are the strain and initial amount of yeast being used, sanitation, and temperature intensity and consistency. For ale yeast, try and maintain temperatures between 65° and 75°. For lagers, temperatures of 65° down to 32° work best to maintain lager characteristics.

GLBS WHEAT BEER
Compliments of Lee Knox
GREAT LAKES BREW SUPPLY—Endicott, NY

Ingredients:
3.3 lbs. GLBS Weizen Extract
3.3 lbs. GLBS Light Extract
1/2 cup Crushed Crystal Malt
1 tsp Gypsum
1/2 tsp Irish Moss
2 ounces Mt. Hood Hops
Wyeast #3056
3/4 cups priming sugar

Brew Info:
Starting Gravity: 1.046
Final Gravity: 1.010

Instructions:
While bringing 4 quarts of water to a boil, steep the grains. Remove grains as water comes to a boil. Remove from heat and add the extracts, all hops, gypsum, and Irish moss. Boil for 30 to 45 minutes.

FERMENTATION

Fill your sanitized primary fermenter with 3.5 gallons of cold water [an empty sanitized milk jug works well as a measure]. Mark the side of the fermenter if you want, so next time you won't have to measure it gallon by gallon. **While the hot wort is still in the brewpot, with the cover on, cool it down to 100 degrees** or less by placing it in the sink and running cold tap water around it. **Spin the brewpot around once in a while** so the cooled wort around the inside edges of the brewpot will mix with the hot wort in the center. From now until fermentation is well under way your wort is very susceptible to contamination so don't let any unsanitized things come in contact with your brew! After some fermentation, the acidity change and lack of available sugars for fermentation discourage bacterial infection, so it is less likely to become inadvertently infected.

Combine your wort with 3.5 gallons of water in your primary fermenter. The final mixture should be less than 80°F before pitching (throwing in) the yeast. If you have a thermometer or a hydrometer, sanitize and take reading(s). This can be accomplished by measuring in the bucket for both readings. An alternate and perhaps more accurate method for the hydrometer readings is to use a test jar. Don't forget to correct your hydrometer reading for temperature, if you want an accurate measurement. The instructions for making the correction are supplied with the hydrometer (or see page 249). **Pitch the yeast. Stir the wort vigorously** (but don't beat it to death)—you want to mix some oxygen into it to help the fermentation. Close the fermenter with the lid (stopper if using a carboy) and **insert the airlock. Fill the airlock with water.** Using vodka instead of water will reduce the possibility of contamination.

If your fermentation takes off vigorously and brew starts blowing out of the airlock, there is nothing wrong. Simply insert your siphon tubing into the opening where the airlock fit. Run the siphon tube into a gallon of water with a tablet of sodium metabisulfite in it. You have an active fermentation. If you are using liquid yeast, it is normal to see no activity for a couple of days. Fermentation is complete when the specific gravity doesn't change for a couple of days. ferment in primary fermenter for 3 to 7 days. Siphon to secondary and let stand for 7 or more days.

The Brewmaster's Recipe Manual

BOTTLING

Sanitize and rinse 48 12 ounce bottles, your siphon tubes, and bottling bucket by soaking them in a sanitizing solution. The bottles should not be the screw type, be sure you can cap your bottles before you go through the trouble of sanitizing them. If the bottles are very clean in the first place, you can get away with a sturdy rinse of a concentrated chlorine and water solution (2 TBSP per gallon of water). **Always rinse your B-Brite or Chlorine solution out of the bottles thoroughly,** a bottle washer is the best apparatus for this.

Take a final hydrometer reading with a sanitized hydrometer. **Boil one or two cups of water with 3/4 cup of corn sugar OR 1-1/4 cups of light dry malt extract. Pour the sugar mixture into the bottling bucket. Siphon the rest of the beer into the bottling bucket.** You can add cold water if you would like to have more beer than what is in the bucket. This just thins the beer a little. NOTE: If you are making a four gallon batch of beer, reduce your bottling sugar to 4/5 of 3/4 cup (or 3/5 cup). Mix the wort gently, be sure not to mix air into the beer as oxygenating the beer at this point may produce undesirable flavors. It is important, however, to have the beer well mixed to avoid inconsistent carbonation.

Place the bottling bucket and bottles in position and **start your siphon with the bottle filler attached.** If you are using a bottling bucket with a spigot, lucky you. If not, fill your siphon hose with water to get it going, just toss out (or drink) the first watered beer. The filler is activated by pushing it on the bottom of the beer bottle. **Fill the beer bottles** to the very top, when you pull the filler out there will be sufficient air space. Cap the beer bottles. **Store the full, capped beer bottles at room temperature and out of the light for two to three weeks** to allow for natural conditioning (carbonation).

Drink your beer at any time during the brewing process. When you like it most, that's when to drink it. After three weeks in the bottle, depending on the beer, an additional three to four weeks will add maturity that you will notice. Sediment will form in the bottom of the bottles due to the fermentation. Careful pouring will keep it in the bottle.

DUNKEL WEISSBIER
Compliments of Dick Foehringer
THE BREWMEISTER—Folsom, CA

"*Dunkel Weissbier* is a darker version of Weizenbier. It is a wheat beer from southern Germany. Dunkel weissbier is refreshing, light-bodied, lightly hopped, yeasty, highly effervescent, slightly sour and with flavor and aroma suggestive of cloves and banana."

8 lbs. Wheat Malt Extract Syrup
1/2 lb. 60L Crystal malt
1/2 oz. Northern Brewer Hops (Boiling) 60 min.
1/2 oz. Cascade Hops (Boiling) 30 min.
1/2 oz. Hallertauer Hops (Aromatic Hops)
1 teaspoon Irish Moss
1 teaspoon Gelatin
1 Bavarian Wheat Liquid Yeast
3/4 cup bottling Sugar

Original Gravity ~1.056
Final Gravity ~1.014

Put the crystal into the boiling bag. Add 1-1/2 to 2-1/2 gallons of cold water and bring to a near boil (~160°F). Shut off heat and let grain steep for 30 minutes. Remove grain bag and drain it completely. Dissolve in extract and return to heat. Bring to a boil and add Northern Brewer boiling hops. Boil 30 minutes. Add Cascade hops. Boil 15 minutes. Add Irish moss, boil 15 minutes. Turn off heat and add Hallertauer aromatic hops. Cover and steep for 15 minutes. Cold break wort by placing into a sink full of cold water. When the wort is below 100°F, strain into primary fermenter. Add cold water to make 5-1/2 gallons. When cooled below 85 °F pitch yeast. (Note: You must start the yeast 1-2 days ahead of time. Follow the instructions on the back of the yeast package.) Also mix the dry hops in 1 cup of hot water. Stir into cooled wort. Ferment in cool, dark place (~65-75°F). Rack into secondary leaving all the hops and sediment behind. Dissolve gelatin in 1 cup hot water. Stir into secondary and replace air lock. When clear (3-5 days) rack again leaving sediment behind. Dissolve bottling sugar in 1 cup hot water. Stir into cleared beer. Bottle and cap. Age a minimum of 3-4 weeks.

SCHWARZRITTER DUNKELWEIZEN
S. SNYDER

INGREDIENTS:

3.3 lbs. Ireks Weizen extract (1/2 of a 3kg. can)
2 lbs. Laaglander Light DME
2 lbs. Laaglander Amber DME
1/2 cup light crystal malt
1 cup Vienna Amber Malt
1 cup Chocolate Malt
1 cup Munich Dark Malt
1/2 oz. Styrian Goldings Plug 5.3% AA (boil) 90 min.
1/2 oz. Saaz Plug 3.1% AA (boil) 30 min.
1/2 oz. Hallertauer Plug 2.9% AA (flavor) 10 min.
1 Yeast Lab Bavarian Weizen #W51 with starter
Six gallons bottled spring water
1-1/4 cups Laaglander light DME for priming

O.G. 1.056 **F.G.** 1.020 **Potential alcohol** 4.75% v/v **IBUs** 15.4

Instructions
(Refer to *General Ale Brewing Procedures* beginning on page 218.)

WHEAT BOCK
Compliments of Sloan S. Venables
BREWMASTER—San Leandro, CA

Ingredients
6 lbs. 90% Wheat Malt Syrup
3 lbs. Light Dried Malt Extract
1 lb. Carapils/Dextrin Malt (Steeped 30 min.)
1/2 lb. Crystal Malt—20L (Steeped 30 min.)
1-1/4 oz. Hallertau Hops—Bittering Hops (Boiled 60 min.)
1 oz. Hallertau Hops—Bittering/Flavoring Hops (Boiled 30 min.)
1 oz. Hallertau Hops—Aromatic Hops (End of Boil)
Lager Yeast—Wyeast #2206 Bavarian Lager or Dried Lager Yeast
3/4 cup Corn Sugar at bottling

Starting Gravity: 1.066　　**Finishing Gravity:** 1.015-1.018
Bittering Units: 35　　**Fermentation Temperature:** 45-55°F

Instructions
(Refer to *General Ale Brewing Procedures* beginning on page 218.)

BELGIAN ALES

"Belgian ale" is possibly the hardest beer term in the world to define because it encompasses a vast array of unique styles, including Dubbel, Tripel, Saison, Oud Bruin, and Witbier, to name but a few. Pierre Rajotte's *Belgian Ale* is an excellent source of recipes and historical information, Michael Jackson's *The Great Beers of Belgium* is required reading for those seeking more in-depth knowledge of commercial brands, and Tim Webb's *Good Beer Guide to Belgium and Holland* is a mandatory travel guide for those visiting this beer lover's paradise.

Belgian Wit Bier, also known as "Bière Blanche" or "White Beer," has its origins in the Flemish region of Belgium, particularly around the town of Louvain. Historically, these beers were made with certain portions of raw wheat and raw oats, but because of the difficulty in milling and mashing these, you might be better served using malted wheat, whole wheat flour, and/or pre-cooked oats instead. These beers should be tart, slightly acidic, and well-carbonated. The aroma should be of malt and wheat, and "Noble" hop varieties are recommended. White Beer is often spiced; with coriander and curaçao bitter orange peel being the clear favorites.

When brewing an "Abbey" or "Abdij" style, the homebrewer should aim for a strong, dark-amber (or golden when brewing a Tripel) beer that is lightly hopped, bottle conditioned, brewed with medium to soft water and, of course, top-fermented. Belgian specialty grains such as caravienne, caramunich, and biscuit malt are suggested, as well as mild European hop varieties such as East Kent Goldings, Saaz, Hallertauer, and Styrian Goldings. These can be used for bittering as well as flavor, but go easy on the hop bouquet; aroma should be malty or neutral. But, of course, there are always exceptions—the Pale Ale-like *Orval Trappist Ale*, for example, is famous for its East Kent Goldings bouquet. Also important is the use of an alcohol-tolerant Belgian Ale yeast if you are brewing high gravity styles.

Belgian brewing law freely allows the use of up to 40% adjuncts, including such unlikely ingredients as raw wheat, candi sugar, coriander and orange peel as previously mentioned, stale hops, and wild yeast. Just a few of the many unique commercial brands include: the imported *Rodenbach, St. Sixtus, Grimbergen, Affligem, Corsendonk, Orval, Chimay,* and *Duvel,* as well as a variety of new American brews including: New Belgium Brewing's *Abbey Trappist Style Ale, Celis White* and *Grand Cru,* and GABF medal winner *Tripel Threat* from Cambridge Brewing Company.

BELGIAN WHITE
Compliments of Dick Foehringer
THE BREWMEISTER—*Folsom, CA*

"Belgian White is an awesome ale with malted wheat, barley, and oats. The style is enhanced by the addition of coriander seed and spicy Hallertauer hops. This delicious brew comes from Belgium, which is sometimes called "the Disneyland of Beer."

4 lbs. Alexander's Wheat Malt Extract
2 lbs. English Light Dry Extract
1 lb. Steel Cut Oats
1-1/2 oz. Hallertauer Hops (60 min.) Boiling
1/2 oz. Hallertauer Hops (15 min.) Aromatic
1 oz. crushed Coriander Seed (5 min.)
1 tsp. Irish Moss (15 min.)
1 teaspoon Gelatin
3/4 cup Bottling Sugar
1 Wyeast Belgian Ale Liquid Yeast

Original Gravity ~1.042   Final Gravity ~1.010

Put the steel cut oats into a grain bag. Add 1-1/2 to 2-1/2 gallons of cold water and bring to a near boil (~160-170°F). Shut off heat and let grain steep for 30 minutes. Remove grain bag and drain it completely. Dissolve in extract and return to heat. Bring to a boil. Add the first addition of Hallertauer hops and boil for 45 minutes. Add the second addition of hops and the Irish moss and boil for 10 minutes. Add the crushed coriander seed and boil for 5 minutes. Cold break wort by placing into a sink full of cold water. When the wort is below 100°F, strain into primary fermenter. Add cold water to make 5-1/2 gallons. When cooled to below 85 °F pitch yeast. (Note: You must start the yeast 1-2 days ahead of time. Follow the instructions on the back of the yeast package.) Ferment in cool (~65-75°F), dark place. When fermentation has ceased, rack into secondary, leaving all the hops and sediment behind. Dissolve gelatin in 1 cup hot water and stir into secondary. Allow beer to clear, typically (3-5 days). Rack again, leaving sediment behind. Dissolve bottling sugar in 1 cup hot water. Stir into cleared beer. Bottle and cap. Allow to age/carbonate in the bottles a minimum of 2-4 weeks.

EAST COAST WIT
EAST COAST BREWING SUPPLY—Staten Island, NY

Makes 5 gallons (5.5 in fermenter)

MALT:
Lactic Mash
0.50 lbs. Belgiam 2 Row
0.50 lbs. Belgiam 6 Row
Main Mash
2.25 lbs. Belgian 2 Row
2.25 lbs. Belgian 6 Row
4.00 lbs. Unmalted, hard red wheat (ground fine)

HOPS:
5.0 HBUs bittering, equal portions of Willamette & Cascade

OTHER INGREDIENTS
0.25 oz. bitter orange quarters, milled (15 mins.)
0.25 oz. fresh whole coriander, milled (15 mins.)

YEAST:
Wyeast 3944 - Belgian White beer yeast

PROCEDURE:
Prepare Lactic mash 48 hours. prior to start. Hold at 120°F.
Main mash

Dough in and acid rest	95°F	30 mins. add sour mash
Protein rest	122°F	30 mins.
Saccharificationrest	150°F	45 mins.
Saccharificationrest	161°F	15 mins.
Mash out	168°F	10 mins.

FERMENTATION

Primary	1 weeek	64-75°F
Secondary	4 weeks	54-59°F

Kegging, correct pH to 3.9 with lactic acid.

WHITE'S BIER
Compliments of Paul White
THE SEVEN BARREL BREWERY SHOP—*Lebanon, NH*

O.G.: 1.040-42   F.G.: 1.010-12

The Mash
4 lbs. 6-Row
4 lbs. Flaked Wheat

Dough into 3 gallons of water @ 132-135°F and rest @ 122-125°F for 30 minutes. Boost temperature to 150°F for 2 hour rest, boosting back to 150°F whenever the temperature falls to 144°F. Mash-out and sparge to collect 6 gallons.

The Boil
After boiling the wort 15 minutes, add <u>6 AAUs of Hallertau Flowers</u> and boil 45 minutes. Add <u>1 teaspoon of Irish moss</u> and <u>3/4 oz. freshly crushed coriander seed</u>, boil 15 minutes, then shut off heat. Stir in another <u>3/4 oz. crushed coriander</u>, cover, and let stand 10 minutes. Chill to 70°F, top up to 5 gallons if necessary and pitch rehydrated <u>Edme Ale yeast</u>. Primary ferment for 5 days, transfer to secondary for 7 days or more. Keg or bottle. Age for at least 2 weeks.

Brewer's Notes: "Do not use 'wheat beer' yeast. I have tried various liquid yeasts with this recipe, but I like what I get with the Edme best."—Paul

ABBEY NORMAL
S. SNYDER

3 lbs. *M&F* Light DME
4 lbs. *Laaglander* Extra Light DME
1/4 lb. Turbinado (Raw Brown Sugar)
1 cup (1/4 lb.) CaraVienne Belgian Light Crystal Malt
1 cup CaraMunich Belgian Medium Crystal Malt
1 cup Belgian Special B Malt, 4 cups (1 lb.) Munich Malt
1 cup Vienna Malt, 1 cup Biscuit Malt, 2 cups Aromatic Malt
5 heaping tablespoons Organic Whole Wheat Flour
1/2 oz. Styrian Goldings Plug 5.3% AA (Boil)--90 min.
1/2 oz. Saaz Plug 3.1% AA (Boil)--90 min.
1/2 oz. Kent Goldings Plug 5.0% AA (boil)--60 min.
1/2 oz. Saaz Plug 3.1% AA (boil)--30 min.
1/2 oz. Saaz Plug 3.1% AA (flavor)--10 min.
1 oz. Hallertau Whole Flowers (aroma)--steeped 30 min.
Yeast Lab "Trappist Ale" with starter
1/2 tsp. Calcium Carbonate added to mash water to reduce acidity
2 tsps. Irish Moss, 6 gallons soft water (bottled spring water), 1 cup corn sugar for priming

O.G. 1.071
F.G. 1.014   Potential Alcohol **7.5%** v/v   **IBUs** 30.5   **HBUs** 8.25

Instructions
(Refer to *General Ale Brewing Procedures* beginning on page 218.)
Special Instructions
- Crack and add cracked malts and specialty grains to 1/2 gallon 150-158°F water. Sprinkle Calcium Carbonate and Whole Wheat Flour over top of the mash and mix in. Mash for 90 minutes before sparging and transferring wort to main brew kettle.
- Cellar condition (50-55°F) 6-12 months.

The Brewmaster's Recipe Manual

NORTH AMERICAN ALES

Besides the uniquely American "Cream Ale," most ales brewed in the United States are creative variations of European classics, often reflecting a combination of German and British brewing traditions. Thankfully, the list of fine microbrews in this category is enormous. Here we have lumped together many styles of "American Ale" for simplicity. Ingredients and water profiles for American-style ales depend largely on the style being brewed, but generally consist of American-grown malts and hops, and a fairly clean, neutral yeast strain, with water that is medium-hard or soft due to the higher hopping rates and the lighter colored malts of American brews.

Good microbrewed American Ales can be found in several style categories including: Brown, Pale/Amber, Wheat, and Cream Ale. A minuscule list of the more popular and acclaimed standouts includes: *Red Seal Ale, Pete's Wicked Ale, Harpoon Ale, New York Harbor Ale, Little Kings Cream Ale, Albermarle Ale, Brooklyn Brown, Dock Street Cream Ale,* and *Genessee Cream Ale.*

BROWN DOG BROWN ALE
THE HOME BREWERY—Ozark, MO

Ingredients:

6.6 lbs. (2 packs) Yellow Dog Malt Extract
1 cup whole Crystal Malt, remove at 170°
1 cup Chocolate Malt, remove at 170°
2 oz. (1/2 cup) Malto-Dextrin (in boil)
1 pack Burton Water Salts
1 pack Yeast Nutrient/Heading Salts
1 oz. Chinook Hop Pellets (12.2% AA) in boil
1 oz. Kent Goldings Hop Pellets (5.5% AA) in last 5 minutes
3/4 oz. Willamette Hop Pellets (5.5% AA) when heat is off
1/2 tsp. Irish Moss added 15 minutes before the end of the boil.
2 packs Doric Ale Yeast or 1 Wyeast Liquid Ale
3/4 cup Corn Sugar for priming

Starting Gravity ~1.048
Final Gravity ~1.012
Alcohol ~5% v/v

Instructions:

Heat 5 gallons of water in a large kettle. Add crushed grains. Many people don't have a kettle that large, but heat as much as you can (at least 2 gallons). When the water is boiling, turn off the heat and add the Malt Extract and water/heading salts to the water. Use a spoon and stir until you are sure no Malt Extract is sticking to the bottom of the kettle. Then turn the heat back on.

Bring the kettle back to a boil, and stir occasionally so the ingredients won't burn on the bottom of the kettle. If your recipe calls for Bittering Hops, now is the time to add them and stir them in. Watch out for a boil-over. In the early part of the boil, the kettle usually tries to boil over once or twice, so control this by adjusting the heat. Later in the boil, the surface tension changes and boiling over is not a problem. Keep stirring occasionally, and let the beer (wort) boil hard for one hour. Stir in the 1/2 tsp. of Irish Moss in your recipe about 15 minutes before the end of the boil.

If Finishing Hops are called for in your recipe, stir them in 2 minutes before the end of the boil. Using Finishing Hops at the end of the boil adds a fresh aroma and flavor to the beer, and the use of finishing hops is appropriate in most beer styles.

Pour the hot beer (wort) into the primary fermenter. It is not necessary to strain the wort if you used hop pellets. Add cold water to bring the total volume up to 5 gallons. If you are using our #B3a Fermenter (the one in the kits) the 5-gallon mark is the bottom ring. Cover the fermenter and wait until the temperature is down to 75°F. If you have a Wort Chiller (#C44), use it to bring the temperature down quickly. At 75° or less, add the Yeast in your recipe. Just tear open the pack(s) and sprinkle it on the wort. Close the fermenter with the lid, stopper, and airlock. Remember to put water (or Vodka) in the airlock. Vodka evaporates more quickly, but bacteria won't live in it.

Fermentation should start within 24 hours, and may continue for between one day and two weeks, depending on the type of yeast, the recipe, and the temperature. Leave the beer alone and don't open the lid. When the airlock has not bubbled for several days and the beer is flat, still, and clearing, it is ready to bottle.

To bottle, siphon about one pint of beer into a pan and warm it on the stove. Add exactly 3/4 cup of Corn Sugar to the pan and stir until it is dissolved. Pour this back into the beer and stir gently but well to distribute the sugar. Siphon or tap into clean sanitized bottles and cap. Keep the bottles at room temperature. After a week, put a bottle in the refrigerator and try it. It will be best in about three weeks.

CREAMY BROWN ALE
Compliments of Ric Genthner
WINE BARREL PLUS—Livonia, MI

"This Brown Ale is a rich, malty brew that has the taste and aroma of fresh hops. A thick, creamy head tops this well-balanced beer."

This brew contains:
   8 lbs. amber and light (mixed) malt extract
   1/4 lb. chocolate malt
   1/4 lb. black patent malt
   1/8 lb. roasted barley malt
   1 lb. crystal malt
   1 oz. Fuggles hops
   1/2 oz. Northern Brewer hops (boiling)
   2 oz. Cascade hops (dry hopping)
   1 package of liquid Wyeast (#3056-Bavarian Wheat)
   1/2 tsp. Fermaid
   1 tsp. Irish moss
   3/4 cup corn sugar

O.G.: 1.069
F.G.: 1.020

Directions

Add the chocolate, crystal, roasted, and black patent malt to 2 gallons of water that is at 158 degrees.
Leave for one hour.
Remove the grain and rinse.
Add the malt extracts and the Fuggles and Northern Brewer hops and boil for 45 minutes.
Add the Irish moss to the boil for the last 15-20 minutes.
Pour immediately into primary fermenter with cold water and top up to 5 gallons.
Add yeast when cool.
After primary fermentation add whole Cascade hops. Leave for 2 weeks.
Bottle with 3/4 cup of corn sugar.

GOLDEN ALE
THE VINEYARD—Upton, Ma

Ingredients:

3.3 lb Munton & Fison extra light malt extract
3 lbs. Laaglander light dry malt extract
1/2 lb. light crystal malt grain
1-1/2 oz. Willamette hop pellets (boiling)
1/2 oz. Willamette hop pellets (last 15 minutes)
1 tsp. Irish moss (15 minutes)
1/2 cup corn sugar for priming
1 package Whitbread Ale yeast

Original Specific Gravity: 1.050 to 1.053
Terminal Specific Gravity: 1.010 to 1.012
Primary fermentation: 4 days at 70°F
Secondary Fermentation: 8 days at 70°F
Boil Time: 40 minutes

Procedure: Crush and put all grains into one quart cold water for ten minutes. Slowly bring to a boil. Once boiling commences, remove from heat. Strain liquid into brew pot. Add 1-1/2 gallons water, malt extract, and bring to a boil. At start of boil add 1-1/2 oz. Willamette hop pellets. Last fifteen minutes of boil time, add 1/2 oz. Willamette hop pellets and one teaspoon Irish moss. Strain into sanitized primary fermenter and add cold water to make 5 gallons, let cool. Pitch yeast when temperature drops below 80°F. At bottling time boil 1/2 cup priming sugar with one cup water for bulk priming.

GOLDEN NUGGET PALE ALE
Compliments of Jim Stockton
HOME FERMENTER CENTER—Eugene, OR

"This is a local favorite," says Home Fermenter's Jim Stockton, who's shop has been in the business since 1980. "This beer has good body and head retention, plus a nice overall hop quality."

Ingredients
7 lbs. Light Malt Extract
1/4 lb. Wheat Malt
1 lb. Amber Crystal Malt
3/4 oz. Nugget Hops, Boiling
3/4 oz. Nugget Hops, Flavoring
1 oz. Kent Goldings Hops, Finishing
1 pkg. Burton Water Salts
1/2 tsp. Irish Moss
1 pkg. Edme Ale Yeast or Wyeast Liquid Culture

Begin with steeping of grains (see paragraph below). Thoroughly mix the malt extract with 2-3 gallons of warm water, and then start the 1 hour boil. Dissolve water salts and add to the kettle. Add 3/4 oz. Nugget boiling hops at the beginning of the boil. Add the other 3/4 oz. of Nugget hops 30 minutes later. Add Irish moss the last 15 minutes of the boil. Add 1 oz. of Kent Goldings finishing (aroma) hops the last 1-2 minutes of the boil. Remove and discard all boiling hops at this time. The aroma hops may also be discarded or added to the fermenter for more hop flavor. Add cold, clean water to make 5 gallons. When temperature drops to 68-75°F, add yeast and ferment until done. Ideal fermentation temperature is 65-75°F.

When adding flavoring grains, such as crystal or black patent malt, a smoother tasting brew will be attained by extracting the flavor and color before the boil. To do this add the grain to cold water and bring almost to a boil. <u>**DO NOT BOIL THE GRAINS**</u>! Turn off the heat, cover and steep the grains for approximately 20 minutes. Strain and rinse (sparge) the grains with 1-2 quarts of hot water (170°F). Do not over-sparge. Add the resulting extract to the boil and discard the spent grains.

YELLOW DOG PALE ALE (AMERICAN STYLE)
THE HOME BREWERY—Ozark, MO

Ingredients:

6.6 lbs. (2 packs) Yellow Dog Malt Extract
1 cup whole Crystal Malt, remove at 170°
1 pack Burton Water Salts
1 pack Yeast Nutrient/Heading Salts
3/4 oz. Chinook Hop Pellets (12.2% AA) in boil
3/4 oz. Kent Goldings Hop Pellets (5.5% AA) in last 5 minutes
3/4 oz. Willamette Hop Pellets (5.5% AA) when heat is off
1/2 tsp. Irish Moss added 15 minutes before the end of the boil
2 packs Doric Ale Yeast <u>or</u> 1 Wyeast Liquid Ale
3/4 cup Corn Sugar for priming
Starting Gravity ~1.047
Final Gravity ~1.012
Alcohol ~4.6% v/v

The Brewmaster's Recipe Manual

Instructions:

Heat 5 gallons of water in a large kettle. Add Crystal Malt. Many people don't have a kettle that large, but heat as much as you can (at least 2 gallons). When the water is boiling, turn off the heat and add the Malt Extract to the water. Use a spoon and stir until you are sure no Malt Extract is sticking to the bottom of the kettle. Then turn the heat back on.

Bring the kettle back to a boil, and stir occasionally so the ingredients won't burn on the bottom of the kettle. If your recipe calls for Bittering Hops, now is the time to add them and stir them in. Watch out for a boil-over. In the early part of the boil, the kettle usually tries to boil over once or twice, so control this by adjusting the heat. Later in the boil, the surface tension changes and boiling over is not a problem. Keep stirring occasionally, and let the beer (wort) boil hard for one hour. Stir in the 1/2 tsp. of Irish Moss in your recipe about 15 minutes before the end of the boil.

If Finishing Hops are called for in your recipe, stir them in 2 minutes before the end of the boil. Using Finishing Hops at the end of the boil adds a fresh aroma and flavor to the beer, and the use of finishing hops is appropriate in most beer styles.

Pour the hot beer (wort) into the primary fermenter. It is not necessary to strain the wort if you used hop pellets. Add cold water to bring the total volume up to 5 gallons. If you are using our #B3a Fermenter (the one in the kits) the 5-gallon mark is the bottom ring. Cover the fermenter and wait until the temperature is down to 75°F. If you have a Wort Chiller (#C44), use it to bring the temperature down quickly. At 75° or less, add the Yeast in your recipe. Just tear open the pack(s) and sprinkle it on the wort. Close the fermenter with the lid, stopper, and airlock. Remember to put water (or Vodka) in the airlock. Vodka evaporates more quickly, but bacteria won't live in it.

Fermentation should start within 24 hours, and may continue for between one day and two weeks, depending on the type of yeast, the recipe, and the temperature. Leave the beer alone and don't open the lid. When the airlock has not bubbled for several days and the beer is flat, still, and clearing, it is ready to bottle.

To bottle, siphon about one pint of beer into a pan and warm it on the stove. Add exactly 3/4 cup of Corn Sugar to the pan and stir until it is dissolved. Pour this back into the beer and stir gently but well to distribute the sugar. Siphon or tap into clean sanitized bottles and cap. Keep the bottles at room temperature. After a week, put a bottle in the refrigerator and try it. It will be best in about three weeks.

TOPSAIL ALE
Compliments of Dick Foehringer
THE BREWMEISTER—Folsom, CA

"*Topsail Ale* offers a reasonably complex (a hint of sweetness along with medium strong hops and a rich malty flavor) taste and aroma in a medium-bodied ale."

7 lbs. Light Malt Extract Syrup
1 lb. Crystal Malt
1-3/4 oz. Chinook Hops (Boiling)
1/4 oz. Chinook Hops (Aromatic)
1/4 oz. Cascade Hops (Aromatic)
2 teaspoons Gypsum
1 oz. Dextrin Malt
3/4 cup Bottling Sugar
1 teaspoon Irish Moss
1 teaspoon Gelatin
1 Ale Yeast

Original Gravity ~1.053
Final Gravity ~1.014

Put the crystal into the boiling bag. Add 1-1/2 gallons of cold water and slowly bring to a near boil. Shut off heat and let the grain steep for 30 minutes. Remove grain bag and drain it completely. Stir in and dissolve completely the extract syrup. Return to heat and add the boiling hops, gypsum, and dextrin malt. Boil for 45 minutes, add Irish moss and aromatic hops. Boil for 15 minutes. Cool the wort and strain into primary fermenter. Add cold water to make 5-1/2 gallons. When cooled below 85°F, pitch yeast and ferment in cool place (~70°F). Rack into secondary and add dissolved gelatin. When clear (3-5 days), rack and add dissolved bottling sugar. Bottle and cap.

Age a minimum of 3-4 weeks. (Hop bitterness will diminish with age.)

McDERMOTT'S GOLDEN ALE
NORTHEAST BREWERS SUPPLY—West Kingston/Narragansett, RI

"This is a great beer for those who say homebrew <u>tastes</u> like it has been brewed at home or that it's too rich for them. This brilliantly clear, golden ale is a favorite at the shop because it's dry and crisp, with a wonderful floral aroma from dry-hopping."

Ingredients

(2) 3.3 lb. cans John Bull Light Unhopped Extract
(2) oz. Northern Brewer whole boiling hops
(1-1/2—2) oz. Northern Brewer whole hops for dry-hopping
(1) Wyeast A3892 #1007 German Ale Yeast
(1) tsp. Irish Moss

1. Boil Water; add cans of extract.
2. Add boiling hops in boiling bag and tsp. of Irish Moss.
3. Boil wort for 25 minutes (short boil keeps beer very clear).
4. Sparge into fermenter.
5. When cool, add yeast. After krausen, put in secondary fermenter.
6. Add dry-hops to secondary and let sit for 2 weeks.
7. Bottle or keg.

AMERICAN WHEAT ALE
Yankee Brewer Recipe of the Month
BEER & WINEMAKING SUPPLIES, INC.—*Northampton, MA*

Ingredients:

6 lbs. American wheat malt extract syrup **OR** 5 lbs. U.S. wheat dry malt
1-1/2 oz. Spalt, Hallertauer, or Tettnanger hop pellets
3/4 cup corn sugar for bottling
10-14 grams ale yeast (dry) OR #3056 Bavarian Weizen liquid yeast.

(Refer to *General Ale Brewing Procedures* beginning on page 218.)

Notes: BWS says, "Using a standard ale yeast will give a soft, neutral flavor to the wheat beer, much like *Anchor Wheat* on tap at the Olde Amherst Ale House. Using the German liquid, which is a blend of ale yeast and S. Delbrückii, gives a notably clovey undertone to the beer, characteristic of southern German Weizens, or Sam Adams Wheat."

EXTRA PALE ALE
Compliments of Dick Foehringer
THE BREWMEISTER—*Folsom, CA*

"This beer is as the name implies, an extra-pale American style beer. Light in color and flavor."

4 lbs. Alexander's pale malt extract syrup
2 lbs. Rice Extract
1/2 teaspoon Citric Acid
2 teaspoons Gypsum
1-1/2 oz. Cascade Hops (boiling)
1/2 oz. Tettnanger Hops (Aromatic)
1 Irish Moss
1 teaspoon Gelatin
3/4 cup Bottling Sugar
1 Ale Yeast

Original Gravity ~1.040
Final Gravity ~1.010

In your brew kettle bring 1-1/2 to 2-1/2 gallons of water to a boil. Remove from heat and stir in extract syrup and rice extract. Return to heat. Add gypsum, citric acid and boil for 15 minutes. Add the boiling hops and boil 30 minutes. Add Irish moss and boil 15 minutes. At 2 minutes before the end of the boil add the aromatic hops. Cold break wort to below 85°F. Strain into primary fermenter and add water to make 5-1/2 gallons. Pitch yeast and ferment in a cool place (~70°). Rack into secondary and stir in dissolved gelatin. When clear (3-5) days rack again and stir in dissolved bottling sugar. Bottle and cap. Age 2-4 weeks.

EAST COAST AMERICAN PALE ALE
EAST COAST BREWING SUPPLY—Staten Island, NY

Makes 6 gallons (5.5 in fermenter) O.G. 1.048-50

MALT:

6.6 lbs.	Northwestern extract
1.0 lb.	Light DME
0.5 lb.	Crystal 40L

HOPS:

Cluster	1.0 oz. for 60 mins.
Cascade	1.25 ozs. for 60 mins.
Cascade	.75 oz. for 20 mins.
Cascade	0.5 oz. steeped for 30 mins. after boil
Cascade	0.5 oz. dry hopped in secondary

OTHER INGREDIENTS
2 tsps. Gypsum in the boil
1 tsp. Irish Moss for 30 mins.

YEAST:
Wyeast 1056 - American Ale

PROCEDURE:
Add Crystal to 6 gallons. Remove at 170°F. Bring to boil, add malts. Boil for 1.0 hour. Add hops as listed. Cool quickly to 78°F. Pitch yeast.

FERMENTATION

Primary	3 - 4 days	64-75°F
Secondary	2 weeks	54-59°F

Keg or bottle with 0.75 cup corn sugar per 5 gallons.

COMMENTS
Deep amber color. Full mouth feel that's well balanced with hops. Lots of hops in flavor and aroma components.

BIG BERTHA PALE ALE
Compliments of Tom Sweeney, Brewmaster, Millrose Brewing Company (Chicago Indoor Garden Homebrew Instructor)
CHICAGO INDOOR GARDEN SUPPLY—Streamwood, IL

Ingredients (for 10 gallons)

20 pounds English Pale Malt
1 pound Brewer's Malt 6-row
1 pound Caramel Malt 40L
1/2 pound Wheat Malt
1/2 pound Munich 10L
1/2 pound Cara-Pils
5-1/2 ounces Northern Brewer Hops (boiling)
1 ounce Cascade Hops (boiling)
1 ounce Willamette Hops (finishing)
1 teaspoon Burton Salts
1 teaspoon Gypsum
500 ml slurry of Wyeast #1056 (American Ale)

Procedure

Infusion mash at 156 degrees F until conversion plus 15 minutes. Raise temperature to 165 degrees F and hold 10 minutes. Rest for 20 minutes. Sparge at 165 degrees F.

Hop schedule: Boil 10 minutes and add Northern Brewer hops. Boil another 70 minutes and add Cascade hops. Boil another 10 minutes and add Willamette hops.

Rest for 30 minutes. Chill to 70 degrees F. Aerate wort and pitch yeast. Ferment at 60-65 degrees F.

Comments
Very hoppy Northwest Coast-type Pale Ale.

AMERICAN CREAM ALE
THE HOME BREWERY—Ozark, MO

Ingredients:

3.3 lbs. (1 pack) Home Brewery Hopped Amber Malt Extract
3.3 lbs. (1 pack) Home Brewery Unhopped Light Malt Extract
1 lb. Corn Sugar, added to the boil
1 oz. Northern Brewer Hop Pellets (bittering)
1/2 tsp. Irish Moss added 15 minutes before the end of the boil
3/4 oz. Cascade Hop Pellets (finishing)
2 packs Doric Ale Yeast
3/4 cup corn sugar for priming

Starting Gravity ~1.055
Final Gravity ~1.013
Alcohol ~5.5% v/v

The Brewmaster's Recipe Manual

Instructions:

Heat 5 gallons of water in a large kettle. Many people don't have a kettle that large, but heat as much as you can (at least 2 gallons). When the water is boiling, turn off the heat and add the Malt Extract to the water. Use a spoon and stir until you are sure no Malt Extract is sticking to the bottom of the kettle. Then turn the heat back on.

Bring the kettle back to a boil, and stir occasionally so the ingredients won't burn on the bottom of the kettle. If your recipe calls for Bittering Hops, now is the time to add them and stir them in. Watch out for a boil-over. In the early part of the boil, the kettle usually tries to boil over once or twice, so control this by adjusting the heat. Later in the boil, the surface tension changes and boiling over is not a problem. Keep stirring occasionally, and let the beer (wort) boil hard for one hour. Stir in the 1/2 tsp. of Irish Moss in your recipe about 15 minutes before the end of the boil.

If Finishing Hops are called for in your recipe, stir them in 2 minutes before the end of the boil. Using Finishing Hops at the end of the boil adds a fresh aroma and flavor to the beer, and the use of finishing hops is appropriate in most beer styles.

Pour the hot beer (wort) into the primary fermenter. It is not necessary to strain the wort if you used hop pellets. Add cold water to bring the total volume up to 5 gallons. If you are using our #B3a Fermenter (the one in the kits) the 5-gallon mark is the bottom ring. Cover the fermenter and wait until the temperature is down to 75°F. If you have a Wort Chiller (#C44), use it to bring the temperature down quickly. At 75° or less, add the Yeast in your recipe. Just tear open the pack(s) and sprinkle it on the wort. Close the fermenter with the lid, stopper, and airlock. Remember to put water (or Vodka) in the airlock. Vodka evaporates more quickly, but bacteria won't live in it.

Fermentation should start within 24 hours, and may continue for between one day and two weeks, depending on the type of yeast, the recipe, and the temperature. Leave the beer alone and don't open the lid. When the airlock has not bubbled for several days and the beer is flat, still, and clearing, it is ready to bottle.

To bottle, siphon about one pint of beer into a pan and warm it on the stove. Add exactly 3/4 cup of Corn Sugar to the pan and stir until it is dissolved. Pour this back into the beer and stir gently but well to distribute the sugar. Siphon or tap into clean sanitized bottles and cap. Keep the bottles at room temperature. After a week, put a bottle in the refrigerator and try it. It will be best in about three weeks.

CREAM ALE
Compliments of Dick Foehringer
THE BREWMEISTER—Folsom, CA

"*Cream Ale's* character is reminiscent of a hoppier, slightly stronger, slightly fruitier cousin to an American Light Beer. Well carbonated and refreshing on a hot day. Similar to *Little Kings* or *Genessee Cream Ale*."

8 lbs. Alexander's Pale Malt Extract Syrup
1/2 lb. Crystal Malt
1/2 Cara-Pils Malt
1/2 oz. Willamette Hops—60 min. (Boiling)
1/3 oz. Hallertauer Hops—60 min. (Boiling)
1/3 oz. Cascade Hops—60 min. (Boiling)
1/2 oz. Hallertauer—2 min. (Aromatic)
1 teaspoon Irish Moss—15 min.
3/4 cup Bottling Sugar
1 teaspoon Gelatin
1 Ale Yeast

Original Gravity ~1.060
Final Gravity ~1.010
Put the crystal and cara-pils into the boiling bag. Add 1-1/2 to 2-1/2 gallons of cold water and bring to a near boil. Shut off heat and let grain steep for 30 minutes. Remove grain bag and drain it completely. Stir in and thoroughly dissolve extract syrup. Return to heat and add the 3 boiling hops. Boil wort for 45 minutes. Add Irish moss, boil for 15 minutes, then during the last 2 minutes of the boil, add the aromatic hops. Remove from heat. Cool the wort and strain into the primary fermenter. Add cold water to make 5-1/2 gallons. Rehydrate the yeast by dissolving into 1/2 cup warm water. Let the yeast mixture sit for 15 min. before pitching. When below 85°F pitch the yeast. Fermentat ~75°F. Rack to secondary and stir in dissolved gelatin. When clear (3-5 days) rack and add dissolved bottling sugar. Bottle and cap. Age a minimum of 3-4 weeks.

CREAM ALE
THE VINEYARD—Upton, MA

Ingredients:

3.3 lbs. Glenbrew hopped light malt extract
2 lbs. light dry malt extract
4 oz. pale malt grain
3 oz. crystal malt grain
1/2 oz. Cascade hop pellets (10 minutes)
1/2 oz. Cascade hop pellets (2 minutes)
1 tsp. Irish moss
1 tsp. ascorbic acid (add at bottling)
1 pkt. Whitbread ale yeast
3/4 cup priming sugar

Original Specific Gravity: 1.042
Terminal Specific Gravity: 1.013
Primary Fermentation: 8 days at 65°F
Secondary Fermentation: 5 days at 65°F
Boil Time: 45 minutes

Procedure: Crush all grains and add to 1 gallon cold water and bring to a boil. Remove from heat and strain liquid into boiling pot and bring to 2.5 gallons with cold water. Add malt, dry malt and bring to a boil for 45 minutes. Add Irish moss last 15 minutes, add 1/2 oz. hops the last 10 minutes, add 1/2 oz. hops for the last 2 minutes. Pour into primary fermenter and add cold water to 5 gallons. Add yeast when temperature gets below 85°F. Rack off solids after 8 days into secondary fermenter. Add 1 tsp. ascorbic acid with priming sugar at bottling.

CREAM ALE
Compliments of Mike Knaub
STARVIEW BREW—Mt. Wolf, PA

Beer Type	Cream Ale	Amount—5 gal.	Boil Time 90 mins
Malt Extracts	M&F	1 lb. 5 ozs.	
Malt Grains	Briess Amer. 6-row Pale Ale	5-3/4 lbs.	
	Hugh Baird Pale Ale	2 lbs.	
	Durst Munich	2 lbs.	
	Ireks Lt. Ger. Crystal	1/2 lb.	
Steep			
Mash In		3 gal. @ 150°	
Protein Rest	25 mins. @ 127°		
Sach. Rest	85 mins. @ 156°		
Mash Out	10 mins. @ 170°		
Sparge		4 gal. @ 170°	
Hops			
Boil	Willamette leaf	5 HBU	45 mins.
Flavor	Hallertau leaf	2.25 HBU	20 mins.
Aroma	Kent Goldings leaf	1-1/2 oz.	5 mins.
Yeast	Ringwood	1-1/2 pint starter	
Water		2 gal. for boil	
Misc.	Flaked Maize	1 lb.	used in mash
	Torrified Wheat	3/4 lb.	
O.G. = 1.050	Primary = 18 days @ 70°		
T.G. = 1.010	Secondary = 16 days @ 40°		

AMERICAN CREAM ALE
Recipe of the Month
BEER & WINE HOBBY—Woburn, MA

Ingredients

1 - 4 lb. can Alexander Pale Malt
1 lb. Light Dutch Dry Malt
4 oz. Malto Dextrin
2 oz. Fuggles Hop Pellets (boil)
1/2 oz. Hallertau Plug Hops (finish)
1 pkg. Burton Water Salts
1 tsp. Irish Moss
1 Muslin Bag
1 pkg. Dry Whitbread Ale Yeast
1 cup priming sugar

S.G 1.035 - 1.040
F.G. 1.010 - 1.012

Instructions

Add 2 gallons of cold water to your pot and bring to a boil. Add 1 can of Alexander Pale Malt Extract, 1 lb. Light Dry Malt, 4 oz. Malto Dextrin and 2 oz. Fuggles hop pellets. Boil for 1/2 hour. During the last 10 minutes, add 1 package of Burton Water Salts and 1 teaspoon of Irish moss. During the last 2 minutes, add 1/2 oz. Hallertauer plug tied in muslin bag. Remove from heat and discard hop bag. Add wort to your primary fermenter containing enough water to bring total volume to 5-1/4 gallons. Pitch rehydrated yeast when wort has cooled to between 65°F and 75°F. Proceed as usual. Finish fermenting. Prime with 1 cup priming sugar and bottle.

XX CERVESA
Compliments of Dick Foehringer
THE BREWMEISTER—Folsom, CA

"This beer is similar in taste and color to the commercial beer *Dos Equis*. It should have a slightly sweet, malty taste. If you taste our version with hot salsa and chips, it makes an even more sweeter and maltier taste. XX Cervesa is designed to go well with hot Mexican food. Enjoy!"

6 lbs. Light Malt Extract Syrup
1 lb. Dark Australian Dry Extract
1/2 lb. Crystal Malt
1/2 teaspoon Citric Acid
2 teaspoons Gypsum
1-1/2 oz. Cascade Hops (Boiling)
1/2 oz. Cascade Hops (Aromatic)
4 oz. Lactose
1 teaspoon Irish Moss
1 teaspoon Gelatin
1 Ale Yeast
3/4 cup bottling Sugar

Original Gravity ~1.053
Final Gravity ~1.014

Put the crystal into the boiling bag. Add 1-1/2 to 2-1/2 gallons of cold water and bring to a near boil (~160°F). Shut off heat and let let grain steep for 30 minutes. Remove grain bag and drain it completely. Dissolve in dry extract, syrup extract, lactose, citric acid, and gypsum. Return to heat and boil for 15 minutes. Add the boiling hops and boil for 30 minutes. Add Irish moss, boil 15 minutes. Turn off heat and add aromatic hops. Cover and let steep for 15 minutes. Cold break wort by placing into a sink full of cold water. When the wort is below 100°F, strain into primary fermenter. Add cold water to make 5-1/2 gallons. When cooled below 85 °F pitch yeast. (Note: Rehydrate your yeast by dissolving in 1 cup warm water. Let stand for 15 minutes.) Also mix the dry hops in 1 cup of hot water. Stir into cooled wort. Ferment in cool, dark place (~65-75°F). Rack into secondary leaving all the hops and sediment behind. Dissolve gelatin in 1 cup hot water. Stir into secondary and replace air lock. When clear (3-5 days) rack again, leaving sediment behind. Dissolve bottling sugar in 1 cup hot water. Stir into cleared beer. Bottle and cap.

Age a minimum of 2-3 weeks.

Lager Recipes

The Brewmaster's Recipe Manual

EUROPEAN LIGHT LAGER

European Light Lager encompasses many styles, with each country on the European continent and around the world offering their own unique interpretation. Dutch Light, Czech Pilsner, Dortmunder Export, and Munich Helles are the most renowned. Australian-style Lager is included in this category also. There are few exceptional imported varieties available in the U.S. because these beers have been bastardized for "American tastes" (German beers for export are not bound by the Reinheitsgebot) and because most suffer from long ocean voyages to get here. A variety of yeast strains are used, but the primary ingredients should be light, lager-type malt or extract, noble hops, and fairly soft water, particularly in regard to bicarbonate levels. We have included recipes here that do not readily fit into the Pilsner, Dortmunder, or Helles categories that follow.

Grolsch, Brand Up, and *Heineken* represent the widely available imports. Microbrewed versions for American homebrewers to sample while waiting out the lagering stage include: Stoudt's *Golden Lager* and Chicago Brewing's *Legacy Lager*.

CLASSIC DUTCH LAGER
Compliments of Dick Foehringer
THE BREWMEISTER—Folsom, CA

"This Heineken taste-alike is a favorite Danish Pilsen Lager. It is dominated by the distinctive signature of Hallertauer hops. Bottle it in green bottles and you will think you are in Holland!"

6 lbs. Pale Malt Extract
1 lb. Dry Rice Extract
1/2 lb. 20L Crystal Malt
1/2 lb. Cara-pils Malt
2 oz. Hallertauer Hops (60 min.) Boiling
1 oz. Hallertauer Hops (30 min.) Boiling
1 oz. Hallertauer Hops (2 min.) Aromatic
1 tsp. Irish Moss (15 min.)
1 tsp. Gelatin
3/4 cup Bottling Sugar
1 Dry Lager Yeast

Original Gravity: ~1.053
Final Gravity: ~1.012

Put the crystal and cara-pils malted grains into a grain bag. Place 1-1/2 to 2 gallons of cold water in your brewpot. Place grain bag in water and bring to a near boil (160-170°F). Turn off heat and allow grain to steep for 30 minutes. Remove grain. Dissolve liquid and dry extract thoroughly and then return mixture to heat. Bring to boil. Add 2 oz. of hops and boil for 30 minutes. Add the second 1 oz. hops and boil 15 minutes. Add Irish moss and boil for 15 minutes. Add the aromatic hops and boil 2 minutes. Cold break the wort to below 100°F. Put the cooled wort into your primary fermenter and add cold water to make 5-1/2 gallons. When cooled below 85°, pitch your yeast. **Note:** You should rehydrate the yeast by dissolving the packet in 1/2 cup warm water. Let it stand for 15 minutes, stir and add to the wort. Ferment in a cool (55-65°F), dark place. When fermentation has ceased, transfer to the secondary, leaving all the sediment behind. Dissolve gelatin in 1 cup hot water and stir into secondary. Allow beer to clear, typically 3-5 days. Rack again and stir in dissolved bottling sugar. Bottle and cap. Allow to age/carbonate in the bottles for 2-4 weeks. Enjoy!

CONTINENTAL LAGER*
Compliments of Peter Hood
BREWING SUPPLIES—*Stockport/Altrincham, England*

*For 5 Imperial Gallons

No. 1—3 lb. Light Powder Malt
No. 2—2 lb. Glucose
No. 3—2 oz. Hallertau Hops
No. 4—1 oz. East Kent Goldings
No. 5—8 oz. Malto Dextrin or Glucose Polymer
No. 6—Lager Yeast

1. Boil No. 1, 3, 4, and 5 in a large pan or boiler with as much water as possible. Use 2 pans if you want.
2. After 30 mins., strain off into clean, sterilised bucket and add No. 2. Stir well to dissolve.
3. Make up to 5 gallons with cold water and leave to cool below 75°F.
4. Add yeast and leave to ferment for about 7 days or until all signs of fermentation have finished (bubbles stop rising).
5. Syphon off into barrel or bottles adding 1/2 tsp. sugar per pint of beer to prime bottles—or 2 to 4 oz sugar to a 5 gallon pressure barrel.
6. Leave in a warm place for 4-5 days, then a cool place to clear—CHEERS!

Notes: It's best to add **Brewing Supplies'** Finings to the barrel. For better head retention, use **Brewing Supplies'** Brewery Heading Powder.

AUSTRALIAN LIGHT LAGER
Compliments of Sloan S. Venables
BREWMASTER—*San Leandro, CA*

Ingredients

6 lbs. Australian Light Malt Syrup
1 lb. Dried Rice Extract
1-1/2 oz. Mt. Hood Hops—Bittering Hops (Boiled 60 min.)
1/2 oz. Mt. Hood Hops—Aromatic Hops (End of Boil)
Lager Yeast—Wyeast #2007 Pilsen Lager or Dried Lager Yeast
3/4 cup Corn Sugar at bottling

Starting Gravity: 1.048
Bittering Units: 25
Finishing Gravity: 1.012-1.014
Fermentation Temperature: 50-55°F

Instructions
(Refer to the General Procedures section beginning on page 218.)

PILSNER

Those who are lucky enough to enjoy a 25¢ *Budweiser Budvar* or a *Pilsner Urquell* in a cafe in Prague's Old Town will often insist that these are the best beers they have ever experienced. Unfortunately, *Budvar* is restricted from import to the U.S. because of its similarity (in name only) to Anheuser Busch's *Budweiser*, and the green bottled *Pilsner Urquell* you get at the local supermarket can be months past its prime or "light-struck." However, the microbrewed Weeping Radish's *Corolla Gold*, Stoudt's *Pilsener*, August Schell *Pils*, Frankenmuth *German-style Pilsener* or *Garten Bräu Special*, if you are fortunate enough to have access to them, are award-winning and much fresher alternatives that will give you good examples to judge your homebrewed Pilsner against.

Suggetsed ingredients of these all-malt lagers are pale Belgian Pils, 2-row German, or "Moravian" Pilsener Malt, Light Crystal Malt, Saazer and Styrian Goldings hops, a Bohemian yeast strain, such as Wyeast #2124 or BrewTek CL-600, and very soft water. The same is true for brewing the less-malty, hoppier German version called "Pils," but a cleaner yeast strain, such as Wyeast #2042, BrewTek CL-660, or Yeast Lab #L31, should be substituted along with slightly harder water.

BOHEMIAN PILSNER LAGER
Compliments of Sloan S. Venables
BREWMASTER—San Leandro, CA

Ingredients

6 lbs. Alexander's Pale Malt Syrup
2 lbs. Light Clover Honey
1 lb. Crystal Malt—10L (Steeped 30 min.)
1-3/4 oz. Saaz Hops—Bittering Hops (Boiled 60 min.)
1 oz. Saaz Hops—Bittering/Flavoring Hops (Boiled 25 min.)
1 oz. Saaz Hops—Aromatic Hops (End of Boil)
Lager Yeast—Wyeast #2124 Bohemian Lager or Dried Lager Yeast
3/4 cup Corn Sugar at bottling

Starting Gravity: 1.050　　　　**Finishing Gravity:** 1.014
Bittering Units: 40　　　　　　**Fermentation Temperature:** 50-55°F

Instructions
(Refer to the General Procedures section beginning on page 218.)

Beer Trivia—*The brewpub U Flecku in Prague's Old Town lays claim to being the world's oldest. It was opened in 1499.*

FEBREWARY LOVER'S LAGER (GERMAN PILSNER)
Courtesy of Bruce Brode
WOODLAND HILLS HOME BREWING—Woodland Hills, CA

GENERAL INFORMATION:
Gravity   1.045
Color   4 SRM
IBUs   20

INGREDIENTS:

Grain Bill	Weight (lb.-oz.)	Mash Time (min.)	Color (SRM)	Specific Gravity
Munich	4 oz.	20	0.1	1.002
Belgian Biscuit	4 oz.	20	0.2	1.002
Belgian Aromatic	4 oz.	20	0.4	1.001

Extracts				
Laaglander-Light DME	3 lbs.	-	1.2	1.026
Rice Solids	1.5 lbs.	-	0.6	1.013

Hopping Schedule	Weight (oz.)	Boil Time (min.)	Alpha Acid	IBUs	Type
Liberty	2.0	75	2.7%	15.1	Leaf
Hallertauer	1.75	20	4.6%	5.3	Leaf
Saaz	0.5	0	4.0%	0.0	Pellet

Finings	Amount
Irish Moss	1 teaspoon

Yeast   Wyeast Danish Mixed

COMMENTS: Ferment at 50-55 degrees for lagers. If not possible, use the 1056 American Ale Yeast and Ferment at 60-65 degrees. Steep grains in 2 quarts water at 150 degrees for 30 minutes. Sparge with 1 quart water at same temp. Use 3/4 cup corn sugar for priming.

GOOD KETTLE WORK:
1—Vigorous, rolling boil.
2—Skim all foam before starting hop seqeunce.
3—Add Irish moss last 20 minutes.

Beer Trivia—*The first American "Budweiser" actually predates the world-class Czech Budweiser Budvar. At the time of the American version's creation, "Budweiser" was a centuries-old generic term for all beers brewed in and around the town of Budweis (Ceské Budejovice).*

GERMAN PILSENER
THE HOME BREWERY—Ozark, MO

Ingredients:

6.6 lbs. (2 packs) Home Brewery Unhopped Light Malt Extract
3 oz. Tettnanger Hop Pellets (bittering)
1/2 tsp. Irish Moss added 15 minutes before the end of the boil
1/2 oz. Hallertauer Hop Pellets (finishing)
1 pack European Lager Yeast
3/4 cup corn sugar for priming

Starting Gravity ~1.048
Final Gravity ~1.013
Alcohol ~4.6% v/v

Instructions:

Heat 5 gallons of water in a large kettle. Many people don't have a kettle that large, but heat as much as you can (at least 2 gallons). When the water is boiling, turn off the heat and add the Malt Extract to the water. Use a spoon and stir until you are sure no Malt Extract is sticking to the bottom of the kettle. Then turn the heat back on.

Bring the kettle back to a boil, and stir occasionally so the ingredients won't burn on the bottom of the kettle. If your recipe calls for Bittering Hops, now is the time to add them and stir them in. Watch out for a boil-over. In the early part of the boil, the kettle usually tries to boil over once or twice, so control this by adjusting the heat. Later in the boil, the surface tension changes and boiling over is not a problem. Keep stirring occasionally, and let the beer (wort) boil hard for one hour. Stir in the 1/2 tsp. of Irish Moss in your recipe about 15 minutes before the end of the boil.

If Finishing Hops are called for in your recipe, stir them in 2 minutes before the end of the boil. Using Finishing Hops at the end of the boil adds a fresh aroma and flavor to the beer, and the use of finishing hops is appropriate in most beer styles.

Pour the hot beer (wort) into the primary fermenter. It is not necessary to strain the wort if you used hop pellets. Add cold water to bring the total volume up to 5 gallons. If you are using our #B3a Fermenter (the one in the kits) the 5-gallon mark is the bottom ring. Cover the fermenter and wait until the temperature is down to 75°F. If you have a Wort Chiller (#C44), use it to bring the temperature down quickly. At 75° or less, add the Yeast in your recipe. Just tear open the pack(s) and sprinkle it on the wort. Close the fermenter with the lid, stopper, and airlock. Remember to put water (or Vodka) in the airlock. Vodka evaporates more quickly, but bacteria won't live in it.

Fermentation should start within 24 hours, and may continue for between one day and two weeks, depending on the type of yeast, the recipe, and the temperature. (Ideally, this beer should ferment at 42°F.) Leave the beer alone and don't open the lid. When the airlock has not bubbled for several days and the beer is flat, still, and clearing, it is ready to bottle.

To bottle, siphon about one pint of beer into a pan and warm it on the stove. Add exactly 3/4 cup of Corn Sugar to the pan and stir until it is dissolved. Pour this back into the beer and stir gently but well to distribute the sugar. Siphon or tap into clean sanitized bottles and cap. Keep the bottles at room temperature. After a week, put a bottle in the refrigerator and try it. It will be best in about three weeks.

CHEXO PILSNER
Compliments of Jim Stockton
HOME FERMENTER CENTER—Eugene, OR

5 lbs. Laaglander Light Dry Malt Extract
1/4 lb. Light Crystal Malt
2-1/2 oz. Cascade Hops, Boiling
1/2 oz. Sazz Hops, Flavoring
1-1/4 Saaz Hops, Aromatic
5 oz. Malto-Dextrin
2 pkgs. Lager yeast or Wyeast Liquid Culture
3/4 cup Dextrose, Bottling

Mix the dry malt and malto-dextrin with cool water, at least 2-1/2 to 3 gallons, and boil for 30 minutes, add the Cascade hops and grain extract* and continue the boil for 30 minutes. Add the Saaz hops at about 15 minutes. Remove the boiling hops at the end of the hour boil, then add the aromatic hops. Boil for 2-3 minutes to sanitize. For extra hop aroma save 1/4 ounce of the Saaz to add during the third day of fermentation. Ferment at 45-55°F and in a 2-stage glass fermenter.

When adding flavoring grains, such as crystal or black patent malt, a smoother tasting brew will be attained by extracting the flavor and color before the boil. To do this add the grain to cold water and bring almost to a boil. <u>**DO NOT BOIL THE GRAINS**</u>! Turn off the heat, cover and steep the grains for approximately 20 minutes. Strain and rinse (sparge) the grains with 1-2 quarts of hot water (170°F). Do not over-sparge. Add the resulting extract to the boil and discard the spent grains.

BOHEMIAN PILSNER
Compliments of Dick Foehringer
THE BREWMEISTER—Folsom, CA

"The original Pilsner beer was brewed in Plzen (which means 'Green Meadows'), Bohemia in 1842. Bohemian was the original style which is pale, golden, and alluring. A creamy dense head tops a well-carbonated brew with an accent on the rich, sweet malt. The medium-bodied Bohemian style gets its aromatic character from the Czech Saaz hops. Flavor Profile: Clean, crisp, hop-spicy, and bitter with malty overtones."

4 lbs. Alexander's Pale Malt Extract
2 lbs. Light Dry Malt Extract
1/2 lb. 20L Crystal Malt
1/4 lb. Carapils Malt
1/4 lb. Flaked Barley
1 oz. Saaz Hops (60 min.) Boiling
1-1/2 oz. Saaz Hops (30 min.) Boiling
1 oz. Saaz Hops (15 min.) Flavor
1/2 oz. Saaz Hops (2 min.) Aroma
1/2 teaspoon Citric Acid
1 teaspoon Calcium Carbonate
1 teaspoon Irish Moss (15 min.)
1 Wyeast Bohemian Lager Liquid Yeast
1 Gelatin
1 Bottling Sugar

Original Gravity: ~1.050
Final Gravity: ~1.012

Put the crystal, carapils, and barley malted grains into a grain bag. Place 1-1/2 to 2 gallons of cold water in your brew pot. Place grain bag in water and bring to a near boil. Steep grains for 30 minutes. Remove grains. Dissolve liquid and dry extract, citric acid, and calcium carbonate thoroughly and return mixture to heat. Bring to a boil. Add 1 oz. hops and boil 30 minutes. Add 1-1/2 oz hops and boil 15 minutes. Add 1 oz hops and the Irish moss and boil 15 minutes. Add last 1/2 oz. hops, boil 2 minutes then turn off heat and steep for an additional 5 minutes. Cold break the wort to below 100°F. Put the cooled wort into your primary fermenter and add cold water to make 5-1/2 gallons. When cooled to below 85°F, pitch your yeast. Note: You must start the liquid yeast 1-2 days prior to brewing to allow it to culture up. Follow the instructions on the package for preparation. Ferment in a cool (55-65°F), dark place. When fermentation has ceased, transfer to the secondary. Dissolve gelatin in 1 cup hot water and stir into secondary. Allow beer to clear, typically 3-5 days. Rack again and stir in dissolved bottling sugar. Bottle and cap. Allow to age/carbonate in the bottles for 2-4 weeks. Enjoy!!!

MID-SUMMER PILSNER
THE VINEYARD—Upton, MA

Ingredients:

6 lbs. Laaglander light dry malt
4 oz. toasted malt grain
3 oz. crystal malt grain
2 oz. Saaz hop plugs (30 minutes)
1 oz. Hallertau hop pellets (5 minutes)
1 tsp. Irish moss (15 minutes)
1 tsp. ascorbic acid (add at bottling)
1 pkt. Whitbread Lager yeast
3/4 cup priming sugar

Original Specific Gravity: 1.038
Terminal Specific Gravity: 1.012
Primary fermentation: 5 days at 65-70°F
Secondary Fermentation: 10 days at 65-70°F
Boil Time: 30 minutes

Procedure: Crush and steep all grains in 1 gallon cold water for ten minutes, then bring to a boil slowly, stirring occasionally. Once boiling commences, remove from heat and strain liquid into boiling pot. Add 1.5 gallons water, 6 lbs. dry malt, and bring to a boil. Add 2 oz. Saaz hop plugs and start timer for the boil (30 minutes). Add Irish moss last 15 minutes. Add 1 oz. Hallertau hop pellets last 5 minutes. Strain into primary and fill up to 5 gallon maximum with cold water, let cool and add yeast. After 5 days, syphon into secondary fermenter. Add ascorbic acid with priming sugar at bottling time.

BOHEMIAN PILSNER
BEER&WINE HOBBY--Recipe of the Month

Ingredients
1 can alexander pale malt, 4 lbs
3lbs. Dutch extra light (german)
2 oz. Hallertauer hop plugs (boiling)
1 oz. Saaz plugs (finishing)
1 tsp. Irish moss
3 muslin bags
Czech pilsner liquid yeast 2278 (cold fermentation)
Or 1007 german pilsner (warmer fermentation)

S.G. 1040-1042
Fg 1012-1014

Important note : please read all instructions before starting

Crack crystal malt, place in a muslin bag and tie. Add cracked grains to 2 gallons cold water and bring to a boil. When water comes to a boil, remove from heat, let steep for 10 minutes. Remove and discard grains. Add can of liquid malt and dried malt. Be sure to save 1-1/4 cups of the dried malt for bottling! Add the hallertauer hop plugs tied in a muslin bag. Boil for 45 minutes. Add irish moss, boil for 10 more minutes. During the last 5 minutes, add the saaz hop plugs tied in a muslin bag. Remove all hops. Have a primary fermenter prepared with 3-1/2 gallons of cold water. Add hot wort to cold water, make up to a total of 5-1/4 gallons. When wort has cooled to between 65-75°F, pitch prepared yeast (instructions included). Proceed as usual. For cold fermentation, see additional instructions.

PIRATES BREW PILSNER
Compliments of Jay Garrison
BREW BUDDYS—Redondo Beach, CA

Ingredients
6 lbs. Light Liquid Extract
1 lb. Cara-Pils
1 oz. Cluster Hops
1 oz. Cascade Hops (Leaf)
Irish Moss
Hop Bag
Wyeast #2124 Bohemian, #2007 Pilsen, or Dry Lager Yeast

Instructions
1) If you selected the Wyeast liquid yeast, you must break the inner packet before you begin to brew. Allow 1 day for each month after the manufacture date printed on the front. If you're using the dry yeast that came with the Pirates Brew Kit, go ahead and get to it.
2) Prepare the grain. The grain should be crushed; if you did not get the grain crushed at the shop, crush it with some sort of rolling pin. You can either mix the grain with 2 quarts of water and heat it until it starts to boil, or heat it to about 165°F and steep for about 15 minutes.
3) Strain the grain, collecting the liquid into your brew pot. Rinse the grain (sparge) with 2 quarts of hot (170-180°F) water.
4) Add the bag of extract and 1 gallon of water to the brew pot. (You might want to rest the bag of extract in hot water for awhile to soften it up.) Bring the wort to a soft rolling boil.
5) Add the Cluster hops to the wort and boil for 40 minutes. Stir occasionally.

6) Add the Irish moss, then, place the Cascade leaf hops in the hop bag and add to the wort, boil for 20 minutes. Stir occasionally.

7) Add the boiled wort to your sanitized, rinsed fermenter. Add ice-cold water to make 5 gallons. When the temperature drops to 75°F or less, add the yeast.

8) If you use liquid yeast, open the swollen packet and add to the wort. If you use dry yeast, add the yeast to 1 cup of 90°F water for a few minutes before adding to the wort. (You can add the yeast directly to the wort and let it sit for a few minutes also, but rehydrating the yeast in warm water will improve the fermentation.) Stir the wort thoroughly with a sanitized spoon.

9) Put the lid on the fermenter tightly, and insert the fermentation lock with the stopper into the hole in the lid and fill it up about 3/4 of the way with water or vodka. Let the wort ferment for a week at 55°F.

10) Transfer to a secondary fermenter, and ferment another two weeks at 40°F. (NOTE: If you have no means to control the fermentation temperature, just ferment at room temperature for a week or two, you will still have a fine beer.)

11) When fermentation is complete, syphon the beer into a sanitized bottling bucket. Boil the corn sugar in about a cup of water; cool; stir gently into the beer. This provides the nutrients necessary for the yeast to carbonate the beer in the bottle.

12) Insert one end of the sanitized and rinsed hose into the bottling spigot and the other end to the bottle filler. Push the bottle filler down onto the bottom of the bottle and open the bottling spigot. 5 gallons of beer will make about 2 cases, so make sure you sanitize this amount beforehand. Leave about 1/2-3/4 inch of space at the top of the bottle. Cap the bottles.

13) Let the beer age for 2 weeks to 6 months. Chill and enjoy.

Note: The normal phase of fermentation will be a lag phase, usually 2 hours to 1.5 days. Followed by a steady increase in intensity, usually lasting anywhere from 1 to 4 days. Fermentation abruptly slows down after this and tapers off to an occasional bubble being pushed out of the fermentation lock every 30 seconds or so. The main contributing factors to these fluctuations are the strain and initial amount of yeast being used, sanitation, and temperature intensity and consistency. For ale yeast, try and maintain temperatures between 65° and 75°. For lagers, temperatures of 65° down to 32° work best to maintain lager characteristics.

EUROPEAN PILSNER
Compliments of Ed Kraus
E.C. KRAUS—Independence, MO

Ingredients
1, 4 lb. can of Alexander Pale Malt Extract
3 cups Light Dried Malt Extract
1-1/2 oz. Saaz Pelletized Hops
1 Tablespoon Irish Moss
1 Teaspoon Gypsum
1 pkg. EDME Beer Yeast
1-1/4 cups DME or 3/4 cups Corn Sugar for Priming
O.G. 1.038-39
F.G. 1.008-10

Boil Malt Extract, Dried Malt and hops for 30 minutes in approximately 1 gallon of water. After 30 minutes add Irish Moss and allow to boil an additional 15 minutes. After boil, stir in Gypsum and allow wort to cool. Prepare a fermentation container by filling with wort and water to 5 gallons. Stir the Yeast into the wort and allow to ferment 5 or 6 days without an air-lock. Then let the wort ferment an additional 7 to 10 days with an airlock on. Syphon beer off the sediment and stir in Bottling Sugar thoroughly and bottle. Store in warm place, 70-80 degrees, for 1 to 2 weeks until carbonated.

DORTMUNDER-EXPORT

Originally brewed in the North Rhine-Westphalia region of western Germany in and around Dortmund, a city with very hard water (TDS over 1,000 mg/l). Dortmunder (now called "Export" in Germany) was one of the four great beers to arise in continental Europe during the lagering revolution; along with Vienna, Pilsner, and Munich Dunkel. Dortmunder is ordinarily a very pale, but full-bodied lager occupying the middle ground between the clean, hoppy dryness of German Pils and the sweeter maltiness of Munich Helles.

Original gravities are usually in the 1.056 range. Use hard water, but beware of high hopping levels, as severe bitterness may result. Aim for an original gravity between 1.048-1.060, IBUs between 23-37, and alcohol by volume from 5-6%. Esters and diacetyl should not be evident, final gravity should be kept very low by highly attenuative yeasts such as Wyeast #2042, BrewTek CL-660, or Yeast Lab #L31. *Ayinger Jahrhundert* is one of the few genuine examples brewed in accordance with the Reinheitsgebot that is exported to the U.S. Stoudt's *Export Gold, Hübsch Lager,* and *Los Gatos Lager* are excellent American microbrewed examples to sample while brewing your first batch.

GERMAN DORTMUNDER
THE VINEYARD—Upton, MA

Ingredients:

4 lb. Heidelburg light malt extract
3 lb. light dry malt extract
1/2 lb. light crystal malt grain
1 oz. German Hallertau hop pellets (40 minutes)
1 oz. Tettnanger hop pellets (30 minutes)
1/2 oz. Styrian Goldings hop plug (10 minutes)
1 tsp. Irish moss (15 minutes)
2 pkgs. Amsterdam lager yeast

Original Specific Gravity: 1.052
Terminal Specific Gravity: 1.010 -1.014
Primary fermentation: 6-8 days at 55°F
Secondary Fermentation: 8-10 days at 55°F
Boil Time: 40 minutes NOTE: After bottling, maintain 55°F for one week, then place bottles in refrigerator for lagering.

Procedure: Crush and steep grain in 1 quart cold water for 10 minutes, then bring to a boil slowly, stirring occassionally. Once boiling commences, remove from heat and strain liquid into boiling pot. Add 1.5 gallons water, Heidelburg malt, 3 lb. light dry malt, and bring to boil. Once boiling, add 1 oz. German Hallertau hop pellets and start timer for 40 minutes. Add 1 oz. Tettnanger hop pellets last 30 minutes. Add Irish moss last 15 minutes. Add 1/2 oz. plug of Styrian Goldings hops last 10 minutes. Strain into primary fermenter and add up to 5 gallons with cold water. Let cool and add yeast. After 6-8 days, syphon into secondary fermenter. Add priming sugar at bottling time.

DORTMUNDER EXPORT
JASPER'S HOME BREW SUPPLY—Hudson, NH

Ingredients:

3 lbs. Munton & Fison Bulk Malt (light)
3.3 lbs. Munton & Fison pale or John Bull light syrup
1 lb. Munton & Fison light DME
1/4 lb. crushed 20 lovibond crystal malt

1 oz. Hallertauer (boil 45 minutes)
1/2 oz. Hallertauer plug (boil 15 minutes)
1 Wyeast 2042 (Danish)
1 muslin bag
1 cup priming sugar

O.G. 1.056-1.060
F.G. 1.011-1.015

Put crystal in muslin bag and put into 1 gallon of cold water. Bring to a boil and remove grains. Take off the flame and add syrups, dried malt extract. Stir until dissolved and put back on the flame. Add 1 oz. Hallertauer hops and boil 30-45 minutes. Add the 1/2 oz. Hallertauer plug and boil for 15 minutes more. Add to four gallons of cold water. Wait until the wort temp. is below 80°F, sprinkle the yeast over the top and wait ten minutes and stir. Cover and let ferment for 10-14 days in the primary fermenter, 2-3 weeks in the secondary (glass) and 6-8 weeks in the bottle. Please remember that the entire fermentation should take place at below 60 degrees (45-55°F works best).

EXPORT LAGER
THE CELLAR HOMEBREW—Seattle, WA

1 can Coopers Lager malt syrup
3 lbs. Extra Light dry malt extract
1/2 lb. German Light Crystal malt (crushed)
1 oz. Tettnang hops (boiling)
1 oz. Hallertau Hersbrucker hops (finishing)
1 pkg. dry lager or German Ale liquid yeast
1-1/4 tsp. Yeast Nutrient

Brewing Directions

1) Place any crushed Specialty Grains in a strainer bag. Add this bag of grain to your brewing kettle, which contains 2 to 2-1/2 gallons brewing water.
2) Bring the brewing water to a boil, then remove the bag of grains.
3) Remove the brewing kettle from the burner and add any Malt Syrup and Dry Malt Extract. Stir thoroughly and return the kettle to the burner. Continue heating and stirring this wort until it boils.
4) At boiling point, add any Yeast Nutrient, Water Salts, and Boiling Hops. Hops can be placed in a hop bag or added loose, to be later strained out after the boil using a strainer bag. Time the boil for about one hour, stirring occasionally. After the first 10 minutes of this boil, remove two cups of wort in measuring cup, and cover with foil or plastic. Cool to 90°F for use in step #5 below.
5) Making the Yeast Starter: For dry yeast, use 1/2 cup warm tap water (90 to 100°F). Sprinkle the contents of yeast packet into that water, cover for at least fifteen minutes, and then add to the two cups of wort you prepared in step #4. Cover and set aside for use in step #9 below. For liquid yeast, prepare one to three days ahead of brewing time per package instructions.
6) After the wort has boiled for that one hour, add Finishing Hops. Place them in the hop bag, which has been emptied of the spent boiling hops, and place them in the boiling kettle or just add the Finishing Hops directly to the brewing kettle.
7) Let the boil continue for 5 minutes. Remove pot from burner and let cool, covered, for about 20 minutes.
8) Pour three gallons of cold water into the sanitized open fermenter fitted with strainer bag, if loose Finishing Hops were used in step #6, strain the warm wort from step #7 into the cold water. Top up the fermenter to 5-1/2 gallons using cold tap water. Cover the fermenter and cool the wort as rapidly as possible.
9) When the wort has cooled to about 80° add the Yeast Starter and ferment as you usually do.

MUNICH HELLES

Helles means "light" in German. This refers to the beer's color, not its body, alcoholic strength, or caloric content. Also called "Munich Light" or "Hell Bier," Helles characteristics include a medium malty flavor, smooth mouthfeel, thirst quenching bitterness, and subtle hop aroma and flavor. For the homebrewer, a Wissenschaftliche yeast strain is recommended, as are O.G.s around 1.050, very pale lager malt or extract, and Hallertau hops. Often considered a blue collar beer, Helles is southern Germany's #1 seller and what you're most likely to be served by the liter in a beer hall such as the Hofbräuhaus. *Kloster Andechs Hell, Paulaner Premium Lager,* and *Spaten Premium Lager* are prime imported versions. Old Dominion's *Hard Times Select* and Pennsylvania Brewing's *Helles Gold* are both award-winning American microbrews to enjoy while you're waiting for your own to mature.

NORTHWESTERN LAGER
Compliments of Paul White
THE SEVEN BARREL BREWERY SHOP—Lebanon, NH

O.G.: ~1.055
F.G.: ~1.014

Ingredients

6.6 lbs. Northwestern Gold Malt Extract
1 oz. Perle or Northern Brewer—Bittering @7-9 AAU
1 oz. Saaz or Hallertau—Flavoring
1 oz. Saaz or Hallertau—Finishing
Lager Yeast

Instructions

- Mix extract well with hot water, then bring to a boil. When the boil is under control, add bittering hops and start timing. Total length of boil will be 60 minutes.
- If using Irish moss, add 2 tsp. 20 minutes before the end of the boil.
- Add flavoring hops 15 minutes before the end of boil.
- Add finishing hops 1-2 minutes before the end of boil.
- Cool to achieve 70 to 80 degrees, after topping up in the fermenter, and pitch yeast.

McHALE'S BEST (MUNICH HELLES)
BEER UNLIMITED—Malvern, PA

Third Place Winner in the 1991 Dock Street Regional Beer Competition—Light Lager Category.

INGREDIENTS:
1 can Mountmellick Light Lager
1 can Munton & Fison Extra Light
3 oz. Tettnang Hops
L32 Yeast Lab Bavarian Lager (requires starter)
1 teaspoon Irish Moss
2 tablespoons Gelatin
3/4 cup Corn Sugar for priming

PROCEDURE:
Boil extracts with 1-1/2 oz. Tettnang for one hour.
At 30 minutes—add Irish moss.
15 minutes before end—add 1/2 oz. Tettnang.
Last 2 minutes—add 1/2 oz. Tettnang.
Dry hop with final 1/2 oz. Tettnang.
Ferment at 68°F for one week.
Rack to secondary fermenter and add 1 tablespoon gelatin in a water solution.
Ferment at cooler temperature for 1-4 weeks.
Prime with 3/4 cup corn sugar and 1 tablespoon gelatin, both in a water solution.
Cheers!

	Specific Gravity
Original	1.048
Final	1.015

MUNICH HELLES LAGER
Compliments of Dick Foehringer
THE BREWMEISTER—Folsom, CA

"Munich Helles is a mildly hopped, malty, pale-colored beer. It is the mainstay of Bavarian festive beer drinking. This lager is traditional to southern German-style and is lower in alcohol, but superb for everyday quaffing!"

6 lbs. Pale Malt Extract
1/2 lb. 20L Crystal Malt
1/4 lb. Flaked Malted Barley
1-1/2 oz. Tettnanger Hops (60 min.) Boiling
1/2 oz. Tettnanger Hops (end of boil) Aromatic
1 teaspoon Irish Moss (15 min.)
1 Wyeast Munich Lager Liquid Yeast
1 teaspoon Gelatin
3/4 cup Bottling Sugar

Original Gravity: ~1.045
Final Gravity: ~1.010

Put the crystal malt and flaked barley malt grains into a grain bag. Place 1-1/2 to 2 gallons of cold water in your brew pot. Place grain bag in water and bring to a near boil (160°F). Turn off heat and allow grains to steep for 30 minutes. Drain and remove grain. Dissolve liquid extract thoroughly and then return mixture to heat. Bring to a boil. Add the 1-1/2 oz. of hops and boil for 45 minutes. Add Irish moss and boil for 15 minutes. Add the "end of boil" 1/2 oz. of aromatic hops. Turn off heat and steep for 15 minutes. Cold break the wort to below 100°F by setting your pan of wort into a sink full of cold water. Put the cooled wort into your primary fermenter and add cold water to make 5-1/2 gallons. When cooled below 85°F, pitch your yeast. (**Note:** You must start the liquid yeast 1-2 days prior to brewing to allow it to culture up. Follow the instructions on the package for preparation.) Ferment in a cool (50-60°F), dark place. When fermentation has ceased, transfer to the secondary, leaving all the sediment behind. Dissolve gelatin in 1 cup hot water and stir into secondary. Allow beer to clear, typically 3-5 days. Rack again, leaving sediment behind. Dissolve bottling sugar in 1 cup of hot water and stir into beer. Bottle and cap.

Allow to age/carbonate in the bottles for 2-4 weeks. Enjoy!

LIGHT LAGER
THE FLYING BARREL—Frederick, MD

Ingredients:

1 four lb. tin Alexander pale
1 Kicker, 1.4 lb. tin Alexander pale
2 ozs. Kent Golding Hops, Alpha ~5 to 5.5 (we prefer Plugs)
1 oz. German Hallertua Hops, Alpha ~3 to 3.5 (we prefer Plugs)
1 tsp. Irish Moss
1 pack Wyeast, Munich Lager, #2308
3/4 cup corn sugar, for priming

Directions for Brewing:

Break yeast pack a day before you are ready to brew (may need more than one day...check date and instructions).
Boil malt and Kent Goldings hops for about 30 minutes in about 1-1/2 gallons of water.
After 15 minutes of the boil, put the Irish Moss in the wort.
After 25 minutes of the boil, put the Hallertau hops in the wort.
Put boiling wort into a fermenter with 3-1/2 gallons of cold water.

Directions for Fermenting:

When temperature drops to below 75 degrees, pitch yeast.
Take hydrometer reading, air lock fermenter and watch the yeast do it's thing.
After 4 days, rack into a clean fermenter (glass if possible), air lock and watch the yeast do it's thing for another 20 days or until fermentation is complete.
Prime and bottle.

Notes: *The Flying Barrel* offers three pieces of advice for homebrewing:
    1. Keep it simple.
    2. Keep everything clean.
    3. Support your local homebrew shop, if you don't have a favorite, give them a call!

MUNICH LIGHT
Compliments of Ed Kraus
E.C. KRAUS—Independence, MO

3.3 lbs. B.M.E. Munich Gold Malt Extract
4-1/2 cups Corn Sugar
1 oz. Hallertau (1 hr. Boil)
1/2 oz. Tettnanger (10 min. Boil)
3 tsp. Irish Moss (10 min. Boil)
1 package Burton Water Salts
1 package Vierka German Lager Yeast
3/4 cups corn sugar (For Bottling)

O.G. 1.036-38
F.G. 1.008-10

(Refer to the General Procedures section beginning on page 218.)

VIENNA

Just prior to Josef Grolle's invention of the Pilsner lager in 1842, legendary brewer Anton Dreher began brewing a malty, amber-red lager in Vienna in late 1840-early 1841 using industrial age brewing techniques of refrigeration, malting, and yeast management. Early records of this beer do not offer specific details of gravity and color, but it is believed that it was similar to the Märzen style. It is known, however, that over the last 150 years since its invention in Vienna, original gravities of the commercial Vienna style fell in relation to the Bavarian fest biers, which are now generally accepted as being stronger and darker than the original auburn-hued Vienna. There are several American microbrews in the Vienna style, such as *Brooklyn Lager, Old West Amber, Rhomberg Classic Amber, etc.,* but true Vienna is fairly rare in Europe.

NORTHWESTERN VIENNA
Compliments of Paul White
THE SEVEN BARREL BREWERY SHOP—Lebanon, NH

O.G.: ~1.042
F.G.: ~1.014

Ingredients

6.6 lbs. Northwestern Amber Malt Extract
1-1/2 oz. Hallertau or Saaz Bittering @5-6 AAU
1 oz. Hallertau or Saaz Flavoring
Lager Yeast

Instructions

Mix extract well with hot water, then bring to a boil. When the boil is under control, add bittering hops and start timing. Total length of boil will be 60 minutes.

If using Irish moss, add 2 tsp. 20 minutes before the end of the boil.

Add flavoring hops 15 minutes before the end of boil.

Cool to achieve 70 to 80 degrees, after topping up in the fermenter, and pitch yeast.

WINTER LAGER
THE VINEYARD—Upton, MA

Ingredients:

3.3 lb. John Bull Hopped Light
4 lb. Laaglander light dry malt
8 oz. Toasted Lager Malt
8 oz. Lager Malt
8 oz. Crystal Malt
1/2 oz. Saaz hop plug (last 10 minutes)
1 teaspoon Irish moss (last 15 minutes)
1 teaspoon ascorbic acid (add at bottling)
1 pkt. Whitbread Lager Yeast
3/4 cup priming sugar

Original specific gravity: 1.042
Terminal Specific gravity: 1.012
Primary Fermentation: 4 days at 60-65°F
Secondary Fermentation: 8 days at 60-65°F
Lager at 55°F for 8 days

Procedure: Crush all grains (toasted lager malt, lager malt, and crystal malt) with rolling pin or short spurts in the blender. Put all crushed grains in 1/1/2 gallons cold water and bring to a boil. Strain liquid into brew boiling pot, add 1/2 gallon water, John Bull Hopped Light, 4 lbs. dry malt, and bring to a boil for 40 minutes. Last 15 minutes add Irish moss. Last 10 minutes add 1/2 oz. Saaz hop plug. Strain into primary fermenter and bring to 5 gallons with cold water. Let cool, pitch yeast. Rack off solids after 4 days into secondary fermenter. Add priming sugar and ascorbic acid at bottling time.

VIENNA AMBER LAGER
S. SNYDER

Ingredients:

1.5 kg. Heidelburg light unhopped extract (3.3 lbs.)
3.5 lbs. Laaglander light spray malt (8.4 cups)
1/8 lb. cracked Crystal malt (1/2 cup)
1/4 lb. cracked Lager malt (1 cup)
6-7 gallons bottled spring water
1 oz. Northern Brewer 8% AA pellet hops (Boil) 60 min.
1\2 oz. Tettnang hops 4.2% AA (Boil) 60 min.
1 oz. Saaz plugs 2.9% AA (Flavor) 10 min.
1 oz. Saaz plugs (Aroma) 2 min.
1 pkg. Wyeast #2308 "Munich" lager yeast
1.25 cups Dutch light spray malt for carbonation

O.G. 1.045
F.G. 1.020 Potential alcohol 3.5%

Instructions
(Refer to General Lager Brewing Procedures beginning on page 223.)

MÄRZEN/OKTOBERFEST

Taken from the German word "März" for the month of March, Märzen (or Maerzen) is a fest bier believed to have been brewed first by Franciscan monks during the season of Lent (which falls during the month of March) and laid down during the summer months. In the middle ages, these were strong, dark ales brewed in anticipation of the late summer/early autumn harvest festivals, but were eclipsed in 1858 when Gabriel Sedlmayr's brother Joseph introduced the Vienna-style fest bier at Munich's Oktoberfest.

Originally, the 19th century version of this beer was the same as Vienna, a reddish-amber lager, and many purists still consider it so. But, in reality, the original gravities and colors of these beers have diverged over the years to the point where the seasonal Oktoberfest/Märzen is now generally accepted as darker and stronger than the traditional Vienna lager as brewed by its inventor, Anton Dreher. Both, however, are increasingly lower in gravity than their predecessors, particularly in Munich where more brewers are offering a golden, standard gravity lager as their fest bier.

Märzen should be a well-carbonated, deep-amber lager, featuring a sweet malt aroma and flavor balanced with the crisp bitterness and subtle finish of German hops. Medium to soft water is recommended, as is a "Munich" or "Bavarian-style" lager yeast (you can use a clean ale yeast in a pinch, but ferment at the lower range of ale fermenting temperatures). Authentic Bavarian versions are usually much sweeter and, therefore, more heavily hopped than their American counterparts. Good commercial examples include Spaten *Ur Maerzen*, Paulener *Oktoberfest*, Hacker Pschorr *Oktoberfest*, Weeping Radish *Fest*, Catamount *Octoberfest*, and Samuel Adams *Octoberfest*.

KRAUT DOG OKTOBERFEST
THE HOME BREWERY—Ozark, MO

Ingredients:

6.6 lbs. (2 packs) Yellow Dog Malt Extract
1 oz. Hersbrucker Pellets (5.3% AA) in boil
No finishing hops
1 pack Wyeast Lager Yeast (your choice)
3/4 cup Corn Sugar for priming

Starting Gravity ~1.048
Final Gravity ~1.013
Alcohol ~4.6% v/v

Instructions:

Heat 5 gallons of water in a large kettle. Many people don't have a kettle that large, but heat as much as you can (at least 2 gallons). When the water is boiling, turn off the heat and add the Malt Extract to the water. Use a spoon and stir until you are sure no Malt Extract is sticking to the bottom of the kettle. Then turn the heat back on.

Bring the kettle back to a boil, and stir occasionally so the ingredients won't burn on the bottom of the kettle. If your recipe calls for Bittering Hops, now is the time to add them and stir them in. Watch out for a boil-over. In the early part of the boil, the kettle usually tries to boil over once or twice, so control this by adjusting the heat. Later in the boil, the surface tension changes and boiling over is not a problem. Keep stirring occasionally, and let the beer (wort) boil hard for one hour. Stir in the 1/2 tsp. of Irish Moss in your recipe about 15 minutes before the end of the boil.

If Finishing Hops are called for in your recipe, stir them in 2 minutes before the end of the boil. Using Finishing Hops at the end of the boil adds a fresh aroma and flavor to the beer, and the use of finishing hops is appropriate in most beer styles.

Pour the hot beer (wort) into the primary fermenter. It is not necessary to strain the wort if you used hop pellets. Add cold water to bring the total volume up to 5 gallons. If you are using our #B3a Fermenter (the one in the kits) the 5-gallon mark is the bottom ring. Cover the fermenter and wait until the temperature is down to 75°F. If you have a Wort Chiller, use it to bring the temperature down quickly. At 75° or less, add the Yeast in your recipe. Just tear open the pack(s) and sprinkle it on the wort. Close the fermenter with the lid, stopper, and airlock. Remember to put water (or Vodka) in the airlock. Vodka evaporates more quickly, but bacteria won't live in it.

Fermentation should start within 24 hours, and may continue for between one day and two weeks, depending on the type of yeast, the recipe, and the temperature. (Ideally, this beer should ferment at 42°F.) Leave the beer alone and don't open the lid. When the airlock has not bubbled for several days and the beer is flat, still, and clearing, it is ready to bottle.

To bottle, siphon about one pint of beer into a pan and warm it on the stove. Add exactly 3/4 cup of Corn Sugar to the pan and stir until it is dissolved. Pour this back into the beer and stir gently but well to distribute the sugar. Siphon or tap into clean sanitized bottles and cap. Keep the bottles at room temperature. After a week, put a bottle in the refrigerator and try it. It will be best in about three weeks.

OKTOBERFEST
THE VINEYARD—Upton, MA

Ingredients:

3.3 lb. Bierkeller Light malt kit
3 lbs. Laaglander light dry malt
4 oz. Toasted pale malt grain
3 oz. Crystal malt grain
2 oz. Roasted barley
2 oz. Hallertau hop pellets (30 minutes)
1 oz. Tettnanger hop pellets (10 minutes)
1 tsp. Irish moss (15 minutes)
Yeast from Bierkeller kit
3/4 cup priming sugar

Original Specific Gravity: 1.042
Terminal Specific Gravity: 1.012
Primary fermentation: 5 days at 60-65°F
Secondary Fermentation: 5 days at 60-65°F
Boil Time: 30 minutes

Procedure: Crush all grains (pale, crystal, and roasted barley) with rolling pin or short spurts in blender. Put all crushed grains in 1 gallon cold water and bring to a boil. Strain liquid into brew boiling pot, add 2 gallons water, Bierkeller kit, dry malt, 2 oz. Hallertau hop pellets and bring back to boil for 30 minutes. Add Irish moss last 15 minutes. Add 1 oz. Tettnang hop pellets the last 10 minutes of the boil. Add to primary fermenter with 2 gallons cold water, let cool, pitch yeast. Rack off solids after 5 days into secondary fermenter. Add priming sugar at bottling time.

OKTOBERFEST
THE HOME BREWERY—Ozark, MO

Ingredients:

3.3 lbs. (1 pack) Yellow Dog Malt Extract
3.3 lbs. (1 pack) Home Brewery Unhopped Amber Malt Extract
2 oz. Saaz Hop Pellets (bittering)
1 oz. Hallertauer Hop Pellets (bittering)
1/2 tsp. Irish Moss added 15 minutes before the end of the boil
1/2 oz. Tettnanger Hop Pellets (finishing)
1 pack European Lager Yeast
3/4 cup corn sugar for priming

Starting Gravity ~1.048
Final Gravity ~1.013
Alcohol ~4.6% v/v

Instructions:

Heat 5 gallons of water in a large kettle. Many people don't have a kettle that large, but heat as much as you can (at least 2 gallons). When the water is boiling, turn off the heat and add the Malt Extract to the water. Use a spoon and stir until you are sure no Malt Extract is sticking to the bottom of the kettle. Then turn the heat back on.

Bring the kettle back to a boil, and stir occasionally so the ingredients won't burn on the bottom of the kettle. If your recipe calls for Bittering Hops, now is the time to add them and stir them in. Watch out for a boil-over. In the early part of the boil, the kettle usually tries to boil over once or twice, so control this by adjusting the heat. Later in the boil, the surface tension changes and boiling over is not a problem. Keep stirring occasionally, and let the beer (wort) boil hard for one hour. Stir in the 1/2 tsp. of Irish Moss in your recipe about 15 minutes before the end of the boil.

If Finishing Hops are called for in your recipe, stir them in 2 minutes before the end of the boil. Using Finishing Hops at the end of the boil adds a fresh aroma and flavor to the beer, and the use of finishing hops is appropriate in most beer styles.

Pour the hot beer (wort) into the primary fermenter. It is not necessary to strain the wort if you used hop pellets. Add cold water to bring the total volume up to 5 gallons. If you are using our #B3a Fermenter (the one in the kits) the 5-gallon mark is the bottom ring. Cover the fermenter and wait until the temperature is down to 75°F. If you have a Wort Chiller (#C44), use it to bring the temperature down quickly. At 75° or less, add the Yeast in your recipe. Just tear open the pack(s) and sprinkle it on the wort. Close the fermenter with the lid, stopper, and airlock. Remember to put water (or Vodka) in the airlock. Vodka evaporates more quickly, but bacteria won't live in it.

Fermentation should start within 24 hours, and may continue for between one day and two weeks, depending on the type of yeast, the recipe, and the temperature. (Ideally, this beer should ferment at 42°F.) Leave the beer alone and don't open the lid. When the airlock has not bubbled for several days and the beer is flat, still, and clearing, it is ready to bottle.
To bottle, siphon about one pint of beer into a pan and warm it on the stove. Add exactly 3/4 cup of Corn Sugar to the pan and stir until it is dissolved. Pour this back into the beer and stir gently but well to distribute the sugar. Siphon or tap into clean sanitized bottles and cap. Keep the bottles at room temperature. After a week, put a bottle in the refrigerator and try it. It will be best in about three weeks.

OKTOBERFEST
Compliments of David Ruggiero
BARLEYMALT & VINE—Newton, MA

Ingredients:

2 containers (6.6 lbs.) malt extract
OR 6.6 lbs bulk amber malt extract
1 lb. Crystal Malt
1/2 lb. Munich Malt
1 oz. Northern Brewer Hops (for bittering)
1 oz. Hallertauer Hops (for aroma)
1 tsp. Irish Moss (for clarifying wort)
1 pkg. Edme Ale Yeast
3/4 cup Corn Sugar (for priming)
1 Muslin Bag

Original Gravity (O.G.) 1.048-1.050   Final Gravity (F.G.) 1.014-1.018
H.B.U.s~8 to 12 or I.B.U.s~20 to 30
Alcohol 5.0% by Volume

Directions for Brewing:
1. Secure grains in muslin bag and place into a pot with 2 gallons of water.
2. Steep the grain while water is heating, remove before a boil commences.
3. Dissolve all malt extracts into the brewpot and re-establish the boil.
4. A total elapsed brewing time of 50 minutes is required in order to:
    - Reconstitute the malt extracts.
    - Sterilize the ingredients.
    - Clarify the wort (this is known as a Hot Break).
    - Extract hop bitterness and aromatic properties.
5. The following additions to the brewpot must be made at each of the specified times:
    ELAPSED TIME: 0 minutes, add the Northern Brewer hops.
                           30 minutes, add 1/2 of the Hallertauer hops & the
                             Irish Moss.
                           50 minutes, add the remaining Hallertauer hops,
                             and remove the brewpot from the stove.
6. Transfer the wort to a sanitized fermenter, straining out hop pellets if possible.
7. Add enough cold water to the fermenter to equal 5 gallons, when the temperature falls below 75°F, add the yeast.
8. Secure the airlock and ferment as usual (refer to General Lager Brewing Procedures beginning on page 223);
    - Single stage fermentation techniques last 7 to 10 days.
    - Two stage fermentation techniques last 3 to 5 days in the primary and 5 days to 3 weeks in the secondary.
    - Influencing factors that can shorten or prolong your beer's fermentation cycle are; temperature, yeast selection and viability, wort gravities, oxygen uptake and general sanitation procedures.
9. When all fermentation activity has ceased, check your final gravity. It should be within .002 degrees of the recipe's suggested reading. Prepare to bottle if it is. (Refer to the *General Bottling Procedures* section beginning on page 232.)

OKTOBERFEST
Yankee Brewer Recipe of the Month
BEER & WINEMAKING SUPPLIES, INC.—Northampton, MA

Ingredients:

7 lbs. German Pale Liquid Malt Extract
1 lb. German Munich Malt Grain
8 oz. Light German Crystal
8 oz. Dark German Crystal
2 oz. German hop pellets (for bittering)
3/4 cup corn sugar for bottling
10-14 grams dry lager yeast OR Brewer's Choice #2308 (Munich), #2206 (Bavarian), or #2124 (Bohemian) liquid yeast culture.

O.G.: 1.050   F.G.: 1.012-14

Notes: "Technically, if using liquid yeast, it should be fermented in the primary at 39-48 °F, followed by a long lagering period at 32-34°F (3-8 weeks). As in the case with most homebrewers (and brewpubs), this simply is not feasible, due to lack of refrigeration, space, time, etc. An alternative is to brew at cool room temperature with dry lager yeast, or do what some brewpubs do, and brew as an ale with the clean liquid yeast cultures from WYeast labs. You can use either #1007 (for a drier beer) or #1338 (for a maltier beer), both accentuate the maltiness. This sounds like heresy, but you'd be surprised to find out how many brewpubs do this.

Note: A great way to cool a carboy during hot weather is to place it in a shallow bath, and place towels over it, into the water. The towel acts as a wick, drawing up moisture, which evaporates and cools the carboy in the process. A fan cools it even faster."—*Beer & Winemaking Supplies, Inc.*

OKTOBERFEST
Recipe of the Month
BEER & WINE HOBBY—Woburn, MA

Ingredients

1 can Ireks Arkady Light (6.6 lbs.)
1 lb. Dutch Amber dry malt
4 oz. Malto Dextrin
1/4 lb. Chocolate Malt
1/2 lb. Crystal Malt, German Dark
1/4 lb. Victory Malt
2 oz. Hallertau Hops (boil)
1 oz. Tettnang Hops (boil)
1/2 oz. plug, Saaz Hops (finish)
1/2 tsp. Sodium Chloride
1 tsp. Irish Moss
1 Muslin Bag
3/4 cup priming sugar
German Dusseldorf Yeast AO6

S.G 1.050 - 1.052
F.G. 1.010 - 1.016

Instructions

Add 2 gallons of cold water to your pot; put 1/4 pound crushed Chocolate Malt, 1/2 pound crushed German Crystal Malt and 1/4 pound crushed Victory Malt into your muslin bag and tie. Place bag in cold water and bring to a boil. When water comes to a boil, remove from heat and let grains steep for five minutes. Remove grains and discard. Return pot to heat and bring to a boil; add Ireks-Arkady malt, 1 pound Dutch Amber Malt, 4 ounces Malto Dextrine, 2 ounces Hallertau, 1 ounce Tettnang hops and 1/2 tsp. sodium chloride—boil for 45 minutes. During the last 15 minutes of your boil, add 1/2 ounce Saaz plug. Remove from heat and cool. Add to your primary fermenter containing enough water to bring to 5-1/4 gallons. Pitch prepared yeast when wort has cooled to between 65°F and 75°F. Proceed as usual. Finish fermenting. Prime with 3/4 cup Corn Sugar and bottle.

WOLFFENFEST
Compliments of Richard & Mark Aumand
RCA DISTRIBUTORS—N. Walpole, NH/Santee, CA

Ingredients

1-3.3 lb. can M&F light liquid malt extract
1-1 lb. bag M&F light dried malt extract
1-1 lb. bag crushed crystal malt
1-1 lb. bag Ireks Munich Dark grain
1-11.5 gram EDME ale yeast
1-GROSS-bottle caps
3/4 cup priming sugar
1 oz. Mt. Hood hops (aroma)
1 oz. Cascade hops (boiling)
2-muslin hop bags

Instructions

Put 1 lb. crystal malt and 1 lb. Munich Dark in muslin hop bags. Tie bags. Place in 1 gallon cold water. Turn stove on high. Bring to a boil. Steep 15 minutes. Discard two bags of grain. Add can of light malt extract and bag of dried malt extract. Add 1 oz. Cascade hops and boil for 35 minutes. Take off stove and add 1 oz. Mt. Hood hops. After 5 minutes add wort to 3.75 gallons cold water or top off to 5 gallons. When wort reaches 70° add yeast and let ferment for 7-10 days. Follow your normal procedure or refer to (refer to the *General Fermentation Procedures* section beginning on page 230.)

Beer Trivia—*The Oktoberfest celebration as we know it today did not become an "official" Bavarian event until 1810 when it was held to commerate the wedding of Ludwig I to Princess Theresa. Modern Oktoberfest celebrations are now held the last week of September through the first week of October.*

OKTOBERFEST LAGER
Compliments of Sloan S. Venables
BREWMASTER—San Leandro, CA

Ingredients

6 lbs. Light Malt Syrup
1 lb. Light Dried Malt Extract
1 lb. Toasted Pale Malted Barley (Steeped 30 min.)
1 lb. Carapils (Steeped 30 min.)
1 lb. Crystal Malt—40L (Steeped 30 min.)
1 oz. Hallertau Hops—Bittering Hops (Boiled 60 min.)
1/2 oz. Hallertau Hops—Flavoring Hops (Boiled 25 min.)
1/2 oz. Tettnang Hops—Flavoring Hops (Boiled 25 min.)
1/2 oz. Saaz Hops—Aromatic Hops (End of Boil)
Lager Yeast—Wyeast #2206 Bavarian Lager or Dried Lager Yeast
3/4 cup Corn Sugar at bottling

Starting Gravity: 1.052 **Finishing Gravity: 1.012-1.014**
Bittering Units: 25 **Fermentation Temperature: 50-55°F**

Instructions
(Refer to General Lager Brewing Procedures beginning on page 223.)

Note—Toast Pale Malted Barley in oven for 15 minutes at 350°F.

MÄRZEN
Compliments of Dick Foehringer
THE BREWMEISTER—Folsom, CA

"Our Märzen is a German Oktoberfest-style lager that has a rich amber-red color with mild, sweet malt character. The aroma is assertively malty, but appropriately balanced with the spiciness of the plentiful Hallertauer and Saaz hops."

Original Gravity ~1.053
Final Gravity ~1.014

7 lbs. Amber Malt Extract
1/2 lb. 60L Crystal Malt
1/4 lb. Carapils Malt
1/4 lb. Chocolate Malt
1 oz. Hallertauer Hops (60 min.) Boiling
1 oz. Hallertauer Hops (30 min.) Boiling
2 oz. Saaz Hops (5 min.) Aromatic
1 teaspoon Irish Moss
1 teaspoon Gelatin
3/4 cup Bottling Sugar
1 Dry Lager Yeast

Put the crystal malt, carapils malt, and chocolate malt grains into a grain bag. Place 1-1/2 to 2 gallons of cold water in your brew pot. Place grain bag in water and bring to a near boil (160-170°F). Turn off heat and allow grain to steep for 30 minutes. Remove grain. Dissolve liquid extract thoroughly and then return mixture to heat. Bring to a boil. Add the first addition of the Hallertauer boiling hops and boil for 30 minutes. Add the second addition and boil for 15 minutes. Add Irish moss and boil for 10 minutes. Add the aromatic hops and boil 5 minutes. Cold break the wort to below 100°F. Put the cooled wort into your primary fermenter and add cold water to make 5-1/2 gallons. When cooled below 85°F, pitch your yeast. **Note:** You should rehydrate the yeast by dissolving the packet in 1/2 cup warm water. Let it stand for 15 minutes, stir and add to the wort. Ferment in a cool (45-65°F), dark place. When fermentation has ceased, transfer to the secondary, leaving all the sediment behind. Dissolve gelatin in 1 cup hot water and stir into secondary. Allow beer to clear, typically 3-5 days. Rack again leaving sediment behind and stir in dissolved bottling sugar. Dissolve the bottling sugar in 1 cup hot water and thoroughly stir into cleared beer. Bottle and cap.

Allow to age/carbonate in the bottles for 2-4 weeks. Enjoy!

BAVARIAN FESTBIER
S. SNYDER

6 lbs. Laaglander Extra Light DME
1/4 lb. Lt. Crystal Malt
3 lbs. Munich Malt
3/4 lb. Vienna Malt
1/4 lb. Carapils
1.5 ozs. bittering hops (.5 oz. ea.) Hersbrucker 3.5%AA, Styrian Goldings 5.3%AA, Tettnang 4.5%AA--60 minutes
1 oz. Hersbrucker aroma hops, 2 minute boil
Wyeast #2308 Munich Lager Yeast in 1.5 liter starter@60 hours
4, 5-Liter Mini-Kegs (or 1-1/2 quarts Speise if bottling)

O.G. 1.060
F.G. 1.016
Potential alcohol 5.75% v/v
IBUs 25

Notes: IBUs reduced 10% by use of hop bags

(Refer to General Lager Brewing Procedures beginning on page 223.)

Special Instructions
Mash grains 1-1/2 hours at 153-155°F. Sparge with 165-168°F water.
Ferment at 46-54°F. Check specific gravity regularly and keg when 80% attenuation is reached. If bottling, ferment to completion then prime with speise.
Cool to 39° for 24 hrs. to settle yeast when fermentation is at 80% or approximately 1.023.
Rack off trub and into kegs and bung. Allow to ferment for 10-14 more days at normal fermentation temperature.
Slowly reduce temperature approximately 1° per day down to 32°F.
Lager six months until Oktoberfest.
Serve at 45-48°F.

The Brewmaster's Recipe Manual

MÜNCHNER DUNKEL

Münchner Dunkel (commonly labelled "Export Dunkel" in Bavaria) belongs to a larger group of styles sometimes referred to collectively as "Continental Dark" which, like its counterpart Continental Light, is an umbrella for many more distinct regional styles such as the chocolatey, coffeish Schwarzbier, the dry, hoppy Dutch Dark, and the soft, malty Münchner Dunkel.

Munich's water profile proved a perfect match for the dark malts in use in Bavaria; and with the isolation of lager yeast strains and the development of refrigeration technology in the mid-1800s, Munich's brewers were able to create the benchmark of dark lagers. Traditional recipes start with light European 2-row lager malts, Pilsener malts, or very light extracts, then add roasted malts such as Vienna, Munich, and Black Prinz for color. The darker malts used require some degree of temporary hardness in the brewing liquor. A smooth, malty, and slightly fruity yeast strain is good for the Munich version, a Danish or other clean lager yeast is best for the other Continental Darks; with Bavarian hops or their derivatives to provide bitterness (~25-35 IBUs), flavor, and aroma. Dunkels should not be black, but a deep, garnet-brown.

There are several imports in the Schwarzbier/Dutch Dark/Dunkel categories, such as *Köstritzer Schwarzbier,* Ayinger *Altbairisch Dunkel,* and *Grolsch Dark,* but like the "Continental Light" imports, may suffer from the long journey. Notable Micros to compare your version to include: Henry Weinhard's *Dark Beer,* Frankenmuth *German Style Dark,* and *Schwarz Hacker.*

MUNICH DUNKEL
Compliments of Dick Foehringer
THE BREWMEISTER—Folsom, CA

"Our Munich Dunkel has a distinctively roasted and chocolate character complimented by malty sweetness and low hop bitterness. A truly great German Dark Lager!"

8 lb. Pale Malt Extract
1/2 lb. 60L Crystal Malt
1/2 lb. Chocolate Malt
1-1/2 oz. Tettnanger Hops (60 min.) Boiling
1/2 oz. Tettnanger Hops (5 min.) Aromatic
1 tsp. Irish Moss (15 min.)
1 tsp. Gelatin
3/4 cup Bottling Sugar
1 Wyeast Munich Lager Liquid Yeast

Put the crushed crystal and chocolate malts into a grain bag. Place bag and 1-1/2 to 2-1/2 gallons of cold water in your brewpot. Bring to a near boil (~160-170°F). Shut off heat and steep the grain for 30 minutes. Remove grains. Stir in extract and thoroughly dissolve. Return to heat. Bring to a boil. Add the first addition of the Tettnanger boiling hops and boil for 45 minutes. Add the Irish moss and boil for 10 minutes. Add the second addiotion of Tettnanger hops (aromatic) and boil for 5 minutes. Cold break by placing the pan into a sink full of cold water. When wort is below 100°F, strain the wort into your primary fermenter. Add enough cold water to make 5-1/2 gallons. When wort is cool (below 85°F), pitch your yeast. (Note: You must start your liquid yeast 1-2 days prior to brewing. Follow the instructions for yeast prep on the back of the foil bag.) Ferment in a cool (~45-65°F), dark place. When fermentation is complete, rack into secondary, leaving all sediment behind. Prepare gelatin by dissolving in 1 cup hot water and stir into secondary. When clear (3-5 days), rack again, leaving sediment behind. Prepare bottling sugar by dissolving in 1 cup hot water. Stir dissolved bottling sugar into clear beer. Bottle and cap. Allow to age/carbonate in the bottles for 2-4 weeks.

MUNICH DARK
Compliments of Ed Kraus
E.C. KRAUS—Independence, MO

3.3 lbs. B.M.E. Munich Gold Malt Extract
5 cups Dark Dried Malt Extract
1-1/2 oz. Hallertau (1 hr. Boil)
1/2 oz. Tettnanger (10 min. Boil)
3 tsp. Irish Moss (10 min. Boil)
1 package Burton Water Salts
1 package Vierka Dark Munich Yeast
3/4 cups corn sugar (For Bottling)

O.G. 1.038-40
F.G. 1.012-14

(Refer to General Lager Brewing Procedures beginning on page 223.)

MÜNCHENER DUNKEL LAGER
S. SNYDER

2 lbs. Munich Malt
1/2 lb. Dark German Crystal Malt
1/4 lb. Carapils
1/4 lb. Vienna Malt
1/4 lb. Chocolate Malt
1 tsp. Calcium Carbonate
5 lbs. M&F light DME
1 oz. Hallertauer plugs@3.5% AA 60 min. (Boil)
1 oz. Hallertauer plugs@3.5% AA 30 min. (Boil)
1.5 oz. Hallertauer plugs 20 min. (Flavor)
1 oz. Hallertauer plugs at knockout (Aroma)
Wyeast Munich #2308 lager yeast with starter

O.G. 1.052   F.G. 1.012   Potential alcohol 5%
IBUs 26 (All hops in bags = 10% reduction in utilization)

- Mash grains:
    Mash in, carefully stirring to mix the liquor and grist. Rest 60 minutes at 148-158°F (65-70°C). Stir occasionally.
    Mash out. Raise mash temperature to 165-170°F (74-77°C) by adding doses of hot water or bottom heat. Rest 5-10 minutes to decrease viscosity.
    Transfer to lauter tun if separate vessel is being used. Slowly sparge with 165-168°F (74-76°C) water and collect wort into brew kettle.
- Add malt extract and bring to a boil. If doing a full wort boil, top up to 6 gallons with good brewing liquor.
- Boil for a total of 1-1/2 hours, adding hops as noted above.
- Let covered brew kettle sit in ice water bath 60 minutes or use wort chiller.
- Rack wort into primary fermenter containing ice-cold water to equal 5 gallons (if necessary).
- Pitch yeast at 64°F, then immediately cool to 48°-52°F and ferment 14 days in primary/14 days in secondary.
- Bottle or keg w/speise pitched with fresh yeast 24-36 hours earlier.
- Condition 14 days at 48°-52°F, step lager 1° per day down to 32°. Lager for 6-8 weeks.

The Brewmaster's Recipe Manual

BOCK

Traditionally brewed in winter for spring consumption, Bock beer's history is shrouded in myth. Many believe that Bock derives its name from its city of origin, Einbeck, Germany, because the city's symbol, a goat, was painted on barrels of the prized brew. Others believe that Bock takes its name directly from the German word for male goat because it is often brewed under the sign of Capricorn. In any event, Munich malt, chocolate malt, and dark crystal malt should dominate the recipe to provide a sweet, malty character. Hop bitterness, flavor, and aroma should be kept low, but evident, and "noble" or Hallertau hybrids are preferred, as are long, cold ferments to keep diacetyl and esters low. Some bicarbonate hardness is desirable to counteract the acidity of the dark malts. Deep copper to dark brown in color, alcoholically strong (6%+ v/v), and very malty in flavor, Bocks taste best when cold lagered several months. When low on homebrew, look for the renowned German originals such as *Einbecker Ur Bock* and the acclaimed (and easier to find) American versions, such as Frankenmuth *German Style Bock,* Catamount *Bock,* or Otter Creek Brewing's *Mud Bock* (a very convincing Bock fermented with ale yeast).

BIG BAD BOCK
THE VINEYARD—Upton, MA

Ingredients:

6.6 lb. Premier pale malt extract
2 lbs. amber dry malt extract
1/2 lb. cara-pils dextrin malt grain
1/2 lb. chocolate malt grain
1/2 lb. toasted malt grain
1 oz. Nugget hop pellets (boiling)
1/2 oz. U.S. Hallertau (boiling)
1/2 oz. U.S. Hallertau (last 15 minutes)
1 tsp. Irish moss (last 15 minutes)
1/2 cup corn sugar for priming
1 pkt. Vierka lager yeast

Original Specific Gravity: 1.066-1.070
Terminal Specific Gravity: 1.016-1.020
Primary Fermentation: 8 days at 55-60°F
Secondary Fermentation: 10 days at 55-60°F slowly raising temp. to 65°F
Boil Time: 40 minutes

NOTE: Lager in bulk when fermentation complete, as cold as 32°F for at least 1 week.
Crush and put all grains into 1-1/2 quarts cold water for 10 minutes. Slowly bring to a boil. Once boiling commences remove from heat. Strain liquid into boiling pot. Add 1-1/2 gallons water, malt extract, dry malt, and bring to a boil. At start of boil, add Nugget hop pellets and 1/2 oz. U.S. Hallertau pellets. Last 15 minutes of boil time add 1/2 oz. U.S. Hallertau pellets and Irish moss. Strain into sanitized primary fermenter and add cold water to make five gallons. Let cool. Pitch yeast when temperature drops below 80°F. At bottling time, boil 1 cup water with 1/2 cup priming sugar for bulk priming.

BOCK TO THE BASICS
Compliments of Steven, Bill, Ken, Will, and Scott
WIND RIVER BREWING COMPANY—Eden Prairie, MN

Ingredients
6 lbs. Dark Malt Extract Syrup
4 lbs. Amber Malt Extract Syrup
1/8 lb. Toasted Barley
1/16 lb. Chocolate Malt
1/2 Cara-pils
1/2 lb. Caramel (Crystal) Malt (40L)
1/2 oz. each, Tettnang/Mt. Hood hops — 90 minutes
1/2 oz. each, Tettnang/Mt. Hood hops — 60 minutes
1/2 oz. each, Tettnang/Mt. Hood hops — 30 minutes
1 oz. each, for Dry-Hopping (4 days in secondary)
1 Pkg. Wyeast Bavarian Lager liquid yeast
1-1/2 cups DME for priming

O.G. 1.070
F.G. 1.028
Potential Alcohol 8% by volume

Instructions
Steep cracked grains in 150°-160°F water (5-1/2 gallons) for 30 minutes. Remove grain—add and dissolve liquid malt extract. Slowly bring to boil. At 90 minutes add hops. At 60 minutes add hops. At 30 minutes add hops. Finish the boil. Use wort chiller. When wort is below 75°F, transfer to carboy and pitch the yeast. Allow primary to continue for 10-14 days at 40°-45°F. Transfer into secondary for 6-8 weeks. At 4th week add your dry hops for 4 days and then remove. At kegging/bottling add 1-1/2 cups dry malt extract which has been boiled in 3 cups of water for at least 10 minutes. Bottle/keg condition for 7 days, then chill and drink. Enjoy!

BOCK AND WHITE
Compliments of Paul White
THE SEVEN BARREL BREWERY SHOP—Lebanon, NH

The Mash
3 lbs. 2-Row Pale
1 lb. Munich
1 lb. Malted Wheat
4 oz. Chocolate Malt
4 oz. Crystal Malt
4 oz. Dextrine

Mash in 2 gallons of water @ 152°F for 1-1/2 hours. Mash out and sparge with 2 gallons of water.

The Boil
Add 6.6 lbs. Ireks Munich Light extract and bring to a boil. Add 10 AAUs of Northern Brewer Flowers, boil for 45 minutes. Add 1 tsp. Irish moss and 1 oz. Hallertau Flowers, boil 15 minutes more. Chill and pitch a Munich Lager yeast. Ferment as a lager. Bottle and age 4 months or more.

Brewer's Notes: "O.G. was not recorded, F.G. was 1.020. The only other recorded notes were, "Wow!, Great!, Do it again!"

GENTHNER BOCK
Compliments of Ric Genthner
WINE BARREL PLUS—Livonia, MI

This brew contains:
  8 lbs. amber plain malt extract
  1/2 lb. chocolate malt
  1 lb. Caramunich malt
  2 oz. German Hallertauer hops (boiling)
  2 oz. Tettnanger whole hops (dry hopping)
  1 Wyeast liquid Bavarian lager yeast
  1 tsp. Irish moss
  1-1/4 cup amber malt extract (for bottling)

O.G.: 1.066 - 1.070
F.G.: 1.014 - 1.020

Directions

Add the chocolate malt and the Caramunich malt to 1-1/2 gallons of water, bring to 158 degrees and hold for 60 minutes. Bring the grain to a boil. Remove the grain when the boiling starts.
Add the malt extract and the Hallertauer hops and boil for 60 minutes.
Add Irish moss to the boil for the last 15-20 minutes.
Pour immediately into primary fermenter with cold water and top up to 5 gallons.
Add yeast when cool.
After initial fermentation, rack into secondary and add 2 oz. of Tettnang hops.
Lager at 51 degrees.
Bottle with 1-1/4 cup of malt when fermentation is complete.

PIRATES BREW BOCK
Compliments of Jay Garrison
BREW BUDDYS—Redondo Beach, CA

Ingredients

6 lbs. Dark Liquid Extract
1 can Alexander Dark
6 oz. Crystal Malt 80L
5 oz. Chocolate Malt
8 oz. Klages Malt (Toasted)
2 oz. Hallertau Hops
1 oz. Mt. Hood Hops
Wyeast #2206 Bavarian Lager, #2308 Munich Lager or Dry Ale Yeast

The Brewmaster's Recipe Manual

Instructions

1) If you selected the Wyeast liquid yeast, you must break the inner packet before you begin to brew. Allow 1 day for each month after the manufacture date printed on the front. If you're using the dry yeast that came with the Pirates Brew Kit, go ahead and get to it.
2) Prepare the grains. First, toast the pale malt in the oven for 20 minutes at 350°F. Then crush them; if you did not get the other grains crushed at the shop, crush them with some sort of rolling pin. You can either mix the grains with 2 quarts of water and heat it until it starts to boil, or heat it to about 165°F and steep for about 15 minutes.
3) Strain the grains, collecting the liquid into your brew pot. Rinse the grains (sparge) with 2 quarts of hot (170-180°F) water.
4) Add the bag and can of extract and 1 gallon of water to the brew pot. (You might want to rest the bag of extract in hot water for awhile to soften it up.) Bring the wort to a soft rolling boil.
5) Add the Hallertau hops to the wort and boil for 40 minutes. Stir occasionally.
6) Add 1/2 of the Mt. Hood hops to the wort and boil for 20 minutes. Stir occasionally.
7) Add the last 1/2 of the Mt. Hood hops to the wort, turn off the heat; stir and let sit (covered, if possible) for 10 minutes.
8) Add the boiled wort to your sanitized, rinsed fermenter. Add ice-cold water to make 5 gallons. When the temperature drops to 75°F or less, add the yeast.
9) If you use liquid yeast, open the swollen packet and add to the wort. If you use dry yeast, add the yeast to 1 cup of 90°F water for a few minutes before adding to the wort. (You can add the yeast directly to the wort and let it sit for a few minutes also, but rehydrating the yeast in warm water will improve the fermentation.) Stir the wort thoroughly with a sanitized spoon.
10) Put the lid on the fermenter tightly, and insert the fermentation lock with the stopper into the hole in the lid and fill it up about 3/4 of the way with water or vodka. Let the wort ferment for a week at 55°F.
11) Transfer to a secondary fermenter, and ferment another two weeks at 40°F. (NOTE: If you have no means to control the fermentation temperature, just ferment at room temperature for a week or two, you will still have a fine beer.)
12) When fermentation is complete, syphon the beer into a sanitized bottling bucket. Boil the corn sugar in about a cup of water; cool; stir gently into the beer. This provides the nutrients necessary for the yeast to carbonate the beer in the bottle.
13) Insert one end of the sanitized and rinsed hose into the bottling spigot and the other end to the bottle filler. Push the bottle filler down onto the bottom of the bottle and open the bottling spigot. 5 Gallons of beer will make about 2 cases, so make sure you sanitize this amount beforehand. Leave about 1/2-3/4 inch of space at the top of the bottle. Cap the bottles.
14) Let the beer age for 2 weeks to 6 months. Chill and enjoy.

Note: The normal phase of fermentation will be a lag phase, usually 2 hours to 1.5 days. Followed by a steady increase in intensity, usually lasting anywhere from 1 to 4 days. Fermentation abruptly slows down after this and tapers off to an occasional bubble being pushed out of the fermentation lock every 30 seconds or so. The main contributing factors to these fluctuations are the strain and initial amount of yeast being used, sanitation, and temperature intensity and consistency. For ale yeast, try and maintain temperatures between 65° and 75°. For lagers, temperatures of 65° down to 32° work best to maintain lager characteristics.

The Brewmaster's Recipe Manual

BOCK
Compliments of Ed Kraus
E.C. KRAUS—Independence, MO

Ingredients

3.3 lbs. John Bull Dark Unhopped Malt
3 lbs. Dark Dried Malt Extract
1/2 lb. Chocolate Malt
1/2 lb. Crystal Malt
3 oz. Hallertau Pellet Hops (45 min. Boil Time)
1/2 oz. Fuggles Pellet Hops (4 min. Boil Time)
2 packages Lager Yeast (your choice)

Crack the Crystal and Chocolate Malt with a mill or crush with a rolling pin. Put the grains in 1 gallon of cold water. Bring it to a boil and immediately strain the grain off the water (wort). Add the rest of the malt extracts to the water along with the 3 oz. of Hallertau hops. Boil for 45 minutes. At the last remaining 4 minutes, add 1/2 oz. of Fuggles for aroma. Let cool with 4 gallons of water, then pitch yeast.

MAI BOCK

Also called "Helles Bock" or "May Bock," this is a full-flavored, but pale, Bock beer. These lagers are brewed in the dead of winter and aged until May—hence the name. Mai Bocks have a big, rich malt flavor balanced by Bavarian hops, but lack the dark roasted or crystal malts that deeply color the better-known styles of Bock. The seasonal *Mai Bock* of the Stoudt Brewing Company represents the rare American-made version of this German classic. Würzburger Hofbräu *May Bok,* Spaten *Premium Bock,* and Ayinger *Maibock* represent notable imports. If cold lagering is a problem, these can be homebrewed successfully with a clean, mild ale yeast strain; however, it is recommended that these beers be aged a minimum of 2 months if using ale yeast and a minimum of 3 months if using lager yeast.

HELLES BOCK
Recipe of the Month
BEER & WINE HOBBY—Woburn, MA

Ingredients

2 cans of Australian Light Plain Malt
2 lbs. English Light Dry Malt
1/2 lb. German Crystal Light Malt
1/4 lb. Victory Malt
2 oz. Hallertau Hop Pellets (boil)
1 oz. Saaz Hop Pellets (boil)
1/2 oz. Saaz Plug (finish)
3 inch Licorice Stick
1 tsp. Irish Moss
1/2 tsp. Sodium Chloride
1 Muslin Bag
3/4 cup Priming Sugar
Yeast Wyeast #1007 (German Ale) or Yeast Lab #L32 (Bavarian Lager)

O.G. 1.050-1.055
F.G. 1.014-1.018

Note: Prepare yeast starter 24 hours in advance.

Instructions
Total Boiling Time: 45 minutes

Add 2 gallons of cold water to your pot, put 1/2 Pound of Crushed German Crystal Malt and 1/4 lb. crushed Victory Malt into muslin bag and tie. Place bag in cold water and bring to a boil. When water comes to a boil, remove from heat and let steep for 5 minutes. Reomve grains and discard, return pot to heat and bring to a boil. Add 2 cans of Light Malt Extract, 2 lbs. of Light Dry Malt, 2 oz. of Hallertau Pellets, 1 oz. Saaz Pellets and 3 inch Licorice Stick. Boil for 45 minutes. During the last 15 minutes of your boil add 1/2 oz. Saaz Plug, 1 tsp. Irish Moss and 1/2 tsp. of Sodium Chloride. Remove from heat and cool. Add to your primary fermenter containing enough cold water to bring total volume to 5-1/4 gallons. Pitch prepared yeast (instruction included) when wort has cooled to between 65° and 75°F. For Ales proceed as usual. For Lager follow further instructions enclosed in Beer & Wine Hobby kit or refer to General Lager Brewing Procedures beginning on page 223. Finish fermenting, prime with 3/4 cup corn sugar and bottle.

HELLES BOCK

Compliments of Daniel Soboti
U-BREW—Maplewood, NJ

Category:	Bock, Helles
Method:	Full Mash
Starting Gravity:	1.066
Ending Gravity:	1.016
Alcohol Content:	6.5%

Recipe Makes: 5.0 gallons
Age Beer: 2 months; better after 4
Color: 5.3 SRM
IBUs: 24

Malts/Sugars:
- 1.25 lb   Crystal 10L
- 11.50 lb.   Pilsner 2-row

Hops:
- 1.00 oz. Hallertauer-German   5.0%   60 min.
- 0.25 oz. Hallertauer-German   5.0%   2 min.

Notes:
Step infusion used. Mash in at 120° for 30 min. Raised to 155° until iodine test came up negative (about 45 min.). Sparged, boiled, force cooled, then yeast pitched from a starter.

"I used Yeast Lab L32 (Munich Lager) for this batch. It is supposed to ferment with a rich, clean flavor and leave a slight malty sweetness. It came out very good and there was a nice residual sweetness."—Daniel Soboti

DOPPELBOCK

Originated in Bavaria in the form of Paulener's *Salvator*, these "Double Bocks" are required to be brewed at original specific gravities of 1.074 or above. Homebrewers should try to keep fruitiness and diacetyl as low as possible, with the malty sweetness from high final gravities dominating hop bitterness, flavor, and aroma. Although lighter, copper-colored examples do exist, dark brown is the most common color. Munich malt and dark German crystal malt are traditional ingredients, as well as the obligatory German hops. Not for the impatient brewer, these beers will need at least three months of lagering at close to 32°F to achieve their true potential. Spaten's *Optimator* is a good, widely available import as is *Celebrator Doppelbock*. Samuel Adams *Double Bock* represents the rare American-made version that is widely distributed.

DOPPELBOCK
Compliments of Sloan S. Venables
BREWMASTER—San Leandro, CA

Ingredients

12 lbs. Light Malt Syrup
1/4 lb. Black Patent Malt (Steeped 30 min.)
1 lb. Toasted Pale Malted Barley (Steeped 30 min.)
1 lb. Carapils (Steeped 30 min.)
1 lb. Crystal Malt—40L (Steeped 30 min.)
1 oz. Northern Brewer Hops—Bittering Hops (Boiled 60 min.)
1-1/2 oz. Hallertau Hops—Flavoring Hops (Boiled 25 min.)
1 oz. Hallertau Hops—Aromatic Hops (End of Boil)
Lager Yeast—Wyeast #2206 Bavarian Lager or Dried Lager Yeast
3/4 cup Corn Sugar at bottling

Starting Gravity: 1.080　　**Finishing Gravity:** 1.016-1.018
Bittering Units: 30　　**Fermentation Temperature:** 50-55°F

Instructions
(Refer to General Lager Brewing Procedures beginning on page 223.)

Note—Toast Pale Malted Barley in oven for 25 minutes at 350°F.

BAVARIAN DOPPELBOCK
THE HOME BREWERY—Ozark, MO

Ingredients:

3.3 lbs. (1 pack) Home Brewery Hopped Dark Malt Extract
3.3 lbs. (1 pack) Home Brewery Hopped Amber Malt Extract
3.3 lbs. (1 pack) Yellow Dog Malt Extract
1 oz. Hallertauer Hop Pellets (bittering)
1/2 tsp. Irish Moss added 15 minutes before the end of the boil
No finishing hops
2 packs European Lager Yeast
3/4 cup corn sugar for priming
Starting Gravity ~1.072
Final Gravity ~1.020
Alcohol ~6.8% v/v

Instructions:

Heat 5 gallons of water in a large kettle. Many people don't have a kettle that large, but heat as much as you can (at least 2 gallons). When the water is boiling, turn off the heat and add the Malt Extract to the water. Use a spoon and stir until you are sure no Malt Extract is sticking to the bottom of the kettle. Then turn the heat back on.

Bring the kettle back to a boil, and stir occasionally so the ingredients won't burn on the bottom of the kettle. If your recipe calls for Bittering Hops, now is the time to add them and stir them in. Watch out for a boil-over. In the early part of the boil, the kettle usually tries to boil over once or twice, so control this by adjusting the heat. Later in the boil, the surface tension changes and boiling over is not a problem. Keep stirring occasionally, and let the beer (wort) boil hard for one hour. Stir in the 1/2 tsp. of Irish Moss in your recipe about 15 minutes before the end of the boil.

If Finishing Hops are called for in your recipe, stir them in 2 minutes before the end of the boil. Using Finishing Hops at the end of the boil adds a fresh aroma and flavor to the beer, and the use of finishing hops is appropriate in most beer styles.

Pour the hot beer (wort) into the primary fermenter. It is not necessary to strain the wort if you used hop pellets. Add cold water to bring the total volume up to 5 gallons. If you are using our #B3a Fermenter (the one in the kits) the 5-gallon mark is the bottom ring. Cover the fermenter and wait until the temperature is down to 75°F. If you have a Wort Chiller (#C44), use it to bring the temperature down quickly. At 75° or less, add the Yeast in your recipe. Just tear open the pack(s) and sprinkle it on the wort. Close the fermenter with the lid, stopper, and airlock. Remember to put water (or Vodka) in the airlock. Vodka evaporates more quickly, but bacteria won't live in it.

Fermentation should start within 24 hours, and may continue for between one day and two weeks, depending on the type of yeast, the recipe, and the temperature. (Ideally, this beer should ferment at 42°F.) Leave the beer alone and don't open the lid. When the airlock has not bubbled for several days and the beer is flat, still, and clearing, it is ready to bottle.

To bottle, siphon about one pint of beer into a pan and warm it on the stove. Add exactly 3/4 cup of Corn Sugar to the pan and stir until it is dissolved. Pour this back into the beer and stir gently but well to distribute the sugar. Siphon or tap into clean sanitized bottles and cap. Keep the bottles at room temperature. After a week, put a bottle in the refrigerator and try it. It will be best in about three weeks.

The Brewmaster's Recipe Manual

NOTE: This beer should be aged at least 3 months before drinking.

BREWER'S DOPPLEBOCK
NORTHEAST BREWERS SUPPLY—West Kingston/Narragansett, RI

"The German word for goat is 'Bock.' So Bock is a German Lager that is intended to be strong like a goat. Dopplebock is as strong as two goats. This brew is distinguished by a strong malt character that is required to support its hefty alcoholic content.

This recipe for 'Brewer's Dopplebock' uses 7.5 lbs. of dry malt extract to make five U.S. gallons of homebrew. Starting specific gravity should be approximately 1.062, with a resulting alcohol content of about 5.8% by volume."

Ingredients

- (6) lbs. Dark Dry Malt Extract—Laaglander Dutch
- (1.5) lbs. Light Dry Malt Extract—Laaglander Dutch
- (1.5) lb. Dopplebock Grain Mix—Crushed (1/2 lb. Crystal Malt, 1/2 lb. Pale Malt, 1/2 lb. Chocolate Malt)
- (4) oz. Hallertau Hop Pellets (Boiling, 16 HBUs)
- (1.5) oz. Hallertau Whole Hops (Finishing, 6 HBUs)
- (2) Hop Boiling Bags
- (1/2) tsp. Irish Moss
- (1) Package Lager Liquid Yeast (#2035 American Lager)
- (1) Sterile Starter Mix
- (58) Bottle caps
- (3/4) cup Corn Sugar (priming)

1. Three days before you're ready to brew, take the liquid yeast out of the refrigerator and prepare according to instructions on the package. In about 24 hours, the foil pouch will expand. Prepare a yeast starter according to the instructions shown below. Add the yeast from the expanded foil pouch. Cover the opening with tin foil and shake well to aerate the starter solution. You'll have a ton of yeast to pitch into your Dopplebock in about a day and a half.

2. Add water to the largest (up to 5 gallon capacity) stainless steel or enameled steel pot you can find, leaving space for the malt (approx. 3/4 gallon) and a couple of inches at the top for the boil. Put the Grain Mix into one of the boiling bags and drop it into the pot while the water is still cool. Apply heat. Remove the grains just before the water starts to boil.

3. When the water starts to boil, stir in the Malt Extract (to avoid scorching, turn off heat before adding malt—turn it back on after malt is well mixed). Put the boiling hops (pellets) into the pot. When the water starts boiling again, set your timer for <u>25 minutes</u>.

4. After 25 minutes have elapsed, add the Irish Moss and set your timer for an additional <u>20 minutes</u>.

5. After you've boiled the wort for a total of 45 minutes, put the Finishing Hops into a hop boiling bag, drop them in and boil for an additional <u>2 minutes</u>. Remove from heat.

6. Cool the wort. There are a couple of ways to do this. If you have a wort chiller this process takes about 10 minutes. If you're boiling a small quantity of wort (1-1/2 to 3 gallons) you can add it to cold water in your primary fermenter to make up 5 gallons. Whatever method you use, remember the time between the end of the boil and pitching the yeast is when your brew is most susceptible to contamination. Therefore, extra care is warranted during this time to protect the wort from exposure to undesirable microorganisms.

The Brewmaster's Recipe Manual

Be sure to sanitize everything that comes into contact with your beer with boiling water, chlorine, or iodophor.

7. When the wort has been added to the primary fermenter and cooled to 70-80° F, add the yeast.

8. To reduce lag time, fermentation should be initiated at room temperature (65-70°F). When signs of fermentation are visable, move to a cooler place (preferably 50-55°F).

9. After about 2 weeks, rack to a secondary fermenter. Most of the yeast will be on the bottom, so be sure to suck some up into secondary fermenter.

10. After another week or two, measure the specific gravity. If its between 1.024-1.030 and holding steady, it's ready to bottle or keg. *Cheers!*

See pages 121 or 240 for instructions on preparing a yeast starter.

Beer Trivia—*Anheuser-Busch produces nearly half of all the beer brewed in the U.S.*

The Brewmaster's Recipe Manual

NORTH AMERICAN LAGERS

This designation once referred to the products of the giant breweries (i.e., *Bud, Coors, Stroh's, Miller*), especially in the beer judging arena. However, the recipes listed here are more pre-prohibition in character than the adjunct-heavy, mass produced versions and are more in the spirit the quality of microbrewed varieties such as *Anchor Steam, Samuel Adams Lager, Harpoon Lager, Rhino Chasers,* etc.

REAL BEER
Compliments of Lee Knox
GREAT LAKES BREW SUPPLY—Endicott, NY

Ingredients:
2 GLBS Unhopped Syrup
2 oz. Mt. Hood Pellet Hops
Liquid or Dry Yeast, Ale or Lager
3/4 cups priming sugar

Brew Info:
Starting Gravity: 1.046
Final Gravity: 1.010

Instructions:
Boil 4 quarts of water. Remove from heat and add syrups. Carefully bring the mixture to a boil. Boil for 30 minutes minimum. 20 Minutes before the end of the boil, add one ounce of Mt. Hood pellet hops. 10 Minutes before the end of the boil, add one ounce of Mt. Hood pellet hops.

FERMENTATION

Fill your sanitized primary fermenter with 3.5 gallons of cold water [an empty sanitized milk jug works well as a measure]. Mark the side of the fermenter if you want, so next time you won't have to measure it gallon by gallon. **While the hot wort is still in the brewpot, with the cover on, cool it down to 100 degrees** or less by placing it in the sink and running cold tap water around it. **Spin the brewpot around once in a while** so the cooled wort around the inside edges of the brewpot will mix with the hot wort in the center. From now until fermentation is well under way your wort is very susceptible to contamination so don't let any unsanitized things come in contact with your brew! After some fermentation, the acidity change and lack of available sugars for fermentation discourage bacterial infection, so it is less likely to become inadvertently infected.

Combine your wort with 3.5 gallons of water in your primary fermenter. The final mixture should be less than 80°F before pitching (throwing in) the yeast. If you have a thermometer or a hydrometer, sanitize and take reading(s). This can be accomplished by measuring in the bucket for both readings. An alternate and perhaps more accurate method for the hydrometer readings is to use a test jar. Don't forget to correct your hydrometer reading for temperature, if you want an accurate measurement. The instructions for making the correction are supplied with the hydrometer (or see page 249). **Pitch the yeast. Stir the wort vigorously** (but don't beat it to death)—you want to mix some oxygen into it to help the fermentation. Close the fermenter with the lid (stopper if using a carboy) and **insert the airlock. Fill the airlock with water.** Using vodka instead of water will reduce the possibility of contamination.

If your fermentation takes off vigorously and brew starts blowing out of the airlock, there is nothing wrong. Simply insert your siphon tubing into the opening where the airlock fit. Run the siphon tube into a gallon of water with a tablet of sodium metabisulphite in it. You have an active fermentation. If you are using liquid yeast, it is normal to see no activity for a couple of days. Fermentation is complete when the

The Brewmaster's Recipe Manual

specific gravity doesn't change for a couple of days. ferment in primary fermenter for 3 to 7 days. Siphon to secondary and let stand for 7 or more days.

BOTTLING

Sanitize and rinse 48 12 ounce bottles, your siphon tubes, and bottling bucket by soaking them in a sanitizing solution. The bottles should not be the screw type, be sure you can cap your bottles before you go through the trouble of sanitizing them. If the bottles are very clean in the first place, you can get away with a sturdy rinse of a concentrated chlorine and water solution (2 TBSP per gallon of water). **Always rinse your B-Brite or Chlorine solution out of the bottles thoroughly,** a bottle washer is the best apparatus for this.

Take a final hydrometer reading with a sanitized hydrometer. **Boil one or two cups of water with 3/4 cup of corn sugar OR 1-1/4 cups of light dry malt extract. Pour the sugar mixture into the bottling bucket. Siphon the rest of the beer into the bottling bucket.** You can add cold water if you would like to have more beer than what is in the bucket. This just thins the beer a little. NOTE: If you are making a four gallon batch of beer, reduce your bottling sugar to 4/5 (or 3/5 cup). Mix the wort gently, be sure not to mix air into the beer as oxygenating the beer at this point may produce undesirable flavors. It is important, however, to have the beer well mixed to avoid inconsistent carbonation.

Place the bottling bucket and bottles in position and **start your siphon with the bottle filler attached.** If you are using a bottling bucket with a spigot, lucky you. If not, fill your siphon hose with water to get it going, just toss out (or drink) the first watered beer. The filler is activated by pushing it on the bottom of the beer bottle. **Fill the beer bottles** to the very top, when you pull the filler out there will be sufficient air space. Cap the beer bottles. **Store the full, capped beer bottles at room temperature for Ales (33-55°F for Lagers) and out of the light for two to three weeks** to allow for natural conditioning (carbonation).

Drink your beer at any time during the brewing process. When you like it most, that's when to drink it. After three weeks in the bottle, depending on the beer, an additional three to four weeks will add maturity that you will notice. Sediment will form in the bottom of the bottles due to the fermentation. Careful pouring will keep it in the bottle.

AMERICAN BACKYARD DRY
May's Brew of the Month
E.C. KRAUS—Independence, MO

Description: A good quenching beer for the warm months ahead. Similar to the larger brewery beers. It is very light in both color and taste, and also has a clean, dry finish. The hops, while noticeable, are not predominant by any means. You may want to add some heading powder for additional foam retention.

General Profile: Starting Gravity: 33-39
Finished Alcohol: 3.5 - 4%
Bittering: 15-20 IBUs
Color: 2-4 SRM/3-6°L

Ingredients: 2.2 lbs. Extra Pale Hopped Malt Syrup
2.2 lbs. Plain Rice Syrup
1.0 lb. Light Dried Malt Extract (2-1/2 cups)
1/2 oz. Cascade Pelletized Hops (30 min. boil time)
1 Tbsp. Irish Moss (15 min. boil time)
2 Tsp. Organic Yeast Nutrient (end of boil)
2 Tsp. Amylase Enzyme (add to fermenter)
1 cup Priming Sugar (Bottling Time)
14 grams Ale Yeast or Wyeast #2278

Directions:

1. Start with 1-1/2 to 2-1/2 gallons of water. Add to that the malt syrup, rice syrup, and the dried malt and bring to a boil.

2. Once boiling, add the Cascade pelletized hops and boil for 30 minutes. During the last 5 minutes of boil, add the Irish Moss. At the end of the boil, stir in the Organic Yeast Nutrient.

3. Once the boiling is complete, the wort to your fermenter and add water to equal 5 gallons. Make sure it has cooled below 80°F and add the yeast and the Amylase Enzyme.

4. Attach air-lock to fermenter and allow to ferment for 7-10 days or until finished fermenting.

5. Bottle with priming sugar as normal and allow to condition for 3-5 weeks.

AMERICAN LIGHT
THE HOME BREWERY—Ozark, MO

Ingredients:

3.3 lbs. (1 pack) Home Brewery Hopped Light Malt Extract
1.1 lbs. (1/3 pack) Home Brewery Unhopped Light Malt Extract
No bittering hops
1/2 tsp. Irish Moss added 15 minutes before the end of the boil
3/4 oz. Cascade Hop Pellets (finishing)
1 pack European Lager Yeast
3/4 cup corn sugar for priming

Starting Gravity ~1.032
Final Gravity ~1.008
Alcohol ~3.1% v/v

Instructions:

Heat 5 gallons of water in a large kettle. Many people don't have a kettle that large, but heat as much as you can (at least 2 gallons). When the water is boiling, turn off the heat and add the Malt Extract to the water. Use a spoon and stir until you are sure no Malt Extract is sticking to the bottom of the kettle. Then turn the heat back on.

Bring the kettle back to a boil, and stir occasionally so the ingredients won't burn on the bottom of the kettle. If your recipe calls for Bittering Hops, now is the time to add them and stir them in. Watch out for a boil-over. In the early part of the boil, the kettle usually tries to boil over once or twice, so control this by adjusting the heat. Later in the boil, the surface tension changes and boiling over is not a problem. Keep stirring occasionally, and let the beer (wort) boil hard for one hour. Stir in the 1/2 tsp. of Irish Moss in your recipe about 15 minutes before the end of the boil.

If Finishing Hops are called for in your recipe, stir them in 2 minutes before the end of the boil. Using Finishing Hops at the end of the boil adds a fresh aroma and flavor to the beer, and the use of finishing hops is appropriate in most beer styles.

Pour the hot beer (wort) into the primary fermenter. It is not necessary to strain the wort if you used hop pellets. Add cold water to bring the total volume up to 5 gallons. If you are using our #B3a Fermenter (the one in the kits) the 5-gallon mark is the bottom ring. Cover the fermenter and wait until the temperature is down to 75°F. If you have a Wort Chiller (#C44), use it to bring the temperature down quickly. At 75° or less, add the Yeast in your recipe. Just tear open the pack(s) and sprinkle it on the wort. Close the fermenter with the lid, stopper, and airlock. Remember to put water (or Vodka) in the airlock. Vodka evaporates more quickly, but bacteria won't live in it.

Fermentation should start within 24 hours, and may continue for between one day and two weeks, depending on the type of yeast, the recipe, and the temperature. (Ideally, this beer should ferment at 42°F.) Leave the beer alone and don't open the lid. When the airlock has not bubbled for several days and the beer is flat, still, and clearing, it is ready to bottle.

To bottle, siphon about one pint of beer into a pan and warm it on the stove. Add exactly 3/4 cup of Corn Sugar to the pan and stir until it is dissolved. Pour this back into the beer and stir gently but well to distribute the sugar. Siphon or tap into clean sanitized bottles and cap. Keep the bottles at room temperature. After a week, put a bottle in the refrigerator and try it. It will be best in about three weeks.

THE HOME BREWERY "FAMOUS" AMBER LAGER
Compliments of Jamie P. Stephens
THE HOME BREWERY—San Bernardino, CA

3 lbs. Laaglander Light Dry Malt Extract
3.3 lbs. Yellow Dog Malt Extract
1.5 oz. Kent Goldings Hop Pellets (Bittering)
.5 oz. Cascade Hop Pellets (Bittering)
.5 oz. Tettnanger Hop Pellets (Finishing)
1/2 cup Crystal Malt 20°L
1/2 cup Crystal Malt 60°L
1/2 cup Crystal Malt 90°L
1/2 tsp. Irish Moss
2 packs Lager Yeast
3/4 Corn Sugar for Priming
O.G. 1.055   F.G. 1.018

Add cracked crystal malt to 2 quarts cold water and raise to a boil. Remove grains when boil commences. Turn off heat, dissolve in dry malt extracts and 2 gallons water. Return to boil, add Kent Goldings hops, and boil for 1 hour. Add Cascade hops after 30 minutes. Add Irish moss after 45 minutes. Add Tettnanger hops after 50 minutes. Cool wort with a wort chiller or place brewpot in ice-water bath for 20 minutes. Strain into primary fermenter, pitch yeast when temperature is below 75°F. When signs of fermentation are evident move to cool, dark place and ferment to completion at 46-58°F. Rack to secondary for 1 to 2 weeks. Bottle with 3/4 cup corn sugar dissolved in 1 pint boiling water. Condition at fermentation temperature for 1 week, then cold lager 3 to 4 weeks. Jamie P. Stephens, General Manager of The Home Brewery, writes, "I have a recipe that will change the world. I created this beer by pure instinct. Looking at my shelves, I began grabbing components that I felt would work together. Everyone is now begging me for the recipe...I had no idea! In summation, this beer...would benefit all of mankind."

FATHERS' DAY SPECIAL LAGER
THE VINEYARD—Upton, MA

Ingredients:

1 Arkells Premium Lager kit
2 lbs. light dry malt
1/2 lb. light crystal malt grain
1/2 oz. Hallertau hop plug (10 minutes)
1/2 oz. Hallertau hop plug (5 minutes)
1 tsp. Irish moss (15 minutes)
1 pkt. yeast from malt kit
3/4 cup priming sugar

Original Specific Gravity: 1.044
Terminal Specific Gravity: 1.012
Primary fermentation: 4 days at 65°F
Secondary Fermentation: 6 days at 70°F
Boil Time: 30 minutes

Procedure: Crush and put grain into 1 gallon cold water for 10 minutes, then bring to a boil slowly. Once boiling commences remove from heat. Strain liquid into boiling pot. Add 1.5 gallons water; bring back to boil and add Arkells kit and 2 lbs. dry malt. Return to boil for 30 minutes. Add Irish moss last 15 minutes. Add 1/2 oz. Hallertau hops last 10 minutes. Add 1/2 oz. Hallertau hops last 5 minutes. Strain into primary fermenter when boil is complete. Add cold water to make 5 gallons. Add yeast when temp. drops below 80°F. Syphon off to secondary in 4 days. At bottling time boil 3/4 cup priming sugar with 1 cup water for bulk priming.

LIGHT AMERICAN #1
THE CELLAR HOMEBREW—Seattle, WA

Ingredients

1—4lb. can Alexander's Malt Extract
1 lb. dry Rice Extract or 20 oz. Rice Syrup
1 cup Honey (optional)
1 oz. Hallertauer Pellet Hops (bittering)
1 oz. Hallertauer Leaf Hops (finishing)
1 pkg. Lager Yeast
3/4 cup Corn Sugar for priming (bottling)

Original Gravity: 1.030-1.035
Terminal Gravity: 1.004-1.010

Instructions: Add Rice Syrup/Extract to 2 gallons of boiling water. Add Honey if desired for more alcohol, malt and bittering hops and proceed with your normal brewing procedures or (Refer to the *General Lager Brewing Procedures* beginning on page 223.)

STEAM BEER
Compliments of Sloan S. Venables
BREWMASTER—San Leandro, CA

Ingredients

6 lbs. Light Dried Malt Extract
1 lb. Crystal Malt—40L (Steeped 30 min.)
3/4 oz. Northern Brewer Hops—Bittering Hops (Boiled 60 min.)
3/4 oz. Northern Brewer Hops—Bittering/Flavoring Hops (Boiled 30 min.)
1/2 oz. Cascade Hops—Aromatic Hops (End of Boil)
Lager Yeast—Wyeast #2112 California Lager or Dried Lager yeast
3/4 cup Corn Sugar at bottling

Starting Gravity: 1.050   **Finishing Gravity:** 1.012-1.014
Bittering Units: 40   **Fermentation Temperature:** 70°F

Instructions
(Refer to *General Lager Brewing Procedures* beginning on page 223.)

CALIFORNIA STEAM BEER
Recipe of the Month
BEER & WINE HOBBY—Woburn, MA

6 lbs. English Dried Malt Extract
8 ozs. Dextrine Malt (Carapils)
1-1/2 ozs. Northern Brewer Hop Pellets
1 oz. Finishing Hops
1 package Burton Water Salts
2 Muslin Bags
3/4 cup Priming Sugar
1 California Lager Yeast

S.G. 1.035-1.040
F.G. 1.008-1.012

IMPORTANT NOTE: Please read all instructions before starting!

This beer ferments at normal room temperature - very important!!!

Prepare yeast starter at least 24 hours prior to starting this beer!

Crack 8 oz. Dextrine Malt Grain, place in muslin bag. To a large stainless steel pot add 1-1/2 gallons of water, add cracked grain and bring to a boil. Remove from heat and let steep for 15 - 20 minutes. Remove grains and dispose. Add dried malt extract and 3/4 oz. of the Hop Pellets to the liquid and boil for 30 minutes. Add the rest of the Hop Pellets and Burton Water Salts; boil for an additional 15 minutes.

Have the Primary Fermenter ready with 3-1/2 gallons of cold water, add the boiled liquid and the 1 oz. Finishing Hops tied in a muslin bag. Bring the liquid level to 5-1/4 gallons, add prepared yeast starter and ferment as usual. Remove finishing hops no later than 48 hours after fermentation starts - regardless of method of fermentation being used.

CALIFORNIA COMMON BEER
Compliments of Dick Foehringer
THE BREWMEISTER—*Folsom, CA*

"Steam Beer is sometimes called California Common Beer. This style originated 100 years ago before cooler lager fermentation conditions were available. It uses lager yeast but is fermented at ale temperatures. Aggressively hopped with a residual sweetness of crystal malt. Real close to Anchor Steam® in taste and color."

4 lbs. Alexander's Pale Malt Extract
2 lbs. Australian Light Dry Extract
1/2 lb. Crystal Malt
2 oz. Dextrin
1-1/2 oz. Northern Brewer Hops (60 min.) Boiling
1/2 oz. Cascade Hops (2 min.) Aromatic
1 tsp. Irish Moss (15 min.)
1 tsp. Gelatin
1 Wyeast American Lager Liquid Yeast
1 Bottling Sugar

Put 1-1/2 to 2 gallons of cold water into your brew pot. Place the grain in a grain bag and put into water. Slowly bring water to a near boil and shut off heat. Steep grain for 30 minutes. Remove grain and drain completely. Dissolve extracts and dextrin and return to heat. Bring to a boil and add boiling hops. Boil 45 minutes and add Irish moss. Boil 15 minutes. Add aromatic hops, boil 2 minutes. Remove from heat and cold break wort to below 140°F. Strain wort into primary fermenter and add cold water to make 5-1/2 gallons. When cooled to below 85°F, pitch yeast. **Note:** You must start the liquid yeast 1-2 days prior to brewing. Follow the instruction on the yeast bag for culturing. After fermentation has ceased (2-4 days), rack into secondary. Dissolve gelatin in 1 cup of hot water and stir into secondary. Allow beer to clear for typically 3-5 days. Rack again and stir in dissolved bottling sugar. Bottle and cap.

Allow beer to age and carbonate for 2-4 weeks. Enjoy!

Original Gravity: ~1.047
Final Gravity: ~1.014

The Brewmaster's Recipe Manual

STEAM BEER
BEER & WINEMAKING SUPPLIES, INC.—Northhampton, MA

Ingredients:
3.5 lbs. American Light Malt Extract
3.5 lbs. American Amber Malt Extract
10 oz. medium amber U.S. crystal malt
4 oz. U.S. Victory malt
2 oz. Chocolate malt
1.5 oz. Bullion hops (bittering)
1 oz. Liberty/Cascade hops (aroma)
3/4 cup corn sugar for bottling
10-14 grams dry lager yeast OR Brewer's Choice #2007 or #2112 liquid yeast culture

O.G.: 1.042   F.G.: 1.010-12

(Refer to *General Lager Brewing Procedures* beginning on page 223.)

AMERICAN BOCK
Compliments of Dick Foehringer
THE BREWMEISTER—Folsom, CA

Ingredients
7 lbs. Amber Malt Extract
1 lb. Dark Dry Malt Extract
1/2 lb. Crystal Malt
1/4 lb. Black Patent Malt
1/4 lb. Munich Malt
1-1/2 oz. Hallertauer Hops (60 min.) Boiling
1/2 oz. Hallertauer Hops (end of boil) Aromatic
1 teaspoon Irish Moss (15 min.)
1 German Dry Lager Yeast
1 teaspoon Gelatin
3/4 cup Bottling Sugar

Original Gravity: ~1.062
Final Gravity: ~1.018

Put the crystal, black malt, and Munich malt grains into a bag. Place 1-1/2 to 2 gallons of cold water in your brew pot. Place grain bag in water and bring to a near boil (160°F). Turn off heat and allow grains to steep for 30 minutes. Drain and remove grains. Dissolve liquid extract thoroughly and then return mixture to heat. Bring to a boil. Add the 1-1/2 oz. of hops and boil for 45 minutes. Add Irish moss and boil for 15 minutes. Add the "end of boil" aromatic hops, turn off heat, and steep for 15 minutes. Cold break the wort to below 100°F by setting your pan of wort into a sink full of cold water. Put the cooled wort into your primary fermenter and add cold water to make 5-1/2 gallons. When cooled below 85°F, pitch your yeast. (**Note:** Rehydrate your yeast by dissolving it in warm water and allowing it to sit for 10 minutes before pitching). Ferment in a cool (55-65°F), dark place. When fermentation has ceased, transfer to the secondary, leaving all the sediment behind. Dissolve gelatin in 1 cup hot water and stir into secondary. Replace airlock and allow beer to clear, typically 3-5 days. Rack again, leaving sediment behind. Dissolve bottling sugar in 1 cup of hot water and stir into beer. Bottle and cap.

Allow to age/carbonate in the bottles for 2-4 weeks. Enjoy!

The Brewmaster's Recipe Manual

Specialty Recipes

CHRISTMAS/HOLIDAY BEER

These beers enjoy a long and proud tradition and are usually heavier, darker and with a more unusual character than the everyday beer. These beers were brewed with the finest ingredients and saved especially for the holiday season. For decades, we Americans had to rely on Europe for such a beer as *Affligem Super Noel, Würzburger Bavarian Holiday, Aass Jule Øl, Scaldis Noel, Samichlaus Bier, Felinfoel Festive Ale* or *Samuel Smith's Winter Welcome*. Thankfully for us, there is now a wealth of specially-crafted holiday beers in America, such as *Pete's Wicked Winter Brew, Harpoon Winter Warmer, Geary's Hampshire Special Ale, Sierra Nevada Celebration Ale, Catamount Christmas Ale,* and *Anchor Christmas Ale*.

MIKE'S SOLSTICE WARMER HOLIDAY ALE
Compliments of Mike Edwards
BEER & WINEMAKING SUPPLIES, INC.—Northampton, MA

7 lbs. British Pale Malt Extract
1 lb. Pale Ale Malt grain
1 lb. Belgian Light Crystal Malt
8 oz. Belgian Aromatic Malt
4 oz. Dark Belgian Crystal Malt
1 lb. Dark Brown Sugar
3 oz. Hallertauer Hops
Optional spices of your choice
3/4 cup corn sugar for bottling
10-14 grams dry ale yeast OR 1 Brewer's Choice #1214 Belgian Ale liquid yeast
O.G. 1.070   F.G. 1.018

"As mentioned earlier, you can custom brew this beer to your own liking where the spices are concerned. Mike brews this as follows: 1/2 oz. coriander, 1-1/2 oz. ginger, and the peel of three oranges, placed into the wort 15 minutes before the end of a one hour boil. At the end, he puts another 1/2 oz. of coriander, and another dose of orange peel (same amount) and lets this steep for at least 15 minutes. Other spices you could use are mint, allspice, nutmeg, lemon peel, or something you think of yourself. Fruit extract could also be added at bottling, in lieu of or in conjunction with complimentary spices. You decide how you want to do it—that's the joy of homebrewing—you can do what you want to make this beer your own. Other fermentables you could add to the boil are corn, cane or light brown sugar, in small amounts."

Use your own favorite brewing methods for this beer or see *General Ale Brewing Procedures* beginning on page 218.

HAMMER HEAD*
Compliments of Peter Hood
BREWING SUPPLIES—Stockport/Altrincham, England

*For 16 Imperial Pints

4 lbs. Light Liquid Malt Extract
8 ozs. Brown Sugar
2 ozs. Fuggles Hops
4 ozs. Crystal Malt
Champagne Yeast

STRONG CHRISTMAS ALE*
Compliments of Peter Hood
BREWING SUPPLIES—*Stockport/Altrincham, England*

*For 5 Imperial Gallons

5 lbs. Light Liquid Malt Extract
2 lbs. Soft Brown Sugar
2 lbs. Glucose Sugar
4 ozs. Fuggles Hops
8 ozs. Crushed Crystal Malt
2 oz. Patent Black Malt
Yeast

Use your favorite extract recipe method for these beers or see *General Ale Brewing Procedures* on page 218, but remember to adjust for volume.

HOLIDAY BEER
THE VINEYARD—*Upton, MA*

Ingredients:

6.6 lb. Premier unhopped pale malt extract
1 lb. honey
1/2 lb. crystal malt grain
2 oz. black patent malt grain
2 oz. Cascade hop pellets (40 minutes)
1/2 oz. Saaz hop plug (5 minutes)
1 oz. grated ginger root
2, 3-inch cinnamon sticks
Grated peels of 4 oranges
1 pkt. Whitbread ale yeast
3/4 cup priming sugar
Original Specific Gravity: 1.045
Terminal Specific Gravity: 1.012

Primary fermentation: 5 days at 65°F
Secondary Fermentation: 8 days at 65°F
Boil Time: 40 minutes

Procedure: To 1.5 gallons cold water add crushed crystal and black patent malts; bring to a boil and remove from heat. Strain out grains, add 1/2 gallon water, malt extract, honey, Cascade hops and boil for 40 minutes. Add ginger, cinnamon, orange peels for last 10 minutes of boil. Add Saaz hops last 5 minutes of boil. Strain into primary fermenter, top up to 5 gallons with cold water, let cool, pitch yeast. Rack off solids after 5 days into secondary fermenter. Add priming sugar at bottling time.

GUTENACHT DOPPELBOCK
Compliments of Jim Willenbecher
CROSSFIRE BREWING SUPPLY—*Broad Brook, CT*

"GUTENACHT is a duplication of a famous Bavarian Monastery's Bock. This double bock is very dark, very high in alcohol, and is brewed in accordance with the Reinheitsgebot. It is an excellent example of a German Christmas Bock."

The Brewmaster's Recipe Manual

Ingredients
13.2 lbs. Amber German Malt Extract
10 oz. Wheat Malt Syrup
1 lb. Dark German Crystal Malt
8 oz. Chocolate Malt
1/2 oz. German Blend at 75 minutes
1/4 oz. German Blend at 25 minutes
1/4 oz. German Blend at 23 minutes
1/4 oz. German Blend at 21 minutes
1/4 oz. German Blend at 20 minutes
1/4 oz. German Blend at 19 minutes
1/4 oz. German Blend at 17 minutes
1/4 oz. German Blend at 15 minutes
1/4 oz. German Blend at 13 minutes
1/4 oz. German Blend at 11 minutes
1/6 oz. German Blend at 7 minutes
1/6 oz. German Blend at 4 minutes
1/6 oz. German Blend at 1 minute
7/8 cup Light Dry Malt for Priming
1 Pack German Lager Yeast, 1 Pack Champagne Yeast

German Blend: Equal parts Hallertau, Tettnang, Saaz, Northern Brewer, Styrian Goldings, and Gold. All imported pellets (whole flowers will get in your way).

Grain Preparation:
1. Crush grain fresh, never buy already crushed grain, it will be stale
2. Add 1 gallon of water
3. Add 1 teaspoon gypsum
4. Bring to 175°F and stir
5. Stir well, let settle
6. Draw off liquid, syphon
7. Rinse with 175°F water

Use grain liquid and rinse water for boiling with malt syrups.

Directions for Brewing:
   Boil for 30 minutes before starting timer shown in ingredients.
   When last hop are in boil, cool very rapidly by adding cold water and placing brew pot in tub of ice water. Transfer to sterile fermenter. Do not remove hop pellets. They will settle with yeast.
   Make up fermenter volume to 4.5 U.S. gallons and aerate with a passion.
   When cooled to 86°F to 94°F rehydrate both yeasts together in 1 quart of water at 93°F to 97°F. After 5 to 10 minutes pitch yeast.
   After Krausen falls, boil 1 quart of water and add 1/2 ounce of German Blend in thirds at 7, 4, and 1 minute. Cool and pour into Bier. Do not strain.
   Let ferment out (3 to 4 weeks).
   At bottling add Priming malt to 1 quart of boiling water. Add 1/2 oz. of German Blend in thirds at 7, 4, and 1 minute. Cool and pour into Bottling bucket through tea strainer to remove all traces of hop pellets. Transfer bier into bottling bucket and stir gently. Bottle immediately.

AGING TIME:	12 to 24 Months
BITTERNESS:	28 IBU Pronounced
HOP FLAVOR:	0.7 CFU Impressive
HOP NOSE:	0.4 CAU Impressive
ORIGINAL GRAVITY:	1.086 to 1.096
TERMINAL GRAVITY:	1.019 to 1.023
ALCOHOL:	7.9% by Weight or 9.8% by Volume

CHRISTMAS ALE
Recipe of the Month
BEER & WINE HOBBY—Woburn, MA

Ingredients

2 cans Light Liquid Malt Extract
2 lbs. Wildflower Honey
2 oz. Cascade Pellets (boil)
1/2 oz. Hallertau Plug (finish)
1/2 lb. German Crystal Malt, Dark
1 pkg. Beer & Wine Hobby Special Spice Blend (contains: sweet orange peel, cinnamon, cloves, and allspice)
1/8 lb. Chocolate Malt
1 Pkg. Burton Water Salts
1 Tsp. Irish Moss
Yeast: Liquid Trappist Ale
3/4 Cup priming sugar
2 Muslin bags

O.G. 1.045-1.052
F.G. 1.008-1.012

Instructions
Total Boiling Time: 45 minutes

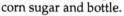

Add 2 gallons of cold water to your pot; put 1/2 lb. crushed German Crystal Malt and 1/8 lb. crushed Chocolate Malt into muslin bag and tie. Place bag in cold water and bring to a boil. When water comes to a boil, remove from heat and let steep for 5 minutes. Remove grains and discard. Return pot to heat and bring to a boil. Add 2 cans of light liquid malt extract, 2 lbs. honey and 2 oz. Cascade hop pellets. Boil for 45 minutes. During the last 15 minutes of your boil, add 1/2 oz. Hallertau plug, 1 tsp. Irish moss, and 1 pkg. Burton Water Salts. Remove from heat and cool, strain out hops. Add to your primary fermenter containing enough water to bring total volume to 5-1/4 gallons. Place special spice blend in muslin bag, tie and place in primary fermenter. Pitch prepared yeast (instructions included) when wort has cooled to between 65°F and 75°F. Proceed as usual. After 4 days in primary, syphon into secondary, leaving spices behind—or take spices out if you are doing it as single stage. Finish fermenting. Prime with 3/4 cup of corn sugar and bottle.

FRUIT/SPICE-FLAVORED BEER

There is no strict definition of this style, although beers made with fruit and other natural flavoring agents probably pre-date the use of barley in most regions of the world. When formulating your own recipes, the best rule of thumb is to use the fruits and spices you like to eat. The fruit can be added to the kettle, the primary, or the secondary, but should be crushed after any seeds or pits are removed. Many microbreweries have taken a shot at fruit-flavored beers, and some of the standouts are: Marin Brewing's *Bluebeery Ale*, Tied House Cafe & Brewery's *Passion Pale*, and Eske's Brewpub *Taos Green Chile Beer*. (See "Tips on Brewing with Fruit" at the end of this section.)

TREE-TOP ALE
Recipe of the Month
BEER & WINE HOBBY—Woburn, MA

INGREDIENTS
6.6 lbs. Light Plain Malt Extract
1 oz. Spruce Essence
   or 1 cup freshly picked Spruce Tips
1 oz. Hallertauer Hop Pellets (boil)
1 oz. Tettnang Pellets (aromatics)
1 oz. loose Finishing Hops
1 pkg. Burton Water Salts
1 tsp. Irish Moss
1 Muslin Bag
Yeast A02 - American Ale, STARTER REQUIRED
3/4 cup Corn Sugar (priming)

S.G 1.035, F.G. 1.008

   Bring 2 gallons of water to a boil. Add 6.6 lbs. Light Plain Malt Extract, 1 oz. Spruce Essence (1/2 bottle) and 1 oz. Hallertauer Hop Pellets; boil for 35 minutes. Add Burton Water Salts and 1 tsp. Irish Moss. Boil for 5 minutes then add Tettnang hops and boil for 10 minutes more. Remove from heat and add hot liquid wort to primary fermenter containing 3 gallons of cold water. Make up to total volume of 5-1/4 gallons. Place finishing hops in Muslin Bag and add to primary fermentor. Pitch prepared and actively fermenting yeast starter into wort and ferment as usual. If using Single Stage Fermentation, remove finishing hops after 2 days of fermentation; if using 2-Stage Fermentation, remove when transferring to Secondary Fermentor. Finish fermenting. Prime with 3/4 cup Priming Sugar. For best results, age at least 4 weeks. This recipe will produce a wonderful, clean and refreshing, crisp beer.

RASPBERRY WEIZEN BEER
THE VINEYARD—Upton, MA

Ingredients:

3.3 lbs. Northwestern hopped Gold Malt Extract
3.3 lbs. Northwestern unhopped Weizen Malt Extract
6 lbs. Raspberries (fresh or frozen)
1 tsp. Irish Moss (last 15 minutes)
2 pkgs. Doric Ale Yeast
3/4 cup corn sugar for priming

Original Specific Gravity: 1.045
Terminal Specific Gravity: 1.010 or less
Primary fermentation: 5 days at 70°F
Secondary Fermentation: 10 days at 70°F
Boil Time: 20 minutes

Procedure: Bring as much water as possible (up to 5 gallons) to a boil and remove from heat. Add the malt extract and stir to dissolve completely and place back on heat to bring to a boil. Boil for 20 minutes, after 5 minutes add Irish moss. Crush raspberries on the bottom of a sanitized primary fermenter. Pour the hot beer wort over the raspberries, cover and allow to cool. When the temperatrure drops below 80°F add yeast. At bottling time boil 3/4 cup corn sugar in 1 cup water for bulk priming.

EASY FRUIT BEER
Compliments of Liz Blades
BLADES HOME BREWERY—Bolton, England

Ingredients
1.8 kg. Munton & Fison Wheat Beer Kit
500 grams Light Dried Malt Extract
0.9 kg. Edme Diastatic Malt Syrup
1 kg. of Fruit per 5 liters of Beer, e.g., Peaches, Raspberries, Strawberries, Blackberries, Apricots—let your imagination go!
1 packet of Yeast provided with kit or your own favorite yeast

Method
1. Sterilise equipment in the normal way (asthmatics should avoid sulphite based products).
2. Remove labels from both cans and place in warm water for 5-10 mins. (this makes contents easier to pour).
3. Place contents of both cans in a large pan, rinse out cans with hot (not boiling) water and empty into pan. Bring the pan to the boil and allow to simmer for 5-10 mins. to sterilise the wort.
4. In the meantime, rehydrate the yeast in a cup of tepid water.
5. Add the sterilised wort and the light dried malt extract to your primary fermenter together with 15 liters of very hot water and stir vigorously until all malt is dissolved.
6. Make up to 22.5 liters with cool water.
7. Pitch in yeast when temperature of wort is around 65°F.
8. Cover and allow to ferment at around 65°F for one week.
9. Transfer to secondary fermenter under airlock with chosen fruit(s) and allow to ferment for around four weeks. I like the temperature at this stage to be around 50-55°F.
10. Bottle in usual way and <u>try</u> to resist drinking for at least 3 months. Remember, patience is a virtue!

Notes: "I've also used this method to produce a reasonable Smoke Beer by fermenting as per 1-8 and at stage 9 adding around 20ml of Liquid Smoke per 5 liters instead of the fruit. The secondary ferment under airlock took around 2 weeks and then I bottled. Do take care with the smoke, otherwise it can be like drinking the residue of the barbeque!!"—*Liz Blades, Chairman of the Home Brewing And Wine Making Trade Asssociation (UK)*

STRAWBERRY PATCH ALE
June's Brew of the Month
E.C. KRAUS—Independence, MO

Description: This brew will win the hearts of many non-beer drinkers as well as the veteran beer connoisseur. The strawberry aroma is well noticeable upon pouring; amber in color with a brilliant red hue. It has a distinct, fruity strawberry flavor that blends perfectly with the tinge of hops, producing a uniquely rounded flavor seldom found in beers.

General Profile:
Starting Gravity: 47-53
Finished Alcohol: 4.5-5.5%
Bittering: 14-18 IBUs
Color: 4-7 SRM/6-10°L

Ingredients:
3.3 lbs. Light Unhopped Malt Syrup
2.0 lbs. Light Dried Malt Extract (5 cups)
8.0 lbs. Fresh Chopped Strawberries
8 ozs. Malto-Dextrin (5 min. boil time)
1 oz. Tettnanger Pelletized Hops (45 min. boil time)
1/2 oz. Hallertau Pelletized Hops (Finishing)
1 Tbsp. Irish Moss (15 min. boil time)
1 Campden Tablet (crushed)
1/4 Tsp. Pectic Enzyme
1 cup Priming Sugar (Bottling Time)
14 grams Ale Yeast or Wyeast #1968

Directions:

1. Start by adding the chopped Strawberries in an open container with 1 gallon of tap water. Add to it 1 Campden Tablet (crushed) and the Pectic Enzyme. Allow mixture to sit in the open for a 24-hour period.

2. The next day, take 1-1/2 to 2-1/2 gallons of water and add the malt syrup and the dried malt. Bring to a boil.

3. Once boiling, add the Tettnanger pelletized hops and boil for 45 minutes. During the last 15 minutes of the boil, add the Irish Moss. At the last 5 minutes of the boil, add the Malto-Dextrin and at the end of the boil, add the Hallertau pelletized hops and allow to steep for 10 minutes with the lid on and the burner off.

4. Once the boiling and steeping is complete, add the wort to your fermenter, then pour in the prepared strawberries. Then add water to equal 5-1/2 gallons. Be sure the mixture has cooled down to below 80°F before adding the yeast.

5. Attach air-lock to fermenter and allow to ferment for 3-4 days, then rack the beer off of the strawberry pulp into a clean fermenter and allow to finish fermentation and clearing.

6. Bottle with priming sugar as normal and allow to condition for 4-6 weeks.

APPLE ALE
Recipe of the Month
BEER & WINE HOBBY—Woburn, MA

INGREDIENTS
1 can Mountmellick Amber Plain Malt
2 lbs. English Dry Malt
1/2 lb. German Crystal Light Malt
2 oz. Lublin Hops (Boil)
1/2 oz. Hallertau Plug (last 10 min.)
1 pkg. Burton Water Salts
1 tsp. Irish Moss
1 Muslin Bag
Liquid Yeast #1056 or #1098
3/4 cup Corn Sugar (priming)
2 bottles *Beer & Wine Hobby* Apple Fruit Natural Fruit Flavoring — add before bottling
Total Boiling Time: 30 minutes

S.G 1.038 - 1.042, F.G. 1.008 - 1.010

Add 2 gallons of cold water to your pot; put 1/2 pound crushed German Crystal Malt into muslin bag and tie. Place bag in cold water and bring to boil. When water comes to a boil, remove grains and discard. Add 1 can Mountmellick Amber Liquid Malt, 2 lbs. English Dry Malt and 2 oz. Lublin Hops. Boil for 30 minutes. During the last ten minutes of your boil, add Irish Moss, Burton Water Salts and 1/2 oz. Hallertau plug. Remove from heat and cool. Strain out Hallertau hops. Add to your primary fermenter containing enough water to bring total volume to 5-1/4 gallons. Pitch prepared yeast when wort has cooled to between 75°F and 80°F. Proceed as usual. Finish fermenting. When beer is done fermenting, siphon into bottling container, add 2 bottles of Apple Natural Flavoring and 3/4 cup of Corn Sugar and bottle.

FRUIT BEER
Compliments of Daniel Soboti
U-BREW—Maplewood, NJ

Category: Fruit Beer
Method: Extract
Starting Gravity: 1.065
Ending Gravity: 1.016
Alcohol Content: 6.3%
Recipe Makes: 5.0 gallons
Age Beer: 4 weeks; better with age
IBUs: 26.0
Malts/Sugars:
  1.00 lb   Crystal 10L
  5.00 lb   Honey
  3.30 lb.   Light Malt Extract Syrup

Hops:
  0.50 oz. Chinook   11.3%   60 min.

Notes:
3 lbs. frozen raspberries added at end of boil and steeped for 20 minutes. Wort and berries added to the fermenter and filled to 5 gallons with cold water. Windsor Ale Yeast added to cooled wort. 3/4 Cup corn sugar added for bottling.

Serve with a wedge of lime or lemon.

"YOUR FAVORITE" FRUIT ALE
Compliments of Dick Foehringer
THE BREWMEISTER—Folsom, CA

"Have you ever tried a Raspberry or Cranberry Ale? How about Cherry, Strawberry, Blackberry or Peach? Well, this is a basic ale recipe that you add 6-8 lbs. of your favorite fruit to. Lightly hopped so the fruit aroma and taste come through. Relatively high in alcohol with 7 lbs. of extract plus the fermentables from the fruit! Try one and you'll make many, many more."

7 lbs. Pale Malt Extract Syrup
6-8 lbs. Fresh or Frozen Fruit of your choice
1-1/2 oz. Hallertauer Hops (boiling)
1/2 oz. Hallertauer Hops (aromatic)
1 Windsor Ale Dry yeast
1 tsp. Gelatin
1 teaspoon Irish Moss
3/4 cups Corn Sugar for bottling

Fruit Prep: Depending upon the type of fruit you are using, there are two methods of preparation. If you are using fruit without big seeds like raspberries, you can prepare them in a blender. Add a small amount of water and blend to a soft, creamy pulp. If the fruit has seeds like cherries, you do not want to grind up the seeds as they are bitter. With this type of fruit, simply mash to a pulp mixture with a potato masher. Collect the fruit in a large bowl and set aside till the end of the boil.

Directions: Put 1-1/2 to 2-1/2 gallons of cold water in your brewpot. Bring to a near boil (~160°F). Shut off heat, stir in extract and thoroughly dissolve. Return to heat and add boiling hops and boil 45 minutes. Add Irish moss and boil 15 minutes. Turn off heat and add the bowl of fruit pulp and aromatic hops. Cover and steep 30 minutes. Cold break the wort by placing the pan into a sink full of cold water. When wort is cooled below 100°F, pour the entire contents into your primary fermenter. Add enough cold water to make 6 gallons. Rehydrate yeast by dissolving in 1 cup warm water and let it sit for 10 minutes. When wort is cool (below 85°F), pitch yeast. Ferment in a cool, dark place. When fermentation is complete, rack into secondary, leaving all fruit pulp and sediment behind. Prepare gelatin by dissolving in 1 cup hot water and stir into secondary. (Note: With some fruits, you may have to repeat the secondary/gelatin clearing procedure a second time to obtain a crystal clear result.) When clear (3-5 days) rack again, leaving sediment behind. Prepare bottling sugar by dissolving in 1 cup hot water. Stir dissolved bottling sugar into clear beer, bottle, and cap. Age a minimum of 2-3 weeks. The fruitiness will be more dominant at first, but will mellow with further aging. Enjoy!!!...We know you will!

Beer Trivia—*Most historians agree that beer was first invented in the ancient civilizations of Babylon, Egypt, and Sumeria—where only women were entrusted with brewing the magical beverage.*

JAMAICAN HONEY AND GINGER BEER*
Compliments of A. Wilkes
RICHMOND HOMEBREW & CRAFT EMPORIUM—Richmond, England

Ingredients for 1 Imperial Gallon

- Beer Yeast Starter Bottle
- Appropriate Water for a Gallon of Beer
- 8 oz. Pure Malt Extract Syrup or 6 oz. Dried Powder
- 2 oz. Ground Ginger
- 1 oz. Cracked Crystal Malt Grains
- 1 lb. Pure Honey
- 1 Tablespoon Strong Tea
- 2 Teaspoons Pure Lemon Juice
- 1 Teaspoon Pure Grape Juice
- 1 Teaspoon Pure Orange Juice

Method

When your **Yeast Starter Bottle** is active and beginning to froth, simmer **5 pints of water** in a large saucepan and stir in **Malt Extract** and 2 oz. **Ground Ginger** until dissolved. Then add **Cracked Crystal Malt Grains**. Cover and **simmer** gently for 15 minutes. Then add all the **Pure Honey**: stir until dissolved, cover and **simmer** for 10 minutes. Then switch off heat and allow to cool. When cool, **strain** your brew into a bucket or brewing bin and cover. **Discard solids.** Add the **activated beer yeast** from your **Starter Bottle** to the brew and the strained **Cold Tea** and **Pure Fruit Juices**. Add sufficient cold water to bring the total amount of liquid to the quantity required. Allow at least 2 inches head space at the top of your Brewing Bin for frothing. Place somewhere **warm** (64°F and covered tightly) for **fermentation (7-12 days)**. Syphon off then bottle. Ready to **drink in two months**.

GINGER ALE
Compliments of Paul White
THE SEVEN BARREL BREWERY SHOP—Lebanon, NH

O.G.: 1.040-42
F.G.: 1.010-12

The Mash

4 lbs. 6-Row Malt
4 lbs. Flaked Wheat

Dough into 3 gallons of water @ 132-135°F and rest @ 122-125°F for 30 minutes. Boost temperature to 150°F for 2 hour rest, boosting back to 150°F whenever the temperature falls to 144°F. Mash-out and sparge to collect 6 gallons.

The Boil

After boiling the wort 15 minutes, add 8 AAUs of Hallertau Flowers and boil 45 minutes. Add 1 teaspoon of Irish moss and 1 oz. freshly grated ginger root, boil 15 minutes, then shut off heat. Chill to 70°F, top up to 5 gallons if necessary and pitch rehydrated Edme Ale yeast. Primary ferment for 5 days, transfer to secondary for 7 days or more. Keg or bottle. Age for at least 2 weeks.

BELGIAN KRUIDENBIER
S. SNYDER

3 lbs. *M&F* Amber DME
3 lbs. *Laaglander* Light DME
2 cups (1/2 lb.) German Light Crystal Malt
2 cups (1/2 lb.) Victory Malt
2 cups (1/2 lb.) Vienna Malt
1.2 cups (1/2 lb.) Corn Sugar
1/2 cup (1/4 lb.) Sucrose
1/2 cup (1/4 lb.) Brown Sugar
1 oz. Hop Bittering Blend (1/4 oz. Styrian Goldings, 1/4 oz. Hallertauer, 1/2 oz. Saaz)
3/4 oz. Hop Flavoring Blend (1/4 oz. ea. Golding, Hallertauer, Saaz)
3/4 oz. Hop Aromatic Blend (1/4 oz. ea. Golding, Hallertauer, Saaz)
1 oz. Oak Chips, 2 Hop Bags, 1 tsp. Irish Moss
Spice Blend (1-1/2 ozs.--cinnamon, nutmeg, allspice, cloves, orange peel, dried apple, star anise, cardamom, coriander)
1 pkg. *WYeast* #1214 liquid Belgian Ale Yeast with starter
1.25 cups DME for priming

O.G. 1.064   **F.G. 1.014**   Potential Alcohol **6.5%** v/v

- Crack and add malts to 2 quarts of 155°F brewing liquor. **Steep 30 minutes.**
- Bring slowly to a 170°F, then immediately sparge into brew kettle.
- Add 2 gallons soft water. Bring to boil. Remove brew kettle from heat before adding extract and DME to avoid sticking or burning.
- Boil for a total of 2 hours, adding hops at **30, 110, & 118** min.
- Add Irish Moss at **105** min.
- Immerse covered brewpot in sink filled with ice water for **30** minutes.
- Put spices in a hop bag and boil separately for 5 minutes in 1 pint of water.
- Rack cooled, strained wort into primary fermenter bucket containing 2-1/2 to 3 gallons ice-cold, soft water to equal 6 gallons.
- Pitch yeast at 75°F, then add spice sack with water it was boiled in to fermenter and 1 oz. of **sanitized oak chips**.
- Ferment between 68°-75°F for 7-14 days.
- Bottle with DME primer, warm condition (68°F) 7 days.
- Cellar condition (56°F) 4-6 weeks.

Tips on Brewing with Fruit—Courtesy Sheaf & Vine Brewing Supply

Adding fruit to beers can be a tricky prospect. It is recommended that the fruit be added to the secondary because adding it earlier will cause much of the fruit aromatics to either be boiled out or scrubbed out by the evolving CO_2 from the primary ferment. The fruit must be sanitized, but boiling the fruit should definitely be avoided. Heating the fruit above 160°F or so will set the pectins and give the beer a permanent haze. One method of fruit sanitation is to put the fruit in water, carefully raise the temperature of the fruit to 150°F for 15-20 minutes, and then drain the water. Campden tablets are another alternative, but they leave sulfites behind to which some people are sensitive. Commercially made fruit juices don't need to be sanitized, but check the label—some are mostly grape juice and others contain preservatives which can kill your yeast. Finally, fruit extracts have recently become available to homebrewers. Many of these, despite reporting to be made from 100% real fruit, add medicinal or unpleasantly bitter flavors to the finished beer. Try adding a few drops of the extract with an eyedropper to a glass of relatively neutral-tasting finished beer and see if the flavors added are indeed what you want before you commit to a full batch.

RECIPE CONTRIBUTORS

Barleymalt & Vine—Newton, West Roxbury, & Framingham, Massachusetts
Beer & Wine Hobby—Woburn, Massachusetts
Beer & Winemaking Supplies, Inc.—Northampton, Massachusetts
Beer Unlimited—Malvern & Conshohocken, Pennsylvania
Blades Homebrewery—Bolton, England
Brew Buddys—Redondo Beach, California
Brewers Resource—Camarillo, California
Brewing Supplies—Stockport & Altrincham, England
Brewmaster—San Leandro, California
The Brewmeister—Folsom, California
The Cellar Homebrew—Seattle, Washington
The Cellars—Cardiff, Wales
Chicago Indoor Garden Supply—Streamwood, Illinois
Crossfire Brewing Supply—Broad Brook, Connecticut
E.C. Kraus—Independence, Missouri
East Coast Brewing Supply—Staten Island, New York
Fermentation Frenzy—Los Altos, California
The Flying Barrel—Frederick, Maryland
Great Lakes Brew Supply—Endicott, New York
The Home Brewery—Ozark, Missouri; San Bernardino, California; Brooksville Florida; North Las Vegas, Nevada; Bardstown, Kentucky; Bogota, NJ; & Grand Forks, North Dakota
Home Fermenter Center—Eugene, Oregon
Jaspers Home Brew Supply—Hudson, New Hampshire
The Jolly Brewer—Wrexham Clwyd, Wales
The Mad Capper—Glastonbury, Connecticut
The Modern Brewer—Cambridge, Massachusetts
Northeast Brewers Supply—West Kingston & Narragansett, Rhode Island
The Seven Barrel Brewery Shop—Lebanon, NH
RCA Distributors—North Walpole, New Hampshire; Santee, California
Richmond Homebrew & Craft Emporium—Richmond, England
Sheaf & Vine Brewing Supply—Countryside, Illinois
Starview Brew—Mt. Wolf, Pennsylvania
U-Brew—Maplewood, New Jersey
Vineyard—Upton, Massachusetts
William's Brewing—San Leandro, California
Wind River Brewing Company—Eden Prairie, Minnesota
Wine Barrel Plus—Livonia, Michigan
Woodland Hills Home Brewing—Woodland Hills, California

Reference Section

The Brewmaster's Recipe Manual

ALE BREWING PROCEDURES

1) If using a liquid yeast or yeast starter, prepare 2-3 days before brewing (see instructions for preparing a yeast starter on page 121). Clean and sanitize all equipment and areas to be used in brewing just prior to starting. Equipment and surfaces left overnight will not be free of germs. It is also a good idea to keep some sanitizing solution in reserve to resanitize contaminated equipment or work areas.

2) Crush any malts, adjuncts or specialty grains and place loose or in a nylon, muslin, or cheesecloth bag. Place this bag in 1 to 4 quarts of cold water (preferably chlorine free), depending on the quantity of grains to be used. If under-modified or unmalted grains are being used, a few tablespoons of highly enzymatic pale malt can be added to the water to provide the necessary enzymes. Although this process can be carried out in your brew kettle, it is highly preferable to steep in a separate pot so the crushed husk particles can be filtered out before the boil.

3) There are two popular ways of doing a steep/partial-mash. The first is to add the crushed grains to the water (in a separate pot), slowly bring the temperature up to just below a boil, then turn off the heat and let them steep for 20-30 minutes; The second, and preferable, method is to heat the water to 150-160°F, then add the grains and let them steep for 20-30 minutes. Some grains, such as crystal malt, require no mashing and their wort can be sparged immediately into your brew kettle. At no point should the mash be boiled. Harsh, grainy, and astringently bitter flavors will be imparted to the beer that will be nearly impossible to mask or lager out.

4) When the steep is completed, remove the grain bag or strain the liquid into your main brewpot, being careful to minimize aeration and catch any solid particles such as grain husks. Add any additional water as is necessary. The higher the percentage of your total batch size that can be boiled the better (i.e., 2.5-5 gallons). This will greatly improve the quality of your beer, but will require a wort chiller to reduce the wort to pitching temperature in the recommended timeframe of 30-60 minutes.

5) Remove the brewing kettle from the burner to prevent sticking and/or burning of residue on the bottom, then add any Liquid or Dry Malt Extract. Cans or bags of liquid extract should be soaked in hot water for 15-30 minutes to facilitate easier pouring. Rinsing the can with hot water helps remove all of the extract. Stir the ingredients to dissolve completely before returning to the heat. For most ales, a hard rolling boil is best. This will result in better clarity, lower DMS, and greater hop utilization. Covering the wort to speed up the boil is not recommended since a boil-over can occur in seconds, and without warning, when the hydrostatic (surface) tension is broken. Covering also reduces the removal of DMS compounds.

6) When the boil commences, add your first addition of kettle (boiling) hops and any necessary yeast nutrients or water salts. (Yeast nutrients are only required in high adjunct beers and are not necessary in all malt beers). Pellet hops can be added loose, their particles will sufficiently settle out in the sediment in your primary. Whole hops or plugs can be placed in a hop bag or added loose to act as a filter bed later when the cooled wort is strained into the primary. Begin timing your boil at this point. 45 to 60 Minutes may be sufficient if pellets are used for bittering; 60 to 90 minutes is preferable when using whole hops or plugs.

7) If using whole hops or plugs for bittering, it is sometimes recommended that you stagger their addition throughout the boil. Often this is done at 90, 60, 45, and 30 minutes remaining in a 90 minute boil; in amounts that will yield the proper IBUs. (See page 247.) Pellets used for bittering can be staggered or added all at once at the beginning of the boil.

8) Flavoring hops should be added 20-10 minutes before the end of the boil, with 15 minutes being the recognized norm to avoid flavor components being boiled away. To avoid boiling off the fragile aromatic components, hops should either be added 1-5 minutes before the end of the boil, steeped for 30 minutes when the heat is shut off and the wort is cooling, placed in the fermenter for 1-3 weeks prior to racking, or even added directly to the cask when making "Real Ale" (the last two methods are referred to as "dry-hopping").

9) When the boil is finished, **cool the wort with a wort chiller** (this will lend better clarity and stability) or as a less desirable alternative, place in a bath of ice-cold water for 20-30 minutes. Be careful not to overfill the cooling bath as the kettle will tip over or water will leak into your wort. The **wort must be cooled to below 80°F before aerating** or oxidation of malt compounds will occur.

10) During this time, pour enough cold water into your sanitized primary fermenter so that total volume, including wort, will equal 5 gallons. This will further ensure that your wort will quickly reach yeast pitching temperature. (Jugs of bottled spring water are ideal for this since they are more likely to be freer of bacteria, chemical contaminants, and chlorine than tap water. They are also easier to place in your refrigerator or freezer for cooling. Reserve some of the spring water for rinsing if you used whole hops or plugs in your boil.) **Never pour hot wort into a cold carboy unless there is cold water in it to absorb the thermal shock; it will shatter!**

11) If you are using dry yeast, you can use this time to rehydrate your yeast in some water that has been boiled for 5 minutes to sterilize, then cooled to between 90-110°F. This rehydration should be carried out in a sanitary place and in a sanitized vessel. After 30 minutes have elapsed since the end of the boil, place a sanitized strainer (and funnel if using a carboy) above your primary. GENTLY strain the wort into your primary, rinsing the hop filter bed with some of the spring water to remove the wort. Stir gently to mix the cooled wort, then take hydrometer and temperature readings.

12) If the wort has cooled to 75-80°F, add your yeast. If the wort is still too hot, place in a tub or somewhere it can be immersed in cold water, but do not add ice unless you are absolutely certain it is sanitary. Stir the wort thoroughly to mix with the yeast, and to aerate enough for a healthy aerobic phase of fermentation. Some yeasts require greater aeration than others (see "Yeast" section.)

13) Cover fermenter, fit with airlock filled with 1 inch of water and move to a dark, quiet place at the temperature recommended for the yeast you are using (typically 60-72°F). If using a carboy, fit with blow-off hose with one end placed in a jug containing clean water.

The Brewmaster's Recipe Manual

LAGER BREWING PROCEDURES

1) If using a liquid yeast, prepare 1-3 days before brewing according to the manufacturer's suggestions. A large yeast starter is highly recommended for all lager recipes and will also require 1-3 days to culture up to pitching levels. A 1 liter starter for 5 gallons of beer would not be too large. See "Tips for Better Homebrewing—Yeast."

2) Clean and sanitize all equipment and areas to be used in brewing just prior to starting. Surfaces left overnight will not remain germ-free. Also, keep a few quarts of sanitizing solution in reserve in case a piece of equipment has to be resanitized.

3) Prepare any malts, adjuncts or specialty grains and place loose or in a nylon, muslin, or cheesecloth bag. Place this bag in 1 to 4 quarts of cold (preferably chlorine free) water, depending on the quantity of grains to be used. If under-modified or unmalted grains are being used, a few tablespoons of crushed, highly enzymatic pale malt can be added to the water to provide the necessary enzymes. It is highly recommended that you mash/steep in a separate pot so the crushed husk particles can be filtered out before the boil.

4) There are two popular ways of doing a steep/partial-mash. The first is to add the crushed specialty grains to the water, slowly bring the temperature up to just below a boil, then turn off the heat and steep the grains for 20-30 minutes; The second, and preferable, method is to heat the water to 150-160°F, then add the grains and let them steep for 20-30 minutes. Some grains, such as crystal malt, require no mashing and their wort can be sparged immediately into your brew kettle. At no point should the mash be boiled. Harsh, grainy, and astringently bitter flavors will be imparted to the beer that will be nearly impossible to mask or lager out.

5) When the steep is completed, remove the grain bag or strain the liquid into your main brewpot, being careful to minimize aeration and catch any solid particles such as grain husks. Add any additional water as is necessary. The higher the percentage of your total batch size that can be boiled the better (i.e., 2.5 to 5 gallons). This will greatly improve the quality of your beer, but will require a wort chiller to reduce the wort to pitching temperature in the recommended timeframe of 30-60 minutes.

6) To avoid darkening the finished product, dissolve all extracts into the brewing water before bringing to a boil. Cans or bags of liquid extract should be soaked in hot water for 30 minutes to facilitate easier pouring. Rinsing the can with hot water helps remove all of the extract. For most light lagers, a short, gently rolling boil of 60 minutes is best (as opposed to 1-1/2 to 2 hours or more for ales). This will also result in lighter color. Covering the wort to speed up the boil is not recommended since a boil-over can occur in seconds and without warning when the hydrostatic (surface) tension is broken. Covering also reduces the removal of DMS compounds.

7) When the boil commences, add your first addition of kettle (boiling) hops and any necessary yeast nutrients or water salts. (Yeast nutrients are not needed except in high adjunct beers.) Pellet hops can be added loose, their particles will sufficiently settle out in the sediment in your primary. Whole hops or plugs can be placed in a hop bag or added loose to act as a filter bed later when the cooled wort is strained into the primary. Begin timing your boil at this point. 60 Minutes may be sufficient if pellets are used for bittering; 60 to 90 minutes is often necessary when using whole hops or plugs. Alternatively, you can compensate for reduced utilization with whole hops by adding more. It is also advantageous to skim the brown resinous scum (hot-break) throughout the boil. This haze-forming coagulated protein can detract from the clarity and delicate flavor of lagers.

The Brewmaster's Recipe Manual

8) If using whole hops or plugs for bittering, it is often suggested that you stagger their addition throughout the boil. Usually, this is done with 90, 60, 45, and 30 minutes remaining in a 90 minute boil; in amounts that will yield the proper IBUs. (See page 247.) Pellets can be added all at once at the beginning of the boil.

9) Flavoring hops should be added 20-10 minutes before the end of the boil, with 15 minutes being the recognized norm. Aromatic hops should be added 1-5 minutes before the end of the boil, steeped for 30 minutes when the heat is shut off and the wort is cooling, or placed in the secondary fermenter 1-3 weeks prior to bottling or kegging.

10) When the boil is finished, **cool the wort with a wort chiller** or as an alternative, place in a bath of ice-cold water for 20-30 minutes. Be careful not to overfill the cooling bath as the kettle may tip over or water will leak into your wort.

11) During this time, pour enough cold water into your sanitized primary fermenter so that total volume, including wort, will equal 5 gallons. This will further ensure that your wort will quickly reach yeast pitching temperature. (Jugs of bottled spring water are ideal for this since they are more likely to be freer of bacteria, chemical contaminants, and chlorine than tap water. They are also easier to place in your refrigerator or freezer for cooling. Reserve some of the spring water for rinsing if you used whole hops or plugs in your boil.) **Never pour hot wort into a cold carboy unless there is cold water in it to absorb the thermal shock; it will shatter!**

12) If you are using dry yeast, you can use this time to rehydrate your yeast in some water that has been boiled for 5 minutes, then cooled to between 90-110°F. This rehydration should be carried out in a sanitary place and in a sanitized vessel. After 30 minutes have elapsed since the end of the boil, place a sanitized strainer (and funnel if using a carboy) above your primary. Strain the wort into your primary, rinsing the hop filter bed with some of the spring water to remove all wort. Stir well to mix the wort, then take hydrometer and temperature readings.

13) If the wort has cooled to 75-80°F, add your yeast. Stir the wort thoroughly to mix with the wort and yeast, and to aerate enough for a healthy aerobic phase of fermentation. If the wort is still too hot, place in a tub or somewhere it can be immersed in cold water, but do not add ice unless you are absolutely certain it is bacteria free.

14) Cover fermenter and fit with airlock, then fill airlock with 1 inch of water or Vodka—do not overfill. An ample 500-1000ml starter will generally allow you to move to fermentation temperatures immediately, otherwise keep at room temperature until fermentation is visually evident (approximately 12-24 hours, depending on the quantity of yeast pitched), then move to the temperature recommended for the yeast you are using. However, be aware that this method may adversely affect the flavor of your beer. If you are using a carboy as your primary, fit with a blow-off hose with one end placed in a jug containing clean water.

The Brewmaster's Recipe Manual

...SION MASHING PROCEDURES

...is by far the most popular all-grain mashing method with
...ewpubs because of its simplicity and relative ease. It is the
...ries in Great Britain, and has gained considerable popularity in
...ion in time, energy cost, and labor a single temperature mash
...technique primarily for brewing with well-modified ale malts,
...ely used in brewing lager beer as well, thanks to the advances in
...oduction of very pale, yet well-modified lager malts.

...red for this mashing method because their lower protein content

...ymes, single temperature infusion mashing is not advised when
..., 15-30% or more).
...num starch conversion and higher fermentability; using from 1 to
...er pound of grain.
...m 148-158°F (65-70°C). Mash pH should be in the 5.0-5.7 range.
...g in small additions of water salts as appropriate.
...inst heat loss.
...ires a longer mash (up to 90 minutes) and will produce a lighter-

...verts faster (30-60 minutes) but will produce a fuller-bodied beer
...es."
...uld be 8-10°F (6-7°C) above what you want the initial heat to be.
...the mash tun back through the mash until the wort runs fairly

...liquor to grist, in a gentle sprinkling motion. Stir gently but

... Typically, sparging is stopped when the wort gravity drops to
...arsh tannins being extracted into the wort.
...covered with hot liquor at all times to keep it from becoming

...hed and sparged with enough brewing liquor for a full wort boil,
...a five-gallon batch.

...easier method than stepped or decoction mashes; and requires less

...es used of 155-158°F (70°C) used to produce greater extract yield
...fermenting dextrins; which may result in more sweetness and

...le Temperature Infusion Mash Schedule

...("dough in"), carefully stirring to mix the liquor and grist. Rest 60-
...occasionally.
...with an iodine tincture by adding 1 drop to a tbsp. of wort on a
...urplish/black), mash out.
...rature to 165-170°F (74-77°C) by adding doses of hot water. Rest 5-

...rate vessel is being used. Slowly sparge with 165-168°F (74-76°C)
...wort into brew kettle.

Correction!

Regrettably, we have discovered a typographical error in the revised edition of *The Brewmaster's Recipe Manual* of which you should be aware. In the all-grain mashing procedures on pages 225, 226, & 227, please note that where the text reads:

(wort turns purple/black) *should read* (wort **no longer** turns purple/black)

Obviously, there is a big difference between the two. When the iodine test produces a purple/black reaction, unconverted starches still remain and the mash should be continued for 30 minutes more then re-checked. Please make a note of this correction in your book.

We apologize for any inconvenience this unfortunate error may cause in your mashing program.

The Brewmaster's Recipe Manual

BASIC STEP-MASHING PROCEDURES

Seen as an alternative to the traditional, labor-intensive decoction method, the stepped-mash or "temperature controlled mash" is better suited for malts with few surplus enzymes, which would be destroyed by boiling, but that still require a protein rest prior to starch conversion. This method is most beneficial for recipes containing higher protein malts, starchy adjuncts and/or "raw" grains, or beers with low serving temperatures.

Basic Points to Remember
- Choose the right type of malt for the beer you're brewing. Step-mashing is a good method for well-modifed, domestic 2-row malt and for well-modified 6-row malts with high tannin levels in their husks that might be extracted in a decoction mash.
- Use fresh grains that are milled properly.
- Experts often advise having a thick mash during the protein rest at 122°F (50°C), which favors the protein-converting proteolytic enzymes, followed by the addition of hot water to give a thinner mash when raising the temperature to 150-158°F, which favors the starch-converting diastatic enzymes. This method allows both types of enzymes to work in their optimum environment.
- Step-mashing elevates the amino acid level of the wort, a factor important to yeast nutrition. However, high malt grists using modern, well-modified barley will naturally have plenty of amino acids; only in high adjunct beers will amino acid deficiency be a problem.
- Step-mashing lends greater colloidal stability (less haze potential) when using higher protein malts such as 6-row, and possibly even American 2-row.

Advantages--Greater extract yields. Allows more control over the balance between fermentable sugars and dextrins than in a single temperature mash. It also allows the use of somewhat cheaper, high protein malts and adjuncts.

Disadvantages--Energy costs, more time is required, lower foam stability may result if your protein rest is too long. Diminished foam stability may also occur when brewing high adjunct/low gravity beers.

Typical Stepped-Mash Schedules

<u>For a Light-Bodied Beer</u>

1st Step--Protein rest. Mash in, stir well. Rest 30 minutes at 122°F (50°C).
2nd Step--Saccharification rest. Rest 20-30 minutes at 150°F (65°C). Stir occasionally. Test for remaining starches with iodine tincture by adding 1 drop to a tbsp. of wort. If negative (wort turns purplish/black), mash out.
3rd Step--Mash out. Raise to 165-170°F (74-77°C). Rest 5-10 minutes to decrease viscosity.
4th Step--Transfer to lauter tun. Slowly sparge with 165-168°F (74-76°C) water over 45-60 minutes and collect wort into brew kettle.

<u>For a Medium-Bodied Beer</u>

1st Step--Protein rest. Mash in, stir well. Rest 30 minutes at 122°F (50°C).
2nd Step--Saccharification rest. Rest 10 minutes at 150°F followed by 20 minutes at 158°F. Stir occasionally. Test for remaining starches with iodine tincture by adding 1 drop to a tbsp. of wort on a white dish. If negative (wort turns purplish/black), mash out.
3rd Step--Mash out. Raise to 165-170°F (74-77°C). Rest 5-10 minutes to decrease viscosity.
4th Step--Transfer to lauter tun. Slowly sparge with 165-168°F (74-76°C) water over 45-60 minutes and collect wort into brew kettle.

The Brewmaster's Recipe Manual

For a Full-Bodied Beer

1st Step--Protein rest. Mash in, stir well. Rest 30 minutes at 122°F (50°C).
2nd Step--Saccharification rest. Rest 20-30 minutes at 158°F (70°C). Stir occasionally. Test for remaining starches with iodine tincture as noted above. If negative (wort turns purplish/black), mash out.
3rd Step--Mash out. Raise to 165-170°F (74-77°C). Rest 5-10 minutes to decrease viscosity.
4th Step--Transfer to lauter tun. Slowly sparge with 165-168°F (74-76°C) water over 45-60 minutes and collect wort into brew kettle.

When Mashing With Pre-cooked Adjuncts

1st Step--Protein rest. Mash in, stir well. Rest 30 minutes at 104°F (40°C).
2nd Step--Protein rest. Add pre-cooked adjuncts and the water they are cooked in. Rest 45 minutes at 122°F (50°C). Stir occasionally.
3rd Step-- Saccharification rest. Rest 60 minutes at 150°F (65°C). Test for remaining starches with iodine tincture as noted above. If negative (wort turns purplish/black), mash out.
4th Step--Mash out. Raise to 165-170°F (74-77°C). Rest 5-10 minutes to decrease viscosity.
5th Step--Transfer to lauter tun. Slowly sparge with 165-168°F (74-76°C) water over 45-60 minutes and collect wort into brew kettle.

When Using Well-Modified Pilsener Malt

1st Step--Protein/saccharification rest. Mash in, stir well. Rest 15 minutes at 140°F (60°C).
2nd Step--Saccharification rest. Rest 15 minutes at 148°F (65°C). Stir occasionally.
3rd Step--Saccharification rest. Rest 30-45 minutes at 150-158°F (65-70°C), depending on attenuation desired in beer. Test for remaining starches with iodine tincture as noted above. If negative (wort turns purplish/black), mash out.
4th Step--Mash out. Raise to 165-170°F (74-77°C). Rest 5-10 minutes to decrease viscosity.
5th Step--Transfer to lauter tun. Slowly sparge with 165-168°F (74-76°C) water over 45-60 minutes and collect wort into brew kettle.

Common Mash Temperatures

	94°F/35°C	122°F/50°C	140°F/60°C	149°C/65°C	158°F/70°C	168°F/76°C	170°F/77°C
Optimum Activity	Phytase optimum --Acid rest temperature for under-modified lager malts	Proteolysis optimum --Protein rest temperature	Beta-amylase optimum --Starch converts to sugars	Diastase optimum --Alpha & beta-amylase work equally well	Alpha-amylase optimum --Starch converts to dextrins	Beta-amylase stopped/ alpha-amylase curtailed	Maximum sparge liquor temperature
Typical Duration	60-120+ minutes	15-60 minutes	15-90 minutes	45-90 minutes	15-30 minutes	5-15 minutes	45-60 minutes
Effect on Mash/Wort	Lowers mash pH when using low calcium brewing liquor	Malt proteins and adjunct starches broken down	Yields wort very low in dextrins, high in fermentables	Wort with well-balanced ratio of dextrins to fermentables	Wort high in dextrins, low in fermentables	Reduces viscosity, aids run-off of mash	Possible tannin extraction from mash if 170°F exceeded

BASIC DECOCTION MASHING PROCEDURES

This is the traditional German method devised in the mid-nineteenth century to deal with under-modified malts and is rarely needed with today's homogenous, well-modified malts. However, decoction is still considered the preferred (but not mandatory) method for certain German beer styles because of the character it lends to the finished product. It is often recommended in brewing Bavarian Weissbiers because the boiling physically breaks down the wheat starch; and in Bock and Märzen brewing because the boiling lends a deeper color, and a maltier flavor and aroma without employing large quantities of the specialty grains that can sometimes impart harshness. There are single decoction, double decoction, and triple decoction programs. It is rare that a triple decoction will ever be required except when mashing poorly modified lager malts or when brewing an authentic Bavarian Doppelbock; nevertheless, a triple decoction schedule has been included for the adventurous brewer.

Basic Points to Remember
- Decoction mashing requires a larger water to grain ratio of up to 3 parts liquor to 1 part grist (3 quarts of water per pound of grain).
- 2-row malts are preferable since 6-row malts may yield high levels of tannins when boiled.
- Decoct the thickest part so the majority of the enzymes residing in the thinner, liquid portion will be preserved.
- Lauter especially gently and slowly when using wheat to avoid a set mash.
- Use fewer coloring grains than you would in an extract brew.
- Remember that you may achieve greater hop utilization in the full wort boil of an all-grain beer.

Advantages--Decoction often provides higher extract yields, better mash pH, less hot break, and a clearer runoff from the lauter tun. Decoction also provides more complete breakdown of starches when mashing adjuncts or malted wheat. It also provides smoother, fuller malt flavors and a traditional deep color to German dark lagers without the use of high percentages of dark malts. These dark malts often lend harsh tannic and astringent flavors to the finished beer.

Disadvantages--There are many. Decoction mashing requires greater time, energy consumption, and skill, as well as more equipment; not to mention the risk of tannin extraction and the likelihood of scorching in a direct-fired homebrew setting. Decoction darkens the wort, which may not be desirable for the beer style that you are brewing.

Typical Decoction Mash Schedules

Single Decoction

1. Mash in at 100°F (38°C) with a 3-1 liquor to grist ratio.
2. Immediately raise the temperature 2°F (1°C) per minute to 122°F (50°C).
3. Maintain protein rest 20-30 minutes (30-45 minutes is sometimes suggested for wheat beers).
4. Pull first thick decoction of roughly 40% of the mash with a 2-1 ratio of liquor to grist.
5. Ladel into second kettle and bring to 160°F (71°C).
6. Maintain saccharification rest 10-15 minutes.
7. Bring to boil for 30-40 minutes.
8. Recombine with the "rest mash" to yield a temperature of 147°F (64°C), applying bottom heat if necessary.
9. Rest 10-20 minutes.
10. Raise to 158°F (70°C) and rest for 10-15 minutes or until iodine test is negative.
11. Raise to 170°F (77°C) and mash out.
12. Sparge with 165-170°F (74-77°C) water.

The Brewmaster's Recipe Manual

Double Decoction

1. Mash in at 100°F (38°C) with a 3-1 liquor to grist ratio.
2. Raise the temperature 2°F (1°C) per minute to 122°F (50°C).
3. Maintain protein rest 10-15 minutes before pulling first decoction.
4. Pull first thick decoction of roughly 40% of the mash with a 2-1 ratio of liquor to grist.
5. Ladel into second kettle and raise heat 2°F (1°C) per minute to 160°F (71°C).
6. Hold saccharification rest for 10-15 minutes.
7. Bring to a boil over 10-15 minutes and boil for 20-40 minutes (depending on desired darkness of wort).
8. Recombine decocted portion slowly into pot with main mash over 10-15 minutes, while stirring.
9. The main mash should now be around 147°F (64°C). Adjust with bottom heat if necessary.
10. Immediately pull a second decoction and perform exactly as in the first.
11. Recombine with main rest mash. Raise temperature with bottom heat to 160°F (71°C).
12. Hold for 10-15 minutes or until iodine test is negative.
13. Mash out. Raise to 165-170°F (74-77°C). Rest 5-10 minutes to decrease viscosity.
14. Transfer to lauter tun and sparge as normal.

Triple Decoction

1. Mash in at 95°F (35°C) with a 3-1 liquor to grist ratio. Stir well. Hold rest 30-60 minutes.
2. Pull first thick decoction of roughly 33% of the mash with a 2-1 ratio of liquor to grist.
3. Ladel into second kettle and raise heat 2°F (1°C) per minute to 150°F (66°C).
4. Hold saccharification rest for 30 minutes.
5. Bring to a boil over 10-15 minutes and boil for 20 minutes.
6. Recombine decocted portion slowly into pot with main mash over 10-15 minutes, while stirring.
7. The main mash should now be around 122°F (50°C). Adjust with bottom heat if necessary. (Carefully maintain correct temperature in main "rest" mash while performing all decoctions.)
8. Hold protein rest for 60 minutes.
9. Pull a second decoction and perform exactly as in the first.
10. Recombine slowly with main rest mash. Raise temperature with bottom heat to 155°F (68°C) if necessary.
11. Hold saccharification rest for 60 minutes.
12. Pull a third decoction and bring to a boil.
13. Recombine with main rest mash. Raise temperature with bottom heat to 160°F (71°C) if necessary.
14. Hold for 10-15 minutes or until iodine test is negative.
15. Mash out. Raise to 165-170°F (74-77°C). Rest 5-10 minutes to decrease viscosity.
16. Transfer to lauter tun and sparge as normal.

FERMENTATION PROCEDURES

1) First and foremost, keep fermenting beer in the dark.

2) Secondly, keep the fermentation temperature constant as much as possible. Studies indicate that fluctuations of 10°F, and sometimes as little as 5°F, can result in off-flavors and poor yeast performance.

3) In most cases, beer should be kept sealed from outside air via an airlock, one-way valve, or blow-off hose system. However, when fermenting certain Wheat Beers, British Ales, and Belgian beers, some believe open fermentation works best in accurately brewing these styles, but this is very risky when homebrewing. The change in pH and the production of alcohol and CO_2, fermenting beer produces an environment unfriendly to most bacteria; nevertheless, keep all fermenting beer in a dark, draft-free area; preferably one that can be sanitized beforehand and kept undisturbed throughout the fermentation process.

4) If using a blow-off hose system to remove resins and fusel oils in the krausen during the primary stages of fermentation, always immerse the free end of the blow-off hose under several inches of clean water. A blow-off hose of at least 1/2 inch (1 inch for fruit beers) inside diameter is recommended.

5) For brewers using a covered primary fermenter with an airlock, fusel oils and resins that can impart harsh flavors to your beer can be removed during the period known as "high krausen." This is the stage approximately 36-72 hours into your fermentation where the yeast forms billowing clumps called "rocky heads." If you lift the lid of your fermenter, you will see these rocky heads topped with the brown resinous scum that should be removed. This residue can be skimmed off the yeast, **but only with a sanitized implement and under strictly sanitary conditions!** The yeast itself should be left on the beer.

6) Follow the directions for proper fermentation temperature provided by the yeast manufacturer <u>not</u> the extract manufacturer. Exceeding these limits may speed up fermentation, but will most likely result in unacceptably high diacetyl and ester levels, stunning higher alcohol levels, and generally poor flavor.

7) Most beers should be allowed to complete their <u>primary</u> fermentation in a single vessel. It is safe to assume that if kept at the proper temperature, the beer will have finished its primary fermentation when the hydrometer readings stay constant for 2-3 days. This will take approximately 5-10 days for ales and 2-4 weeks for lagers, aiming for a final gravity of about 25% of your original gravity. If you prefer not to expose your beer to bacterial risk by repeatedly taking readings, let your ales ferment a full 10 days before bottling and your lagers 14 days before racking to the secondary for at least 2 more weeks of secondary fermentation.

8) Longer ale fermentation times (10-14 days) where the beer is allowed to sit on its yeast sediment for a few extra days will help reduce the diacetyl that gives beer a buttery flavor note that is inappropriate for many styles. But it is advised that, if the fermentation extends beyond 14 days, the beer be transferred off the yeast sediment to another container.

9) For ales, the beer can now be racked to a bottling bucket and packaged. For lagers, it is highly recommended that the beer be racked to another vessel for an extended period of "secondary fermentation" at temperatures slowly brought down to 32°F. Because plastic fermenters are permeable to oxygen, this stage should be done in a glass carboy. This secondary fermentation can last for 1-8 weeks (depending on temperature used—beer conditions faster at warmer temperatures, but should not exceed 45°F) and allows more complete settling of the yeast and other haze causing matter, resulting in a clearer and cleaner tasting finished product.

10) Clarifying aids can be added to the beer during its final week in the secondary, as well as any aroma hops. Dry hops can be placed in your secondary either loose or in a hop bag. The hop bag will keep loose bracts from clogging your racking tube and bottle filler, but may be difficult to remove through a narrow carboy neck. Longer dry hopping times (2-3 weeks) and careful movement of your carboy will promote better settling of loose hops.

11) A possible, although unlikely, side-effect to very long periods of secondary fermentation is that too much of the yeast may settle out or die, making bottle or keg conditioning with priming sugar unsuccessful or sluggish. Homebrewers can rectify this by force carbonating the flat beer with CO_2 or by adding a fresh dose of the yeast you used for primary fermentation along with the priming solution at bottling time (see next section).

Beer Trivia—*Bavaria's 750 breweries represent 75% of the breweries in Germany and approximately 20% of the world total.*

The Brewmaster's Recipe Manual

BOTTLING PROCEDURES

Before starting any bottling procedure, it is best to check your beer's final gravity to be sure it is ready to be bottled, ideally within .002 specific gravity points of what your recipe predicted. If you have no clear guidlelines for the style or a particular recipe, a good rule of thumb is to shoot for a final gravity of 25% of your original specific gravity. Sometimes yeast will stop fermenting if they have been exposed to adverse conditions, then begin fermenting again when they are racked or the fermenter is disturbed. Bottling with too high a ratio may result in an inappropriately unattenuated beer or a bottle that resembles the "Old Faithful" geyser when opened.

1) The first thing to do is collect enough bottles and caps/Grolsch gaskets to hold all your beer. If you brewed 5 gallons that will equal 54-12 oz. bottles, 40-16 oz. pints, or 37-half-liters. Rarely will you be able to get a full 5 gallon yield, but it's better to be prepared. Screw-cap, non-returnable bottles require special caps and a different type of bottle capper than what homebrew shops sell.

2) The next step is to make sure the bottles are visually clean. That is to say, free from sediment, visible dirt, etc. If they are not clean, they should be thoroughly washed and rinsed.

3) Finally, the bottles should be carefully sanitized. You can use any of the popular sanitizers on the market, or stick with the standard 30-minute chlorine bleach and water soak (1 tbsp. per gallon). Another alternative is to sterilize the bottles in a household dishwasher—if it has a sanitary cycle. However, it is important to make sure there are no food particles in the drain that might be splashed onto or inside the bottles. This sterilizing should be done without soap and rinsing agents.

4) If you used the chlorine bleach method or other harsh chemicals, it is recommended that you thoroughly rinse the bottles 2-3 times with hot water to remove the residual chlorine.

5) All instruments, gadgets, containers, hoses, buckets, etc. that will come in contact with the beer in any way should also be thoroughly sanitized and rinsed, as well as the area to be used for the bottling procedure. (Bathrooms are usually the most convenient.) The room should also be free of drafts carrying airborne germs.

6) At this point, unless you will be force-carbonating your beer with CO_2, you need to prepare a priming solution of corn sugar or dried malt extract dissolved in water. For added security, this water should be boiled at least 5 minutes to kill any germs and to remove chlorine odors. The recommended amount of water is 1 or 2 pints, with 1/2 to 3/4 cups of corn sugar or 1.2 to 1.5 cups dried malt extract. Adding individual doses to each bottle is highly discouraged.

Another popular method of priming is one in which sterile, unfermented wort (called "Speise"—German for "food") is added to the beer. In homebrewing, this Speise can be taken from your wort before the yeast is pitched, then kept refrigerated in a sterile, airtight container until ready for use, or it can be made up fresh on bottling day (but this requires removal of the trub). This method is sometimes incorrectly called "Krausening;" a method German brewers use whereby a portion of actively fermenting beer (containing a high yeast cell count and unfermented sugar) in the Krausen stage is added to fully fermented beer in order to facilitate carbonation. With ales, the addition of new yeast is usually not necessary, so a sterile, filtered malt extract and water solution can be used. However, with lagers that have been subjected to very long periods of cold conditioning, the initial yeast colony may be dead or completely settled out. A new yeast addition to lagers is considered by some to be a measure of security for ensuring adequate fermentation in the bottle or keg, and a more rapid absorbtion of air in the headspace.

The Brewmaster's Recipe Manual

Rates for 5 gallons equal roughly 1.5 quarts of Speise for high O.G. beers (>1.060) and 3 quarts for lower O.G. beers (<1.030). The approximate amount of Speise needed (depending on fermentability of the malt you use) is listed below (in quarts):

O.G.	Speise Needed
1.070	1.00-1.50 quarts
1.060	1.50-1.75 quarts
1.050	1.75-2.00 quarts
1.040	2.00-2.50 quarts
1.030	2.50-3.00 quarts
1.020	3.00-3.50 quarts

Although this method of adding wort may make your beer "all malt" and in accordance with the Reinheitsgebot, it does have its drawbacks. **1)** Malt takes longer to be processed by the yeast than sugar, resulting in slower conditioning. **2)** This new malt has not fermented and aged as long as the rest of the beer, and therefore, may contribute minor "new beer" characteristics that will require slightly more time to dissipate. **3)** This method is less exact and may require more trial and error than simply dosing out 3/4 cup of corn sugar. **4)** This method often results in residue in your bottles if the trub from the Speise is not filtered.

7) Now that you've prepared your priming solution you can add it to your bottling bucket. This solution may be very hot, so be careful not to pour it directly onto a fresh dose of yeast. Set your fermenter above the bottling bucket, insert one end of the racking tube into the beer and begin your siphon.

8) The safest way to start a siphon is to fill the siphon tube with water, pinch the "out" end, then first insert the "in" end in the beer and then the "out" end in the bottling bucket. When you release the bottling bucket end, the siphon will begin.

9) Try not to aerate or splash the beer during any racking procedure. This will result in oxidation of the hops, resulting in a possible loss or deterioration of aroma and stale flavors in the beer. When the siphoning is complete, gently mix the priming sugars, new yeast, and beer.

10) From here you can begin filling your bottles. Most bottling buckets now have spigots from which to run a racking hose, if yours doesn't or you're siphoning directly from the fermenter, you'll have to pinch the tube between fills. If you have a rigid racking cane and bottle filler, insert into the bottle and fill until the beer reaches the top rim. When the racking tube is removed, proper headspace will be created.

11) Cap the bottles, rinse to remove spilled beer, then dry and move to a dark space for conditioning.

The Brewmaster's Recipe Manual

GENERAL KEGGING PROCEDURES

KEGGING SYSTEMS
by Paul White
Head Brewer, *The Seven Barrel Brewery*, Lebanon, New Hampshire

Most serious brewers will consider a kegging system at some time. The best, but most expensive, is the "Cornelius" type. They are 5 gallon stainless steel kegs with a CO_2 cylinder, regulator, and in and out hoses. Kegs may be either ball lock or pin lock. Ball lock kegs usually have a pressure relief valve that you can operate manually. Pin lock keg relief valves usually cannot be manually operated.

Cleaning

1. Rinse the keg with hot water and inspect. Put the lid in a pan of hot water.
2. Fill keg halfway with hot water then add 1/4 ounce of BTF. Install the lid and shake the keg to coat all surfaces.
3. Pressurize the keg with 5 psi of CO_2, shake again to re-coat surfaces.
4. Run about a cup of sanitizer out through the dispensing line. Shake again.
5. When the keg has had 20 minutes of contact with the sanitizer, remove all lines, relieve the pressure, open the keg and pour off the sanitizer. It may be saved and reused.
6. Depress the "out" poppet to drain sanitizer from the pick-up tube.
7. Rinse once, then fill halfway with clean, hot water. Reseal, pressurize, and run some water through the dispensing line, then remove the line.
8. Relieve the pressure, open the keg and drain. Keep the keg upside down until cooled. It's now ready to fill.

Filling

Syphon your finished beer into the keg. Be sure your hose is long enough to reach the bottom of the keg. While the beer is running, put the lid in a small pan of water and bring to a boil. This sanitizes the lid and softens the O ring for a better seal. Do not fill the keg so full that the short "in" stem is in the beer. Install the lid and pressurize with 5-10 psi. Check for leaks. Then pull the relief ring or lever in the center of the lid. This removes air from the keg and replaces it with CO_2. Do this three times; waiting a few minutes each time. To remove air from pin lock kegs, remove the disconnect and depress the poppet with a blunt tool.

Carbonating

Method 1: Treat the keg like one big bottle, but use 1/3 cup of corn sugar boiled in one cup of water. Add this to the keg before filling. Pressurize to 5 psi, leaving the pressure on for the first two days. Store at 70 degrees for 7 days.

Method 2: After sealing and bleeding the air out, raise the regulator pressure to 25 psi. Shake the keg for 20 seconds, take a break, then shake again. Repeat a third time. Disconnect the CO_2 line, shake, then store in a cool dry place.

Method 3: You will need a place that has a constant temperature below 60 degrees—the colder the better. On the carbonation chart find your temperature and desired carbonation level (usually 2.5 to 3.0). Set the regulator to the proper psi and leave connected. Allow two weeks for conditioning.

The Brewmaster's Recipe Manual

Tips

- Check poppets for leaks any time you disconnect. A drop or two of beer on a leaker will foam. Flick the poppet with a fingernail to stop most leaks.
- If carbonating by Method 1, you may want to shorten the pick-up tube by 1/2 inch.
- The clearer the beer going in, the clearer the finished product will be. I use Irish moss in the boil, 4-8 days in a secondary at 55 degrees, and if it's not clear by then, I add some gelatin finings.
- A new toilet brush works well for getting to the bottom of kegs when cleaning.
- All types of faucets come apart. Clean them and beer lines regularly.
- Bleach is not recommended for sanitizing kegs as it corrodes stainless steel, especially at the weld.

Gadgets

Jumper Cable—This allows you to move clear, carbonated beer from one keg to another under pressure. Your second keg ends up with sediment-free beer that can be transported without getting cloudy. You can also blend beers.

Pressure Checker—A pressure guage connected to an "in" side disconnect. Just pop the checker onto the keg to check pressure.

Pressure Bleeder—A disconnect with a bleeder valve connected. Used with a jumper cable to keep flow going.

Combination Pressure Checker/Bleeder—The two units above on one disconnect.

Counter-pressure Bottle Filler—A pain-in-the-butt device for filling bottles from the keg under pressure.

Other Systems

There are several optional kegging systems on the market. I will do a short description of them based on my order of preference.

The 5-liter Party Kegs—Four 5-liter plastic-lined metal kegs that will hold a 5 gallon batch. Tappers are either air pump or CO_2 bulb injectors.

The Party Ball—2-1/2 or 5 gallon plastic balls. May be tapped by full CO_2 system, CO_2 bulb injectors, or air pumps.

The Party Pig—A 2-1/4 gallon brown plastic ball. The beer is dispensed by an inside bladder filled with a special soda and salt combination that swells as the keg empties.

Pressure Kegs by Edme, Rotokeg, and Others—White plastic barrels in various sizes and shapes. Beer is dispensed by CO_2 bulb injectors or natural pressure.

Headpacks—A 5 gallon plastic bag in a cardboard box. Beer is drawn off a spigot at the bottom by natural pressure and gravity.

Carbonation Chart

Pounds per Square Inch / Temperature of Beer (degrees F.)

To use the chart, look up the temperature of the beer, and read across to the desired level of carbonation. Follow up the line to find what pressure to set your regulator. © 1994 Byron Burch, The Beverage People.

°F \ PSI	0	1	2	3	4	5	6	7	8	9	10	11	12	13	14	15	16	17	18	19	20	21	22	23	24	25	26	27	28	29	30
30	1.82	1.92	2.03	2.14	2.23	2.36	2.48	2.60	2.70	2.82	2.93	3.02																			
31	1.78	1.88	2.00	2.10	2.20	2.31	2.42	2.54	2.65	2.76	2.86	2.96																			
32	1.75	1.85	1.95	2.05	2.16	2.27	2.38	2.48	2.59	2.70	2.80	2.90	3.01																		
33		1.81	1.91	2.01	2.12	2.23	2.33	2.43	2.53	2.63	2.74	2.84	2.96																		
34		1.78	1.86	1.97	2.07	2.18	2.28	2.38	2.48	2.58	2.68	2.79	2.89	3.00																	
35			1.83	1.93	2.03	2.14	2.24	2.34	2.43	2.52	2.62	2.73	2.83	2.93	3.02																
36			1.79	1.88	1.99	2.09	2.20	2.29	2.39	2.47	2.57	2.67	2.77	2.86	2.96																
37				1.84	1.94	2.04	2.15	2.24	2.34	2.42	2.52	2.62	2.72	2.80	2.90	3.00															
38				1.80	1.90	2.00	2.10	2.20	2.29	2.38	2.47	2.57	2.67	2.75	2.85	2.94															
39					1.86	1.96	2.05	2.15	2.25	2.34	2.43	2.52	2.61	2.70	2.80	2.89	2.98														
40					1.82	1.92	2.01	2.10	2.20	2.29	2.38	2.47	2.56	2.65	2.75	2.84	2.93	3.01													
41						1.87	1.97	2.06	2.16	2.25	2.34	2.43	2.52	2.60	2.70	2.79	2.87	2.96													
42						1.83	1.93	2.02	2.12	2.20	2.29	2.39	2.47	2.56	2.65	2.74	2.82	2.91	3.00												
43						1.80	1.90	1.99	2.08	2.16	2.25	2.35	2.43	2.52	2.60	2.69	2.78	2.86	2.95												
44							1.86	1.95	2.04	2.12	2.21	2.30	2.39	2.47	2.56	2.64	2.73	2.81	2.90	2.99											
45							1.82	1.91	2.00	2.08	2.17	2.25	2.34	2.43	2.51	2.60	2.68	2.77	2.85	2.94	3.02										
46								1.88	1.96	2.04	2.13	2.21	2.30	2.39	2.47	2.55	2.63	2.72	2.80	2.89	2.98										
47								1.84	1.92	2.00	2.09	2.17	2.26	2.34	2.42	2.50	2.59	2.67	2.75	2.84	2.93	3.02									
48								1.80	1.88	1.96	2.05	2.13	2.22	2.30	2.38	2.46	2.55	2.62	2.70	2.79	2.87	2.96									
49										1.93	2.01	2.09	2.18	2.25	2.34	2.42	2.50	2.58	2.66	2.75	2.83	2.91	2.99								
50									1.85	1.90	1.98	2.06	2.14	2.21	2.30	2.38	2.45	2.54	2.62	2.70	2.78	2.86	2.94	3.02							
51									1.82	1.87	1.95	2.02	2.10	2.18	2.25	2.34	2.41	2.49	2.57	2.65	2.73	2.81	2.89	2.97							
52										1.84	1.91	1.99	2.06	2.14	2.22	2.30	2.37	2.45	2.54	2.61	2.69	2.76	2.84	2.93	3.00						
53										1.80	1.88	1.96	2.03	2.10	2.18	2.26	2.33	2.41	2.48	2.57	2.64	2.72	2.80	2.88	2.95	3.03					
54											1.85	1.93	2.00	2.07	2.15	2.22	2.29	2.37	2.44	2.52	2.60	2.67	2.75	2.83	2.90	2.98	3.03				
55											1.82	1.89	1.97	2.04	2.11	2.19	2.25	2.33	2.40	2.47	2.55	2.63	2.70	2.78	2.85	2.93	2.98	3.01			
56												1.86	1.93	2.00	2.07	2.15	2.21	2.29	2.36	2.43	2.50	2.58	2.65	2.73	2.80	2.88	2.93	2.96			
57												1.83	1.90	1.97	2.04	2.11	2.18	2.25	2.33	2.40	2.47	2.54	2.61	2.69	2.76	2.84	2.88	2.91	2.99		
58												1.80	1.86	1.94	2.00	2.07	2.14	2.21	2.29	2.36	2.43	2.50	2.57	2.64	2.72	2.80	2.84	2.86	2.94	3.01	
59													1.83	1.90	1.97	2.04	2.11	2.18	2.25	2.32	2.39	2.46	2.53	2.60	2.67	2.75	2.80	2.81	2.89	2.96	3.03
60													1.80	1.87	1.94	2.01	2.08	2.14	2.21	2.28	2.35	2.42	2.49	2.56	2.63	2.70	2.75	2.77	2.84	2.91	2.98

The Brewmaster's Recipe Manual

GENERAL CONDITIONING & LAGERING PROCEDURES

1) Most **ales** require about 5-7 days to produce CO_2 in the bottle at normal fermentation temperature when corn sugar is used as the priming agent, longer with malt extract or Speise. This process of bottle or cask re-fermentation is known as "conditioning." The term "carbonated" is used to refer the process where CO_2 is injected artificially into the beer from an outside source.

2) **Lagers** usually require a few days more to condition, especially if they are primed with malt extract or Speise, and depending on the temperature of the room where they are stored. Lagers should be conditioned as close to the fermentation temperature as possible, typically in the 46-58°F range, for a minimum of 10-14 days to let the slower-acting lager yeasts to work.

3) When you are satisfied with the CO_2 level of your beer, you can now move it to a cooler environment for maturation. This is a period where any "green beer" flavor qualities in hops or malt can mellow. Traditional English cask conditioned ales often receive as little as two days **"cellaring"** before being served up in a pub, but it is accepted wisdom that 3 weeks is best for standard gravity homebrewed ales. Ideally, this should be done at temperatures in the 50-55°F range—and as cold as 32°F for German ales such as Alt or American Cream Ale. Higher gravity ales, such as Barleywine, Strong Ale, and Belgian Tripel, for example, benefit from even longer aging times of 6 months to several years. Some off flavors and aromas in lagers can take 4 months to lager out, and beers using bacteria, such as Berliner Weisse, often require long 6 to 12 month aging times. The time needed is very yeast strain dependent.

4) Lagers universally require a <u>minimum</u> of 3 weeks of cold **"lagering"** at 32-45°F to achieve their best flavor. Temperatures higher than this have been shown to deteriorate flavor and aroma. Light lagers with a higher malt content, such as Munich Helles or Czech Pilsner, require a minimum of 4 weeks of lagering, and preferably 7-8 weeks as noted by George Fix in *Vienna, Märzen, Oktoberfest* (Brewers Publications, 1991). Many experts agree that darker lagers, such as Oktoberfest and Bock, benefit from even greater lagering periods ranging from 8 weeks to 1 year.

After CO_2 has been produced in the packaged beer, the main purposes of lagering beer are for clarification and to allow the flavor to mature, especially in regards to the mellowing of hop bitterness. Although this may be considered unnecessary in filtered, artificially carbonated lagers brewed with sophisticated techniques, this time is absolutely vital for "living beers" with active yeast sediment.

Carbonating With Residual Sugars

A simpler method of priming can be used with casked beers which involves racking the beer while it is still fermenting and allowing the residual sugars to provide carbonation. One disadvantage is that the original and final gravities must be precisely known, another is that the transfer must occur when the proper level of sugars (approximately 20%) remain. Excess CO_2 can be bled off if the pressure gets too high in a Cornelius keg, but other bulk systems, such as 5 liter mini-kegs, will require guess work and experience. As with other natural carbonation methods, avoid excessive head space above the beer.

The formula for this method involves subtracting the projected final gravity from the original gravity, then calculating 80% of the result and subtracting that figure from original gravity. <u>For example: a beer with a 1.050 original gravity and a 1.014 final gravity would be calculated 1.050 - 1.014 = 1.036. 1.036 x 80% = 1.029. 1.050 - 1.029 = a gravity of 1.021 when the beer is racked.</u> This translates roughly to 1.007 specific gravity points above expected terminal gravity for lagers and well-carbonated ales. Less-carbonated British ales are typically racked to cask when there are roughly 1.004 points remaining.

The Brewmaster's Recipe Manual

TIPS FOR BETTER HOMEBREWING

Alcohol Level & Beer Body
•You may notice that the liquid malt extract instructions (hopped or unhopped) call for the use of corn or cane sugar in large quantities. We strongly urge that you ignore this and use only pure (dried or liquid) barley malt extract, except for purposes of carbonating, where it is appropriate to the style (e.g., high alcohol Belgian Ales), or where it is to be used in small amounts to lighten body.

Boiling
•Except where noted, it is advised that the wort be boiled for at least one hour in all of the recipes, regardless of the malt extract manufacturer's instructions.
•Remove the brew kettle from heat source prior to adding malts to avoid burning or sticking of ingredients, which may impart a burnt flavor and darker color to your beer.
•Stir in extracts before applying heat to kettle water. This will keep the wort color lighter. Another way is to place a diffuser under the kettle to distribute heat evenly.
•A technique once used in brewing dark, heavy, German beers is to boil the wort for up to three or four hours. Using this method, the protein coagulated in the hot break is eventually dissolved back into the wort, resulting in an extremely smooth, velvety, and full-bodied beer. A longer boil also lend a darker color and more toasted/caramel flavors. The bittering hops should be added just 90 to 60 minutes before the end of such a boil.

Beer Clarity
•Use of a secondary fermenter, preferably a 5-gallon glass carboy for 5-gallon recipes, is practically mandatory in successful lager brewing. In 2-stage fermenting, the beer is racked off the sediment formed in the after primary fermentation is complete, therefore reducing the time that dead yeast and trub stay in contact with the beer, as well as lessening the chance that this sediment will make it into your bottling bucket.
•In his book *Continental Pilsener* (Brewers Publications, 1989), David Miller suggests racking your homebrew off the cold trub before pitching your yeast (or 8 to 12 hours afterward) to further eliminate unwanted sediment. According to Miller, this procedure lowers fusel alcohol production and eliminates the need to skim the krausen off the beer. A simple method for homebrewers is described in the following paragraph. **Note:** <u>This trub sediment is not the same as the yeast sediment that forms during fermentation. Fermenting beer should not be racked off this yeast sediment until fermentation is complete, except where specifically called for in a recipe.</u>
•For added beer clarity, you can perform a homebrewer's version of what the commercial brewers call cold trub removal. They do it in a whirlpool or by floating these coagulated proteins out with forced air; you can do it by racking your beer into another fermentation vessel anytime before active fermentation begins (less than 12 hours is best). Simply put your wort and yeast in a vessel other than what you'll use for primary fermentation (preferably a glass carboy so you can see when the layer of sediment forms at the bottom). In as little as an hour you'll see the trub settle to form a whitish layer about 1/2 inch thick. You can now very carefully siphon off the beer into your primary, leaving the trub behind.
•Another very effective method for achieving brilliantly clear beer is the addition of fining agents. One of the best (besides using high quality malts and proper sanitation) is <u>Irish Moss</u>, which should be added for 10-20 minutes at the end of your boil. Another very good product, especially for light lagers, is <u>Polyclar</u>, which can be stirred into your secondary 2 to 5 days prior to bottling or kegging. <u>Gelatin</u> and <u>Isinglass</u> are two other popular and effective means of achieving clarity without the expense of filtration.

Water
•Most tap water in United States is suitable for homebrewing, whether on a city water line or taken from a private well. The common wisdom is, "If it tastes good, it's o.k." However, municipal/public water that has a strong chlorine taste or smell should be corrected by a vigorus boil before adding specialty grains or

The Brewmaster's Recipe Manual

TIPS FOR BETTER HOMEBREWING
(Continued)

extract. Just make sure the water is cooled again to the proper temperature for grain treatment (150-170°F). (Remember that carbonate hardness will be removed after 10 minutes of boiling, then decanting the water off the precipitated sediment.)

- Your City Water Board can provide you with a detailed analysis of your water, usually for free. If you live in a rural area with a private well, the Health Department in your county can do a water sample, but this will almost always require a fee.
- Another easy, though slightly costlier, solution to water worries is to use <u>bottled water</u>. Bottled water is freer of contamination and can be chilled in bulk if you have the refrigerator space, and you also have the freedom to purchase the water that tastes best to you. Nevertheless, always sterilize water used in yeast starters or for priming.
- The two most popular forms of bottled water for brewing are <u>spring water</u> and <u>distilled water</u>. Unless you insist on only the best from the French Alps, spring water can be had for 50¢ to $1 per gallon.
- Spring water is usually soft to medium-soft and small additions of water salts or gypsum can be made without great concern. (A sampling of spring water parameters is listed on page 33.)
- Distilled water is created by boiling water to steam, the steam condenses in a still, then is collected again as a liquid, leaving the precipitated water salts behind. Distilled water is the softest water available and therefore makes a good starting point for creating the exact water profile you desire for a particular beer style. Distilled water costs approximately $1 per gallon.
- Mineral water will usually be prohibitively expensive and should be avoided unless you know its ion content.

Hops
- Regardless of the form in which you purchase hops, always keep them in the refrigerator or freezer (for long-term storage) until you ready to use them.
- Always tightly re-wrap and refrigerate opened packages of hops. Aluminum foil and plastic bags used together will offer some protection against oxidation and freezer burn.
- To be sure of maximum freshness, many experts advise against purchasing <u>whole</u> hops later than 8 months after the most recent harvest, particularly since most whole hops are not packaged in oxygen-barrier gas-purged bags. In most hop growing regions, this would be 8 months after late August/early September, i.e., around April 30th. Properly stored hops in <u>unopened</u> gas-purged oxygen-barrier bags will stay fresh for well over a year.
- Bittering hops should be added 90 to 60 minutes before the end of the boil when using Plugs or Whole Hops; 60 to 45 minutes before the end of the boil when using pellets.
- Use of a carboy/blow-off hose system for primary fermentation may reduce your beer's bitterness because many of the bitter resins will be ejected with the krausen. Save the carboy for secondary ferments or increase your IBUs in the boil.

Yeast
- Use liquid yeast or quality name-brand dry yeast whenever possible. The dry yeasts included with cans of malt extract may be old or damaged by exposure to temperature extremes; and even when fresh, rarely compare with the consistent quality and variety of liquid cultures. Besides, the vast majority of award-winning brews are made with liquid yeast. Name brand dry yeasts will give satisfactory results, but should be rehydrated.

Yeast Rehydration
- Yeast Lab™ suggests this method for rehydrating yeast. 1) Dissolve the dry yeast in 1/2 cup of warm water (105°F/40C) without stirring. 2) After 15 minutes, mix well to suspend all the yeast before adding to the wort. 3) Do not keep the yeast in the water longer than recommended.

The Brewmaster's Recipe Manual

TIPS FOR BETTER HOMEBREWING
(Continued)

Yeast Quantity
- The homebrewer should consider using 2 packs of liquid yeast (100ml) or 7-14 grams of rehydrated dry yeast when brewing higher gravity beers (i.e., 7 lbs. or more total Malt Extract). A better alternative is to prepare a yeast starter of 1 to 2 liters.

Methods for Pitching Lager Yeast—Courtesy Sheaf & Vine Brewing Supply
There are two methods for pitching yeast into a lager. For lack of better terminology, let's call them "Traditional" and "Shortcut." The Traditional method of pitching yeast into a lager is to slowly cool the large starter to 50-55°F and then pitch that into the wort when it has cooled to the <u>same</u> temperature. Pitching a 70°F starter into a 50° wort will kill some of the yeast and shock the rest so you have a long lag time and possibly an incomplete and sluggish ferment. The Shortcut method is to pitch a large 65° starter into 65° wort and then wait for activity before beginning to slowly (5° per day) cool the wort down to the 50-55° range. The advantages of the Shortcut method are faster starts and the ability to get by with a smaller starter. The disadvantages are that you will get a fruitier beer than the Traditional method since part of your fermentation has occurred at ale temperatures.

Cooling
- An easy way to quickly cool your wort to yeast-pitching temperatures if you don't have a wort chiller is to put 2-1/2 to 3 gallons of commercially bottled spring water in the refrigerator at its lowest setting overnight, then pour into fermenter just prior to adding wort.
- Another way to cool down your wort before adding to fermenting vessel is to let the brew kettle sit <u>COVERED</u> in a sink or tub of ice-cold water for up to 30 minutes.
- REMEMBER! A basic scientific principal states: liquids cool faster in ice-cold water than in ice (or snow) because more surface area is covered, resulting in faster, more efficient heat transfer.

Flavor
- Never allow any grains to reach a boil when steeping or mashing. Ideally, specialty grains should be mashed or steeped at 150-170°F in a separate pot when extract brewing, and only the wort derived from them added to your brewpot and boiled. Boiling draws out tannins from grain husks, which will impart harsh flavors to your brew.
- Avoid pulverizing specialty grains or malts that will be used in your brew. Turning the husks into flour will greatly increase the possibility that tannins will make their harsh flavor presence known in your final product.
- Avoid over-sparging of grains. This can wash out the dreaded tannins in the husks that lend a harsh, bitter flavor. One good rinse is usually enough for specialty malts. Also, do not use water above 170°F.
- Avoid over-stirring of wort or mashed grains. Also avoid violent "casting out" of <u>hot</u> wort into your fermenter. Oxidation of malt components results in sherry-like or wet cardboard aromas in the finished beer.

Fermentation
- Keep fermentation temperatures steady. Fluctuations of only 5°F can cause off-flavors and premature yeast flocculation; and always keep fermenting beer in the dark.
- Whenever possible use a secondary fermenter. Even when crafting the fastest turnaround British ales, a day or two in a secondary can greatly improve a beer's maturation time and smoothness of character. In lager brewing, a secondary is mandatory in achieving clarity and clean flavor profiles without the use of artificial aids.

The Brewmaster's Recipe Manual

TIPS FOR BETTER HOMEBREWING
(Continued)

Bottling
• Brown vs. Green Bottles—Although it's hard to beat the convenience and beauty of those Grolsch bottles, serious homebrewers should consider weaning themselves off of green bottles. Green glass does not filter out the harmful high-energy (e.g., ultraviolet) rays that exist in sunlight and florescent light. This leads to a chemical reaction with the hops resulting in a skunky taste and aroma—sometimes after only a few minutes of exposure. If at all possible, use brown bottles, but try to keep all beer away from direct light until it is served, and if you must hold it up to a light to check the clarity, etc., use incandescent light.
• Since most Homebrew Competitions will not accept entries in anything except green or brown 12 oz. bottles with no raised lettering, designs or identifying features, make sure you always put at least half a dozen of your beers in 12 oz. bottles just in case you come up with a real winner!
• PureSeal™ bottle caps (a.k.a. "Smartcaps") absorb oxygen in the headspace and have been proven to make hop aroma last much longer. It is important to note that boiling these caps in order to sanitize them will ruin their oxygen-absorbing capabilities.

Cask Conditioning and Cellarmanship
• Leave casks well-secured and undisturbed in serving position until empty. Once in this position, allow to settle at least 1 day before serving. Use only whole or plug hops to dry hop. Place in a sanitized hop bag and leave for 7-10 days.
• Select the correct cask size; i.e., for the quantity of beer to be consumed in 1 or 2 days once tapped.
• Maintain a temperature in the cellar between 50-57°F. Temperature significantly affects the CO_2 level, which for a traditional cask conditioned ale should be 0.75-1.5 volumes. High temperatures will result in flat beer and a degredation of finings. Excessively low temperatures may result in a permanent chill haze or an overly gassy beer.
• Cellars should be ventilated, but devoid of any drafty areas. Sudden temperature changes (hot or cold) can cause sediment-disturbing convection currents to be set up in your cask.

Conditioning, Lagering, and Aging
• One of the hardest parts of homebrewing is waiting for the beer to be ready to drink. Although some ales mature very quickly and can be enjoyed after one to two weeks of conditioning, you've no doubt noticed how your beer improves with age. Many lagers slowly turn more golden and less red as they age, and hop bitterness mellows as the beer evolves from week to week. Most experts agree that ales require a <u>minimum</u> of 5 weeks from start to finish: 1 week to ferment; 1 week to condition; and 3 weeks to mature. Lagers generally require a <u>minimum</u> of 10 weeks: 2 weeks in the primary; 2 weeks in the secondary; 2 weeks to condition; and 4 weeks to mature. Higher gravity beers, such as Bock usually require at least 8 weeks of maturing; and Barleywine, from 6 months to several years. Homebrewed Lambics can require 1 to 3 years to reach maturity. Maturation time can be reduced by minimizing tannin extraction and by the use of low-alpha boiling hops instead of high-alpha varieties.

Refrigeration
• Regardless of whether you prefer ales or lagers, the serious homebrewer should also seriously consider obtaining a second "beer-designated" refrigerator. Even a small fridge with constant temperatures can vastly improve the conditioning of ales; and is absolutely essential for brewing and storing lagers in warm weather—when they are most appropriate. Check your local yellow pages for used appliance dealers. Second-hand refrigerators can be had for as little as $50 to $100.

Serving Temperature
• British ales are generally served at "cellar" temperatures (i.e., 50-57°F). Quality lagers, wheat beers, and most other ales should be served in the 45-50°F range. Ice-cold beer deadens the taste-buds and detracts from the flavor. The internationally accepted definition of "room temperature" is 68°F/20°C. Dry Stout is served at this temperature, but usually only in Ireland. Generally, it is served at cellar temperatures or colder.

The Brewmaster's Recipe Manual

BREWING RECORD & EVALUATION FORM
(Photocopy For Personal Use)

Batch Name/Number:_____ Volume:_____
Original Gravity:_____ °Plato_____
Final Gravity:_____ °Plato_____
Style:_____ Sub-style:_____

Ingredient Mashed & Amount   *Temperature & Time*   *Method*
_____   _____   _____
_____   _____   _____
_____   _____   _____
_____   _____   _____
_____   _____   _____

Primary Fermentation Ingredients/Techniques: Date:_____
_____
_____
_____
_____
_____
_____

*Hops Used/Form:*_____ *AA%:*____ *Quantity:*____ *Purpose:*____ *Time:*____
*Hops Used/Form:*_____ *AA%:*____ *Quantity:*____ *Purpose:*____ *Time:*____
*Hops Used/Form:*_____ *AA%:*____ *Quantity:*____ *Purpose:*____ *Time:*____
*Hops Used/Form:*_____ *AA%:*____ *Quantity:*____ *Purpose:*____ *Time:*____

*Yeast:*_____ *Brand/No.*_____ *Liquid/Dry/Rehydrated*_____ *Quantity:*____
*Length of Ferment:*_____ *Special Ingredients/Instructions:*_____

Secondary Fermentation and Lagering Ingredients/Techniques: Date:_____
_____
_____

*Length of Secondary Ferment:*_____
*Dry Hops Used/Form:*_____ *AA%:*_____ *Quantity:*_____ *Time:*_____
*Length of Lagering Phase:*_____
*Notes/Other Important Information:*_____

Apparent Attenuation:_____
Bottling Date:_____ Priming Method:_____
Number of Pints/12 oz. Bottles:_____
Other (Party Pig™, RotoCask™, Cornelius Keg™, etc.):_____

EVALUATION—*Based on the 50 point maximum scale used in AHA competitions*

	6 pts.	10 pts.	19 pts.	5 pts.	10 pts.	50 pts.	
Date	Appearance	Aroma	Taste	Condition	Overall	Total	Comments

The Brewmaster's Recipe Manual

WEIGHTS & MEASURES
(All measures are in U.S. equivalents unless otherwise noted)

LIQUID MEASURES
1 gallon = 3.785 liters
1 gallon = 4 quarts = 128 fl. oz.
1 gallon of water weighs 8.35 lbs.
1 Imperial (British) gallon x 0.833 = 1 U.S. gallon
1 Imperial gallon = 1.20095 U.S. gallons
1 quart = 2 pints = 4 cups = 32 fl. oz. = .95 liters
1 pint = 16 fl. oz = 2 cups = 1/2 quart
1 ounce = 2 tablespoons = 6 teaspoons
1 barrel = 31-1/2 gallons
1/2 barrel = 1 keg = 15.5 gallons = approximately 7 cases
1/4 barrel (pony keg) = 7.75 gallons

1 tablespoon = 3 teaspoons = 1/2 fluid oz.
1 cup = 16 tablespoons = 8 fluid oz.
1 teaspoon = 1/3 tablespoon or 1/8 fluid oz.
1 fluid oz. = 2 tablespoons or 6 teaspoons
1 liter = 100 centiliters = 1,000 milliliters
1 liter = 2.11 pints = 1.057 quarts = .264 gallons
1 hectoliter = 100 liters

Gallons x 3.8 = liters
Liters x 0.26 = gallons

Miscellaneous British Beer Cask Sizes (In Imperial Gallons)
1 Hogshead = 54 gallons (1.5 barrels)
1 Barrel = 36 gallons
1 Kilderkin = 18 gallons
1 Firkin = 9 gallons
1 Pin = 4.5 gallons

DRY WEIGHT MEASURES
1 pound = 16 ounces = 454 grams
1 ounce = 28.349 grams
1 kilogram = 1,000 grams = 35.27 ozs. = 2.21 lbs.
1 gram = 100 centigrams = 1,000 miligrams
1,000 mg = 0.35 oz.

Pounds x 0.45 = kilos
Kilos x 2.2 = pounds

The Brewmaster's Recipe Manual

WEIGHTS & MEASURES
(Continued)

MEASUREMENT CONVERSION

Known Quantity	To Find	Mutiply By
Teaspoons	Milliliters	4.93
Teaspoons	Tablespoons	0.33
Tablespoons	Milliliters	14.79
Tablespoons	Teaspoons	3.00
Cups	Liters	0.24
Cups	Pints	0.50
Cups	Quarts	0.25
Pints	Cups	2.00
Pints	Liters	0.47
Pints	Quarts	0.50
Quarts	Cups	4.00
Quarts	Gallons	0.25
Quarts	Liters	0.95
Quarts	Pints	2.00
Gallons	Liters	3.79
Gallons	Quarts	4.00

TEMPERATURE CONVERSION

Celsius = 0.556 x (F° - 32) Subtract 32 from Fahrenheit degrees, then multiply by five-ninths (0.556).

Fahrenheit = (1.8 x C°) + 32 Multiply Celsius degrees by nine-fifths (1.8), then add 32.

CONVERSION OF SOME COMMON TEMPERATURES
Mashing—148-158°F = 64-70°C
Sparging—160-170°F = 71-77°C
Boiling—212°F = 100°C
Pitching (Ale)—65-75°F = 18-24°C   Pitching (Lager)—55-60°F = 13-16°C
Fermenting (Ale)—60-80°F = 16-27°C   Fermenting (Lager)—40-60°F = 4-16°C
Lagering—32-45°F = 0-7°C
Cellaring—50-55°F = 10-13°C
Serving (Ale)—50-55°F = 10-13°C   Serving (Lager)—45-50°F = 7-10°C

SUGAR AND MALT CONVERSIONS
Dry Malt Extract (DME) & Brewer's (Corn) Sugar:
  1 lb. = 2.4 cups
  1 cup = 6.5 ozs.
Cane Sugar:
  1 lb. = 2 cups
  1 cup = 8 ozs. = 1/2 lb.
  1 oz. = 2 level tablespoons
Note: 3/4 cup corn sugar for priming = 1.20-1.5 cups light DME—depending on fermentability. For example: *Laaglander DME* is typically 55% fermentable; *Munton & Fison* is typically 75%.

WEIGHTS & MEASURES
(Continued)

SPECIFIC GRAVITIES OF WORT INGREDIENTS
(1 pound per gallon of water at 60°F)

Variations from these figures will depend on a variety of factors including: the vigorousness and length of the boil, efficiency of your mashing/brewing techniques, and the quality and modification of your ingredients. An extract efficiency of approximately 80% is assumed here for malt and grain adjunct values.

Amber Malt—1.025-28
Black Patent Malt—1.023-26
Cane Sugar—1.042-45
Chocolate Malt—1.024-27
Corn (Brewer's) Sugar—1.035-40
Corn Syrup—1.034-37
Crystal Malt—1.015-26

Dextrine Malt—1.015-20
DME/Spray Malt—1.038-45
Flaked Barley—1.023-26
Flaked Maize—1.027-30
Flaked Rice—1.027-30
Flaked Wheat—1.024-27
Invert Sugar—1.036-39

Lager Malt—1.027-30
Malt Extract Syrup—1.027-39
Malto-Dextrin—1.036-39
Mild Ale Malt—1.026-29
Munich Malt—1.020-25
Pale Ale Malt—1.027-30
Pilsener Malt—1.027-30
Roasted Barley—1.024-27

Torrefied Barley—1.023-26
Torrefied Wheat—1.024-27
Turbinado—1.041-44
Vienna Malt—1.025-28
Wheat Flour—1.026-29
Wheat Malt Extract Syrup—1.022-25
Wheat Malt—1.025-28

Der Müller.

A MALT EXTRACT ANALYSIS—MUNTON & FISON
(Infusion Mashed)

LIQUID MALT EXTRACT

	Light	Amber	Dark
Color (EBC)	3-7	12-16	24-28
Flavor	medium	full	strong
Lactic Acidity	0.4-1.0	0.4-1.0	0.4-1.0
Alpha Amylase	negligible	negligible	negligible
Diastatic Power	negligible	negligible	negligible
pH	5.1-5.4	5.1-5.4	5.1-5.4
IBUs (Hopped Versions)	25-35	20-26	20-26
Fermentability % *	55-80	55-80	55-80

DRIED MALT EXTRACT

	Light	Amber	Dark	X-Dark	Diastatic	Hopped Amb.	Hopped Lt.
Color (EBC)	4-10	16-24	40-80	80-120	4-12	35-40	4-10
Flavor	mild	full	strong	very full	mild	strong hopped	med. hopped
Diastatic Power	—	—	—	—	50-120[a]	—	—
Moisture %	3-5	3-5	3-5	3-5	3-5	3-5	3-5
Reducing Sugars[b]	65-75	65-75	65-75	65-75	70-90	65-80	65-80
Lactic Acidity %	.4-.9	.4-.9	.4-.9	.4-.9	.4-1	.4-1	.4-1
pH	5-6	5-6	5-6	5-6	5-6	5-6	5-6
TFS[c]	55-80	55-80	55-80	55-80	55-80	50-80	55-80
Fermentability %*	60-85	60-85	60-85	60-85	60-85	55-85	60-85
Mg[d]	350-700	350-700	350-700	350-700	350-800	350-700	350-700
Na[d]	200-600	200-600	200-600	200-600	200-600	200-600	200-600
Ca[d]	150-400	150-400	150-400	150-400	200-450	150-350	150-350

* Expresses as a dry weight percentage. The average is typically 75%.
(a)—Expressed as °Lintner.
(b)—As Maltose.
(c)—Total Fermentable Solids as a dry weight percentage.
(d)—Expressed as ppm dry weight.

FORMULAS

DETERMINING SPECIFIC GRAVITY USING MALT EXTRACT
When using malt extract, it's nice to know how much malt you will need to produce the ORIGINAL SPECIFIC GRAVITY of your wort before you start to brew, especially if you intend to brew a specific style of beer. Dry Malt Extract (DME) produces about 44 degrees per pound/per gallon of water. Liquid Malt Extract produces approximately 35 degrees. To predetermine the Original Gravity of your beer when designing recipes, use this simple formula to determine how much malt extract to use: (degrees of extract) times pounds of malt used divided by gallons of beer to be brewed. For instance: if we use 4-1/2 pounds of DME to make 5 gallons of beer we would have 44 x 4.5 = 198...so, 198 divided by 5 (gallons of beer to be made) = 39.6, or an Original Gravity of about 1.040.—*Courtesy Brewer's Resource, Camarillo, CA*

DETERMINING ALPHA ACID UNITS (AAUs)
Add the Alpha Acid % per ounce of hops you will be boiling for more than 15 minutes and then divide by the number of gallons to be made. For instance: 1-1/2 oz. of hops with 5.5% AA = 1 oz. hops with 45 AA = 12.25 total Alpha Acid Units. Divide the AAUs by the gallons of beer to be made, 5 gallons would yield 2.5 AAUs per gallon of beer.—*Courtesy Brewer's Resource, Camarillo, CA*

DETERMINING INTERNATIONAL BITTERNESS UNITS (IBUs)
This formulation (Courtesy—*The Beverage People,* Santa Rosa, CA) is based on a model used by Byron Burch in *Brewing Quality Beers: The Home Brewer's Essential Guidebook* (Second Edition, Joby Books, Fulton, CA 1994). Ounces of hops x alpha acid x percent utilization (as a function of boil time) divided by 7.25. For instance: If we brew a Pale Ale with 1-1/2 ozs. of Fuggles (4.8AA) boiled 60 minutes for bittering and 3/4 oz. of Goldings (5.5AA) boiled 15 minutes for flavor we would have the following; 1.5x4.8 = 7.2 & 7.2x30 = 216. 216 divided by 7.25 = 29.79 IBUs. Add to this the Flavoring hops; .75x5.5 = 4.13; 4.13x8 = 33.04; 33.04 divided by 7.25 = 4.56 IBUs for a total of 34.35 IBUs. Percent utilizations are:

up to five minutes 5%;
6 to 10 min. 6%;
11 to 15 min. 8%;
16 to 20 min. 10.1%;
21 to 25 min. 12.1%;
26 to 30 min. 15.3%;
31 to 35 min. 18.8%;
36 to 40 min. 22.8%;
41 to 45 min. 26.9%;
46 to 50 min. 28.1%;
51 to 60 min. 30%.

FORMULAS
(Continued)

Note: Although professional brewers and some homebrewers can achieve hop utilization rates as high as 40% with hop pellets, it is safer to assume that you will only achieve a maximum of 30% with pellets and 25% when using Plugs or Whole Flowers. Using these figures, as well as aiming for the mid-range of IBUs in the style you are brewing, will improve your chances of achieving appropriate bitterness. Some of the other factors that <u>increase</u> hop bitterness utilization, according to Gerard W.C. Lemmens, B.Sc. in his treatise "Hop Utilisation" (*American Brewer*, Spring 1993), include:

1. High Wort pH
2. Long Boil Times
3. Low Wort Gravity
4. Using "Fresh" Hops
5. Strain of Yeast Used

Conversely, it also should be noted that the factors that <u>decrease</u> hop utilization include: short boil times, high wort gravity, hop bags, stale hops, and the strain of yeast used.

DETERMINING HOMEBREW BITTERING UNITS (HBUs)
Homebrew Bittering Units, or HBUs, is a formulation invented by the *American Homebrewers Association*, and equals the total <u>ounces</u> of hops to be boiled for 15 minutes or more multiplied by their <u>alpha acid</u> rating.

<u>Example:</u> 3 oz. of 4.4% AA hops = 3 x <u>4.4</u> (not 4.4<u>%</u>!) = 13.2 HBUs

DETERMINING PERCENTAGE OF ALCOHOL BY VOLUME
Subtract alcohol percentage of Terminal Specific Gravity reading from alcohol percentage of Original Specific Gravity reading:
<u>Example:</u> 7% (1.055) - 1% (1.010) = 6%
<u>OR</u> Original Specific Gravity minus Terminal Specific Gravity (without decimal points) divided by 7.5.:
<u>Example:</u> 1055 - 1010 = 45 ÷ 7.5 = 6%

DETERMINING PERCENTAGE OF ALCOHOL BY WEIGHT
Mutiply alcohol by volume figure by .80 or 80%:
<u>Example:</u> Alcohol by volume = 6 x .80 = 4.8%

The Brewmaster's Recipe Manual

HYDROMETERS

The **Specific Gravity Scale** refers to the weight of a liquid in relation to the weight of water, which is set at 1.000 or 1000. This is the scale used by British Brewers and is the scale used by the majority of American Homebrewers.

The **Balling** or **Brix Scale** (a saccharometer) expresses the percentage of sugar in the liquid (by weight) and is usually expressed in degrees **Plato** (°P). This is the scale used by American and German brewers.

The **Alcohol Scale** measures the <u>approximate</u> amount of alcohol expressed as a percentage that will be present in the beer when fermentation is complete. Two readings must be taken; one before yeast is pitched, and one when fermentation has ceased. (See example #2 below.)

Temperature Corrections for Standard Hydrometers
Most hydrometers are calibrated to read accurately at 60°F. If your wort is not at this temperature, you'll need to adjust your readings according to the correction figures below. (See example #1.)

Temp. in Degrees F.	S.G. Correction
40	Subtract 1
50	Subtract 1/2
60	Add 0
70	Add 1
77	Add 2
84	Add 3
88	Add 4
95	Add 5
100	Add 6
105	Add 7

Example #1:
Wort temperature is 77°F.

Specific Gravity:	1.053
Correction Figure:	+2
Actual Specific Gravity:	1.055

Determining potential alcohol: Subtract the second alcohol reading (young beer) from first alcohol reading (wort).

Example #2:
1st Reading (Original Gravity): 1.055   Corresponding alcohol %: 7.0
2nd Reading (Terminal Gravity): 1.014   Corresponding alcohol %: 1.5

Therefore; 7.0 - 1.5 = 5.5% alcohol by volume

TRIPLE SCALE HYDROMETERS
(Continued)

TRIPLE SCALE HYDROMETER READINGS:

Potential Alcohol %	Specific Gravity	Degrees Plato	Potential Alcohol %	Specific Gravity	Degrees Plato
0.00%	1.002	0.50	11.50	1.090	22.50
0.25	1.004	1.00	11.75	1.092	23.13
0.50	1.006	1.50	12.00	1.093	23.25
0.75	1.008	2.00	12.25	1.095	23.75
1.00	1.010	2.50	12.50	1.097	24.25
1.25	1.012	3.00	12.75	1.098	24.50
1.50	1.014	3.50	13.00	1.100	25.00
1.75	1.016	4.00	13.25	1.102	25.50
2.00	1.018	4.50	13.50	1.104	26.00
2.25	1.020	5.00	13.75	1.105	26.25
2.50	1.022	5.50	14.00	1.107	26.75
2.75	1.024	6.00	14.25	1.109	27.25
3.00	1.026	6.50	14.50	1.111	27.75
3.25	1.028	7.00	14.75	1.113	28.25
3.50	1.030	7.50	15.00	1.115	28.75
3.75	1.032	8.00			
4.00	1.034	8.50			
4.25	1.036	9.00			
4.50	1.038	9.50			
4.75	1.040	9.88			
5.00	1.041	10.25			
5.25	1.043	10.75			
5.50	1.045	11.25			
5.75	1.047	11.75			
6.00	1.049	12.25			
6.25	1.051	12.75			
6.50	1.053	13.25			
6.75	1.055	13.38			
7.00	1.056	14.00			
7.25	1.058	14.50			
7.50	1.060	15.00			
7.75	1.061	15.38			
8.00	1.063	15.75			
8.25	1.065	16.25			
8.50	1.067	16.75			
8.75	1.069	17.25			
9.00	1.071	17.75			
9.25	1.073	18.50			
9.50	1.075	18.75			
9.75	1.076	19.13			
10.00	1.078	19.50			
10.25	1.080	20.00			
10.50	1.082	20.50			
10.75	1.084	21.00			
11.00	1.086	21.50			
11.25	1.088	22.00			

NOTE: As you can see from the above figures, there are roughly 4 points of specific gravity per degree of Plato. **Example:** .5°P x 4 = S.G. 1.002.

The Brewmaster's Recipe Manual

Homebrew Supply Shops

The Brewmaster's Recipe Manual

ALABAMA

Home Winemakers
2520 Old Shell Road
Mobile, AL
205-478-9387

Black Warrior Brewing Supply
University Station
P.O. Box 1487
Tuscaloosa, AL
205-752-2999

ALASKA

Arctic Brewing Supply
5915 Lake Otis Parkway #3
Anchorage, AK 99507
907-561-5771

ARIZONA

Brewmeisters Supply Co.
3522 W. Calavar Rd.
Phoenix, AZ 85023
602-843-4337

Brewkettle Homebrew Supply
6915 Lorton Lane
Flagstaff, AZ 86004
602-526-8374

GunnBrew Supply Co
16627 N Cave Creek Rd
Phoenix, AZ 85032
602-788-8811

ARKANSAS

Whee Must Wort
919 Lindell
Fayetteville, AR
501-442-0304

Simple Pleasures
115 N. 10th St., #C103
Ft. Smith, AR
501-783-2500

The Big Rock Malt Co.
921 W. 7th St.
Little Rock, AR
501-372-2337

The Treasure Chest
2300 Parkway
N. Little Rock, AR
501-758-6261

Spices Unlimited
2118 State Line
Texarkana, AR
501-772-3445

CJ's Old Time Depot
373 CC 607
Rt. 3 Bx 712
Jonesboro, AR 72410
501-935-3857

CALIFORNIA

The Brewmeister
303 Riley St.
Folsom, CA 95630
916-985-7299

Brew Buddys
1509 Aviation Blvd.
Redondo Beach, CA 90278
1-800-372-3433

Brewer's Resource
404 Calle San Pablo, No. 104
Camarillo, CA 93012
805-445-4100
1-800-827-3983

Fermentation Frenzy
991 N. San Antonio Road
Los Altos, CA 94022
415-941-9289
FAX 415-941-0924

Woodland Hills Home Brewing
22836 Ventura Blvd.
Woodland Hills, CA 91364
818-884-8586

RCA Distributors
9229 Allano Way St.
Santee, CA 92701
619-448-6688
FAX 603-445-2018

William's Brewing
2594 Nicholson Street
P.O. Box 2195-AN
San Leandro, CA 94577
510-895-2739
1-800-759-6025

Ninkasi's Brewing Supplies
5969 El Cajon Blvd.
San Diego, CA 92115
619-287-8976
FAX 619-287-1938

The Beverage People
840 Piner Road, #14
Santa Rosa, CA 95403
707-544-2520
1-800-544-1867

Brewmaster
2315 Verna Court
(On Marina Blvd.)
San Leandro, CA 94577
510-351-8920
1-800-288-8922
FAX 510-351-4090

Home Brew Mart
5401 Linda Vista Rd.,
Suite 406
San Diego, CA 92110
619-295-2337

Brew Mart
1630 F St.
Eureka, CA 95501
707-445-4677
1-800-286-2739

MCC
707 Hwy 175
Hopland, CA 95449
707-744-1704
1-800-392-7129

The Home Brewery
24723 Redlands Blvd. Suite F
San Bernardino, CA 92408
909-796-0699
1-800-622-7393

Napa Fermentation Supplies
724 California Blvd.
Napa, CA 94559
707-255-6372
1-800-242-8585

R&R Home Fermentation Supplies
8385 Jackson Rd.
Sacramento, CA 95826
916-383-7702

Bucket of Suds
317-A Old County Rd.
Belmont, CA 94002
415-637-9844

Beer Makers of America
1040 N. 4th St.
San Jose, CA 95112
408-288-6647
1-800-994-BREW

Bencomo's Homebrew Supply
1544 N. Palm
Fresno, CA 93728
209-237-5823

Modesto Homebrew Supply
1424 Carver, #G
Modesto, CA
1-800-297-BREW
209-521-9995

B.R.E.W.
1965 Marina Blvd.
San Leandro, CA
510-483-2267

Barley & Wine
Home Fermentation Supply
1907 Central Avenue
Ceres, CA 95307
209-538-BREW
1-800-500-BREW

Oak Barrel Winecraft, Inc.
1443 San Pablo Avenue
Berkeley, CA 94702
510-849-0400

Fun Fermentations, Inc.
640 E. Katella
Orange, CA 92007

Great Fermentation of Marin
87 Larkspur
San Rafael, CA 94901
415-459-2520
1-800-542-2520

Doc's Cellar
470 Price St.
Pismo, CA 93449
805-773-3151

Portable Potables
1011 41st Ave.
Santa Cruz, CA 95062
408-476-5444

Santa Cruz Homebrew
616 California Street
Santa Cruz, CA 95060
408-459-0178

Home Brew Outlet
3233 Elkhorn Blvd. #4
N. Highlands, CA 95660
916-348-6322
1-800-959-2648

The Brew Club
2535 7th Ave., Unit #1
Santa Cruz, CA 95062
408-464-2337
1-800-995-BREW

Bliss Brewing Co.
PO Box 179
Yucca Valley, CA 92286
619-365-1082
1-800-470-BREW

Hop Tech
PO Box 2172
Danville, CA 94506
510-736-2350
1-800-DRY-HOPS
FAX 510-736-7950

Brimhall Brew Barn
1852 A St.
Antioch, CA 94509
1-800-414 BREW
510-778-HOPS

South Bay Homebrew Supply
P.O. Box 3798
Torrance, CA 90510
310-517-1841

Double Spring Homebrew Supply
4697 Double Springs Rd
Valley Springs, CA 95252
209-754-3217

Ruud Rick's Homebrew Supply
7273 Murray Dr. #17
Stockton, CA 95210
209-957-4549

Stein Fillers
4180 Viking Way
Long Beach, CA 90808
310-425-0588

Ocean Beach Home Brewery Supply
1922 Bacon St.
San Diego, CA 92107

COLORADO

The Homebrew Hut
555 I Hwy. 287
Broomfield, CO 80020
303-460-1776

The BREW-IT Co.
120 Olive Street
Fort Collins, CO 80524
303-484-9813
1-800-748-2226

North Denver Cellar
3475 W. 32nd Ave.
Denver, CO 80211
303-433-5998

Doc's Brew Shop
3150-B1 S. Peoria
Aurora, CO 80014
303-750-6382

Front Range Bierhaus
3117 N. Hancock Ave.
Colorado Springs, CO 80907
719-473-3776

Brew Ha Ha!
708 Eight Street
Greeley, CO 80631
303-356-1566
1-800-257-1566

Rocky Mountain Homebrew
7292 No. Federal Blvd.
Westminster, CO 80038
303-427-5076

Silverthorne Homebrewers Supply
301 Lagoon Lane
P.O. Box 978
Silverthorne, CO 80498
303-468-8330

Highlander Home Brew, Inc.
151 Mineral Ave, Suite 113
Littleton, CO 80120
303-794-3923
1-800-388-3923

Old West Homebrew Supply
303 East Pikes Peak Ave.
CO Springs, CO 80903
719-635-2443
1-800-ILV-BREW

What's Brewin'
2886 Bluff Street
Boulder, CO 80301
303-444-9433

Wine & Hop Shop
705 E. 6th Ave.
Denver, CO 80203
303-831-7229

The Wine Works
5175 W. Alameda Ave.
Denver, CO 80219
303-936-4422

CONNECTICUT

Great American Homebrew
1720 West St.
Southington, CT 06489
203-620-0332

The Mad Capper
P.O. Box 161
Glastonbury, CT 06033
203-659-8588

B.Y.O.B. Brew Your Own Own Beer
847 Federal Rd.
Brookfield, CT 06804
203-444-2962

Just Brew It, LLC
946 Hope St., Suite 156
Stamford, CT 06907
203-329-8668
1-800-953-BREW

Crossfire Brewing Supplies
17 Kreyssig Road
Broad Brook, CT 06016
203-623-6537

Brother Logan Brewing Supplies
60 Jerry Daniels Road
Marlborough, CT 06447
203-295-8620

Maltose Express
391 Main Street
Monroe, CT 06864

Homemade Libations
25 Ely Avenue
South Norwalk, CT
203-855-7911

Brew-Your-Own-Beer
1550 Randolph Road
Middletown, CT 06457
203-347-4127

S.E.C.T. Brewing Supply
c/o SIMTAC
20 Attawan Road
Niantic, CT 06537
203-489-4560

Wine and Beer Art of Smith Tompkins
1501 E. Main St., Rt 202
Torrington, CT 06790
203-489-4560

DELAWARE

Wine Hobby U.S.A.
2306 West Newport Pike
(Delaware Rt. 4)
Stanton, DE 19804
1-800-847-HOPS

FLORIDA

The Home Brewery
416 S. Broad St.
P.O. Box 575
Brooksville, FL 34601
904-799-3004
1-800-245-BREW

The Home Brewery
1313 East 8th Ave.
Ybor City
Tampa, FL 33601
813-241-BREW

A Home Brew
1236 Whitfield Ave.
Sarasota, FL 34243
813-758-5022

Brew Shack
4025 W. Waters Ave.
Tampa, FL 33614
813-889-9495
1-800-646-BREW

Worms Way Florida
4402 N. 56th Street
Tampa, FL 33610
1-800-283-9676

S.W. Florida Homebrew Supply
4527 Del Prado Blvd
Cape Coral, FL
813-945-4220

Homebrewers Mart
11760 SE Dixie Hwy
Hobe Sound, FL
407-546-9108

Brew Bayou
4330 Lake St.
Leesburg, FL
904-728-5250

Bahama Winery Supply
4708 Hwy 389
Lynn Haven, FL
904-265-0882

Lagerhead Brewing Co.
205 Government St.
Niceville, FL
1-800-505-2739

Heart's Liquors & Homebrew
5824 N. O. B. Tr
Orlando, FL
407-298-4103

The Homebrew Den
1635A N. Monroe St.
Tallahassee, FL
1-800-923-2739

Barley & Hops
1217 E. Hanna Ave.
Tampa, FL
813-237-2965

Home Brewer's Outlet
4734 Okeechobee Blvd
West Palm Beach, FL
407-686-4019

GEORGIA

Wine Craft of Atlanta
5920 Roswell Rd.
Parkside Shopping Center
Atlanta, GA 30328
404-252-5606

Brew Your Own Beverages Inc.
20 E. Andrews Dr. N.W.
Atlanta, GA 30305
404-365-0420
1-800-477-BYOB

Brewtopia
3573 Atlanta Hwy.
Athens, GA 30606
706-546-6258
1-800-540-MALT

Home Brewing Supply
1383 Prince Ave.
Athens, GA
706-548-5035

Midtown Brewers Supply
1033 Peachtree St.
Atlanta, GA
404-607-7980

Amber Waves
2808 La Vista Rd.
Decatur, GA
404-315-1100

Sweetwater Package Store
3900 Peachtree Ind.
Duluth, GA
404-476-4556

ABC Beverage
501 Indian Trail Rd.
Lilburn, GA
404-923-0250

Coastal Homebrewing & Winemaking Supplies
20 Braclakin Rd.
Richmond Hill, GA
912-756-5066

ILLINOIS

Sheaf & Vine Brewing Supply
5425 S. LaGrange Rd.
Countryside, IL 60525
708-430-HOPS

Home Brew Shop
307 W. Main St.
St. Charles, IL 60174
708-377-1338

Chicago Indoor Garden Supply
297 N. Barrington Rd.
Streamwood, IL 06107
708-885-8282
1-800-444-2837
FAX 708-885-8634

Crystal Lake Health Food Store
25 E. Crystal Lake Ave.
Crystal Lake, IL 60014
815-459-7942

Evanston First Liquors Homebrewing
1019 W. Davis St.
Evanston, IL 60201
708-328-9651

Fleming's Winery
Rural Route 2, Box #1
Oakwood, IL 61858
217-354-4555
1-800-832-4292

Lil' Olde Winemaking Shoppe
4 S. 245 Wiltshire Lane
Sugar Grove, IL 60554
708-557-2523

You-Brew Country Food & Liquor
19454 S. Route 45
Mokena, IL 60448
708-479-2900

Chicagoland Winemakers Inc.
689 W. North Ave.
Elmhurst, IL 60126-2132
708-834-0507
1-800-226-BREW

Home Brewing & Wine Making Emporium
28 W. 685 Rogers Ave.
Warrenville, IL 60555
708-393-2337
1-800-455-BREW

Koski Home Brew Fixen's Ltd.
1415 5th Ave.
Moline, IL 61265
303-797-2130
1-800-788-BREW

Chicago Homebrew Supplies
1444 Chicago Ave
Chicago, IL 60622
312-243-BEER
1-800-213-BEER
FAX 312-243-2881

Rock River Brewing Supply
P.O. Box 6242
Rockford, IL 61108
812-227-HOPS

INDIANA

Old Mill Wine & Spirits Shoppe
3123 Blackiston Mill
New Albany, IN
812-941-1350

Worm's Way Indiana
3151 South Highway 446
Bloomington, IN 47401
812-331-0300
1-800-274-9676

LOUISIANA

The Beersmith
1818 Wooddale Blvd.
#18
Baton Rouge, LA
504-926-2337

The Beerslayer
3956 Fire Tower Rd.
Grand Cane, LA
318-858-2219

Piper's Haven
248 W. Congress St.
Lafayette, LA
318-235-4757
1-800-682-5413

Brew Ha Ha Homebrewing
4505 Magazine St.
New Orleans, LA
504-895-5745

Brewers Choice
3600 MacArthur Blvd.
#N
New Orleans, LA
504-368-2337

Bootleg Brew
574 Goode St.
Thibodaux, LA
504-446-6774

KANSAS

Ale-N-Vino
925 N. Kansas Ave.
P.O. Box 8155
Topeka, KS 66608
913-232-1990

Bacchus & Barleycorn Ltd.
8725Z Johnson Drive
Merriam, KS 66202
913-262-4243

CJ's Beer & Wine Hobby Shop
539 E. Santa Fe
Olathe, KS 66061
913-764-5717
1-800-858-0664

KENTUCKY

Winemakers Supply & Pipe Shop
9477 Westport Road
Westport Plaza
Louisville, KY 40221
502-425-1692

The Home Brewery
1446 N. 3rd Street
Bardstown, KY 40004
502-349-1001
FAX (SAME)
1-800-992-BREW

Nuts N Stuff Inc. Bulk Foods
2022 Preston St.
Louisville, KY 40217
502-634-0508

The Party Source
95 Riviera Dr.
Bellevue, KY
606-291-4007

Liquor Outlet
4048 Dixie Hwy
Louisville, KY
502-447-6590

Liquor Outlet
3420 Fern Valley Rd.
Louisville, KY
502-968-1666

Liquor Outlet
1800 S. Hurstbourne Pkwy
Louisville, KY
502 491-0753

MAINE

The Purple Foot Down East
116 Main Street
Waldoboro, ME 04572
207-832-6286 (Info)
1-800-829-6280 (Orders)

The Hop Shop
P.O. Box 900
Gray, ME 04039
207-657-5550

Cookin' With Spirits
Squire Hill Plaza
Upper Main St.
Winthrop, ME 04364
207-377-3237

HomeBrew Emporium
Rural Route #1, Box 1815
Upper Main St.
Winthrop, ME 04364
207-377-3128
1-800-400-MALT (in Maine only)

MARYLAND

Brew Masters Ltd
12266 Wilkins Avenue
Rockville, MD 20850
1-800 466-9557

The Flying Barrel
124 South Carroll Street
Frederick, Maryland 21701
301-663-4491

Bierwerks Inc.
8141 Telegraph Rd.
Severn, MD 21144
410-551-6000
1-800-619-6660

Cellar Works
7542 Belair Rd.
Baltimore, MD 21236
410-665-2900

Happy Homebrewing Supply Co.
Wicomico Shoppers Bazaar
Rt. 13
Fruitland, MD 21826
410-651-9795

Chateau Wine Supplies
8120 Main Street
Ellicott City, MD 21043
410-465-6628

Brew n' Kettle
100 S. Light Street
Baltimore, MD 21230
410-783-1258

The BrewKeg
822-C Frederick Road
Catonsville, MD 21228
410-747-2245

HomeBrew Connection
19000 Alpenglow Ln.
Brookeville, MD 20833
301-570-4014
FAX 301-774-4260

Chesapeake Brewing Co.
1930 Lincoln Dr., Unit C
Annapolis, MD 21401
410-268-0450
FAX/ANS. 410-268-3705

The Brew Pot
13031 11th St.
Old Bowie, MD 20715
301-805-6799

Bel Air Homebrewer's Connection
15 Churchville Rd.,
Suite 113-168
Bel Air, MD 21014
410-638-1454
1-800-982-BREW

Maryland Homebrew
6770 Oak Hall Lane, #115
Columbia, MD 21045
410-290-FROTH

Fullerton Liquors
7542 Belair Rd.
Baltimore, MD
410-665-2900

MASSACHUSETTS

Beer & Winemaking Supplies, Inc.
154 King Street
Northampton, MA 01060
1-800-473-BREW (Orders)
413-586-0150 (Advice)

The Keg & Vine
697 Main Street
Holden, MA 01520
508-829-6717

Barleymalt & Vine
4 Corey Street
West Roxbury, MA 02132
617-327-0089
1-800-666-7026

Barleymalt & Vine
280 Worcester Rd. (Rt. 9)
Framingham, MA 01701
508-820-3392
1-800-666-7026

Barleymalt & Vine
26 Elliot Street
Newton, MA 02161
1-800-666-7026

The Vineyard
123 Glen Avenue
P.O. Box 80
Upton, MA 01568
1-800-626-2371

The Modern Brewer
2304 Massachusetts Ave.
Cambridge, MA 02140
1-800-SEND ALE

Beer & Wine Hobby
180 New Boston Street
Woburn, MA 01801-6206
1-800-523-5423 (orders)
617-933-8818 (info)
FAX 617-662-0872

Stella Brew Discount Homebrew Supplies
Route 20
Charlton City, MA 01509
508-248-6823

Stella Brew Discount Homebrew Supplies
197 Main Street
Marlboro, MA 01752
508-460-5050

Marty's
675 Washington Street
Newton, MA 02160
617-332-1230

Boston Brewers Supply
48 South Street
Jamaica Plain, MA 02130
617-983-1710

Marty's
193 Harvard Avenue
Allston, MA 02134
617-782-3250

Brewers Choice
120 W. Center Street, Rt. 106
Howard Farms Marketplace
W. Bridgewater, MA 02379
508-580-6850

The Witches' Brew
25 Baker Street
Foxboro, MA
508-543-2950

Barnstable Brewers Supply
P.O. Box 1555
Windmill Square, Route 28
Marstons Mills, MA 02648
508-428-5267

Biermeister
P.O. Box 9334
Lowell, MA 01853
508-458-5899

The Hoppy Brewer Supply Co.
550 Central Ave.
Seekonk, MA 02703
508-829-6717

The Malt Shop
P.O. Box 81005, Box 139
Springfield, MA 01108
413-783-0242

Frozen Wort
P.O. Box 988
Greenfield, MA 01302
413-773-5920

MICHIGAN

Wine Barrel Plus
30303 Plymouth Rd.
Livonia, MI 48150
313-522-9463

True Brew Homebrewing Supply Co.
P.O. Box 125
Algonac, MI 48001
810-794-1038

Arrowhead Nursery Inc. Beer & Wine Making Supplies
G-5138 Corunna Rd.
Flint, MI 48532
313-732-4900

Brew & Grow
33523 W. 8 Mile #F-5
Livonia, MI 48152
313-442-7939

Midwest Brewing Supply
P.O. Box 6215
Saginaw, MI 48608
517-793-9420
FAX (same as above)
1-800-644-BREW (Orders)

MINNESOTA

America Brews
9925 Lyndale, Ave S.
Bloomington, MN 55420
612-884-2039

Von Klopp Brew Shop
Hwy 52 South
Pine Island, MN 55963
1-800-596-2739

BeerMasters Supply Company
2515 4th Avenue N.
Anonka, MN 55303
612-323-9781

The Brew Shop
3406 Dakota Ave.
St Louis Pk, MN 55416
1-800-BREWIT2

Semplex
4159 Thomas Ave N.
Minneapolis, MN 55412
1-800-488-5444

Brownstone Beer
2202 Boom Road
Stillwater, MN 55082
612-439-9058

Wind River Brewing Company
7212 Washington Ave. South
Eden Prairie, MN 55344
1-800-266-HOPS (Orders)
612-942-0589 (Advice)
FAX 612-942-1981
Compuserve 73071,1754
Prodigy XXXB32A

Brew-N-Grow
8179 University Ave. N.E.
Fridley, MN 55432
612-780-8191

James Page Brewing Company
1300 Quincy Street NE
Minneapolis, MN 55413-1541
1-800-347-4042

MISSISSIPPI

Eurobrew
2650 Beach Blvd. #27
Biloxi, MS
601-388-2991

MISSOURI

E.C. Kraus
733 S. Northern Blvd
Independence,
MO 64053
816-254-7448

The Home Brewery
P.O. Box 730
Ozark, MO 65721
417-485-0963
1-800-321-BREW
FAX 417-485-0965

Third Fork Station
345 Cedar St.
Union Star, MO
816-593-2357

Johnny Brew-Meister's
Crossroads West
Shopping Center
2101 W. Broadway
Columbia, MO 65203
314-446-8030
FAX 314-446-8031

St. Louis Wine & Beer Making
251 Lamp & Lantern Village
St. Louis, MO 63017
314-230-8277

Winemaker's Market
4349 N. Essex Ave.
Springfield, MO 65803
417-833-4145

Witt Wort Works
1032 S. Bishop Ave.
Rolla, MO 65401
314-341-3311

Worm's Way Missouri
2036 Concourse
St. Louis, MO 63146
314-994-3900
1-800-285-9676

Cool Stuff
120 S. Ninth St.
Columbia, MO 65201
314-875-7912

MONTANA

Homebrew Etcetera
2143 Hwy. 2 W.
Libby, MT 59923
406-293-4942

Hell Roar Homebrew
517 East Aspen St.
Boseman, MT 59715
406-585-0090
1-800-995-HELL

NEBRASKA

Fermenters Supply
8410 "K" Plaza #10
Omaha, NE 68127
402-593-9171

NEVADA

The Home Brewery
4300 N. Pecos Road, #13
No. Las Vegas, NV 89115
702-644-7002
1-800-288-DARK

NEW HAMPSHIRE

The Seven Barrel Brewery Shop
Colonial Plaza
Exit 20, Interstate 89
West Lebanon, NH 03784
603-298-5566

Brewer, Cook & Baker
104 Congress Street
Portsmouth, NH 03801
603-436-5918

Amber Waves Homebrew Supply
5 Central Ave.
Rochester, NH 03867
603-335-4707

Great Bay Brewing Supply
692 Lafayette Park
Seabrook, NH 03874
603-474-3227

Let's Brew
8 Franklin Plaza
Dover, NH 03820
603-749-1240

Jasper's Home Brew Supply
11D Tracy Lane
Hudson, NH 03051
603-881-3052

RCA Distributors
10 North St.
North Walpole, NH 03609
603-445-2018
1-800-RCA-BREW
FAX 603-445-2018

Brewers Market
10 N. Main Street
Ashland, NH 03217

Stout Billy's
61 Market Street
Portsmouth, NH 03801
603-436-1792
1-800-392-4792

Beer Essentials
92 Renshaw Road
Weare, NH 03281
603-529-4664

Granite State Natural Food Inc.
164 N. State St.
Concord, NH 03301
603-224-9341

The Stout House
Eastern Slope Plaza
P.O. Box 2561
North Conway, NH 03801
603-356-5290

Hops & Things
170 Main Street
Tilton, NH 03276
603-286-7209
BBS 603-286-4677

NEW JERSEY

U-Brew
319-1/2 Millburn Ave.
Millburn, NJ 07041
201-376-0973
FAX 201-376-0493

The Barnegat Bay Brewing Co.
215 Route 37 W.
Toms River, NJ 08755
1-800-HOP-ON-IT

Beercrafters Inc.
110A Greentree Rd.
Turnersville, NJ 08012
609- 2 BREW IT

The Brewer's & Vintner's Supply Co. Inc.
290 Cassville Rd.
Jackson, NJ 08527
908-928-4045
1-800-322-3020

Hop & Vine
11 DeHart St.
Morristown, NJ 07960
201-993-3191

Hunterdon Homebrew Shoppe
10 Bridge Street
Frenchtown, NJ 08825
908-996-6008

The Home Brewery
56 W. Main Street
Bogota, NJ 07603
201-525-1833
1-800-426-BREW (orders)

Red Bank Brewing Supply
67 Monmouth Street
Red Bank, NJ 07701
908-842-7507

Brew Quarters
504 Kinderkermack Road
River Edge, NJ 07661
201-262-0097

The Brewmeister
115 North Union Avenue
Cranford, N.J. 07016
1-800-322-3020

Ale & Mead Brewing
181 Willowdale Ave.
Montclair, NJ 07042
201-744-5498

Brunswick Brewing Supply
727 Raritan Ave.
Highland Park, NJ 08904
908-572-5353
1-800-884-2739

Wine Rack
293 Route 206
Flanders, NJ 07836
201-584-0333

Tully's Brew-N-Barrel
476B Bloomfield Ave.
Verona, NJ 07044
201-857-5199

NEW YORK

Great Lakes Brew Supply
310 Adams Avenue
Endicott, NY 13760
1-800-859-GLBS (4527)
607-785-4233 (Advice)
FAX 607-786-3450

East Coast Brewing Supply
124 Jacques Avenue
P.O. Box 060904
Staten Island, N.Y. 10306
718-667-4459
FAX 718-987-3942

Hennessy Homebrew Inc.
470 N. Greenbush Rd. (Rt. 4)
Rensselaer, NY 12144
1-800-HOBREWS

The Brew Shop @ Cornell's
310 White Plains Road
Eastchester, NY 10707
1-800-961-BREW
FAX 914-961-8443

Brew By You Inc.
119 Rockland Center, Suite 293
Nanuet, NY 10954
1-800-9-TO-BREW
FAX 914-732-8213

Brewers Den
24 Bellemeade Ave.
Smithtown, NYY 11787
516-979-3438
1-800-499-BREW

Lager 'N Suds Homebrew Supply
RD 3 Box 325 Burlingham Rd.
Bloomingburg, NY 12721
914-733-1093

Niagra Tradition Homebrewing Supplies
7703 Niagra Falls Blvd.
Niagra Falls, NY 14304
716-283-4418

East End Brewing Supply
35E Middle country Road
Coram, NY
516-698-0579

Bathtub Brews
240 Main Street
Beacon, NY
1-800-314-BREW

Party Creations
RD 2 Box 35 Rokeby Road
Red Hook, NY 12571
914-758-0661

Brierton's Malt Supplies
P.O. Box 48
Great River, N.Y. 11739-0048
1-800-638-MALT
FAX 516-224-4751

Staten Island Homebrew & Grow
439 Castleton Ave.
Staten Island, NY 10301
718-727-9300
FAX 718-727-9313

America's Brewing Co.
100 River Rd.,
Triangle Plaza, Suite 8
Harriman, NY 10926
914-782-8586

Arbor Wine & Beermaking Supplies, Inc.
74 W. Main St.
East Islip, NY 11730
516-277-3004

Adirondack Brewing Supply
301 Grand Street
Amsterdam, NY 12010

D.P. Homebrew Supply
1998 E. Main St., Route 6
Mohegan, NY 10547
914-739-0977

E.J. Wren Homebrewer Inc.
Ponderosa Plaza
209 Oswego St.
Liverpool, NY 13088
315-457-2282

Heimstatte Homebrewers Supply
RD #1, Box 354
Livingston Manor, NY 12758
914-439-4367

Mountain Malt and Hop Shoppe
54 Leggs Mills Rd.
Lake Katrine, NY 12449
914-336-7688
1-800-295-MALT

S&R Homebrewing & Winemaking Supplies
P.O. Box 5544 Union Station
Endicott, NY 13763
607-748-1877

U.S. Brewing Supply
815 Madison Ave.
Albany, NY 12208
1-800-383-9303

Kedco
564 Smith Street
Farmingdale, NY 11735-1168
1-800-654-9988

The Brewery
11 Market Street
Potsdam, NY 13676
1-800-762-2560

Two Drews Homebrew Supply
307 Quaker Road
Chappaqua, NY 10514
914-238-0333
203-380-1363

Milan Laboratory
57 Spring Street
New York, NY 10012
1-800-BEERKEG

Little Shop of Hops
11 East 37th Street
New York, NY
212-685-8334
1-800-343-HOPS
FAX 212-704-9611

New York Homebrew
36 Cherry Lane
Floral Park, NY 11001
1-800-YOO-BREW

NORTH CAROLINA

**Ale & Beer
Supply Co.**
1600 Spring Garden St.
Greensboro, NC
910-275-1226

Assembly Required
142 E. Third Ave.
Hendersonville, NC
704-692-9677

**Xtract Xpress
Hop Shop**
109 Barden, Drive
Kernersville, NC
910-643-7798
1-800-X70-7XXX

City Beverage
915 Burke St.
Winston-Salem, NC
910-722-2774

Brew Better Supply
103 Covington Square Dr.
Cary, NC 27513
919-467-8934

Asheville Brewers Supply
2 Wall Street, #117
Asheville, NC 28801
704-285-0515

American BrewMasters
3021-7 Stoneybrook Drive
Raleigh, NC 27604
919-850-0095

Alternative Beverage
114-O Freeland Lane
Charlotte, NC 28217
1-800-365-BREW

NORTH DAKOTA

The Home Brewery
P.O. Box 1662
Grand Forks, ND 58201
701-772-2671
1-800-367-BREW (orders)

**Happy Harry's Polar
Package Inc.**
1125 19th Ave. N.
Fargo, ND 58103
701-235-4661

OHIO

The Grape and Granary
1302 E. Tallmadge Ave.
Akron, OH 44310
216-633-7223
1-800-695-9870

OKLAHOMA

Professional Brewers LLC
2917 W. Hefner Rd.
Oklahoma City, OK 73120
405-752-7380

Bob's Brewhaus
724 W. Cantwell Ave.
Stillwater, OK 74075
405-372-4477

Mollers Craft Brew Supply
9717 N.W. 10th St. Lot #87
Oklahoma City, OK 73127
1-800-682-5460

OREGON

**Wasson Bros. Winery &
Beer and Wine Supply**
41901 Hwy. 26
Sandy, OR 97055
503-668-3124

Homebrew Heaven
1292 12th St. S.E.
Salem, OR 97302
503-375-3521

Home Fermenter Center
123 Monroe St.
Eugene, OR 97402
503-485-6238

F.H. Steinbart Co.
234 S.E. 12th St.
Portland, OR 97214
503-232-8793

**Herbs & Spice
and ev'rything nice**
Robinwood Shopping Center
19145 Willamette Drive
West Linn, OR 97068-2092
503-636-4372

**Johnston's Home Brew
and Wine Supply**
164 Columbia Loop Rd.
Roseburg, OR 97470
503-679-4645

Oregon Specialty Company
7024 N.E. Glisan St.
Portland, OR 97213
503-254-7494
FAX 503-251-2936

PENNSYLVANIA

Mr. Steve's Homebrew Supplies
4342 N. George St.
Manchester, PA 17345
717-266-5954

**Neibert's Spielgrund Wine
& Gift Shop**
3528 E. Market St.
York, PA 17402
717-755-3384

The Brewsmith Ltd.
323 E. Main St.
Collegeville, PA 19426
610-489-8986

Starview Brew
51 Codorus Furnace Rd.
Mt. Wolf, PA 17347
717-266-5091

Beer Unlimited
Routes 30 and 401
Great Valley Shopping Center
Malvern, PA 19355
610-889-0905

Beer Unlimited
515 Fayette Street
Conshohocken, PA 19428
610-397-0666

Homebrewer's Outlet
10 Lincoln Circle
Fairless Hills, PA 19030
215-943-8569

Home Sweet Homebrew
2008 Sansom Street
Philadephia, PA 19103
215-569-9469

Ambler Brewer's Connection
(at Ambler Stove & Fireplace)
903 E. Butler Pike
Butler & Bethlehem Pikes
Ambler, PA 19002
215-643-3565

Brew by You
3504 Cottman Ave.
Philadelphia, PA 19149
215-335-BREW

Keystone Homebrew Supply
Montgomeryville
Farmers Market
Route 63
Montgomeryville, PA 18936
215-641-HOPS

RHODE ISLAND

Northeast Brewers Supply, Inc.
PO Box 232
West Kingston, RI 02892
401-789-9635
FAX 401-789-9646

Northeast Brewers Supply, Inc.
140 Pt. Judith Road
Narragansett, RI 02882
1-800-352-9001
FAX 401-789-9646

Brew Horizons
884 Tiogue Ave.
Coventry, RI 02816
401-826-3500

Pawtucket Homebrewing Supply
66 Downes Ave.
Pawtucket, RI 02861
401-723-3938

Basement Brew-Hah Inc
P.O. Bx 7574
Warwick, RI 02887
401-727-1150
1-800-213-BREW

SOUTH CAROLINA

Carolina Wine & Cheese
54-1/2 Wentworth St.
Charleston, SC
803-577-6144

Charleston Beer Works
845-D Savannah Hwy
Charleston, SC
1-800-225-2910

The Brewers Barrel
401 W. Martin Town Rd
North Augusta, SC
803-279-7998

U-Brew
1207 Hwy 17 S.
N. Myrtle Beach, SC
803-361-0092

Home Winemaking & Beer Brewing Supplies
113 Delmar Dr.
Simpsonville, SC
803-967-4399

SOUTH DAKOTA

Medicine Rock Division Dakota Supply
HCR-2, Box 2A
W. HWY 212
Gettysburg, SD
605-765-9400

TENNESSEE

Allen Biermakens
4111 Martin Mill Pike
Knoxville, TN 337920
615-577-2430
1-800-873-6258

The Winery & Brew Shoppe
60 S. Cooper St.
Memphis, TN 38104
901-278-2682

The Beverage Barn
4700 Hixson Pike
Chattanooga, TN
615-875-8918

The Hagermeister
P.O. Box 10126
Clarksville, TN
615-431-4717

Home Brew Shoppe
3712 Walker Blvd.
Knoxville, TN
615-689-9064

Squash Blossom Market
5101 Sanderlin
#124
Memphis, TN
901-685-2293

Cork & Stein
114 E. Division Rd.
Oak Ridge, TN
615-483-3619

The Brewhaus
4955 Ball Camp Pike
Knoxville, TN 37921
615-523-4615
1-800-638-2437

TEXAS

The Winemaker Shop
5356 W. Vickery
Fort Worth, TX 76107
817-377-4488
FAX 817-732-4327

Austin Homebrew Supply
306 E. 53rd Street
Austin, TX 78751
512-467-8427

Home Brewers Supply
2307 Texas Av. So.
College Station, TX 77840
409-764-8486

Bulldog Brewing Supply
2217 Babalos
Dallas, TX 75228
214-324-4480
1-800-267-2993

Homebrew Headquarters--West
900 E. Copeland, Suite 120
Arlington, TX 76011
817-792-3940
1-800-862-7474

Homebrew Headquarters--North
13929 North Central Expressway
Suite 449
Dallas, TX 75243
214-234-4411
1-800-966-4144

DeFalco's Home Wine & Beer Supplies
5611 Morningside Dr.
Houston, TX 77005
713-523-8154
FAX 713-523-5284

Homebrew Supply of Dallas
777 South Central Expressway,
Suite 1-P
Richardson, TX 75080
214-234-5922

St. Patrick's of Texas Brewers Supply
12922 Station Drive
Austin, TX 78727
512-832-9045

Bonehead Brewing Company
10417 Broken Shoe Tr.
Austin, TX
1-800-299-2337

St. Patrick's of Texas Brewers Supply
401A Guadalupe St.
Austin, TX
512-499-8544

Homebrew Headquarters
2810 Greenville Ave
Dallas, TX
214-821-7444

UTAH

Mountain Brew Retail
2793 S. State Street
South Salt Lake City, UT 84115
801-487-2337

VERMONT

Vermont Homebrewer's Supply, Inc.
37 Hillside Terrace
Shelburne, VT 05482
1-800-456-BREW

Vermont Homebrewer's Supply, Inc.
1341 Shelburne Rd.
South Burlington, VT 05403
802-985-9734

Something's Brewing
196 Battery St.
Burlington, VT 05401
802-660-9007

Brew Lab
94 N. Main Street
St. Albans, VT 05478
802-524-2772

VIRGINIA

James River Brewing Co.
2602 W. Main St.
Richmond, VA 23220
804-353-5006

Schneider's of Capitol Hill
3117 Duke St.
Alexandria, VA 22313
703-823-4600
FAX 703 823 4605

The Brewers Club
P.O. Box 504
Locust Grove, VA 22508
703-972-7467
1-800-U-Brew-It

Brew America
138 Church Street N.E., Suite F
Vienna, VA 22180
703-938-4805

Wine Seller
302 Elden St.
Herndon, VA
703-471-9649

Wine Seller
9912-C Georgetown Pike
Great Falls, VA
703-759-0430

Vintage Cellar
1313 S. Main St.
Blacksburg, VA
1-800-672-WINE

Hop & Vine
7577 Alleghany Road
Manassas, VA 22111
703-335-2953

Easy Brewing
181 Kings Hwy
Fredericksburg, VA
703-372-6850
1-800-745-BREW

WASHINGTON

The Cellar Homebrew
14411 Greenwood Ave. N.
P.O. Box 33525
Seattle, WA 98133
206-365-7660
1-800-342-1871

The Hop Shoppe
7526 Olympic View Drive
Suite F
Edmunds, WA 98026
206-776-2237

Cascade Brewing Supplies
224 Puyallup Ave.
Tacoma, WA 98421
206-383-8980

Brewer's Warehouse
4520 Union Bay Place N.E.
Seattle, WA 98105
206-527-5047

Evergreen Brewing Supply
12121 N.E. Northup Way,
Suite 210
Bellevue, WA 98005
206-882-9929
1-800-789-BREW

**Jim's 5¢ Home Brew Supply &
Traditional Beer Emporium**
N. 2619 Division St.
Spokane, WA 99207
509-328-4850
1-800-326-7769

**Liberty Malt Supply Co./
Pike Place Brewery**
1432 Western Ave.
Seattle, WA 98121
206-622-1880
FAX 206-622-6648

Northwest Brewers Supply
915 6th Street
Anacortes, WA 98221
206-293-8070

**West Seattle Homebrew
Supply Co.**
4720 S.W. California Ave.
P.O. Box 16532
Seattle, WA 98116
206-938-2476

WASHINGTON, D.C.

**Columbia Home
Brewing Company**
3220 N Street N.W.
Washington, D.C. 20007
1-800-473-7293
202-3330-7293

WEST VIRGINIA

R.J. Goods
3555 Route 60 E.
Barboursville, WV 25504
304-736-3010

Tent Church Vineyard
RR 1, Box 218
Colliers, WV 26035-9723
304-527-3916
1-800-336-2915

The Brewing Station
405 Fairview Dr.
Charleston, WV 25302
304-343-0350
304-343-0439

**Hofburg Homebrewers &
Vintners Supply**
Rt. 1 Box 39BB
Cairo, WV 26337
1-800-718-2718
304-628-3172

WISCONSIN

The Malt Shop
N 3211 Highway S
Cascade, WI 53011
1-800-235-0026

Nort's Worts
7625 Sheridan Rd.
Kenosha, WI 53143
414-654-2211

The Wine and Hop Shop
434 State St.
Madison, WI 53703
608-257-0099

B. Bros. Brewing Supply
1733 Charles St.
LaCrosse, WI 54603
608-781-WINE

**Hedtke's IGA-
Homebrewing &
Winemaking Supplies**
308 Charles St.
Hatley, WI 54440
715-446-3262

**The Market Basket Homebrew
& Wine Supplies**
14835 W. Lisbon Rd.
Brookfiled, WI 53005
414-783-5233

North Brewery Supplies
9009 S. 29th St.
Franklin, WI 53132
414-761-1018

Brew City Supplies
P.O. Box 27729
Milwaukee, WI 53227
414-425-8595

The Purple Foot
3167 S. 92 St.
Milwaukee, WI 53277
414-327-2130
FAX 414-327-6682

WYOMING

Whole Foods Trading Co.
1239 Rumsey Ave.
Cody, WY 82414
307-587-3213

CANADA

Spagnol's Wine and Beer Making Supplies Ltd.
1325 Derwent Way
Annacis Island
New Westminster,
BC V3M 5V9
604-524-9463
FAX 604-524-1327

Gordon's Cave a Vin
Montreal, Quebec
H4A 1X2
514-487-2739

Better Bitters
Fairview Road
Burlington, Ontario
905-681-BREW

Wine Line and Beer Gear
433 Academy Road
Winnipeg, MB R3N OC2
204-489-7256

The Hopping Grape Vine
171 Speers Rd. Unit #13
Oakville, ON L6K 2E8
905-845-5716

UNITED KINGDOM

AVON

Maurice D. Chant
519 Fishponds Road
Bristol BS16 3AJ
England
0272 653916

Home Brewing Centre
35 High Street
Keynsham
Bristol BS18 1BS
England
0272 868568

BEDFORDSHIRE

Luton Winemakers Stores
125 Park Street
Luton
Beds LU1 3HG
0582 25490

The Happy Brewer
15 Union Street
Bedford MK40 2SF
0234 353856

BERKSHIRE

Hop In
48 Erleigh Road
Reading RG1 5NA
0734 667265

BUCKINGHAMSHIRE

J.P. Homebrew Centre
Deer Walk
Central Shopping Building
Milton Keynes
Buckinghamshire
0908 670592

CHESHIRE

Brewing Supplies
13 Oxford Road
Altrincham WA14 2DY
061 9282347

Brewing Supplies
48 Buxton Road
Stockport SK2 3NB
061 4804880

Whitby Homebrew Centre
245 Whitby Road
Ellesmere Port
South Wirral L65 6RT
051 3552365

P&M Osbourne
4 Hazelwood Road
Hazel Grove
Stockport
Cheshire
061 4833568

Wayside Choice
16 Hightown
Crewe CW1 3BS
0270 257046

Sale Homebrew
7 Northenden Road
Sale
Cheshire
061 9734859

CORNWALL

Geoff's Homebrew Centre
47A Cross Street
Camborne TR14 8ET
0209 715708

DERBYSHIRE

Eezee Brewing
9 Low Pavement
Chesterfield S40 PF
0246 279382

Heanor Homebrew
29 Ray Street
Heanor
Derby DE75 7GE
0773 760808

DEVON

Hop Shop
22 Dale Road
Mutley
Plymouth
0752 660382

Quay Side Home Brew
8 Leatside
The Quay
Exeter
0392 427271

Felixwood Homebrew
30-33 The Market
Newton Abbot
0626 56690

DORSET

Kinson Homebrew & Health Foods
1434 Wimborne Road
Kinson
Bournemouth
0202 574351

DURHAM

Hop & Grape
15 Duke Street
Darlington
Durham
0325 380780

ESSEX

Meads Homebrew Centre
500 London Road (A13)
Westcliffe-on-Sea SS0 9LD
0702 345474

The Cellar
at Chase Road Post Office
472 Southchurch Road
Southend-on-Sea SS1 2QA
0702 465512

GLOUCESTERSHIRE

Pops Homebrew
10 Grosvenor Street
Cheltenham GL52 2SG
0242 232426

HAMPSHIRE

The Home Brew Shop
10 Alexandra Road
Farnborough
Hants GU14 6DA
0252 540386

The Brewmaster's Recipe Manual

**Harvey Wine &
Beer Making Centre**
174 West Street
Fareham PO16 0EQ
0329 233253

Easy Brew
133A Southampton Road
Poulner
Ringwood
0425 479972

HERTFORDSHIRE

What's Brewing
Stand No. 112
Watford Indoor Market Hall
Watford
Herts, England
0923 677019

HUMBERSIDE

Mr. Kits Homebrew Shop
2 Posterngate
Market Place
Hull HU1 2JN
0482 224775

Preston's Homebrew
51 Prince's Avenue
Hull HU5 3QY
0482 42092

KENT

Maidstone Winemaking Centre
53 Hardy Street
Maidstone ME14 2SS
0622 677619

LANCASHIRE

Blades Home Brewery
115 Market Street
Farnworth
Bolton
Lancs BL4 8EX
Tel/FAX 0204 72130

The Witches Brew
20 Briercliffe Road
Burnley
0282 24841

Brian's Homebrew
Accrington 3 Day Market
Lancashire
0254 394092

**Washbrook's Specialist
Home Brew Centre**
59 Halifax Road
Rochdale OL12 9BD
0706 41590

LEICESTERSHIRE

Matchless Homebrew
32 Belvoir Road
Coalville LE67 3PN
0530 813800

Aaron Shally's
50 Baxtergate
Loughborough LE11 1TH
0509 263092

LONDON (EAST)

Janet's Homebrew
12 The Broadway
Highams Park
London E4 9LQ
081 5270664

LONDON (NORTH)

Barleycorn
97/99 Lancaster Road
Enfield
Middx EN2 0JW
081 363 2956

LONDON (SOUTH)

Wimbledon Home Brew Centre
19 Kingston Road
London SW19 1JX
081 5429520

GREATER MANCHESTER

Blades Home Brewery
115 Market Street
Farnworth
Bolton
Lancs BL4 8EX
Tel/FAX 0204 72130

Brewtopia
20 Silver Street
Bury
061 7977698

Julies Homebrew
875 Oldham Road
Newton Heath
Manchester M40 5BH
061 2056513

MANCHESTER

Salford Homebrew
96 Fitzwarren Street
Salford M6 5RS
061 745 9488

Something Brewing
51 Manchester Road
Chorlton-Cum-Hardy
Manchester M21 1PW
061 8607698

MERSEYSIDE

The Wine Loft
Northern House
North Road
St. Helens WA10 2TL
0744 29881

Brewit Home Brew Centre
8 East Prescot Road
Old Swan
Liverpool L14 PW
051 2202365

Cheers! Homebrew Centre
60 Bridge Road
Litherland
Liverpool L21 6PH
051 9205552

MIDDLESEX

Whytes Homebrew
8 Church Street
Staines
Middlesex
0784 451576

NOTTINGHAM

Eezee Brewing
32 West End Arcade (off Angel Row)
Nottingham NG1 6JP
0602 411035

Flagon & Cask
202 Main Street
Bullwell
Nottingham
0602 271368

Home Brewers' Centre
31 Ratcliffe Gate
Mansfield
Notts NG18 2JA
0623 655431

Brewcraft
186 Gateford Road
Worksop S81 7JT
Notts
0909 477939

SHROPSHIRE

The Sign of the Vine
Unit 40
The Gallery
General Market Hall
Shoplatch
Shrewsbury SY1 1HQ
0743 368345

STAFFORDSHIRE

Pink Elephant
35 Marston Road
Stafford
0785 47486

SURREY

Richmond Homebrew & Craft Emporium
92 Kew Road
Richmond
Surrey TW9
Tel/FAX 081 3329349

Art of Brewing
42 Richmond Road
Kingston KT2 5EE
081 549 5266

Cheers Health & Homebrew
94 Priory Road
Cheam
Surrey
081 644 0934

SUSSEX

Bung Ho
Norman Road
St. Leanord's on Sea TN38 0ER
0424 437045

Noggins
18 Felpham Road
Felpham Village
Bognor Reigns PO22 7AZ
0243 82968

TYNE & WEAR

Union Homebrew Centre
19 Derwent Street
Sunderland SR1 3NT
091 567557

Brewin Ales
Gateshead Indoor market
Trinity Square
Gateshead NE8 1AG
4877275

Cheers—Houghton Home Brew Centre
17a New Bottle Street
Houghton-le-Spring DH4 4AP
091 5845055

WARWICKSHIRE

Hamsted Home Brew
37 Newton Road
Great Barr
Birmingham B43 6AD
021 3586800

Studley Home Brew
4 High Street
Studley B80 7HJ
0527 854198

WEST MIDLANDS

Coventry Homebrew Centre
115 Radford Road
Coventry
0203 598460

Bloxwich Home Brew
107 High Street
Bloxwich
Walsall
0922 404739

Brewer Bill
Stall 11
Coventry Retail Market
Coventry
0203 550876

Youngs Homebrew Ltd.
Bilston
West Midlands
WV14 8DL
0902 353053

WILTSHIRE

Lew's Brews
182 Victoria Road
Swindon SN1 3DF
0793 485760

WORCESTERSHIRE

Bromsgrove Home Brew
70 Birmingham Road
Bromsgrove
Worcs B61 0DD
0527 875202

YORKSHIRE

M&D Homebrew Supplies
The Old Malthouse
5 Avison Yard
Kirkgate
Wakefield WF1 1UA
0924 369547

The Ale Shoppe
205 Lockwood Road
Huddersfield
West Yorkshire HD1 3TG
0484 432479

Cellarcraft
28 Waterhouse Street
Halifax HX1 1UQ
0422 330667

Doncaster Homebrew
Unit 5, Odeon Arcade
Hallgate
Doncaster DN1 3LZ
0302 768030

Betterbrew
8 Corporation Street
Rotherham S60 1NG
0709 369278

SW SCOTLAND

Dumfries View N' Brew
17 Glasgow Street
Dumfries DG2 9FA
Scotland
0387 57990

LOTHIAN

The Village Home Brew
24 Corstorphine High Street
Edinburgh
Scotland
031 3341821

TAYSIDE & FIFE

Forfar Homebrew
2 East High Street
Forfar DD8 2EG
Scotland
0307 63854

WALES

The Cellars
114-116 Albany Road
Cardiff CF2 3RU
0222 493567

Jolly Brewer
1 College Street
Wrexham
Clwyd LL13 8NA
0978 263338

Home Brew Centre
2 Park Crescent
Barry
South Glam CF6 8HD
0446 732765

NORWAY

Centrum Vin & Essenser
Youngs gt. 11
0181 Oslo

Korketrekker'n
Majorstua
Kirkevelen 50
0368 Oslo

Korketrekker'n
Manglerud Senter
Postboks 51
0612 Oslo

E.I. Kristiansen & Co
Hagegt 36 (Tøyensenteret)
0653 Oslo

Rowi Trading
Trondhelmsveien 47
Postboks 4634 Soflenberg
0506 Oslo

ASSOCIATIONS & PUBLICATIONS

Associations

American Homebrewers Association
736 Pearl Street
P.O. Box 1679
Boulder, CO 80306-1679
(303) 447-0816
FAX (303) 447-2825

Brewlab—The Life Science Building
University of Sunderland
Chester Road
Sunderland SR1 3SD
England
0 (1) 91 515 2535

CAMRA Ltd. (Campaign For Real Ale)
230 Hatfield Road, St. Albans
Hertfordshire AL1 4LW, England
727-867201 (from the U.S., first dial 011-44)
FAX 727-867670 (from the U.S., first dial 011-44)

De Objectieve Bierproevers (OBP)
(Belgian Beer Consumer's Organization)
Postbus 32
2600 Berchem 5
Belgium

Home Wine and Beer Trade Association
604 N. Miller Road
Valrico, FL 33594
813-685-4261

Association of Bottled Beer Collectors
c/o Bob Heath
4 Woodhall Road, Penn,
Wolverhampton WV4 4DJ
England
0 (1) 902 342 672

British Beermat Collectors Society
c/o Brian West
10 Coombe Hill Crescent
Thame
Oxfordshire OX9 2EH

The Brewer's Society
(Brewers and Licensed Retailers Association)
42 Portman Square
London W1H 0BB
0 (1) 71 486 4831

The Inn Sign Society
2 Mill House, Mill Lane
Countess Wear, Exeter
Devonshire EX2 6LL
0 (1) 392 70728

Institute of Brewing
33 Clarges Street
London W14 8EE
England

Promotie Informatie Traditioneel Bier (PINT)
(Dutch Beer Consumer's Organization)
Postbus 3757
1001 AN Amsterdam
Netherlands

Siebel Institute of Technology
4055 W. Peterson
Chicago, IL 60646
312-463-3400
FAX 312-463-4962

Society for the Preservation of Beers from the Wood (SPBW)
61 De Frene Road
London SE26 4AF

Svenska Ölfrämjandet (SO)
(Swedish Beer Consumer's Organization)
Box 16244
S-10325 Stockholm
Sweden

Magazines

Zymurgy/New Brewer
736 Pearl Street
P.O. Box 1679
Boulder, CO 80306-1679
(303) 447-0816
FAX (303) 447-2825

Brewing Techniques
P.O. Box 3222
Eugene, OR 97403
(503) 687-2993
1-800-427-2993
FAX (503) 687-8534

Suds 'n Stuff
Bosak Publishing Co.
4764 Galicia Way
Oceanside, CA 92056
(619) 724-4447
FAX (619) 940-0549

American Brewer—The Business of Beer/
Beer: The Magazine
P.O. Box 717
Hayward, CA 94543-0717
(510) 538-9500

All About Beer
Chautauqua, Inc.
1627 Marion Ave.
Durham, NC 27705
(919) 490-0589
FAX (919) 490-0865

American Breweriana Journal
American Breweriana Association
P.O. Box 11157
Pueblo, CO 81001

The Malt Advocate
3416 Oak Hill Road
Emmaus, PA 18049
(610) 967-1083
E-Mail: maltman999@aol.com

Beer Magazine
102 Burlington Cr.
Ottawa, Ontario K1T 3K5
Canada
613-737-3715

ASSOCIATIONS & PUBLICATIONS

Newspapers

Ale Street News
P.O. Box 1125
Maywood, NJ 07607
(201) 368-9100
FAX (201) 368-9101

BarleyCorn
P.O. Box 2328
Falls Church, VA 22042
(703) 573-8970

Brew Hawaii
P.O. Box 852
Hauula, HI 96717-9998
808-259-6884

Celebrator Beer News
P.O. BOX 375
Hayward, CA 94543
(510) 670-0121
FAX (510) 670-0639
Compuserve 70540,1747

Midwest Beer Notes
339 6th Avenue
Clayton, WI 54004
715-948-2990

Rocky Mountain Brews
251 Jefferson
Fort Collins, CO 80524
303-224-2524

Southern Draft Brew News
702 Sailfish Rd.
Winter Springs, FL 32708
407-327-9451

Southwest Brewing News
11405 Evening Star Drive
Austin, TX 78739
512-467-2225
512-282-4935

**What's Brewing
(CAMRA Newspaper)**
230 Hatfield Road, St. Albans
Hertfordshire AL1 4LW, England
727-867201 (from the U.S., first dial 011-44)
FAX 727-867670 (from the U.S., first dial 011-44)

**What's Brewing
(CAMRA - Canada Newspaper)**
P.O. B ox 30101
Saanich Centre Postal Outlet
Victoria, B.C. V8X 5E1
Canada
604-386-2818

The Yankee Brew News
Brasseur Publications
P.O. Box 8053
J.F.K. Station
Boston, MA 02114
(617) 846-5521
(617) 361-6106 (Ads)
Compuserve 70571,3252

Beer & Tavern Chronicle
277 Madison Ave.
New York, NY 10016
FAX 914-227-5520

Newsletters

Alephenalia
140 Lakeside Ave.—Suite 300
Seattle, Washington 98122-6538
(206) 448-1228

Northwest Brew News
22833 Bothell-Everett Hwy, Suite 1139
Bothell, WA 98021-9365
206-742-5327

On Tap: The Newsletter
P.O. Box 71
Clemson, SC 29633
803-654-3360

The Pint Post
12345 Lake City Way N.E. #159
Seattle, WA 98125
206-365-5812

What's On Tap
P.O. Box 7779
Berkeley, CA 94709
1-800-434-7779

BIBLIOGRAPHY

Burch, Byron, *Brewing Quality Beers: The Home Brewer's Essential Guidebook*, Second Edition, Joby Books, Fulton, CA 1994.
Collins, Marie & Davis, Virginia, *A Medieval Book of Seasons*, Harper Collins Publishers, NY, NY 1992.
Cyperrek, Rudolf, *Das Andere Bier*, optimum Verlag für Wirtschaftsschrifttum und Werbung, Wiesbaden, Germany 1975.
Eckhardt, Fred, *The Essentials of Beer Styles*, Fred Eckhardt Communications, Portland, OR 1989.
Eliel, Andrew, Managing Editor, *Egon Ronay's Heineken Guide 1994: Pubs & Inns*, Leading Guides Ltd.; St. Martin's Press, NY, NY 1993.
Fix, George and Laurie, *Vienna, Märzen, Oktoberfest*, Classic Beer Style Series, Brewers Publications, Boulder, CO 1991.
Foster, Terry, *Pale Ale*, Classic Beer Style Series, Brewers Publications, Boulder, CO 1990.
Graves, M., *A Modern Herbal*, Dover Publications, NY, NY 1971.
Hutchens, Alma R., *Native American Herbalogy*, Shambhala Publications, Inc., Boston, MA 1973.
Jackson, Michael, *Michael Jackson's Beer Companion*, Running Press Book Publishers, Philadelphia, PA 1993.
Jackson, Michael, *The Simon & Schuster Pocket Guide to Beer - Fourth Edition*, Fireside/Simon & Schuster, New York, NY 1994.
La Pensee, Clive, *The Historical Companion to House Brewing*, Montag Publications, Beverley, U.K. 1990.
Lees, Graham, *Good Beer Guide to Munich and Bavaria*, CAMRA Books, the Campaign for Real Ale, St. Albans, England 1994.
Miller, David, *The Complete Handbook of Homebrewing*, Garden Way Publishing, Storey Communications, Pownal, VT 1988.
Miller, David, *Continental Pilsener*, Classic Beer Style Series, Brewers Publications, Boulder, CO 1989.
New York Public Library and The Stonesong Press, Inc., *The New York Public Library Desk Reference*, Webster's New World, NY, NY 1989.
O'Neill, P.J., editor, *Cellarmanship—Caring for Real Ale*, CAMRA, the Campaign for Real Ale, St. Albans, England 1994.
Papazian, Charlie, *The Complete Joy of Homebrewing*, Avon Books, NY, NY 1984.
Protz, Roger, *The European Beer Almanac*, Lochar Publishing Ltd., Moffat, Scotland 1991.
Rajotte, Pierre, *Belgian Ale*, Classic Beer Style Series, Brewers Publications, Boulder, CO 1992.
Rajotte, Pierre, *First Steps in Yeast Culture: Part One*, Alliage Éditeur, Montreal, Canada 1994.
Roberston, James D., *The Connoisseur's Guide to Beer*, Caroline House Publishers, Inc., Aurora, Illinois 1982.
Warner, Eric, *German Wheat Beer*, Classic Beer Style Series, Brewers Publications, Boulder, CO 1992.
Webb, Tim, *Good Beer Guide to Belgium and Holland*, CAMRA Books, the Campaign for Real Ale, St. Albans, England 1994.
Wheeler, Graham, *Home Brewing -- The CAMRA Guide*, CAMRA Books, St. Albans, England 1993.
Willenbecher, James F., *Concoction of a Beer Engineer*, CEI Publications, Broad Brook, CT 1992
Yenne, Bill, *Beers of the World*, Chartwell Books, Inc., Secaucus, NJ 1994.

Periodicals

"Factors Affecting Hop Production, Hop Quality, and Brewer Preference," Alfred Haunold and Gail B. Nickerson, *Brewing Techniques*, Vol. 1 No. 1, May/June 1993. Eugene, OR.
"Nibbling Away at Bavaria's Great Heritage" Graham Lees, *What's Brewing—Newspaper of The Campaign For Real Ale*, June 1994, St. Albans, Herts, England.
"Hop Utilisation," Gerard W.C. Lemmens, B.Sc., *American Brewer—The Business of Beer*, No. 55, Spring 1993, Hayward, CA.
"1994 Homebrew Competition Rules and Regulations—Style Guidelines," *Zymurgy*, Elizabeth Gold, editor, Vol. 16 No. 5, Winter 1993. Boulder, CO.
"Witbier, A Belgian Specialty," Bill Metzger, *All About Beer*, Volume 14 No. 2, May 1993. Oceanside, CA.

BIBLIOGRAPHY

"Special Malts for Greater Beer Type Variety," Ludwig Narziss, Ph.D., *Zymurgy*, Vol. 16 No. 5, Winter 1993. Boulder, CO.

"The Art and Science of Decoction Mashing," Eric Warner, *Zymurgy*, Vol. 16 No. 4, Special Issue 1993. Boulder, CO.

"Why Old Black Magic Still Casts a Spell" Roger Protz, *What's Brewing—Newspaper of The Campaign For Real Ale*, May 1994, St. Albans, Herts, England.

"Beer of the Month: Saison DuPont," *BarleyCorn*, George Rivers, editor, July/August 1993, Falls Church, VA.

"Beer and Brewing in Boston," *The Improper Bostonian*, Tobin Street, editor, Vol. II, Issue, 4, January 20, 1993, Brookline, MA.

"History of German Brewing," Karl J. Eden, *Zymurgy*, Vol. 16 No. 4, Special Issue 1993. Boulder, CO.

"Scots Light: Beer Burns Raved About" Charles McMaster, *What's Brewing—Newspaper of The Campaign For Real Ale*, May 1994, St. Albans, Herts, England.

"Festivals, Tastings, & Brew Ha Ha," *Celebrator*, Thomas E. Dalldorf, editor, Vol. 6 No. 4, August/September 1993, Hayward, CA

"Beer, Women, and History—Part I," Alan D. Eames, *Yankee Brew News*, Brett Peruzzi, editor, Fall 1993, Boston, MA.

"The CAMRA Fact Sheet," published by *What's Brewing—Newspaper of The Campaign For Real Ale*, Iain Loe, Research Manager, Roger Protz, editor, St. Albans, Herts, England.

"A Lambic Beer Tour Through Payottennland," Christopher Kenneally, *Yankee Brew News*, Vol. 4 No. 4, Winter 1993-94, Boston, MA.

"Mt. Hood, a New American Noble Aroma Hop," Alfred Haunold and Gail B. Nickerson, *ASBC Journal*, American Society of Brewing Chemists, Inc., 1990.

"The Celis Brewery—A Belgian Oasis in Texas," Bill Metzger, *Ale Street News*, Vol. 2 No. 4 August/September 1993, Maywood, NJ.

"The Brews of Ski Country," Gregg Smith, *All About Beer*, Volume 15 No. 1, March 1994. Oceanside, CA.

"Old Spanish Custom is at the Root of Shep's Dark Brew" Roger Protz, *What's Brewing—Newspaper of The Campaign For Real Ale*, March 1994, St. Albans, Herts, England.

"How Sweet It Is—Brewing with Sugar," Jeff Frane, *Zymurgy*, Vol. 17 No. 1, Spring 1994. Boulder, CO.

"Hops: The Brewer's Bitter Balancer," Rob Haiber, *Ale Street News*, Vol. 2 No. 2 April/May 1993, Maywood, NJ.

"Back from the Dead," Graham Wheeler, *What's Brewing—Newspaper of The Campaign For Real Ale*, May 1994, St. Albans, Herts, England.

"Cask-Conditioned Ales," Jim Busch, *Zymurgy*, Vol. 16 No. 4, Special Issue 1993. Boulder, CO.

"The British Brewing Scene," David C. Hanbury, *Zymurgy*, Elizabeth Gold, editor, Vol. 16 No. 4, Special Issue 1993. Boulder, CO.

"Beer Styles No. 1—Pilsener," *Ale Street News*, Rob Haiber, Vol. 2 No. 4 August/September 1993, Maywood, NJ.

"Why Stout was Once the Fat Man of Brewing" Charles McMaster, *What's Brewing—Newspaper of The Campaign For Real Ale*, March 1994, St. Albans, Herts, England.

"Holiday & Winter Beers," James Robertson, *All About Beer*, Volume 14 No. 6, January 1994. Durham, NC.

"Letters," *What's Brewing—Newspaper of The Campaign For Real Ale*, Roger Protz, editor, June 1994. St. Albans, Herts, England.

"Off The Lees," *Better Winemaking*, Paul Jean, Jr., editor-in-chief, Volume 5 No. 1, Winter 1994. Nepean, Ontario.

"Ask the Trouble Shooter," Dave Miller, *Brewing Techniques*, Vol. 2 No. 5, Sept./Oct. 1994. Eugene, OR.

"Stepping Up to Advanced Techniques," Jim Busch, *Brewing Techniques*, Vol. 3 No. 2, March/April 1995. Eugene, OR.

"The Lagering of Lagers," Dan Gordon, *Zymurgy*, Vol. 16 No. 4, Special Issue 1993. Boulder, CO.

The Brewmaster's Recipe Manual

BREWER'S NOTES

The Brewmaster's Recipe Manual

BREWER'S NOTES